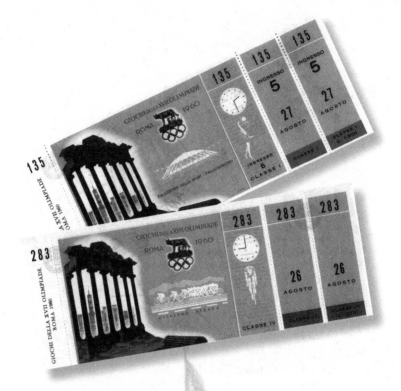

DAVID
MARANISS

ROME
1960

THE OLYMPICS
THAT CHANGED
THE WORLD

SIMON & SCHUSTER New York • London • Toronto • Sydney

Insert photo credits: David Lees/Time & Life Pictures/Getty Images: 1, 9, 24, 45; Mark Kauffman/Time & Life Pictures/Getty Images: 2, 6, 15, 16, 25, 38; Linda Maraniss: 3; Hulton Archive/Time & Life Pictures/Getty Images: 4; IOC: 5, 26, 28, 33; Central Press/Time & Life Pictures/Getty Images: 7; United Press International Photo: 8; Bettmann/CORBIS: 10; *Sporting News* Archive/ZUMA Press: 11; John G. Zimmerman/*Sports Illustrated*: 12, 31, 39; Jerry Cooke/*Sports Illustrated*: 13, 20, 21, 48; Italian National Olympic Committee (CONI) Archive: 14, 29, 42, 46, 47; University of Illinois Archive: 17, 18; IOC/Lothar Rübelt: 19; George Silk/Time & Life Pictures/Getty Images: 22, 30, 40, 44; *The Tennessean*: 23, 36; Keystone/Time & Life Pictures/Getty Images: 27, 43; Washington Post Library/AP Wire Photo: 32; Marvin E. Newman/*Sports Illustrated*: 34, 37; FPG/Staff/Time & Life Pictures/Getty Images: 35; AFP/Staff/Time & Life Pictures/Getty Images: 41.
End Papers: Italian National Olympic Committee (CONI) Archive

SIMON & SCHUSTER
1230 Avenue of the Americas
New York, NY 10020

First Simon & Schuster hardcover edition July 2008

SIMON & SCHUSTER and colophon are registered trademarks of Simon & Schuster, Inc.

For information about special discounts for bulk purchases, please contact Simon & Schuster Special Sales at 1-800-456-6798 or business@simonandschuster.com.

Designed by Dana Sloan

Manufactured in the United States of America

10   9   8   7   6   5   4   3   2   1

Library of Congress Cataloging-in-Publication Data

Maraniss, David.
    Rome 1960 : the Olympics that changed the world / David Maraniss.
—1st Simon & Schuster hardcover ed.
        p.   cm.
    1. Olympic Games (17th : 1960 : Rome, Italy)   2. Olympics—Political aspects.   3. Olympics—Social aspects.   4. Cold War.   I. Title.
    GV7221960   .M37   2008
    796.48—dc22   2008013013

ISBN-13: 978-1-4165-3407-5
ISBN-10:   1-4165-3407-5

To Linda, my quirky saint

CONTENTS

A BRIEF PREFACE

THIS book is shaped around eighteen days in the summer of 1960 when the Olympics came to Rome. In the history of the modern Games, other times and places have drawn more notice, but none offers a deeper palate of character, drama, and meaning. The contests in Rome shimmered with performances that remain among the most golden in athletic history, from Wilma Rudolph in the sprints to Abebe Bikila in the marathon; from Cassius Clay in the boxing ring to Rafer Johnson in the decathlon. But beyond that the forces of change were everywhere. In sports, culture, and politics—interwoven in so many ways—one could see an old order dying and a new one being born. With all its promise and trouble, the world as we see it today was coming into view.

Television, money, and drugs were bursting onto the scene, altering everything they touched. Old-boy notions of pristine amateurism, created by and for upper-class sportsmen, were crumbling in Rome and could never be taken as seriously again. Rome brought the first commercially broadcast Summer Games, the first doping scandal, the first runner paid for wearing a certain brand of track shoes. New nations and constituencies were being heard from, with increasing pressure to provide equal rights for blacks and women as they emerged from generations of discrimination and condescension.

The singular essence of the Olympic Games is that the world takes the same stage at the same time, performing a passion play of nations, races, ideologies, talents, styles, and aspirations that no other venue, not even the United Nations, can match. The 1960 Games came during a notably anxious period in cold war history; almost every action in Rome was viewed through the political lens of those tense times.

One week before the Opening Ceremony, a Moscow trial brought the conviction of an American pilot, Francis Gary Powers, on espionage charges after his high-altitude U-2 reconnaissance plane was shot down over Soviet territory. Two days before the Closing Ceremony, Soviet Premier Nikita Khrushchev set sail for New York for a dramatic appearance at the U.N. General Assembly, where he pounded his fist and railed against America and the West. In between, even as athletes from East and West Germany competed as a unified team in Rome, officials in East Berlin closed their border temporarily, laying the first metaphorical bricks for what months later would become the all-too-real Berlin Wall.

The pressures of the cold war played an underappreciated role in forcing change in culture and sports, all much in evidence in Rome. At the opening Parade of Nations at the Stadio Olimpico, the crowd was stirred by the sight of Rafer Johnson marching into the arena at the head of the U.S. delegation, the first black athlete to carry the American flag. Johnson's historic act reflected his unsurpassed status as a world-class decathlete, but it also served as a symbolic weapon at a time when the United States was promoting freedom abroad but struggling to answer blatant racism at home, where millions of Americans were denied freedom because of the color of their skin. One of the new battlegrounds in the cold war was black Africa, where fourteen nations came into being that year. The ambitions of a postcolonial world were played out at the Olympics when marathoner Abebe Bikila of Ethiopia became the first athlete from sub-Saharan Africa to win a gold medal, running barefoot through the Roman streets less than a quarter century after Italy had invaded his homeland.

Early formulations of the individualism that came to define the sixties could also be seen in Rome, most notably in a cocky German sprinter, Armin Hary, and an eighteen-year-old light-heavyweight boxer from Louisville named Cassius Marcellus Clay, whose gold medal performance marked the first step onto the world stage of a character soon to gain renown as Muhammad Ali. And finally, it was at the 1960 Olympics that American women athletes took a more prominent role. Sexism still dominated the Olympic Movement, as it did the entire world of sports, but the realities of the cold war helped force progress for the simple reason that success of U.S. women could boost the medal count versus the Soviets. On the Stadio Olimpico track, in the late-summer heat, the rise of women was helped immeasurably by the radiance of sprinter Wilma Rudolph and the Tigerbelles, who came out of Coach Ed Temple's little program at Tennessee State University to capture the world's admiration and inspire women athletes for generations thereafter.

It is with the Tigerbelles and Rafer Johnson, two years before Rome, that the story begins.

ROME 1960

1

ALL THE WAY
TO MOSCOW

DARKNESS fell slowly in midsummer Moscow, but the Americans arrived so late that the chartered buses needed headlights to illumine the ride from the airport. Every now and then, for no readily apparent reason, the Russian drivers clicked off the lights, drove a few blocks through the crepuscular murk, then turned on the beams again. The most mundane events can be charged with mystery the first time around, and this was a first for the passengers entering the Soviet capital on the Monday evening of July 21, 1958. They were members of the first U.S. track-and-field team to visit the USSR since the start of the cold war. Out the windows, flashes of light and shadow flitted by, a hypnotic passing scene: drunken men slouched in dimly lit doorways; armed soldiers at intersections; broad avenues with little traffic other than buses whose exhaust fumes fouled the humid air; and the occasional black sedan claiming the VIP lane. When the Americans reached their hotel and checked into their rooms, they were struck by how heavy everything seemed. Bulky bedposts and thick, ponderous curtains.

Edward Stanley Temple had seen worse back home. As someone who had spent a lifetime dealing with alien environments because of his skin color alone, this one was not quite so unnerving. Moscow, to him, was just a stop on the road, another way for the coach and his athletes to get where he wanted them to go, past Russia and into history at the 1960 Olympic Games in Rome.

This leg of Temple's improbable journey had begun three weeks earlier with a gesture of audacious confidence. As he was preparing to leave his home in Nashville for the Fourth of July weekend, he asked his wife, Charlie, to pack his suitcase with enough clothes for him to spend several weeks overseas. The request surprised her, since the schedule called for Temple, the women's track coach at Tennessee Agricultural and Industrial State University, to be away for only four days at the national championships in Morristown, New Jersey. That was just the first stop, he explained. Although nothing had been decided yet, he predicted that he and his Tigerbelles would be chosen to go from there all the way across the Atlantic for the first-ever dual track meet between the United States and the Soviet Union.

The fact that Temple booked a Ladd Bus Company charter for the ride to New Jersey underscored his conviction of better things to come. For years his track team had traveled in two clunky station wagons—four or five girls per car—one driven by him, the other by his friend, the photographer Earl Clanton, who had coined the team's evocative Tigerbelles nickname, a felicitous melding of *tiger* and southern *belle*. Their traditional road trips ventured deeper into Jim Crow territory, to track relays at Tuskegee Institute or Alabama State, and followed a familiar pattern. Late on a Friday, often around midnight, they broke away from the hilly campus in north Nashville, the waybacks jumbled with gym duffels, starting blocks, hammers, spikes, purses, curling irons, and meals of peanut butter and jelly sandwiches and apples packed in brown paper bags. It was best if they filled the gas tank beforehand; getting service at a station along the way could be a dicey proposition. And the fewer stops, the safer.

Temple grew up in Harrisburg, Pennsylvania, and he recruited a few athletes from the projects in Chicago and New York, but most of his runners came out of rural Georgia towns like Jakin, Griffin, and Bloomingdale. They had seen Whites Only signs all their lives and knew how to keep on going. At some point there would be a shout from the back: time to "hit the fields." It was both polite code and bleak reality, meaning pull over to the shoulder of the highway so they could scramble into the darkness for relief. As the caravan approached its destination, an order would come from the front: "Get your stuff together." This meant rollers off, lipstick on, everything brushed and straightened. The sprinters were a free-spirited group; some chafed at Coach Temple's rules of behavior but grudgingly obliged. "I want foxes, not oxes," he told them. The Tigerbelles had perfected the art of emerging from the least flattering conditions looking as fresh as a gospel choir, for which they were often mistaken.

The Independence Day expedition north to what the track world called the nationals was different from the usual road trip. There was no need to hit the fields; the Ladd bus had its own lavatory. And no more peanut butter and jelly sandwiches. Once they escaped the borders of the old Confederacy, Coach Temple and his team could find more possible places to stop and eat, within means of their paltry budget, which allowed about $6 per athlete for breakfast and dinner. His top-flight runners—including Lucinda Williams, Barbara Jones, Isabelle Daniels, and Margaret Matthews—brought along suitcases even bigger than his. Like him, they figured victory would come their way in Morristown, and after that they would go on to the Soviet Union.

All of his best sprinters, that is, except the one who was not there. As a sixteen-year-old high school girl two years earlier, Wilma Glodean Rudolph had run with the Tigerbelles on the bronze-medal-winning 4 X 100 meter relay team at the 1956 Summer Olympics in Melbourne, Australia. Since then, she had trained regularly at Temple's clinics for high school girls at Tennessee State and had graduated from Burt High in Clarksville, a tobacco town forty-five miles northwest of Nashville, where she also starred in basketball. All of her accomplishments had been stunningly against the odds, from the time she had been born two months premature, weighing less than five pounds. At age four, she had endured scarlet fever, double pneumonia, and polio, crippling her left leg and forcing her to wear orthopedic shoes and metal leg braces for several years. By her adolescence, after years of weekly bus trips for treatments at a clinic in Nashville, she had overcome all that and blossomed into a lithe, flowing runner. Now her freshman year in college was approaching, and Wilma was about to become a full-fledged Tigerbelle, but for the time being she was out of action. If outsiders asked about her, Temple told them she had appendicitis. In fact, she was about to give birth to a baby girl. She had gone from Olympic medalist heroine to expectant unmarried mother, alone and mortified.

Temple had another saying: "It's a short distance between a pat on the back and a kick in the ass." He had seen how people had soured on Rudolph when she got pregnant. And one of his own ironclad rules was no mothers allowed on the team. But Wilma was so different, the sweetest girl he had ever met, and she ran with such beautiful ease. Her older sister Yvonne in St. Louis would take the baby temporarily, she said, if Coach let her come back. Temple relented. Wilma could join the Tigerbelles when they returned from this trip.

Women's track and field was an odd little outpost on the frontier of sports in 1958 America, forlorn and largely scorned. Female athletes were not recognized by the National Collegiate Athletic Association. Only a few colleges, most of them historically black schools in the South, had track-and-field programs, but even they competed under the rules of the Amateur Athletic Union, not the NCAA.

When Temple was named head coach at Tennessee A&I State after graduating in 1950, it was because nobody else wanted the job. His starting salary was $150 a month, which, when added to his pay for teaching social science courses, brought in a yearly sum of $5,196. His only other enticement was that he could move from East Dormitory room 305 (where he had survived four years on the boisterous floor with the sarcastic motto "Three-o-five will keep you alive") down to a larger room on the first floor. His first team budget was under $1,000. The campus's old cinder track encircled a football field and was often torn up by behemoths' cleats; Temple was constantly raking it himself. When weather forced his Tigerbelles indoors, they ran in a gym barely fifty yards long where they were in danger of slamming into a wall if they failed to negotiate a double doorway leading out to the hall.

By the mid-fifties, even after Temple had established his program and led it to a national title, the athletic department still would not give him a desk, let alone an office. He shared a cramped cubbyhole with his wife, who was campus postmistress, and borrowed her desk. There were no scholarships for his athletes, so he found them work-study jobs at the post office. As minimal as these conditions were, Tennessee State at least had a program, more than most schools could say, and a winning one at that. Tuskegee had paved the way in the 1940s, but by the late fifties, the Tigerbelles dominated.

Aside from those two black Southern colleges, most of the teams competing at the nationals were northern big-city AAU clubs: Queens Mercurettes, Chicago Comets, New York Police Athletic League, Cleveland Recreation Department, Liberty Athletic Club of Boston, South Pacific Association of Los Angeles, German-American Athletic Club of New York. None of those squads had enough talent or depth to mount a challenge to Tennessee State at Morristown. By the end of the day on July 5, the Tigerbelles had won the team title by amassing 110 points, more than twice as many as the second-place Mercurettes, and all of their top sprinters had won, including the relay foursome of Daniels, Williams, Jones, and Matthews, who set a new American women's record at 46.9 seconds.

Along with the winning relay team, the top two finishers in each of nine events qualified for the combined squad of men and women competing in the unprecedented track meet against the Soviets to be held in Moscow at the end of the month.

By the end of the tournament, AAU officials had yet to name a coach for the women's squad. Temple had heard that they were leaning toward a white coach from the New York Police Athletic League. He also believed that he had one key ally on the board making the decision that night, Frances Sobczak Kaszubski of Cleveland. Like him, Kaszubski carried her own outsider's burden in the world of amateur sports. Only ten years earlier, when she had competed as a discus thrower at the 1948 Olympics, she had been so disregarded by the male-dominated U.S. Olympic Committee that she had to pay her own way, an experience that at once demoralized her and drove her to devote her life to ensuring that girls coming later had more support. Now, as the top woman representative on the AAU track-and-field committee, she respected Temple and what his women had endured in the face of prejudice. She also realized that, for all practical purposes, without the Tigerbelles there would be no U.S. women's team. Temple looked up to Big Kaszubski, who stood 6-foot-1, towering 5 inches over him. Mutt and Jeff, he called them. She was tough, with her Kaszubski Rules of Order, and could use her size to intimidate, he thought, but she was also sympathetic.

To emphasize how much he wanted the coaching job, he presented his case to her in dramatic terms that night. "The brass came in from New York," Temple later recalled. "They had this big tent, and they were going in this tent, and Frances was going to be there, and I wasn't. And I said, 'Frances, you going to that meeting?' She said yes. I said, 'Well, now, let me tell you something.' And this is exactly what I told her. I said, 'I got eight people on this team: everybody in the hundred, everybody in the two hundred, the relay, long jump, hurdles.' I said, 'We came up here on a chartered bus, and that bus is leaving here at eight o'clock tomorrow morning.' I said, 'Now, you go in there and tell them that if I am not on this trip, all eight of 'em will be on the bus going back to Nashville, Tennessee.' Her eyes got as big as fish, and when they came out of the meeting, she said, 'Ed Temple, you're the coach!' "

THE OLYMPIC ideal was of pure athletic competition separated from the ideologies and international disputes of the modern world. But that was an impossible notion, and there was no pretense of separating sports and politics in the first dual track-and-field meet involving the two superpowers of the cold war era. Sports officials first broached the subject during an informal summit meeting at the Soviet quarters in Melbourne at the 1956 Olympics. A long night of food, drinks, and conversation about future head-to-head competitions ended with a firm handshake between team leaders Daniel Ferris of the U.S. and Russian Leonid Khomenkov. But the reality could not take shape without political diplomacy, and that came later, on January 27, 1958, when Soviet ambassador Georgi Zaroubin and U.S. ambassador S. B. Lacy concluded three months of negotiations by signing the US-USSR Exchange Agreement. After icy relations for so many years, with little cultural contact between the two nations, finally there would be regular exchanges in industry, agriculture, medicine, music, art, film, theater, and athletics.

The home and away exchange pattern had been arranged in sports even before the pact was officially signed. In the first year, ice hockey and basketball teams would play in Russia, while wrestlers and weight lifters competed in the U.S.—all culminating with a titanic track-and-field meet at Lenin Stadium in Moscow in late July. Both governments praised the agreement. The newspaper *Pravda* welcomed it as "part of the principle of peaceful coexistence," and Soviet Olympic officials were quoted in *Izvestia* saying that the sports teams had "a lot to learn from each other." The only vocal opposition came from right-wing critics in the U.S. who denounced any accommodation of the Communists. In response, the State Department argued that the exchanges could only help the image of the United States, which, as one internal memo stated, "had been distorted beyond any pretense of accuracy" by Soviet propaganda. One of the most troubling images had to do with race, America in black and white.

By the time the roster of the U.S. track team was set at the national championships in early July, there were few signs of a cold war thaw. No sooner had David Edstrom, a young decathlete from the University of Oregon, made the team than he began to wonder what was in store. Leafing through a New York newspaper, Edstrom saw photos of a Russian mob outside the West German embassy on Moscow's Bolshoya Gruzinskaya Street pelting the building with slabs of concrete and splattering the walls with bottles of purple ink. Two days later the papers showed a similar crowd gathered at the U.S. embassy in Moscow, waving placards and denouncing America as a land of fascist dogs. Both rallies were carefully directed by Soviet officials—a bit of propagandistic stagecraft meant to counterbalance earlier demonstrations in Bonn and New York protesting the recent execution by hanging of former Hungarian leaders Imre Nagy and General Pal Maleter. Nagy and Maleter had become martyrs in the West: Communists who had turned against their Soviet overseers to help lead the ill-fated Hungarian Revolution of 1956.

All of this was strange and unsettling to Edstrom, who, like his teammates, had never been to the Soviet Union. "I thought, What is going on there?" he recalled. "It was kind of scary thinking about going over. I didn't know what to expect."

American officials were more concerned about the prospects of the track meet itself, how the results might be used by them—or, to their minds, misused by the Soviets—for propaganda purposes. Here the ironies of different concepts of equality came into play. Following a long-standing tradition among European nations, the host Russians declared that the point totals of men and women would be counted together to determine a winner. U.S. officials feared that their women, considered inferior to their Soviet counterparts, would drag them to defeat, and wanted to split men and women into separate competitions. This was the norm in the States, where the role of women was so minimized that *Track & Field News,* the bible of the sport, did not even cover the women's championships in Morristown. Renewed negotiations got so sticky that one day, as Temple was putting his team through twice-a-day drills at a high school track in New Jersey, where it had set up training camp awaiting the overseas trip, Kaszubski approached him with grim news. "Ed," she said, "we might not go on this tour to Russia." Another form of segregation, Temple thought. Maybe he wouldn't need that big suitcase after all.

In the end, after keeping the women's team in limbo for a few days, U.S. officials concluded that they would look foolish refusing to participate because of the gender issue. Among other things, that would provide the Soviets with more rhetorical ammunition, reinforcing their accusations that under capitalism many athletes were treated like second-class citizens. As the Soviets waged a propaganda struggle for the hearts and minds of people around the world, they consistently pounded away at the theme of racial segregation in the American South. State Department officials and foreign policy advisers in the Eisenhower White House were reluctant to provide them with yet another equality issue. A National Security Council task force on international communism had concluded that summer that one of the most effective ways to counteract Soviet propaganda was to show the world more than white males. "We should make more extensive use of nonwhite American citizens," the task force report stated. "Outstanding Negroes in all fields should be appealed to in terms of highest patriotism to act as our representatives." It was partly with that in mind that the White House financed the trip to Moscow with funds from the President's Special International Program for Cultural Presentations.

"CLIPPER AAU" was painted on the side of the Pan American Airways DC-7C that rumbled down the runway of New York's Idlewild Airport on the morning of July 20 and charted a northern arc across the Atlantic. The U.S. team was seventy-three strong counting coaches and officials. Uncertainty about what lay ahead was evident in the cargo hold, which contained four hundred pounds of extra food in case the Russian fare was inedible. It was the largest delegation of American track-and-field stars ever assembled outside the Olympics. Six previous Olympic gold medal winners were aboard, including shot-putter Parry O'Brien, who captained the squad, and hurdler Glenn Davis, who had been chosen to carry the American flag. But the best among them, still looking for his first gold medal, fit whatever notion the government might have had of an "outstanding Negro."

This was Rafer Lewis Johnson, who had won the U.S. decathlon championship in Palmyra, New Jersey, on the same day the Tigerbelles swept the sprints up in Morristown. Rafer Johnson was considered an exemplar of sound mind and sound body—a student body president at UCLA, intelligent, movie-star handsome, classically sculpted at six-three and two hundred pounds, with long legs and a muscular frame. There was an aura about Johnson that lifted him above the crowd. He was ferociously competitive yet not as self-centered as most athletes, with a universal perspective that came from growing up black, the son of a factory worker at an animal food processing plant, in a historically Swedish town in central California. Johnson boarded the plane with an unopened letter from his college coach, Ducky Drake, in his pocket, and failure etched in his mind.

It was at the 1956 Olympics in Melbourne that Johnson had suffered the most painful loss of his young career. He had gone down to Australia as a gold medal favorite, so talented that he qualified for the team not only in the ten-event decathlon but also separately in the long jump, then called the broad jump. While warming up, he pulled a muscle in his right leg, an injury that forced him out of the broad-jump competition but did not sideline him completely. He battled on in the punishing two-day decathlon, but was slowed just enough that he finished second behind teammate Milt Campbell, an oft-overlooked champion who had been the first black to win the decathlon. From his earliest days in Kingsburg, out in the flats of California's San Joaquin Valley, Rafer had always been the golden boy, superior in anything he tried, from football to basketball to the broad jump. His showing in Melbourne shattered him. Normally stoic, a model of athletic poise, the twenty-one-year-old broke down in the arms of Coach Drake at the end, crying inconsolably.

Drake talked to his star long into the night, and from the depths of that discussion Johnson emerged with a deeper understanding of what it took. "When you finish second, you have to take a real close look at how you performed, how you thought, and how these thoughts caused you to feel, and how you reacted to that," Johnson said later. "We broke those things down. So often with a victory and another victory and another, you are just kind of doing the same thing." He had heard the words before, but now he absorbed them: "You have to do it on that day. You have to do it at the time when they fire the gun. You have to do it on the hour when play is to start. You have to be fully aware and prepared for anything that might happen."

Johnson sensed a transformation. He became a different athlete, mentally stronger, his foundation totally rebuilt. He would not boast, but his confidence transcended words; he felt an indomitable will to win. He waited a year and a half after Melbourne to compete again in a decathlon. Still favoring his right leg, and taking only one try in the broad jump, high jump, and pole vault, he nonetheless easily won the

Kingsburg Invitational in his hometown in June 1958, then defeated his UCLA teammate C. K. Yang and Oregon's Edstrom in the nationals a month later in Palmyra. Since Yang, who finished second, was a citizen of Taiwan, Edstrom qualified as the other decathlete on the squad heading for Moscow. Edstrom's assignment was to fight for third-place points against the second-best Russian, Yuri Kutenko. Johnson would face a more formidable challenge in a battle with Vasily Kuznetsov, who had finished third in Melbourne but now held the pending world decathlon record of 8013 points, the first ever to exceed the 8000 mark. The Johnson versus Kuznetsov decathlon battle was the most anticipated event in what the Soviet press was already calling the Match of the Giants.

Pan Am took Johnson and his teammates as far as Oslo, Norway, overnight, where they stopped for fuel and picked up a handful of U.S. athletes already touring Europe. The transatlantic flight had been a fifteen-hour party back in the coach section, with the Tigerbelles and shot-putter Earlene Brown of Los Angeles singing, clapping, and whooping it up with the boys. Someone hauled out a guitar; they danced in the aisles. Then on to Helsinki, where they lingered at the airport all day, bored and weary in Finland. When someone asked why they had to wait around so long, the answer came back that the Soviets wanted them to arrive after dark. "They sat us on the tarmac for hours, just wouldn't let us in," remembered Rink Babka, a University of Southern California athlete who made the team as a discus thrower. Finally they boarded three smaller planes, one Finnish and two Russian Aeroflots, for the final leg to Moscow. The strangeness of the scene stuck in the memory of David Edstrom: "It was a two-engine plane, and the seats were like what you would find in a Blue Bird bus for schoolkids. Rigid. And they served us vodka and caviar."

When the Americans landed in Moscow, there was another hour on the runway, far from any gate, before they could get out. Little Eddie Rosenblum, a Washington lawyer who ran the AAU's foreign relations committee as a combination cheerleader and promoter, stood at the plane's exit door, his bald head topped by a fedora, and proclaimed that he was going to march down the stairs carrying an American flag. As Ed Temple recalled the moment: "Eddie was a dyed-in-the-wool USA person. 'Give me the flag,' he says. Sounds good to us. I was third or fourth in line behind him. Then the door opened, and there were these two Russians standing out there with tommy guns on their shoulders, and Ed Rosenblum passed that flag back so fast . . . the flag went along past me; move that flag right on! I was scared. These people mean business over here."

In the official delegation waiting on the tarmac stood Gavriel Korobkov, coach of the Soviet team. With his heavy-framed glasses and slouched posture, Korobkov looked more like an intellectual than a jock, and in fact he was both. Track and field was his passion, but he spent much of his spare time at the apartment he shared with his mother in suburban Moscow, listening to the BBC on the radio and poring over English language magazines. As he watched the Americans descend, Korobkov searched with keen interest for Payton Jordan, head track coach at Stanford University. He introduced himself and then asked, "Do you remember receiving a letter from a Russian many years ago? That was me!" More than a decade earlier, when Jordan himself was a top sprinter at Southern Cal, Korobkov had written him saying that he too was a sprinter, but with a lot to learn. "I would like to know very much everything you do," Korobkov wrote. "I beg of you, please, tell me your training program. I'd be gracious to you forever if you help me."

Jordan, later described by one of his runners as a "Paleolithic conservative with . . . ultra-right-wing views," did indeed remember, for he had responded to the unusual request by outlining his track regimen in detail to the young Russian. At the time, back in the late 1940s, the Soviets were an unknown quantity in track and field. They had dropped out of the Olympic Games in the 1920s, deriding them as a capitalist enterprise, and only gradually reentered international competition after World War II, appearing in various European track-and-field meets. But they did not return to the Olympics until 1952 in Helsinki. By then the Soviets had decided that they could use sports as propaganda to prove the superiority of the socialist system, and track and field, with its objective and irrefutable times and distances, became an essential part of that effort.

After the eerie bus ride into central Moscow, the Americans had five full days in the city before the dual meet. Much of that time was spent dozing at the hotel or training at the stadium track, where their practice routines were filmed by Russian observers. One night the athletes were invited to the American embassy, which was monitoring the visit, sending regular dispatches to Washington on whether the tour was serving its intended purpose of counteracting Soviet propaganda. ("Team members were consistently well dressed, breezy, and friendly," one diplomatic file to the State Department noted. "But what very evidently made the greatest impression was the indiscriminate comradeship between Negro and white team members, which gave lie in dramatic fashion to the regime's propaganda about segregation in U.S. life.") Another night bulky Rink Babka, all 270 pounds of him, attended his first ballet, the Bolshoi, the only male in a small group of Americans who took up an offer for free tickets. Babka, Parry O'Brien, Glenn Davis, and Rafer Johnson visited Red Square one afternoon, hiding their cameras under their sport coats, thinking they could take pictures of Lenin's Tomb. "We got in line and finally got up to the tomb and started taking pictures, acting like no one could see us," Babka recalled. "They grabbed us and took our cameras away and scared the heck out of us."

Dallas Long, a shot-putter who had just finished high school in Phoenix and was the baby of the team, rarely strayed from the hotel lobby and never spent a ruble of the expense money the athletes were given. He did notice that the well-dressed Russian men hanging around the lobby seemed to speak English fluently. Must be spies, he thought. Gordon McKenzie, a distance runner, enjoyed interacting with the Russian bus drivers, and often played or kibitzed when they staged impromptu chess matches on the sidewalk outside the coach. Edstrom, thrilled just to share a room with Rafer Johnson, who had been his athletic hero for years, parked himself at Red Square for hours and took notes on the unfamiliar sights.

The Tigerbelles came down to the lobby one day and encountered a black American expatriate from New York with his Russian wife and their two little girls. He wanted his children to meet some Americans with the same skin color and hair texture. Not only did the Tigerbelles talk to the girls, they invited them up to one of their rooms and fixed their hair in a curl and twist that no one in white Moscow knew how to do. The women runners brought their own curling irons, along with compact sterno cans to heat them. "We ran out of sterno one day," recalled Lucinda Williams, "so I asked one of the Russian maids, 'Can you get me a hot plate?' We thought we could plug in the hot plate and heat up the curling iron with that. Well, the maid understood but she didn't understand. She comes back with this bath towel and unwraps it to show us a dinner plate that they had heated up in the oven! That was the hot plate."

The extra food U.S. officials brought along never materialized. Perhaps the solicitousness of the hotel's kitchen staff made the Americans realize that hauling out their own care packages would create an untoward international incident. The Russian food in any case was a constant source of conversation. On the flight over, the Tigerbelles debated whether it was true that Russians ate horsemeat, the thought of which gave them the creeps. Lucinda Williams was relieved to eat borscht for a week, as long as it came with "a lot of that good Russian bread." At breakfast, the athletes were told that the hotel cooks had been trained to prepare dishes American style, so they could order any kind of eggs they wanted for breakfast. They placed their orders through an interpreter—sunny-side up, over easy, scrambled—but it seemed that no matter what they ordered, the results came out the same. Babka grew sick of the chicken: "boiled chicken, broiled chicken, chicken broth soup . . ." His parents were both immigrants from Czechoslovakia who loved the new world out on the plains of Nebraska, but it was not until Rink reached Moscow, he said, that he started to appreciate their lectures about how lucky he was to be American.

Ed Temple experienced a starkly different variation on that theme. Two days before the meet, a press conference was arranged for the coaches. The Americans were represented by George East-ment of Manhattan College, Larry Snyder of Ohio State University, and Payton Jordan of Stanford for the men, Temple for the women. The room buzzed with foreign correspondents, photographers, interpreters. Everyone there was white, except the coach from Tennessee State. All the questions were about the men. Manipulating the expectations game, as coaches naturally do, the Russians said they expected the Americans to win. Eastment said that six of his athletes were recovering from sore throats. There was much talk about the Johnson versus Kuznetsov match. Temple sat there, feeling ignored, for nearly a half hour until finally a reporter turned to him and asked, "Coach Temple, on your United States team, how many Negro athletes do you have as compared to white athletes?"

Temple paused; he had never counted them before. He was running through the roster in his mind when George Eastment jumped in. "I'll take that," Eastment said. "We don't consider them Negro or white on this team. We're all Americans."

The interruption was well-intentioned, but surprised Temple nonetheless. He could remember back to his first trip south from Pennsylvania down to school at Tennessee State, and how when the train passed Cincinnati and neared Louisville he was moved to the colored car; and how on the trolleys in Nashville he had to ride in the back; and how at the two downtown theaters in Nashville, Loew's and the Paramount, the "colored" had to walk up three flights of stairs to the top balcony after entering from a back alley. On the very day of this press conference in the capital of the Soviet Union, the next governor of Tennessee was campaigning back in the United States, in the city of Franklin, and a reporter for the *Nashville Banner* was typing out the lead: "Buford Ellington said here today that it is in the best interests of all Tennesseans to prevent the mixing of the races . . ."

"I'll be damned," Temple said to himself after being spoken for at the press conference. "We have to come all the way to Moscow for me to hear 'We're all Americans.' "

ON THE EVE of the track meet, Rafer Johnson opened the letter from Ducky Drake, his coach. Drake, who also served as the football trainer at UCLA, had not been selected for the U.S. coaching staff, but he knew how important his presence had been in Melbourne, and he wanted to remind Johnson that he was there with him in Moscow, in spirit at least.

"You thought 7,000 miles or so could separate us, but they can't," Drake wrote. "These next couple of days I'll be just as much with you as at Palmyra . . . Remember you're the champion. You're the one *they* have to beat, so let them worry. Go about your work with a quiet confidence that cannot be shaken . . . No matter what happens, remember if you have faith as a grain of mustard seed, you can move mountains. Remember, victory is sweet. World records come when least expected. Work and think on each event as it comes up. Do your best. No one can ask or expect more."

Soccer usually captivated sports fans in Moscow during the heat of summer, but the athletic singularity and political symbolism of the historic confrontation created a feverish interest in the track meet against the United States. A huge, clamorous crowd filled the vastness of Lenin Stadium on the gray, humid Sunday afternoon of July 27 for the first day of competition. There was no official ticket count, but estimates ranged from seventy-five thousand to a hundred thousand people.

For the athletes, this was more than an exhibition, and the tension was comparable to the Olympics. "We felt a lot of pressure to beat the Russians," David Edstrom recalled. Igor Ter-Ovanesyan, a twenty-year-old broad jumper from Kiev, who had been the youngest member of the Soviet team in Melbourne, said the pressure on his side was even more stressful than the Olympics. "There was definitely pressure on the Soviet team to beat the Americans. It extended beyond sports into politics. So there was some brainwashing going on, as usual, of the athletes, and we on the Soviet team realized the responsibility we had. It was like we were coming out of the trenches and fighting fist to fist, face to face." The Soviet motto, in fact, was: "Fight every point. Fight from the start right up to the last moment of competition."

After reading day after day how lightly regarded his American women were, Ed Temple arrived at the stadium with a positive feeling, anticipating that his Tigerbelles-led team had been underestimated. Rather than tightening up, his charges had appeared lighthearted on the bus ride over from the hotel. Big Momma Brown, as the foreign press called Earlene Brown, the shot-putter, was so loose that she marched onto the field wearing an oversized Uzbek hat, a gesture that immediately won over the Russian audience. The warmth they showed Brown was not felt by Rink Babka, who marched in with his discus teammate, Al Oerter, and their two Russian counterparts. It seemed that whenever he walked close enough to the stands for fans to see his name on a placard, he would hear disapproving whistles. "Guess they're just booing us," Babka said to Oerter. Tamara Press, the big, friendly discus thrower and shot-putter on the Russian women's team, finally came over to Babka, put her arm around him, and said, "Rink, don't feel bad. They're just kidding you." The word *Babka*, she explained, sounded like a kind of Russian slang for a good-looking chick.

The athletes exchanged miniature stars-and-stripes and hammer-

and-sickle flags and tolerated the protocol of perfunctory official speeches, and then the background buzz and bustle suddenly dissolved into silence for the playing of the U.S. national anthem. "That never left my mind," Ed Temple said later. "A hundred thousand people stood up, and you didn't hear a pin drop."

As the afternoon wore on, it became clear that Temple was astute about his team. Of all the matches that first day, the most electric was the women's 100-meter dash. The winner in a blur was Barbara Jones, who barely nosed out Russian Vera Krepkina, with Jones's teammate Isabelle Daniels finishing a close third. A Chicago native who had transferred to Tennessee State after losing her scholarship at Marquette University, Jones was the most headstrong of the Tigerbelles, often complaining about the rigorous training regimen Temple imposed. "I felt the work was too strenuous and the rules were ridiculous," she once said. But she stuck with the program and eventually came to believe that Temple helped her evolve "from a child to a woman." Later that first day, she and Daniels teamed with Lucinda Williams and Margaret Matthews to win the 4 x 100 meter relay. In perhaps an even bigger upset, Earlene Brown, who had gained strength and lost 15 pounds (from 235 down to 220) after three weeks of training under Temple, won the shot-put competition, outdistancing the favored Tamara Press.

The most disconcerting event of the day was the men's 10,000-meter run. Both American entrants, Jerry Smartt and Gordon McKenzie, struggled with cramps halfway through the race. Smartt slackened to a feeble trot but kept moving forward and eventually finished the race. McKenzie hurt so much that he slowed to a walk and at one point apparently stepped off the track. He was sick and sore (the worst of the sore throats) and didn't want to finish, but his coaches were adamant. Even if he came in last, the Americans would get one point; only by dropping out would they get zero. Every point counted in the match of the giants. Keep going, the coaches shouted, and McKenzie tried to resume, but a Soviet official intervened and said that he had been disqualified. The only dispute of the games ensued, a minor one at that, and the disqualification was upheld.

The Russians cheered wildly for their victories in the distance race and 20-kilometer walk, but by the end of the day the Americans held a slim lead in total points, 83–75. And midway through the decathlon, Rafer Johnson had soared ahead of his rival Kuznetsov, winning the 100, the 400, and the shot put, and scoring decently in the broad jump and high jump. He had followed the instructions in Ducky Drake's letter event by event, and expressed confidence about what was to follow. "I'm going to win," he said. "I have to."

The crowd the next afternoon, a drizzly Monday, was less than half of Sunday's turnout, down to thirty thousand or so, leaving large swaths of empty seats in the cavernous stadium. The rain transformed the discus circle, dirt rather than cement, into a muddy pit. Though the Russian women pulled into a larger lead, the Tigerbelles and Earlene Brown continued to excel. Brown came in a close second to Tamara Press in the discus, and Lucinda Williams, entering her senior year at Tennessee State and captain of the U.S. women's team, streaked to the tape in the 200-meter dash in a photo finish with Maria Itkina. "It was my first experience with a real photo finish," Williams said later. "We had to wait around for the photo because we didn't know who had won. I knew I had done the lean, the Tennessee State lean that Coach Temple always taught us; keep running through the tape and lean. I knew I had done that. But I said to myself, 'I know they are not going to give it to me. Here in Moscow.' And all of a sudden they flash something on the scoreboard marquee. I couldn't understand most of it, but I knew it said 1—USA!" Williams and Itkina hugged each other at the news. They had bonded by then, and Williams said to herself that someday she would name a daughter after her Russian friend. (Years later, she took pleasure in explaining to Kimberly Maria Adams the derivation of her middle name.)

For the men, Babka won the discus, Glenn Davis the hurdles, and O'Brien and Long swept the shot put, but the Russians surprised in the high jump and gained points in the javelin and 5000-meter run. Now all attention was focused on the decathlon. Kuznetsov began the day favored in three of the final five events: the 110-meter hurdles, pole vault, and 1500 meters. If he could get to that final race, the metric mile, within range, the Soviet press thought, he might win the match. Correspondent Max Frankel, covering the event for the *New York Times,* noted that the Russians had "made something of a cult of personality in their cheering for Vasily Kuznetsov." But nothing could disrupt Rafer Johnson, mind alert, body relaxed, deep in an athletic trance. He carried with him the lessons of Melbourne. Whatever happened, he was mentally ready. Rather than being exhausted and out of breath, he seemed to gain momentum from the fact that the Russians shortened the intervals between events from a half hour down to twenty minutes. In the second-to-last event, the javelin, Drake's message stuck in his mind: "Check the wind. Get a good angle of flight." On his third and final throw, despite the sloppy conditions, he heaved the javelin 238 feet 1⅞ inches. With that single extraordinary effort, more than 20 feet farther than his opponent and worth nearly 300 points, Johnson clinched victory and at the same time overtook Kuznetsov's brief world record—and he had another event still to go.

The metric mile, run in the darkness late that night, was neither tense nor anticlimactic, but rather a long, steady victory lap for the world champion, who stayed at Kuznetsov's heels the entire way— and the Russian fans rose as one to cheer him on to the then-stunning total of 8302 points.

David Edstrom did his job too, edging out Kutenko for third place. But it was not quite enough. Soviet sportswriters took note of the electronic stadium scoreboard that glowed with the final team scores. USSR 172, US 170. In a contest that could not have been closer, the scoreboard indicated that the Russians had won. Like all disputes between the superpowers, victory was subject to interpretation. The U.S. men won their half 126–109, but the women, despite the brilliance of the Tigerbelles, lost 63–44. Even then, as R. L. Quercetani argued in *Track & Field News,* only an anomaly in the scoring system allowed the Soviets to claim a win. At most European meets, the losing relay team in a dual meet received two points, but here it was three. "The results of the 'combined match'—what a ridiculous thing!—would have been 170 to 169 USA instead of 172 to 170 if the scoring had been different," Quercetani wrote. That exclamation-pointed desultory aside was his only acknowledgment that women participated in the meet.

An honored truism in sports holds that teams come before individuals, and that what matters, what is remembered in history, is the final score, not how a single athlete performs. This truism often proves false, as it did in Moscow on that summer night in 1958. Not the Soviet point total but the memory of Rafer Johnson is what endures. "One can never forget the brilliant performance of Rafer Johnson," declared *Pravda* sports commentator Lev Lebedev. "It will dignify the history of world athletic records for a long time to come." Quercetani called Johnson's performance "no doubt the most spectacular feat in the history of the decathlon since the days of Jim Thorpe."

The atmosphere at the end was established by Kuznetsov himself, who admired Johnson and had written him several friendly notes since they had first met at Melbourne two years earlier. Now, the match of the giants done, the remaining fans standing and roaring their approval, he walked over to Johnson, squeezed his hand, kissed him on the cheek, and embraced him. Another roar burst out when Johnson ascended the victory platform and waved a bouquet of flowers. "*Spasibo,*" Johnson said, thanking his hosts in Russian. A short time later, after the American had gathered his gear and was on his way to the idling bus, a throng of a few hundred Russian fans swarmed around him. He was frightened at first. Could this be like the angry mob that had thrown purple ink at the American embassy in Moscow less than a month earlier? "I didn't really know what was happening," he recalled. "I didn't know what they were going to do with me."

Outside Lenin Stadium, in the darkness of that late July night in Moscow, amid all the tension of the cold war, the Russian people hoisted Rafer Johnson onto their shoulders and paraded him around, chanting boisterously for the greatest athlete in the world.

2

ALL ROADS TO ROME

T wo weeks before the opening of the 1960 Rome Olympics, in the midst of one of the hottest summers of the cold war, a press counselor for the Italian embassy in Washington paid a courtesy call on his counterpart at the U.S. Department of State. With diplomatic politesse, Gabriele Paresce said that he was there to remind American officials that Italy, as the host country, hoped to keep the Rome Olympics "free from activity of a political or propaganda nature."

After reaching into his briefcase, Paresce handed John G. Kormann a document known as an aide-memoire. It included part of a speech on the Olympic spirit delivered by Italian defense minister Giulio Andreotti, president of the Organizing Committee for the Games of the XVII Olympiad. Other Italian press attachés were undertaking similar missions at capitals around the world, Paresce said. He wanted to assure the Americans that in their case the visit was a mere formality. The Italians expected no problems from them. On the other hand, they were "seriously concerned that the Iron Curtain countries should be admonished not to exploit contacts at the Games for propaganda purposes." When it came to the communists, according to Paresce, it would be a case of "No propaganda, or we throw you out!" Before leaving, he asked Kormann to relay his message to the United States Olympic Committee. Kormann explained that American Olympic officials were not controlled by the government and could not be told what to do, but he happened to be on friendly terms with the press director, Arthur Lentz, and would be happy to pass along the word. He said he was certain that both the State Department and the USOC "wanted to maintain the true spirit of the Games." After Paresce left, Kormann called Lentz in New York, where the U.S. team was assembling in preparation for Rome. Lentz promised him that the Americans would do all they could to respect the Italian request.

The next morning, Saturday, August 13, David Sime, a sprinter on the U.S. team, was alone in his room at the Vanderbilt Hotel in Manhattan, weakened by the flu, when the telephone rang. "Is this David Sime?" a man asked. He said he was from the government and wanted to talk.

"About what?" Sime wondered. He was not in a sociable mood. If he had felt better, he would have been at Van Cortlandt Stadium, in the Bronx, going through the training regimen with the rest of the track-and-field team. Instead, he remained at the delegation's hotel at Park Avenue and 34th Street, preserving his strength for his moment of truth. That would come eighteen days later inside Stadio Olimpico in Rome, when the red-haired Duke University medical student was scheduled to race in the 100-meter dash, one of the premier events of the Olympics.

But this caller was insistent, and already knew enough to pronounce his name so that it rhymed with *rim*. Scottish. Forget the *e* on the end.

Come on up, Sime said.

Once inside the room, the federal agent told Sime that the United

States of America could use his help. After analyzing intelligence from European contacts and carefully observing Soviet stars who had been in Philadelphia for the second US-USSR dual track meet in 1959, they had targeted an athlete who might be approachable in Rome, an interesting prospect for defection.

Is this a hoax? Sime asked. As an amateur athlete, one could never tell what was real and what was a joke. Almost every week, some decision made by the brass at the Amateur Athletic Union seemed unreal. Who could believe it when they suspended the eligibility of his friend Lee Calhoun, the champion high hurdler from North Carolina College at Durham, for a year because Calhoun and his wife, Gwen, got married on the *Bride and Groom* television game show? That was a joke, or should have been, but it was not. Then there were the athletes themselves. Sime knew enough prankster teammates, especially his pals from that summer's Olympic Trials and practice meets, pole-vaulter Don Bragg and javelin thrower Al Cantello, to suspect that they might be setting him up.

Deadly serious, the visitor flashed a government ID. "We'd like you to come to Washington," he said. "We'll have you back tonight."

There was a flight to Washington, a black car waiting, a ride to a nondescript building, a brisk walk to a secured room—it was all a strange blur. "I had no idea where I was. There were three of us in the room. 'Here's the guy's name,' they said." It was Igor Ter-Ovanesyan. " 'Here's what he looks like. We will contact you in Rome and go from there if you do it.' They wanted me to meet with him because they figured I was a medical student, and it would have more merit to it."

That Dave Sime was on his way to Rome at all signified how far along an unlikely comeback track he had traveled. There was a time, in the year leading up to the 1956 Olympics, when he was considered the world's fastest human. That is what the track writers called him after he had won the indoor sprints at the Millrose Games in New

York earlier that year. Big Red could run anything: 60-yard dash, 70-yard dash, 100, 200, low hurdles, high hurdles. He was white lightning, a flash from Fairview, New Jersey, so talented that as a thirteen-year-old he had won the Silver Skates prize for speed skating at Madison Square Garden, making the front page of the New York *Daily News*—and he didn't even like to skate. A few years later, he showed enough potential in football to be recruited to play at the U.S. Military Academy at West Point by an assistant coach named Vince Lombardi. He might have gone into the services but decided against it when he realized that colorblindness would prevent him from becoming an air corps pilot. Basketball was truly his favorite sport (his father had played for the old New York Celtics), but when it came to selecting a college, he decided on Duke, lured there by baseball coach Ace Parker, who wanted him to play center field.

It was not until he reached Duke that Sime became interested in track. His raw speed far outpaced his technique at first, but he schooled himself in the art of sprinting by reading every book on running at the university library, eventually patterning his style on the stride of a dash great from an earlier era, Ralph Metcalfe. He spent hours thumbing through the pages of a flip book of photographs depicting Metcalfe running, creating the sensation of a moving picture. By the end of his sophomore year, Sime had streaked to national stardom in the track world and was a favorite to win gold in the sprints in '56, but he hurt his leg before the Olympic Trials and never made it to Melbourne. This disappointment, he said later, was the "best thing that happened" in his life, forcing him to redirect his attention to premed courses. He also concentrated on baseball. During his junior season, Sime led the Atlantic Coast Conference and was named a second-team all-American. He might have abandoned track altogether until a test of his amateurism at once infuriated him and turned him around. After that stellar junior season, he had landed a summer job playing semipro baseball in Pierre, South Dakota, but before the opening game, he received an emergency telephone call from Dan Ferris, the head of the AAU, who had somehow learned of his intentions and whereabouts.

"If you play one game, you will be ineligible for all amateur athletic events in track and field," Ferris told him.

"So I am stuck," Sime recalled. "I could have said, 'Fuck, I'm going to do it,' and give up my amateur athletics. But I still was pissed that I didn't get to go to Melbourne. Bobby Morrow, who I beat every time when I was healthy, wins the gold medals, and I'm sitting back home . . . So now I didn't know what to do." Sime was without money, and the Pierre ball club was of no help; it wouldn't pay him unless he played in the first game. In desperation, he called Eddie Cameron, Duke's athletic director, who said the NCAA would penalize Duke if he sent money to bring Sime home, but that he could arrange transportation to an AAU track meet in Dayton. Sime flew to Ohio, worked out for a day, did well in the meet, and soon found himself on a national squad touring France—and back on a course that eventually led him toward the race he had always wanted to run, for an Olympic gold medal. Even Ace Parker, his baseball coach, thought it was the right decision. When Sime debated with him whether to try pro ball or keep his Olympic dream alive, Parker said that out of the few billion people in the world, only a handful get a chance to run in the Olympics, and that if he had that one-in-millions chance, he should seize it.

Now Sime, at age twenty-four, was an Olympian with an extra assignment: run for your country, and bag a defector for your country as well. Dave was all for it. He considered himself a patriot. To get a high-profile athlete to switch sides and leave the Soviet Union for America seemed a thrilling thing to do.

The airlift of American athletes from New York to Rome began the same day as Sime's whirlwind secret round-trip mission to Washington. First to leave were the swimmers and members of the water polo team, along with an advance deputation of coaches and officials.

Another planeload departed the next day. As each group assembled at Idlewild and waited for the Pan American props that would haul them on the vibrating, seemingly endless fifteen-and-a-half-hour flights, Arthur Lentz, the press officer, moved through the throng of athletes distributing materials. He had already made Berlitz tutors available to teach them how to say phrases like "Your sister is very beautiful" in Italian. Now he was handing out copies of the U.S. Declaration of Independence and a thirty-three-page booklet on the virtues of American life—all printed in Russian. So much for any pretense of keeping the Olympics free from politics. In the propaganda struggle of cold war superpowers, neither side would disarm unilaterally.

The booklet, published by a CIA front called Freedom Fund Inc., noted, among other things, that there were nearly a million people from the Soviet Union now living in America, and that here even the Communist Party could run a candidate for president. Another section discussed common misperceptions of the U.S., one being that only the privileged class benefited from the capitalist system. In emptying his supply of three hundred booklets, Lentz told the athletes that they should pass along their copies to members of the Soviet team at the Olympic Village in Rome.

TO IGOR Ter-Ovanesyan, not quite twenty-two, who had made the Soviet team in the broad jump for the second straight Olympics, competing against athletes from the United States remained an intimidating prospect. Igor was the Soviet version of a gym rat, a lifelong product of the state-run athletic system. His father, an Armenian-born discus thrower, and his mother, a Ukrainian volleyball player, had met at the Kiev State Institute of Physical Education, and both taught there while he was growing up. Although he did not turn to track and field until he was fifteen, Ter-Ovanesyan showed uncommon early talent, breaking the broad-jump record for his age group in his first competition. From then on, his idols were not Soviets but Americans who dominated track and field, starting with the great Jesse Owens, who set the Olympic long-jump record at the 1936 Games in Berlin and a world record a year before at an event in Ann Arbor, Michigan, with a remarkable leap that was still unmatched a quarter century later. "They were like gods for me, the American jumpers," Igor said later. First at Melbourne and then at the historic dual meets in Moscow in 1958 and Philadelphia in 1959, he had felt psychologically overmatched by the U.S. athletes and struggled to overcome an inferiority complex.

But the Western world, and all things American, intrigued him. Bored and lonely during a track tour in Sweden in 1958, he picked up an old English textbook and studied it at night in his Stockholm hotel room. Back in Kiev, he began tuning in Voice of America broadcasts and listened to "everything that wasn't jammed." On every trip to a European capital, he bought American jazz records, books, magazines, as many totems of Western culture as he could find, and smuggled them home in his suitcase. "Did you ever see Louis Armstrong?" he once asked the sportswriter Dick Schaap. "He is wonderful. He is the best. I collect all his records." Schaap found it hard to believe that Igor—who "looked like an Ivy Leaguer and acted like a beatnik"—could be a Russian. But though Ter-Ovanesyan was flirting with what seemed new and unfettered, there remained much about the West that he did not understand, and he still felt a deep imprint of love and loyalty for his fatherland.

Nineteen-sixty had been a difficult year in Soviet relations with the West. Tension seemed to be building month by month, starting in May, when an American U-2 reconnaissance plane piloted by Francis Gary Powers was shot down over Soviet airspace. That was followed by Premier Khrushchev's staged walkout from a four-powers summit meeting in Paris, the cancellation of a future visit to Russia by President Eisenhower, a Soviet promise to defend socialist Cuba with missiles if need be, surrogate battles in Africa and Asia, more pressure over the status of West Berlin, and now, on the eve of the Olympics, a public show trial, in Moscow, where Powers faced espionage charges.

From the Soviet perspective, all of life was an ideological test, and in this context Ter-Ovanesyan was reminded again and again of the political importance of his mission. With his teammates, he was taken on a pilgrimage to Lenin's Tomb. They walked in silence in a slow, somber circle around the mausoleum, a ritual meant to instill a deeper sense of camaraderie and patriotism. He attended daily meetings of the Komsomol, the young people's branch of the Communist Party. He listened to rambling lectures on the role he and his teammates would play in building friendships with athletes from around the world.

Their performance in Rome, Igor was told, would reflect the triumph of a new socialist society where sports was an essential part of the culture. A send-off column from one of the writers he respected at *Pravda* read in part: "Our sportsmen represent the new socialistic order where mental health and moral purity are harmonically tied with physical development. Sports and physical development are the habit of the nation. They are the source of the good spirit, happiness, hard work, and long lives of the Soviet people." It was the same for writers as it was for athletes, Ter-Ovanesyan thought. Just as there was pressure on him to reach certain standards during his training regimen in order not to be regarded negatively by his coaches, so in their sphere his sportswriter friends had to deal with expectations from officials monitoring them and what they published.

Pravda accounts said there were 24 million active athletes in the Soviet Union and that there would be 30 million by the end of the year. From those tens of millions, 299 were selected for the Olympic team that assembled in Moscow and started leaving for Rome on the same mid-August day that the American delegation began departing from New York. The Soviet athletes included blacksmiths, builders, doctors, lawyers, engineers, fishermen, printers, miners, farmers, scientists, and students, but most were connected to the military. In preparing them for Rome, their official handlers placed an emphasis on how best to impress the rest of the world. This meant, among other things, overcoming prevailing Russian stereotypes.

At Helsinki in 1952 and Melbourne in 1956, the world press had written disparagingly of the poor dress and general unattractiveness of many of the Soviet women athletes. If the characterization reflected the prevailing sexist attitude of sportswriters, it nonetheless mirrored an unpleasant portrait of grim Soviet life that Kremlin officials desperately wanted to erase. From the time the first planeload of Russian athletes marched through the airport in Rome, the physical appearance of both the men and women was noted by foreign journalists. Readers from Paris to London to San Francisco were informed that the Soviet women came off the plane wearing sharp beige suits, hosiery, high-heeled brown pumps—and lipstick.

Whatever their dress, the Soviets arrived in Rome with instructions to exude an outward confidence. The doubts that nagged at Ter-Ovanesyan and many of his teammates were smothered by a constant publicity drumbeat of inevitable socialist victory. Since the 1958 dual meet in Moscow, Gavriel Korobkov, the Soviet coach, had been maintaining a meticulous scrapbook detailing the accomplishments of U.S. track-and-field athletes, and knew precisely their best times in the sprints and distances and heights in the jumps. Korobkov was a realist, not prone to political rhetoric, but he was also a clever strategist. If the Americans had the superior athletes, he also believed that they had some of the most fragile ones and that he might be able to find ways to make them crack under pressure. While the Soviets were still far below world standards in swimming, dominated by the U.S. and Australia, if they could battle the Americans to a draw in track and field, they thought they could take enough medals in various other sports—from weight lifting to cycling to gymnastics to canoeing—to win the overall point total and gain world bragging rights over the Americans.

When a bus carrying the first Soviets from the airport pulled up to the Olympic Village, an Italian journalist rushed over and asked if there were any celebrities on board. "As many as you would like," came a half-joking translated reply. "Take down names of all of us and then after the Games we'll reconfirm."

That day in Washington, a memorandum reached the desk of President Eisenhower from his Committee on Information Activities Abroad. "The Communists are now putting more emphasis on propaganda through deeds than through words," the memo stated. This revised approach reflected "an understanding that Sputnik, the Soviet ICBM, the Bolshoi Ballet, or a Soviet victory at the Olympics has more propaganda value than mere words." More precisely, the Soviets viewed the Olympics as an extraordinary opportunity to weave words and action together.

MORE THAN half of the U.S. contingent of 305 athletes were still in New York on Monday, August 15, when Mayor Robert Wagner feted them at a send-off rally at city hall. Along with a military color guard and a stairwell of politicians urging the young men and women to win for their country, retired five-star general Omar Bradley was there, a visage from the past, stirring echoes of a time when young Americans swept through Europe as liberators. The Second World War was a mere fifteen years gone, and its aftereffects were still evident and relevant in Italy, yet it seemed as remote as the Roman Empire to many of the U.S. athletes, whose lives had been shaped by a relentlessly forward-looking postwar culture. Some of the female swimmers were not even born when the war ended.

Rafer Johnson was designated to speak for his teammates at city hall. "It is the goal of each of us to win a gold medal. Naturally, that's not possible for all. But we do hope to do the best job possible of representing our country." Simple words, even prosaic, but with Johnson, as a person and as a decathlete, the whole often was greater than the parts. He sounded self-assured yet humble. No one looked sharper in the U.S. Olympic team's travel dress uniform—McGregor-Doniger olive green sports coat, Hagger slacks, Van Heusen beige knit shirt. He had a firm grasp of the occasion and his surroundings, once flawlessly calling out the name of each of the dozens of teammates who stood at his side. Team officials could not help noticing. It was Rafer Johnson's off-the-field performance in New York, along with his stature as a gold medal favorite in the decathlon, that convinced them that he should be the U.S. captain and the first black athlete to carry the American flag when the delegation marched into the stadium at the Opening Ceremony in Rome. There could be no more valuable figure in the propaganda war with the Soviets, who wasted no opportunity to denounce the racial inequities of the United States.

Beneath his composed exterior, Johnson was a jumble of emotions: joy, pride, anticipation, gratitude, determination, and some anger. He refused to feel manipulated, yet he could not escape the burden of carrying other people's expectations and dealing with their contradictory demands. He was aware, he later said, of the irony of representing a nation that treated people of his color like second-class citizens, but he also felt that he could advance the cause most effectively by doing what he did best, which was to excel at his sport and comport himself with dignity.

The same U.S. amateur officials who wanted him to be the symbol of the American team had just upset him with what he viewed as a capricious restriction. While working out on the track at UCLA earlier that year, Johnson had encountered Kirk Douglas, one of many Hollywood actors who occasionally ran there. As they chatted and jogged around the oval, Douglas told Johnson that he was getting ready to do a film called *Spartacus* about a slave revolt in ancient Rome. Stanley Kubrick would be directing. There were many character roles for athletic types. "Why don't you come and read for it?" Douglas asked. Johnson immediately took to the idea. His track days were nearing an end; no matter what happened at the Olympics, he had told himself, that was it, no more decathlons. He had always enjoyed acting; nothing noteworthy, but the junior and senior plays back in high school in Kingsburg, and some community theater. And what better way to break in than with a film that takes place in Rome, of all places? Following Douglas's advice, Johnson read for a part and got it. He was to play Draba, a rebellious Roman slave from Africa who was killed in the ring and had his body hung in chains upside down as a gruesome warning to others.

Before accepting the role, Johnson called the AAU to make sure he was not violating amateur rules. He talked with Dan Ferris, the same official who had kept Dave Sime from playing semipro baseball in South Dakota. But this case seemed different. What did acting have to do with sports? Weren't amateur athletes allowed outside jobs? Ferris said no, not in this instance. According to the AAU's interpretation, acting in *Spartacus* would make him a pro. Johnson was stunned and issued another appeal to Ferris later. If you take the part, Ferris insisted this time, forget about getting on the plane with your teammates and competing in Rome. He had consulted with other AAU officials, and they agreed. Johnson was being hired not because he knew how to act, they said, but because he was a famous athlete. From their perspective, that was no different than if he were paid for a track meet. For the moment, Johnson could empathize with Draba; overlords were threatening to hang him upside down in chains as a warning to others. But in his mind the choice was not close. The *Spartacus* role went to Woody Strode, a black actor and former UCLA athlete himself, and Johnson stayed with the Olympics. After all the obstacles he had overcome since the disappointment of Melbourne, nothing could divert him on his path to redemption.

There had been some unexpected twists since Johnson's moment of exhilaration two years earlier at the historic dual meet in Moscow, when he had set a new world decathlon record and been hoisted onto the shoulders of appreciative Russian fans. On a late spring morning less than a year later, as Rafer and his brother Jimmy, a star football player at UCLA, were driving back from Los Angeles to Kingsburg for the high school graduation of their sister Erma, they got in a traffic accident near Bakersfield that left Rafer with a bruised spinal cord, a pulled hamstring, and spasms in his lower back. No serious accident is a blessing, but this one, he believed, ended up helping him in ways that he could not have foreseen.

Realizing that Johnson could not resume his running regimen, Craig Dixon, the assistant track coach at UCLA, proposed that he start lifting weights, a practice that was barely respectable in most sports during that era. Johnson remembered that in high school at Kingsburg two football players had been kicked off the team for lifting. Over at Southern Cal, weight lifting was so discouraged that the discus thrower Rink Babka would slip over to a house in Watts and pump iron with a group of black bodybuilders who used barbells made from water pipes and weights that were coffee cans filled with concrete. But Dixon believed in weight lifting, so Johnson tried it. Week after week he felt himself getting stronger and even more co-ordinated. As his recovery progressed, and he began preparing for the 1960 Olympics, his results in the three throwing events of the decathlon—shot put, discus, and javelin—improved substantially.

The positive effect of his weight training became evident to the world at his first decathlon since Moscow, the Olympic Trials at the University of Oregon track in Eugene on July 8 and 9, 1960. The pain from the traffic accident still lingered; he needed two shots of Novocain before the competition. But with the three throwing events putting him over the top, Johnson amassed a record total 8683 points, obliterating both the mark he had established at the 1958 dual meet with his Soviet foe, Vasily Kuznetsov, and Kuznetsov's subsequent new record set a year later at the second dual meet between the superpowers, this time held in Philadelphia (where Johnson, because of his injury, did not compete). Even then, Johnson was in danger of losing both the Eugene competition and the world record going into the final event, the 1500 meters. His challenger was his UCLA team-mate C. K. Yang, who would be representing Taiwan at the Olympics. Because of his ties to the UCLA program, Yang was invited to the U.S. decathlon Trials, just as he had been in 1958 at Palmyra, New Jersey, where he also finished second. Johnson and Yang ran in separate heats of the 1500, with Johnson going first and then having to wait thirty-five minutes before Yang's run. It was within the realm of possibility that Yang could run a metric mile fast enough to overcome Johnson's impressive total, but he was slowed by a muscle cramp midway around the second lap.

In their relationship as teammates and competitors, there was always a tug between the powerful will to win and a deep friendship. At the end in Eugene, Johnson found himself shouting words of encouragement as Yang labored around the track. C.K. finished the race, but far slower than his personal best, leaving the record for Rafer and providing decathlon aficionados with the delicious prospect of an Olympic rematch. Neither decathlete could know then that the memory of Yang's muscle cramp in the last of the ten grueling events would follow them all the way to the stadium in Rome.

As Johnson spoke for his teammates at city hall, he was thinking about the rematch. He was "very pleased" that his friend C.K. would be pushing him at the Olympics. And he was looking forward to the chance to make up for his 1956 loss. None of this worried Johnson, but instead filled him with elation, he said later. "I had to be one of the happiest people at city hall that day."

That night, after an informal reception at the Waldorf-Astoria Hotel, three more busloads of athletes set out for Idlewild and the trip across the Atlantic. Every flight had its own profile. Only one plane was a jet, and it carried mostly dignitaries and USOC officials. For years and decades thereafter, the athletes took great delight in reports that some officials got looped on the flight and were let off in Paris. The story, probably apocryphal, accurately delineated the rift between the young competitors and the older men in suits telling them what they could and could not do. A prop DC-7C carrying the cyclists and weight lifters was delayed on the runway for hours while a mechanic scrambled out on the wing and worked on the engine. When the plane finally took off, it was so cramped with bulky athletes jammed into uncomfortable seats that some ended up sleeping in the aisle. In his diary, Jack Simes, a cyclist, wrote: "I get up because I wanted to go visit the head in the back anyway. The whole plane is pretty dark except for the noisy section where there is much activity. As I pass on the way to the head I see, in the middle of it all [four cyclists] mixed in with the big guys. They're playing cards, and there are beer bottles and money all over the place and lots of laughter. This is the Olympics we're going to? Up late drinking beer and gambling?"

The passenger manifest for a plane departing the night of August 15 listed the heavyweight crew and the women's track team, including eight Tigerbelles and Ed Temple, who had been named the women's coach. The white rowers and black sprinters played whist and pinochle together on the long flight. There had been no threat from Temple this time to take his team back to Nashville on a Ladd bus if he didn't get the job; everyone had come to realize how vital his program was to the U.S. hopes.

The fleetest of his sprinters now was Wilma Rudolph, who had missed the 1958 trip to Moscow because of her pregnancy. Yolanda, her daughter, now two, was back living with her parents in Clarksville. Rudolph, known to her friends as Skeeter, a nickname her high school basketball coach had given her because she was "always buzzing around like a mosquito" on the court, seemed to be nearing her ultimate performance level just in time for Rome. Earlier that summer, when she had first put up a world-class time in the 100 at the AAU nationals in Corpus Christi, Texas, Temple could not believe it. The official time down on the field precisely matched his own stopwatch up in the stands, but it was so good he thought something must have been wrong. Maybe the cinder track was a few yards short. "I said, 'People, this child's running a little too fast. I mean, something's the matter with the track or something.' " Then Rudolph ran her best-ever time in the 200, and a week later the same thing happened at the Olympic Trials. Skeeter was on the move.

Still, Temple was not overly confident. He wanted his runners to think they would win gold, but kept lower expectations to himself. On the flight to Rome, he was thinking, "Just get to the finals. If only we can get Wilma and maybe another Tigerbelle to the finals. That would mean they were among the best six in the world. Then, maybe by some miracle, they could get a third place. Just get up on the stand." A bronze medal would get a Tigerbelle to the podium.

The third plane carried the Olympic boxing team, including an obstreperous eighteen-year-old light heavyweight from Louisville named Cassius Marcellus Clay. In retrospect, it is not surprising that the memories of many who took that flight focus on Clay, who was still four years away from renaming himself Muhammad Ali. His personality would not change, only the size of his audience and his larger meaning. In Manhattan that week, the Olympic long jumper Bo Roberson, who had been an all-round sports star at Cornell University when the journalist Dick Schaap was a student there, introduced the kid boxer to the young sports editor of Newsweek, and they hung out together one day and night, in Harlem and back at the delegation hotel. "I'll be the greatest of all time," Clay repeatedly told Schaap, who would never forget those improbable words. They were nothing new to Clay's Olympic teammates, who had heard Clay boast so much that they often tuned him out. But on the plane to Rome, what made him stick out was an unusual fusion of confidence and fear. He was certain about what would happen in the ring in Rome, just not certain he would get there. His fear of flying was so strong that it took the persuasion of all his teammates to get him to board the plane.

Jerry Armstrong, a bantamweight from Idaho State College, said "Cassius was scared to death. We said, 'Well, you can either fly or stay home.' " The boxers were seated up near the cockpit, which did nothing to soothe Clay's apprehension. Over and over again, he repeated his mantra, "*If God wanted us to fly, he would give us wings.*" To which Wilbert McClure, a light middleweight from the University of Toledo, would respond, "Well, we're flying, and we ain't got no wings, so how do you explain that?" Nikos Spanakos, a featherweight from Brooklyn, who boxed collegiately at the College of Idaho, remembered that Clay was screaming the entire flight. "So the coach gave us a sleeping pill to knock us all out, and Cassius was able to overcome the sleeping pill and was *still* screaming." In this case, screaming meant talking. By McClure's account, Clay spent several hours "talking about who would win gold medals and dada-dada-dada, and he had good ideas and picked the guys who were going to win." He based his predictions on who "had the Olympic style and were furthering the Olympic image." There was some method to the madness of this kid yapping his way across the Atlantic, McClure decided. Not for the last time, he was talking and boasting to overcome his own fears.

THE ETHIOPIANS came early to Rome, leaving heavy thunderclouds behind as they departed Addis Ababa. There were twelve men on their Olympic team: six runners and six cyclists. After coming down from the mountain altitudes, the runners had trained in the final weeks on dusty grounds near an air base at Debre Zeit, south of the capital city. They were coached there by a Swede named Onni Niskanen, director of athletics in the government of Haile Selassie, or H.I.M., as the reverential local newspapers referred to His Imperial Majesty. Three days before the Olympians left Addis Ababa, they had been ushered inside the gates of the imperial palace for the first time for an audience with the emperor. It had taken more than coaching skills for Niskanen to get to this moment. The Olympic team had been underfunded, lacking money for training or to pay for the stay

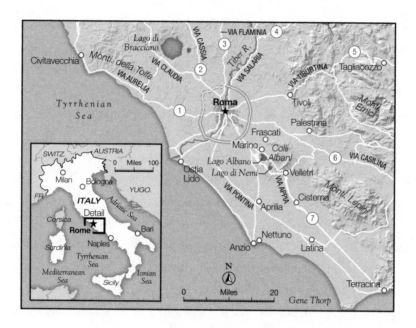

in Rome, until His Imperial Majesty was persuaded that his nation's distance runners could bring him honor—perhaps even a medal. "You have all recorded good results in the athletic competition of the armed forces this year," Haile Selassie told them. "The question is whether such victory will continue as well as it has so far. You, athletes, are the ones to answer that question."

It had been twenty-five years since the Fascist legions of Benito Mussolini had invaded Ethiopia, devastating the civilian population with bombing raids and poison gas. In 1936 Il Duce's troops occupied a mountain village in Debre Birhan, forcing out Wudinesh Beneberu and her family, including her four-year-old son, Abebe Bikila. The next year, the Italians seized the Axum Obelisk, one of Ethiopia's cherished religious and archeological treasures, and shipped the seventy-eight-foot monument of antiquity back to Rome, where it was stationed prominently along a main thoroughfare as a reminder of colonial European supremacy. Now Il Duce was long dead, and H.I.M. remained, and Abebe Bikila, just turned twenty-eight, a private in Haile Selassie's Imperial Guard, was landing in Rome with the modest delegation of Ethiopian Olympians, preparing to run a marathon route that would lead him past his nation's stolen obelisk. The experts of distance running had never heard of him. In the materials being prepared for the world press, his name was transposed as Bikila Abebe.

The small teams from Burma and Romania were already in Rome when Abebe Bikila and his Ethiopians arrived. They were so anxious to enjoy the city, and this gathering of peers from around the world, and to train away from their homelands, that they settled into the Olympic Village more than two weeks before the Opening Ceremony. The Japanese were next to join them, then the Ghanaians, Sudanese, and Indonesians. The world order was transmuting in 1960, with nations being born, regressing, progressing—and out of all that, an unprecedented eighty-three National Olympic Committees were sending a record total of 5,338 athletes to Rome. None was from the world's most populous nation, the People's Republic of China, which officially withdrew from the Olympic Movement in 1958 and had isolated itself from international athletic competition for most of the fifties. The main reason the Communist Chinese were not in Rome was because of their opposition to the Olympic community's recognition of another team that was already there, a 45-athlete delegation led by decathlete C. K. Yang from Taiwan, which the Communist Chinese considered a rightful part of their territory. Ten hours of fog had delayed the team's takeoff from Taipei, and it still seemed shrouded in a fog of war over what it rightfully should be called, Taiwan or the Republic of China. Nonetheless, the first cable from team officials in Rome back to the island was a request for two thousand more China Olympic pins to distribute.

Suriname came with the smallest possible number of athletes (a solitary Siegfried Esajas, an 800-meter runner allegedly destined to oversleep and miss his one and only heat), and Germany with the largest contingent, 321. The Germans also most obviously embodied the internal tension of the Olympic movement: political and apolitical, united and divided.

Since the end of World War II, Germany had been a riven domain, with the western sector of the country and West Berlin reconstructing a democratic government under the supervision of the U.S., England, and France, while the eastern sector and East Berlin were in the Soviet orbit. Now the chief of mission for the German Olympic delegation was Gerhard Stoeck of the Federal Republic of Germany, and the deputy chief was Manfred Ewald from the German Democratic Republic. West and East, two political systems, contested borders and checkpoints, but one supposed unified team. Stoeck and Ewald arrived in advance of their athletes and spent considerable time together trying to figure out how they could survive. While their relationship played out in a larger political theater, it had the intimate awkwardness of parents from a nasty divorce showing up at their child's wedding and being forced to sleep in the same hotel room. There had been no athletes from East Germany, or the Soviet zone, at the Helsinki Olympics, and only 37 in Melbourne, where they had trained and lived separately from their Western counterparts. This time, with 141 Eastern athletes on the team, Stoeck and Ewald agreed that they would live and train together, or at least within the same areas, and that overt politics would be taboo.

Years of intense negotiations, ten rounds' worth, concluded near midnight August 9 at a session in Dortmund, Germany, at the Hotel Westfalenhalle, the two sides finally agreeing on the composition of the unified team and its accepted symbols. It was a merger of athletic necessity, not political choice, forced upon them by officials from the International Olympic Committee who had ruled that the Germans would compete as one team or not at all. Their Italian hosts had placed the German men in block 30 of the Olympic Village, not far from Piazza Grecia, a square outlined by flagpoles. When the team flag was hoisted there, it was the traditional German red, black, and gold, but replacing politically tinged emblems preferred by East or

West were the five Olympic rings. And instead of a national anthem, the music played at the flag raising—as it would at any future medal ceremony where a German athlete won—was the "Ode to Joy" from Beethoven's Ninth Symphony.

Ewald, at age thirty-six, had moved from one ideological extreme to another in his young life. Born in Podejuch, Germany, later part of Poland, he had been a Hitler Youth and was trained at an elite Nazi school. He fought in World War II as a teenager and near the end of the war was taken prisoner by the Soviets on the Eastern front. Returning to what became the Soviet zone of East Germany, he joined the Communist Party and rose through the ranks of sports and politics. It was part of the daily rhetoric of East Germany to denounce West German leaders as former Nazis, but Ewald seemed to get a pass on that account. Now, in Rome, when two reporters from the *Frankfurter Allgemeine Zeitung,* a leading newspaper in West Germany, visited him at the German quarters in the Olympic Village, they noted "the most polite way" he assessed the odd situation. The team was comprised of "equal partners from East and West, with equal rights and duties," he told the visiting journalists. He had even instructed athletes from his eastern side to avoid wearing blue GDR sweatshirts and instead don the black-and-white unified team outfits when they stepped outside their rooms. "He went on for fifteen minutes enthusiastically painting a beautiful picture," they observed.

At the end, they asked why a plaque on his door happened to say "Team Leader of the GDR." Ewald claimed that he had just noticed it and would have it swiftly replaced.

If ostensibly unified in Rome, the German squads arrived separately. The Easterners made much of an elderly gentleman they brought along with them. Carl Galle, eighty-seven, the oldest living German Olympian, was an East Berliner who had run the metric mile at the first modern Olympic Games in 1896. The Olympic fire had burned inside him ever since, Galle said, and he followed the Games wherever he could. The Olympics, or at least the prospect of a

Roman holiday punctuated by drinking songs and orchestrated stadium cheers, also inspired a horde of West Germans to caravan down to Italy by the thousands. Karlheinz Vogel, a writer for the Frankfurt paper, got stuck in horrible traffic near the Italian border and characteristically berated the inefficiency of the Italians. "In Bale, German and Swiss customs waved people through like traffic police," Vogel noted. "In Chiasso, the Swiss customs could hardly be seen. But the Italians at the border force people to leave their cars, fill out forms, put stamps in travel documents, and do not care if the line of cars is getting longer and longer."

A traffic jam at the Italian border sounded preferable to what the large and confident Australian delegation endured on its trip to Rome. First there was hydraulic trouble in one of the jets, causing a twenty-four-hour delay after refueling in Bahrain. With another stop in Cairo, it took the two hundred Aussie athletes and their handlers two and a half days to reach their destination. They were exhausted upon arrival, and the blast-furnace heat of late-summer Rome, now soaring over ninety degrees, did not help their adjustment. A pack of journalists waited for them at the airport, eager to hear the latest in the relationship between Herb Elliott, the world's greatest miler, and his eccentric coach, Percy Cerutty. "There never was a rift," Cerutty claimed when asked if Elliott had soured on him. Then, in his pugnacious style, he added: "And I'll flatten anyone who says there is."

While Cerutty, known for his special diets and sand dune training, was the personal guru of Elliott and other distance runners, he was not part of the official Australian coaching team and had to scramble for credentials and housing in Rome. The regal Elliott himself was granted special privileges, allowed to spend most of his time with his wife and baby outside the Olympic Village gates. Cerutty, always frugal if not broke, talked his way into lodging in a dorm with the cyclists. But he was summarily expelled after a few days because he had transformed the suite into a boisterous day-and-night runners' salon, taking in disciples from around the world who solicited his wisdom. Disarray was the early watchword for the unfortunate Australians; soon after they arrived, many of their world-class swimmers came down with conjunctivitis, which they attributed to the chlorine and the blistering sun.

AS GERMAN tourists streamed south through the Alps, the last of the American athletes to leave New York—the men's track-and-field squad and the basketball team—were just arriving in Switzerland, drained and leg weary, after their own fourteen-hour flight. U.S. Olympic officials had arranged for a track meet in Bern and basketball exhibition games in Geneva and Lugano as warm-ups for Rome in the week before the Opening Ceremony. Harold Connolly, the veteran hammer thrower, spoke aloud for many of his teammates when he groused about this side trip. It would interfere with serious training, he said, and was "simply a sightseeing trip for officials who want to see the Alps." Here again, there was little sympathy from the athletes for their overseers; word spread among them that the real reason the Swiss trip was booked was because the foreign hosts had agreed to pay the charter travel costs.

Pete Newell, the U.S. Olympic basketball coach, nevertheless welcomed the games in Switzerland, which he hoped would prepare his young team for the vagaries of international officiating. Newell, who had just retired as head coach at the University of California, Berkeley, after leading the Bears to an NCAA championship in 1959 and a loss to Ohio State in the finals that spring, had the luxury of working with his Olympic squad since early April, when selections were made after Trials in Denver. The team was busting with talented college players unfamiliar with the international style, starting with the stellar trio of Oscar Robertson from the University of Cincinnati, Jerry West from West Virginia University, and Jerry Lucas from Ohio State, along with Walt Bellamy of Indiana University,

Terry Dischinger of Purdue University, Jay Arnette of the University of Texas, and Darrall Imhoff of UC Berkeley. But the other players were chosen by an AAU-dominated Olympic selection committee influenced by corporations like Phillips Petroleum in Tulsa and Caterpillar in Peoria, Illinois, which sponsored ostensibly amateur teams and enjoyed the publicity that came with helping finance the Olympic effort. A few of their players were both experienced in international play and good enough to demand playing time, but others took roster spots that might have gone to more talented collegians, including two future Hall of Famers unable to make the team, John Havlicek of Ohio State and Lenny Wilkins of Providence College.

The first exhibition game, played in Geneva on Saturday, August 20, taught Newell little about his team. Not much to learn when the score is 122–37, and the Swiss opposition is a makeshift squad of local university students. But the Americans did get some benefit from playing with an official Olympic ball, which was bald and slippery, and made from eighteen pieces of leather, unlike the seamless one-piece American ball, with its sticky little pebble grains. The one-sided match served one other purpose: it sent a message to officials of Soviet basketball, who until then knew nothing about Robertson and West and Lucas, and so had been talking confidently about taking on the American neophytes. A face in the crowd was Semyon K. Tsarapkin, chief Soviet delegate to the three-power U.S.-British-Soviet A-bomb test ban talks in Geneva, which the next day would adjourn for two months. Reports from courtside portrayed Tsarapkin, a veteran diplomat who later would negotiate the nuclear hotline with the U.S., sitting in the front row "looking glumly at the exhibition of American superiority."

The track-and-field team faced equally unimposing competition at its weekend meet in Bern against second-tier athletes from England, Poland, Italy, Switzerland, France, Germany, and Austria. There was no decathlon, so Rafer Johnson competed instead in a few individual events, refining his technique in the javelin and long jump. Don Bragg, favoring a sore leg, took it easy in the pole vault, as did John Thomas, the heralded young high jumper. The talk of the meet was Lee Calhoun, who ran the 110-meter high hurdles in 13.2 seconds, tying the world record set by Germany's Martin Lauer. Calhoun seemed to be rounding into form nicely after his year-long suspension in 1958, punishment for breaking amateur rules by marrying his wife on national television and accepting the show's wedding gifts. Glenn Davis, the multitalented low hurdler, ran free and easy in the 200-meter hurdles, an event that was not in the Olympics, and established another record at that rarely run distance. And Ralph Boston, a long jumper from Tennessee State, the adopted big brother of the Tigerbelles, also broke a world record, flying twenty-six feet, eight and seven-eighths inches. The 100-meter dash followed what had become a familiar recent pattern. Ray Norton, from the track club at San Jose State College, had won the Olympic Trials at Stanford in July and was the heavy favorite in Rome. In most pre-Olympic write-ups, in fact, Norton was labeled a likely triple gold medal winner—for 100, 200, and relay. But shortly after the trials, Dave Sime had started beating him in practice meets, and Sime outran him again in Bern. The coaches seemed unconcerned about Norton. He would come around for Rome, they said.

No one seemed worried about Jim Beatty, either, especially since he won his event in Bern. Beatty had made the Olympic team in the 5000-meter run with the same deep motivation that drove Dave Sime, his friend and roommate. He had been at his prime as a college runner at the University of North Carolina in 1956 but failed to make it to Melbourne that year, and essentially quit running until the lure of Rome drew him back. In October 1959 he drove across the country to California to train with the renowned distance coach Mihaly Igloi, a Hungarian exile. The journey itself would remain burnished in his mind: turning twenty-five on the road, stopping in Reno, Nevada, to hear the Four Aces sing "Love Is a Many Splendored Thing," heading down the highway to San Jose. Overweight, out of running shape, but with a bundle of heart, Beatty trained to Olympic standards, running all the distance races, from the metric mile to the 5000. By May 1960 he had clocked a sub–four-minute mile and a 13:51 in the 5000. He could have run either, but chose the 5000 for the Olympics. Rome was a week away. And now, as he propelled into his kick to victory on the straightaway in Bern, he hit a soft pocket in the cinder track, and a jolt of electricity shot up his leg as he crossed the finish line.

Everything in Switzerland could be deceiving. All traces of the flu that had leveled Dave Sime in New York seemed gone now. Saturday night in Bern had been cold and blustery, but a bright sun burnished a becalmed blue sky as the meet came to an end Sunday afternoon. When the team bus stopped near a glacier-fed river, Al Cantello, the javelin thrower, and Bill Nieder, a shot-putter, led a stampede out the door to dive in. "It wasn't very deep, but the river was moving," Rink Babka, the discus thrower, recalled. "If you put your ear in, you could hear the gravel moving." Babka sensed at one point that Rafer Johnson was having trouble with the current and pulled him off to the side. Sime luxuriated in the bracing water. One of the coaches instructed him to rest that night, but the med student paid no attention. He had brought his wife along, and they stayed out until three in the morning. "That," he said later, "is when I got the chills."

Like many of his colleagues in the sportswriting fraternity, Fred Russell, veteran columnist at the *Nashville Banner,* had spent the summer touring the continent. In Spain he wrote about Picasso. In Germany he posed in a Kaiser Wilhelm helmet. In Paris he wore a beret. Russell was a prankster with a light touch, but when he reached Switzerland he wrote in awe of the juggernaut he was joining. "In 32 years of sports writing, no experience I've had has been more rewarding than the privilege of joining the Olympic squad. [Now] it's a trip into the Alps, then the train ride to Rome Tuesday." The train arrived in Rome Tuesday, but the journey began Monday, and quite a ride it turned out to be. The track-and-field athletes boarded first and took up several compartments, settling in for a long overnight trip. No one slept, according to Rafer Johnson, the team captain. "It was all fun, and we laughed and talked the whole time."

Laughed and talked and tossed furniture, to be more precise. Hour by hour, piece by piece, chairs and cushions went flying out into the alpine darkness; even fixtures ripped from the wall. One car, by dawn, was stripped bare, with not a single bit of furnishing left.

The basketball team boarded at six-thirty that morning in Lugano, closer to the Italian border, and the chaos continued. Coach Newell and his men had trouble getting aboard because of language problems. "No one could understand when we asked where our compartments were," Newell said later. "We'd go one way and get a no. We'd start the other way and get another no. Finally we let down a window and piled all our luggage into the first empty compartment, except that it wasn't empty. There was a guy asleep in one corner. We piled our bags all around him, and it was a wonder he didn't smother. When we finally discovered where we belonged, it was ten cars away. When we got the last bag out, I was relieved to see the guy in the corner still breathing and still asleep."

Some people—like the sleeping stranger and Oscar Robertson— cannot be flustered. The Big O was thrilled by the sights out the window, coming down through Northern Italy's mountains, hills, and valleys. He also was quietly practicing Italian, all the words and phrases he learned listening to a record every night when the team trained at West Point earlier that month. As a child, Robertson often rode trains between his grandparents' house near Nashville and his home in Indianapolis, but he had never seen anything like this. "Indianapolis," he told NBC later, "is very flat."

It was afternoon by the time the last Americans reached the Olympic Village. They checked into Buildings 7 and 8, not far from the Brits. Larry Snyder, the track coach, reported that his team was in excellent shape except for a few minor aches and bruises. That is how coaches talk to the press. Dave Sime recalled it this way: "We get into Rome, and I feel like shit. Sore throat. And it's one hundred three degrees or something." Not his body temperature, but the weather. "I go see Doc Hanley." Daniel F. Hanley, from Bowdoin College, was one of the team physicians. "He says strep throat. So I get a shot in the ass. Both cheeks."

3

NO MONARCH EVER
HELD SWAY

WHEN Avery Brundage, president of the International Olympic Committee, arrived in Rome a week before the Opening Ceremony, he was met at the airport by his guide and chauffeur, Edward Cernaez, who was fluent in French, English, and Italian, and available for assistance around-the-clock. Also there, hovering to the side, was Ambassador Yu Tsun-chi from the Republic of China, who had come unannounced with the hopes of grabbing a few minutes of Brundage's time. Soon enough Brundage was surrounded by a scrum of reporters armed with questions—first and foremost whether he intended to step down as president, as he had been hinting at for months. "I merely said I was ready for some peace and quiet, nothing more," Brundage responded. His interrogators persisted: what did that mean? "I don't want to enlarge upon my previous remarks," he said. They took that as a no, he did not intend to resign after all. Where he would find peace and quiet was another matter entirely.

Brundage was seventy-two now, blocky, balding, and bespectacled, with crumpled dark gray suits, the very model of an old-fashioned Midwestern Republican millionaire businessman, which is what he was, yet so much more. From his roots in American athletics—as a trackman at the University of Illinois, U.S. decathlete at the 1912 Olympics in Stockholm (where he dropped out after eight events, finishing in sixteenth place, far behind winner Jim Thorpe), and president of the AAU and the American Olympic Committee in the late 1920s and 1930s—Brundage had evolved by 1960 into the personification of the Olympic Movement. His insistence on capitalizing those two words hinted at the grandiosity of his design. He believed that the Olympic Movement, in its reach and meaning, far surpassed any government, religion, or philosophy. The briefcase he carried when he reached Rome held the text of a speech he was to deliver at the solemn opening of the 57th Session of the IOC. In it he asserted that while the greatest political empires all crumbled, his world of sport only grew stronger year by year, expanding to scores of countries on all six continents, even without wealth or armies. "No monarch," he wrote, "ever held sway over such a vast expanse of territory."

Yet as Brundage finished his eighth year as high priest of this secular empire of sweat, the modern world was closing in on him from all sides. His rigid rules on amateurism were being ridiculed by journalists and tested by an increasing number of athletes, who saw everyone making money from their efforts but themselves. New nations were lobbying for more participants and a wider variety of events, while Brundage and his old guard wanted fewer of both. Women wanted to run longer distances, while Brundage and some other traditionalists thought that anything beyond once around the oval track was unladylike. Civil rights activists in South Africa and Great Britain were urging the IOC to live up to its Olympic Creed and expel the apartheid delegation from South Africa, while Brundage took

South African leaders at their word that they were letting all citizens compete for roster spots, but colored natives simply were not talented enough.

And more: in a bid for power conveniently disguised as a democratic movement, the Soviet Union was mounting a challenge to the very structure of the International Olympic Committee, hoping to take it over by transforming the membership selection process. Brundage believed that members of the committee had to remain autonomous and nonideological, devoted not to their countries but to the Olympic cause—even if that meant running the IOC like a secret society, the selection of members determined by a coterie of upper-class gentlemen and various counts, princes, and marquesses, the last dying vestiges of European royalty. From the other side of the cold war came attacks from within his own home country, with the Eisenhower administration and conservative factions in the U.S. accusing Brundage of being wrong, if not traitorous, on the central political issue of the Olympics: whether a delegation should be called the Republic of China or Taiwan.

All of these matters were so pressing that Brundage could not avoid them, even at meetings where he controlled the agenda. The first forum was a meeting of the IOC executive board held on Friday, August 19, at the Hotel Excelsior, where Brundage and other Olympic leaders were staying, up the street from the American embassy on the pulsating Via Veneto. With its Belle Epoque decor of gilded chairs, pink marble, and high ceilings, the Excelsior was the grande dame of Rome hotels, befitting the elite nature of the IOC's inner circle. Here sat Dr. Armand Massard of France and the Marquess of Exeter, also known as Lord David Burghley, of England, a former Olympic hurdler who had coveted the presidency since 1952, when Brundage beat him out. Massard and Burghley were the two vice presidents. Also on hand were Count Paolo Thaon di Revel of Italy; Sir Arthur Porritt of New Zealand; Dr. Karl Ritter von Halt of Germany; Bo Ekelund of Sweden, a former high jumper; and General

Vladimir Stoichev of Bulgaria, the lone Eastern bloc member. Helping Brundage run the meeting was Otto Mayer, chancellor of the IOC, who oversaw its daily affairs from the Mon Repos headquarters in Lausanne, Switzerland, with the mannerisms of a snobbish tennis and riding club director. This was the crowd that once got into a harrumphing snit at the outlandish suggestion to forgo the wearing of formal top hats at an outdoor function. Brundage himself was not from the upper class, having made his money in Chicago hotels and office buildings, but he felt at home in the high society world and acted more baronly than any of them.

The first order of business was consideration of new members of the committee, among them Reginald Stanley Alexander of Kenya, who was in Rome as head of the Kenya Olympic Association. Alexander was a former colonial mayor of Nairobi and had played field hockey for Kenya during his younger days. Most important, he had the blessing of Otto Mayer, who had once dined with him in Lausanne. His stamp of approval came in a 1959 note Mayer sent the Marquess of Exeter. "My idea is he would be a very good member for us," Mayer wrote then. "He is young, very Olympic minded; he is British (not a coloured man!), and I wonder if it would not be a good idea to have once a member in that section of the world, that means Africa? What do you think?" Good enough for the marquess, and Brundage as well, and Alexander was in. The last thing the inner circle wanted was someone who might be different or take up a cause beyond the Olympic Movement itself. Nearly a decade earlier, when Lord Burghley (he was not yet elevated to marquess by his father's death) sent along the name of Lord Killanin of Ireland for committee membership, it was with this testimonial: "His history is that, although an active Irishman, he went to Cambridge . . . I feel that his views on the Irish questions would not be to stir up continual trouble, but rather as far as possible to 'let sleeping dogs lie.' "

• • •

THE MAIN agenda item for the executive board involved China, a big dog that would not stop barking. No issue proved more difficult for Brundage than China—or the two Chinas. There was Mao Ze-dong's People's Republic of China, or Red China, Communist and controlling the mainland; and the Republic of China, or Nationalist China, based on the island of Taiwan and run by the authoritarian anticommunist Chiang Kaishek. In 1956 both sent delegates to Mel-bourne, but Mao's China, which had participated in the 1952 Hel-sinki Games, refused to compete unless the team from Chiang's China, which it considered illegitimate, was banned. Two years later, in 1958, when the IOC still would not accede to that demand, the Communist Chinese summarily withdrew from the Olympics and all other international athletic federations. They denounced Brun-dage as "a tool of the Imperialistic State Department of the United States."

Then, at a decisive session in Munich on May 25, 1959, the IOC voted to force the Republic of China Olympic Committee to compete under the name Taiwan (or the other name for the island, Formosa) or not at all, arguing that it could no longer use China in its name because it did not physically represent the vast territory of China. Brundage and the Marquess of Exeter, the strongest Western propo-nent of the name change within the IOC, said it was a practical deci-sion arrived at free from ideological pressure and without political overtones. The political act came from those who insisted on calling it China when it was not China, they argued. "We cannot recognize a Chinese committee in Taiwan any more than we can recognize an Italian committee in Sicily or a Canadian committee in Newfound-land," Brundage said. But the U.S. government, which recognized Chiang's Nationalist China but not Mao's mainland government, viewed this as a major symbolic victory for the Communist bloc, and thought Brundage had been naive and manipulated by the Soviets, who had initiated the proposal.

The first American press dispatches from Munich lent support to this view with their hyperbolic interpretation, reporting that the IOC had bowed to pressure from Moscow and had expelled Nationalist China with the intent of paving the way for the return of the Communist Chinese. For the next year, Brundage was attacked not as an imperialist tool but as a Communist sympathizer. He withstood vitriolic attacks from right-wing radio commentators, a letter-writing campaign launched by the John Birch Society and various church groups, and critical editorials from mainstream newspapers and magazines.

The direction of the attack befuddled Brundage, who took pride in being a staunch anti-Communist. His hard-line political views on China were set out bluntly years earlier in a speech he delivered to the Detroit Economic Club in February 1955: "Why was China betrayed? Why was MacArthur held back in Korea? Right then and there we—I say we—made Red China a major power, destroyed what was left of not only the United States' but the entire white man's prestige in the Orient, and snuffed out the light of freedom for Asia's helpless millions." Those were still his views on the larger question, yet his position on the nomenclature issue had given him a far different image. Allen Guttman, an Olympic historian and Brundage biographer from Amherst College, uncovered a haiku-like note that Brundage scribbled to himself during the heat of the controversy:

AB
Clever fellow
Imperialist
Fascist
Capitalist
Nazi
& now Communist

While not going to that extreme, the *New York Times* denounced Brundage and said he had "succumbed to the rawest sort of political blackmail." "Avery Brundage Must Go," blared a headline in the *Detroit Times*. And *Sports Illustrated* said "politics have entered Olympic affairs with a vengeance at the Olympians' own invitation."

Among Brundage's few defenders in the press was, surprisingly, Red Smith of the New York *Herald Tribune,* who once called him "the greatest practicing patsy . . . of this century" and commonly lampooned him as an out-of-date autocrat. "The role of dissenter is not one to be coveted," Smith wrote, yet he felt compelled to dissent from conventional wisdom. Even if the "agitation leading up to the decision" came from "a source that is repugnant to us," that did not mean that the decision was wrong, or political. "In this instance the [politics charge] might more properly be brought against the critics of the IOC than against that organization."

The U.S. State Department lined up strongly against the IOC and began an intense effort to reverse the Munich decision. Foreign service officers in all European capitals were instructed to lobby local contacts on the issue. Cable traffic flowed regularly between Washington and embassies in Rome and Taipei, the Taiwan capital. One airgram from Rome to State early that summer suggested an attempt at sensual diplomacy: The Italians should invite Otto Mayer down from Lausanne "to discuss technical aspects of Games and then after showing him some of the fleshpots of Rome" try to persuade him to back down from the name change. Although Brundage was more prone to weaknesses of the flesh—*Sports Illustrated* would later call him "a philanderer of enormous appetite"—no similar strategy was broached for him. In terse telegramese, one dispatch from State to Rome and Taipei read: "Department has concluded it inadvisable attempt directly influence him this matter at this juncture. Basis past experience, such efforts would probably have negative effect. Department however continuing attempt influence issue through Roby and others." Roby was Detroit business executive Douglas F. Roby, one of the two U.S. members of the IOC, who spoke out against the

Munich decision and had become the key Olympic contact, feeding inside information to State and doing its bidding.

In the run-up to the Olympics, State sent a confidential memo to its embassy in Rome instructing it to contact Roby as soon as he arrived, "informing him of current situation and offering all appropriate assistance in his efforts to obtain support for ROC [Republic of China] among non-US members." The memo was dated August 11, the day before the press counselor for the Italian embassy in Washington was reassured by a State Department diplomat that the U.S. would do everything possible to keep the Olympics free from partisan politics or propaganda. Roby reached Rome on the Thursday evening of August 17 and was met at the Hotel Excelsior by an embassy officer. They had "a long and satisfactory talk," a telex to Washington reported. Roby was said to be "tentatively mildly optimistic" and agreed to "attempt informal approaches with delegates from Venezuela, Canada, Greece, Netherlands, Iceland, Mexico, Spain and India." On the other hand, Roby was "disturbed by a precedent"—that in a preliminary basketball tournament held in Bologna, Italy, for teams that had to play their way into the Olympics, the Republic of China had already agreed to use the name Taiwan.

There was no question what the executive board would say about the China issue, though its decision could still be overturned by the full IOC at its meeting a few days later. Led by the Marquess of Exeter and Brundage, the board decided to "maintain the decision in Munich." In specific, this meant that "the athletes and officials will take part in the parades and in the competitions under the appellation Taiwan. They will also figure under this name in the programmes, and will be announced under this name at all the ceremonials pertaining to the protocol."

At the American embassy down the street from the executive board meeting, a confidential memo arrived at 4:49 that afternoon.

Officials in Washington had learned "from high levels" that the fight, for all practical purposes, was over. The Republic of China had decided to "take part in Rome Games regardless of IOC decision on nomenclature"—even if it had to be called Taiwan. This was still a secret, they were trying to keep it out of the press, and some miracle might change things. The Americans were still trying to persuade the Taiwanese to boycott Rome rather than give in. But here was the private word. Two reasons were given for the decision, combining sports and politics: "(1) in order to permit decathlon champion C. K. Yang take part in hope he will win China's first Olympic medal and (2) because presence of free China even as Taiwan would result in continued Chicom (Red China) political boycott of Olympic movement."

BARON PIERRE de Coubertin, the Frenchman who founded the modern Olympics, or at least the version that stuck, had always wanted his Games to be staged in Rome, from whence he claimed his ancestors came. After Athens in 1896, Paris in 1900, and St. Louis in 1904, he tapped Rome for the IV Olympiad, seeing it as a return to monarchical glory after a sullying in the democratic New World. He explained later that he "desired Rome because it is only there that, once it has returned from its excursion into utilitarian America, the Olympic ideal will once again wear its sumptuous toga, clothed in art and thought in which right from the beginning I had always wanted to see it attired." But an eruption at Mount Vesuvius two years before the 1908 Games forced Italy to decline as hosts, turning attention instead to the rebuilding of devastated Naples, and the Games went to London. Benito Mussolini had aspirations for Rome hosting the 1944 Olympics, but the world was in no mood for games with World War II raging, and Il Duce had been overthrown by then in any case, soon to meet his ignominious death. Now, at last, Rome had its Games, and Avery Brundage was as overcome by the majesty of the setting as his baronial predecessor had been.

The opening dinner of the 57th Session of the IOC was suitably solemn, ornate, all puffery and pomp. The setting was the Palazzo dei Congressi, built by Mussolini just before the war as part of his grand design for a second Roman republic—a modern Fascist version—in the EUR section of Rome that featured ponderous new government offices, apartment buildings, and museums. On a warm Saturday night, the Italian head of state arrived, the Honorable Giovanni Gronchi, ushered in by silver trumpets from the valets of Vitorchiano blasting Roman fanfares. Other important guests and committee members moved toward their seats with more trumpeters from the Carabinieri Band playing repetitions of the Olympic motif. And there came Avery Brundage, looking comfortably at home in this exalted milieu. He stood above the crowd, poised on a raised podium, ready to deliver the speech he brought with him to Rome. The Orchestra of the National Academy of Santa Cecilia and a hundred robed singers were arrayed behind him, framed by a long row of the five-ringed Olympic flags, the wall covered by a vast banner proclaiming *"Citius Altius Fortius,"* the Latin motto of the Olympics, meaning "Faster Higher Stronger."

"New glory has been added to the Eternal City," Brundage declared. He was talking about the architectural designs produced by Pier Luigi Nervi especially for the Rome Olympics, including the nearby Palazzo dello Sport, where the boxing matches and basketball finals would be held, comparing Nervi's structures to the majesty of "Bernini and Michelangelo, and the monuments left by Hadrian, Trajan, and the other Caesars." But he also meant the glory of his own design. The Rome of Augustus, the greatest of ancient times, he boasted, "is dwarfed by the world of sport today, which includes all five continents . . . practically the entire globe." And the sporting domain, his Olympic realm, exceeded not only political empires but also spiritual ones, he said. "No philosophy or religion . . . has spread so widely and so quickly as the Olympic Movement in its modern development."

It was a movement that had "neither armies nor money, but in sixty years it has enlisted the enthusiastic support of the peoples of more than four score countries," Brundage continued. "It has spread with this amazing speed solely through the efforts of unpaid but dedicated and devoted volunteers. Christians, Moslems, Hindus, Buddhists, and atheists, all respect its basic principles of common honesty, mutual regard, fair play, and good sportsmanship, which are the essence of all religion." To maintain its integrity, he said, the Olympic Movement could allow "no deviation . . . from the fundamental and basic principle that there shall be no discrimination because of race, religion, or politics. The Olympic Games are, and must be kept, open to the youth of all the world if they are fully to serve their purpose."

The trumpeters sounded the Olympic motif again as dignitaries and Mr. Brundage took their leave into the Roman night.

The next morning, in his room at the Hotel Luxor, Michael Scott took out a sheaf of stationery stamped *The Africa Bureau, Vauxhall Bridge Road, London,* and jotted a note that he would hand deliver to the president of the IOC across town.

"Dear Mr. Brundage," he wrote. "I have come to Rome at the request of the South African Sports Association and the Campaign Against Race Discrimination in Sport in order to make representations to your committee concerning the South Africa Olympics team, which is not representative of the best achievements of the South African people—that is to say of all the people, including the Africans and the coloured people of South Africa." Scott said he was there in place of Dennis Brutus, the head of the South African Sports Association, who was unable to appear because the Union of South Africa government had not granted him a passport to leave the country. Accompanying Scott was Nana Mahomo, a recent South African émigré, who would provide firsthand accounts of "the artificial handicaps in sport under which his people labor . . . which have prevented the inclusion of any of them in the present team and make necessary the protest which we have come to Rome to voice."

Brundage and his inner circle knew about Scott's mission to Rome and had tried to discourage it, despite their hollow rhetoric of "no deviation" from the Olympic principle against racial discrimination. Otto Mayer, the IOC chancellor, had been instructed to write a letter earlier that month to officials at the British antiapartheid organization that Scott represented. In his letter to Antony Steel in London, Mayer avoided the issue of race and said simply that Scott was not the right messenger and Rome was not the right time or place. "I think this would not be very suitable, as the situation should be explained by a person living in South Africa and not someone staying in Europe," Mayer wrote. "As a matter of fact, we are already very well informed on the situation as it is, and I don't think that a representative from your committee might say more than what we know . . . Therefore your delegate might take the risk to undertake the journey for nothing."

The eight months of 1960 leading up to the Rome Olympics had been tumultuous in South Africa, delineating a historic turning point in the indigenous revolution against the white supremacist state and how the government was regarded by the world of nations. On March 21 black Africans had staged protests around the country against pass laws, which required them to carry documents listing details of their lives, including their name, tax code, and employer. At a protest in Sharpeville, thirty miles south of Johannesburg, white police officers fired into the massive crowd, leaving 69 dead and 176 wounded. The Sharpeville massacre became the symbol and rallying cry of the movement against apartheid. The United Nations Security Council condemned South Africa and called on it to bring about racial equality. An incipient boycott began, led by Britain and black African nations. The government responded with another crackdown, imposing a state of emergency, detaining 1,700 political prisoners without trial and outlawing the main party of opposition, the African National Congress.

Twenty days after the Sharpeville massacre, Dennis Brutus, secretary of the South African Sports Association, wrote a letter to Brundage from his home office in Port Elizabeth. He said that it was difficult for him to secure information about the Olympics in South Africa, but he hoped the IOC, at its next regular session, would allow him to make the case for the "excluded nonwhite sportsmen" of his country. He applied for a passport so that he could meet Brundage and his committee in Rome. That very day, April 13, South African Security Branch detectives raided Brutus's home, interrogated him about the goals and activities of his association, and seized his files of letters, pamphlets, and documents.

The next day, not coincidentally, a letter came to Brundage from Brutus's nemesis, Ira Emery, secretary of the all-white South Africa Olympic Committee. Appended to Emery's letter were news clippings from the *Johannesburg Star* about the raid on Brutus's organization. Understanding Brundage's rhetorical antipathy toward anything overtly political, Emery argued that Brutus was more interested in politics than sports. With Orwellian logic, he added: "The action of the security police bears out this statement very completely, as no other nonwhite sports body has been screened, to our knowledge."

Without speaking to each other, Brutus and Emery lobbied their antithetical causes in letters to Brundage over the remainder of the spring and summer. Brutus insisted that he had fresh evidence of racial discrimination in the selection of the South African team. Emery insisted that "not a single Nonwhite South African athlete was anywhere near international standard." In a May 28 letter to a Swedish member of the IOC, Brundage tipped his hand toward Emery. "We have complete confidence in the South African Olympic Committee," he wrote. In a circular letter to all IOC members, Brundage and

Otto Mayer went a step further, attaching a reprint of an article Emery sent them that purported to represent the interests of nonwhites in South Africa. "Sadly, we must shake our heads and admit it," the article concluded. "The truth is we don't yet quite make the grade." The publication, *Drum,* was owned by a white South African, but the writers were predominantly black.

In early July Brutus sent a telegram to the South African Department of Interior asking for information about the passport. He had not heard a word, except that the local passport office had referred his application to Pretoria. Finally, on Wednesday, July 27, he received a telegram from Interior: "Application of passport not successful." No reason was given. It was then that antiapartheid activists in South Africa and Great Britain scrambled for a backup plan that led Michael Scott to Rome, where on a Sunday morning he would hand deliver his letter to the Hotel Excelsior, pleading for a hearing before Brundage and the IOC.

NEVER WRITE anything down, Brundage once advised his long-time chief financial assistant, Frederick J. Ruegsegger. Yet Brundage was a chronic doodler, constantly scribbling notes to himself—idle thoughts, aphorisms, bits of philosophy, lists of people and material things. His paper trail offered a window into the peculiarities of his life and mind. During the two-day sessions of the IOC on Monday, August 22, and Tuesday, August 23, Brundage had a pad of paper at his side the entire time, and his scribbles, like a multitude of other letters from his life, were saved for posterity, ending up in an archive at his alma mater, the University of Illinois. During those two days, among other things, the full IOC seconded the executive board decision on Taiwan, rebuffed Soviet attempts to transform the committee structure, heard from a delegation from Tokyo, where the next Olympics would be staged, and agreed to have the executive board see Michael Scott on the South Africa question, but only in accompaniment with the South African committee member, Reginald Honey.

While all this was going on, Brundage's scribble pad was filling up with a list of European royals he had recently encountered:

Duke Ruspoli, head of Italian Tennis Association
Prince San Faustino, or Bourbon del Monte, married to an American
*   with house at Santa Barbara*
Story of Countess from Vienna. Most people in Vienna monarchists.

And a list of wines he had heard about recently:

Domaine d la Croix rose
Veronese vino
Clastidio Italian rose wine

Odds and ends of his social life:

Soap becomes man
Learn how to walk on the ceiling
Girl in Excelsior bar "Since Americans are here the price is 30,000
*   clear"*

And various political thoughts:

Social legislation and high taxes have reduced everyone to semi-
*   poverty and mediocrity*
More Jews than ever demanding restitution of everything lost and
*   lot more*
Warren Magee, attorney for Douglas Stewart, on plane . . .
*   defended German banker, Rasche, for whom I wrote statement*
[a reference to Karl Rasche, chairman of Dresdner Bank,

which helped fund the Third Reich, and who was held responsible for it at the Nuremberg trials after the war].

Those last two jottings, in combination, lead into the deeper hypocrisy of Brundage's notion of keeping the Olympic Movement above politics. In the mid-1930s, after Hitler and the Nazis seized power in Germany, a strong movement arose for a U.S. boycott of the 1936 Olympics in Berlin. Brundage, then head of the American Olympic Committee, fought vigorously to send a team. He said politics should not be a factor and that the IOC would extract promises from Hitler to adhere to the Olympic Creed against discrimination based on race or religion. But beneath that argument ran a deep river of anti-Semitism. In a September 27, 1935, letter to Carl Diem, chief organizer of the Berlin Games, Brundage complained of a "renewed outburst from our Jewish friends" against the Berlin Olympics. He insisted that the boycott effort "pushed by Jews" was based on irresponsible propaganda, and asked Diem for data showing "Jews going about their business in Germany as far as sports [are] concerned."

This was not a one-time slip; disparagement of Jewish leaders of the boycott movement was a consistent theme of Brundage's correspondence with German officials. As another example, in an October 28, 1935, letter to Hans von Tschammer und Osten, sports director of the Third Reich and a member of the Nazi Party, he included a packet of clippings of Nazi misdeeds and the proposed boycott, adding: "The most vicious of these articles are reprinted and circulated in sports circles by the thousands in order to add to our difficulties. Altho all visitors to Germany report courteous and hospitable treatment, the stories from [American] news writers on the Reich almost entirely go to the other extreme. The huge Jewish population in the large cities of America, particularly New York, and the importance of Jewish merchant advertisers, perhaps account for this fact."

Brundage ultimately prevailed and brought a strong U.S. team to

Berlin led by the great black athlete from Ohio State, Jesse Owens. In the American Olympic Committee report of 1936, Brundage referred to Owens as a "boy." In the manuscript of an autobiography Brundage later prepared, he took note of Owens's triumph, but paid greater attention to an elaborate fest staged by Hermann Goering, then commander in chief of the Luftwaffe and mastermind of the German economy. "This was arranged as an 'al fresco' buffet for several hundred guests in the huge park surrounding what was Goering's house in the heart of Berlin," Brundage wrote. "The food prepared by the best chefs in Berlin was arranged on tables on one side of the area, which must have been more than 200 meters square. One end of the area was enclosed by a high curtain, which, after the dinner, was drawn to expose an opera company with the finest Berlin orchestra. This was not the end of the entertainment, however, since after the opera performance, another long curtain on the other side of the area was drawn, and the guests were invited into a typical Bavarian amusement park with all the side shows and other usual forms of entertainment. Karl von Halt and I, 1912 competitors in the same event, renewed our competition in the various strength tests . . . The Nazis might not have adopted all the high principles of the Olympic Movement—but, they were converted to the fact that the Olympic Games are of such world-wide significance that all the power of the mighty German state should be placed behind them."

A week after he returned to America, Brundage came to New York for the German Day celebration held October 4, 1936, at Madison Square Garden. The event, run by a committee dominated by members of the American German Bund, an organization of German American citizens sympathetic to Nazi Germany, drew more than twenty thousand people. The honored guests included Karl Strolin, mayor of Stuttgart, who spoke of "the miracle which we owe to our leader Adolf Hitler and his unshakable belief in Germany." The German ambassador to the U.S., Hans Luther, said, "Germany is rearming not to make war but to make peace secure." When

Brundage took the microphone, he defended the Olympics and praised Germany. No country since ancient Greece, he said, "has displayed a more truly national public interest in the Olympic spirit in general than you find in Germany today." He thanked German Americans for helping fund the U.S. Olympic team when others threatened a boycott. "The question then was whether a vociferous minority highly organized and highly financed could impose its will on one hundred twenty million people." And he brought the huge crowd to its feet with a lesson he brought home from Berlin: "We can learn much from Germany. We, too, if we wish to preserve our institutions, must stamp out Communism. We, too, must take steps to arrest the decline of patriotism."

Madison Square Garden reverberated with the sounds of thousands in full voice. They sang the "Star-Spangled Banner," "Deutschland, Deutschland Über Alles," and the Nazi anthem, "The Horst Wessel Song."

NOW, A QUARTER of a century later, across the cataclysm of the Holocaust and World War II, Brundage sat at the front of the conference room at the Hotel Excelsior in Rome, scribbling his random thoughts. He could look out to the rows of IOC members and see his old friend, Dr. Karl von Halt, the German with whom he had jovially competed in tests of strength that night at Hermann Goering's outlandish mansion.

On the afternoon of the second session, Brundage was elected to a third term. The Soviets decided not to challenge him, and the Marquess of Exeter, the ambitious vice president who had wanted the top job since 1952 and now hoped to offer himself as a compromise candidate, instead rose to make the nomination. There was a loud cheer, and the monarch of sport still held sway over his vast expanse of territory.

4

MAY THE BEST
MAN WIN

On the day before the Olympics began, Paolo Pedinelli and his
father made a pilgrimage down to Rome from the ancient Umbrian
town of Amelia to see the world's great athletes. Paolo was five years
old then, and the scene he encountered at the gates of the Villagio
Olimpico was so magical that he would remember it the rest of his
life. There was a crush of humanity on the wide concrete expanse
outside the main gate to the village; joyous crowds seeking autographs, elbowing for better views inside, shouting out the names of
recognizable stars from Germany, Italy, Australia, Russia, and the
United States. It all seemed exotic even before the Pedinellis came
upon a good-natured group of turban-wearing Sikhs, who turned
out to be members of the wrestling squad from India. One of them
scooped up little Paolo, hoisted him onto his shoulders, and carried
the boy around, his head bobbing above the throng. Paolo had that
familiar childhood sensation of feeling giddy and a bit scared at the

same time. He felt like he was riding atop Hercules, he said later, and the world from up there seemed fresh and beautiful.

Until a few years earlier, when Rome began a massive construction campaign in preparation for the Olympics, the territory within sight of the shoulder-boosted youngster had looked only fetid and ugly, a reminder of the scars of war. Since the end of World War II, this flat swampland at a bend in the Tiber River on the northern rim of Rome had been a shantytown of old railcars, truck beds, and tin and cardboard shacks housing the poor and dispossessed who had been uprooted from their homes during the intense fighting at Anzio and Cassino. Now the squatters had been dislocated again, replaced by a sprawling modernist village of yellow-brick apartment buildings replete with recreation rooms, drugstores, telephone and telegraph offices, a bank, an outdoor movie theater, a hospital, and a row of restaurants and sidewalk cafés, all contained and connected by twelve kilometers of new roads and pedestrian walkways, and protected by a private police force. The apartment buildings, two to four stories, with enough beds for eight thousand residents, would serve as public housing after the Olympics. They looked the part, except for a signature feature: all were raised one story off the ground by rows of cement stilts, providing shaded breezeways underneath that gave some relief from the sweltering August heat.

The U.S. men's team was housed in two of the larger buildings in the middle of the village, sharing fifty suites that held three to eight athletes each. They tended to bunch up by sporting specialty: cyclists here, boxers there, trackmen across the way. "With three big guys, you had trouble moving around a little bit, but we were used to that," recalled Oscar Robertson, the basketball star, whose roommates included the nearly seven-foot Walt Bellamy. Although Olympic officials boasted that some beds were long enough even for Big Bells (the beds were called de Gaulles, in reference to the towering French leader), none seemed adequate. At whatever length, Lance Larson, a swimmer from California, also thought the beds were scratchy, as though the mattresses were made from straw.

Much like American GIs who had helped liberate Europe a generation earlier, U.S. Olympic athletes brought a bountiful supermarket culture with them to Rome. Richard Cortright, a veteran cyclist from Buffalo, entered the village with a stash of supplies, clothes, and foodstuffs to sell and trade. "He sets the stuff up in his bedroom closet cabinets so when he opens the double doors it's all on display on the shelves and hanging on the inside of the doors," his teammate Jack Simes recorded in his journal. "We call it Dick's Store. And it quickly becomes known to the Italians who work in the village, and other athletes. So, at odd times it's not unusual for strangers to be walking down the hall in search of a deal." There was one crucial item missing from Dick's Store, according to Bob Tetzlaff, a fellow cyclist: toilet paper. The Italians had two kinds, one like wax paper and another like a paper towel, neither pleasant.

The Americans had their own dining unit open twenty-two hours a day, from five in the morning to three in the morning. It was operated by an Italian chef with seventy-six employees, but the menu was quintessentially red-meat American long before the era of health foods and carbo loading. Beef was always available as the first option. "They fed us steak, steak, steak," said Ed Temple. Also liver, roast baby lamb, turkey, and veal. Each part of the world had its own restaurant, ten in all, and many of the Americans quickly grew sick of their fare and experimented with more exotic foods, especially Indian curries. "We would run the track managers crazy because they would say you can't eat foods from other countries," Ray Norton, the sprinter, later said. "So they would sort of follow us around . . . We'd go where the Russians were . . . and then we'd go visit the Indians, the Italians, all over the place."

One place the men could not go was inside the women's quarters, a separate sector on the other side of a raised highway and cordoned off by an iron gate and eight-foot wire fence. Village guards roamed the perimeter, and a no-nonsense Italian matron, Signora Ernestina Cabella Nardi, was stationed at the entry gate, deputized to separate the 611 female Olympians from the thousands of eager young men on the other side. There were jokes about Don Bragg, the self-styled Tarzan of the Americans, pole-vaulting over the fence, and of John Thomas, the buoyant young high jumper, making the leap. Janis Krumins, a Soviet basketball giant, almost seven foot three, could reach his hands over the top. The *Nashville Banner*'s Fred Russell, touring the village with some of his sportswriter pals, took note of the "rigid precautions" to "make the encampment man-proof" and said that a snooper "would have to hire a helicopter."

Not quite, as it turned out. Three young Italian men tricked their way past the gatekeeper; armed with pesticides, they claimed they were there to kill pesky mosquitoes.

There was also the problem of a raised highway.

Before the U.S. delegation left for Rome, some parents of girls on the swim team (and they were girls, aged thirteen to seventeen) expressed concern about them staying in alien quarters so far from home. After a few days at the village, one of the swimmers, fifteen-year-old Anne Warner, wrote a letter to her parents in Northern California reassuring them: "Mom and Dad, I'll be great because we have a guard and a guardhouse and a big fence." A few days later Warner received a telegram from her mother with the urgent message "CLOSE THE DRAPES!" She had been mortified by a story in the local paper about Roman Peeping Toms who had staked out positions on the raised freeway, where they peered down with binoculars and telephoto lenses. "From sundown until past midnight, dozens and dozens of motorists park opposite the girls' windows," the story reported. Sure enough, Warner and her roommates looked out and noticed the unwelcome snoops for the first time. Many of the windows lacked curtains, so they covered them with sheets.

There was a decidedly sexist tone to the Rome Olympics, reflecting not just the aggressive manner of Italian males, but also the tenor of the times and the sensibilities of the sportswriting tribe presenting the event to the public. Abie Grossfeld, a gymnast on the American team, was invited to a pre-Games cocktail party at the home of Gina Lollobrigida on the Appian Way, where the guest of honor was American actor Rock Hudson, who was working with the Italian actress in the film *Come September.* As Grossfeld was observing the scene, he was approached by a group of reporters who wondered whether he would object if they asked his young wife, nineteen-year-old gymnast Muriel, her measurements. They were struck by her figure and wanted to compare it with Lollobrigida's. An ensuing story went out on the wires saying that the hostess "has quite an Olympian figure herself" but was "almost outpointed in her own home" by Muriel Grossfeld (36-22-35 for the actress, 37-21-34 for the gymnast). "Male guests at the party had it right," the account continued. "They watched both girls."

Arthur Daley, a prominent columnist for the *New York Times,* took to ogling Dawn Fraser, a top swimming star for the Australians. In a column under the headline "Dawn Fraser's 'Strip Tease' Stopped by Official," he noted that she once took off her warm-up outfit only to discover that she did not have her suit on underneath. "There is an appealing scrubbed look to this likeable twenty-two-year-old," he wrote. "She is a pretty girl in spite of the fact that she staunchly refuses to wear either lipstick or make-up. This hasn't slowed her down romantically, however. She is wearing a diamond engagement ring." As it turned out, Australian officials were not so charmed by Fraser. While she could bring them reflected glory in the pool, "they were troubled by her independent frame of mind," according to Dennis H. Phillips, a history scholar from Sydney who studied Aussie women and the Olympics. "She was accused of assorted crimes in Rome. Among other things, she was seen with a cigar poking from the side of her mouth."

Female Olympians felt constant pressure to conform to imposed standards of modesty even as they were being portrayed as sex symbols. At its meeting in Rome, the International Swimming Federation (FINA) voted to prohibit women swimmers from racing in bikinis, demanding that "the suit must be modest." At the same time, Art Rosenbaum of the San Francisco *Chronicle* was writing a column about how his tour group, before reaching Rome, had spent time on the French Riviera, where George F. Bineer, "the swimming expert with the *Chronicle* party," joked that he "should have brought along a tape measure—an itty-bitty one—to figure the lack of size in bathing costumes he has observed on his way to Rome." At Nice, Rosenbaum reported, George F. was "the first to hit the beach, and appointed three other men assistant BW's—bikini watchers."

The women on the U.S. team had to follow a dress code established by the team's director of activities, the Comtesse de Morelos, who in an earlier life, before marrying into Italian nobility, had been an American athlete known as Brenda Helser. With her refined continental sensibilities, the comtesse directed her sartorial hostility at Bermuda shorts. "I have lived in Europe for more than ten years, and I know that Bermuda shorts have become a symbol to Europeans of everything that is unpleasant about the U.S. woman," she said. She banned them not only from the streets of Rome but also from the village. The U.S. women besieged her with complaints, to which her reply was: "Do you think those flapping bottoms are beautiful?"

But what angered them more than being kept out of Bermudas was being ordered to stop dancing. This edict came down from none other than Ed Temple, the track coach, and his no-frills team manager, Frances Kaszubski. A few days after the women's track team reached Rome, Temple became concerned when his runners showed up for a morning workout "beat, and I mean really beat." What was wrong? Word came back to him that they had been up late the night before at the village recreation hall showing the world how to dance to American rock-and-roll tunes playing on the jukebox. "The Russians and Germans and Italians sat there for hours watching our boys and girls dancing and cheering them on," Temple said. "So I laid down the law right then and there." Everyone wanted to dance with Wilma Rudolph, but the real swingers were Willye White, an irrepressible long jumper from Chicago, and Earlene Brown, the discus thrower and shot-putter from Los Angeles.

The women felt their coach was being too restrictive and ignored his orders when they thought he wouldn't find out, but his mind was focused solely on performance on the track. "I told them we can dance in the United States," Temple said later. "If they start giving out gold, silver, and bronze in dancing, then we can jump in and dance. They said they wanted to get in some recreation and go to the dance hall with all the countries, and I said, 'No, we ain't dancing over here.' I said, 'Whoever goes to dance, you going to catch the next plane home. We didn't come all the way to Rome to dance.' [At least] one of them tried, Willye White. We called her Red because she had red hair. Red was always a defiant type person. Red went up there and danced and everything."

If the women seemed like good copy off the field, even they could not compete with the young boxer Cassius Clay. After yakking his way through his flying phobia on the long flight across the Atlantic, he found everything in Rome new and exciting, even the bidet in his suite at the village, which according to teammate Nikos Spanakos he first mistook for a drinking fountain, and tried to take a swig from it. Within a few days, Clay had established himself as the gregarious clown prince of the world athletes. He seemed to be everywhere, shaking hands, telling tall tales, boasting about his boxing prowess, joshing with Olympians from Europe, Asia, and Africa.

"He was always preaching, no matter where it was—in the cafeteria, out on the grounds, in the enormous village, downtown, over at the boxing venue. He was always talking," recalled Paula Jean Myers Pope, an American diver. One American official said that in four days, Clay had already posed with twenty-eight different delegations and signed countless autographs. Francis W. Nyangweso, a boxer from Uganda, recalled coming back from training one afternoon and being approached by athletes wearing USA uniforms. "One of them, very tall and big, spoke to us in an American accent. When I got used to his English, our conversation ranged over topics including wild animals, forests, and snakes," Nyangweso said. "Before we parted, this gentleman advised us that the boxer on our team who happened to be drawn against him should duck on medical grounds and should not try to fight him, for he, Cassius Clay, would not like to demolish a young brother from Africa."

Members of the press corps quickly dubbed Clay "Uncle Sam's unofficial goodwill ambassador," and were especially taken by his "solid Americanism"—a trait he reinforced in an exchange with a foreign journalist. "With the intolerance in your country, you must have a lot of problems," the reporter said to Clay. "Oh, yeah, we've got some problems," Clay was quoted in response. "But get this straight—it's still the best country in the world." Clay's political sensibilities would change dramatically within a few years, but his personality at age eighteen was essentially the same as it would be the rest of his life. In retrospect, because of the worldwide fame he gained later as Muhammad Ali, there is a temptation to present him as a larger figure at the Rome Olympics than he really was. He was ebullient and memorable from the start, but he was not a leader of the U.S. delegation. It was Clay seeking out people, not people seeking out Clay.

"They try to rewrite history," Rink Babka, the discus thrower from Southern Cal, said later, reflecting a common feeling among Olympic veterans. "When I think of 1960 and hear people say Cassius Clay was Mr. Olympics and everyone went to see him—bullshit." The most respected athletes on the American squad, according to their teammates, were, first, Rafer Johnson, the captain, and, second, Wilma Rudolph, the leader of the Tigerbelles. Ray Norton, the sprinter, and John Thomas, the high jumper, held star status because of the expectation that they would shatter world records and bring home gold medals. With basketball more popular in the U.S. than track and field, the brilliant triumvirate of Oscar Robertson, Jerry West, and Jerry Lucas had a special aura even though their sport was considered an Olympic sideshow. Glenn Davis, the determined 400-meter hurdler from Ohio State, and Bo Roberson, the long jumper and three-sport star at Cornell, radiated dignity and intelligence and also had larger internal followings than Cassius Clay.

IGOR TER-OVANESYAN and his Soviet teammates were kept busy with the work of comradeship on the day before the Olympics opened. On that Wednesday morning, they were called to an assembly on the square near their dormitory to listen to a special greeting from their leader back in Moscow, Nikita S. Khrushchev. With earnest oratorical flourishes, Nikolai Romanov, the head of the Soviet delegation, read aloud a letter from Khrushchev which that same day had been printed on the front pages of *Izvestia* and *Pravda*. A correspondent from Tass, the Soviet news agency, reported that "with warm applause our sportsmen greeted the warm message from the head of the Soviet government, which was full of ideals of friendship of the youth of the world."

Khrushchev's message was meant not just for the Soviets but for all athletes gathered in Rome, even if it was boilerplate Soviet rhetoric. In Russian, he welcomed the "life-loving sports youth" of the world. He said the Olympic flame "fires in the hearts of people the spirit of camaraderie." The progress of humankind, he said, depended "on mental richness, moral cleanliness, and physical development." Those characteristics, he claimed, were evident in both the Olympic Movement and the Soviet Union, where "the government takes care of strengthening the health of workers and also the physical and mental development of the nation." The Olympic Games were worthy because they improved "brotherly contact among sportsmen of different countries," he noted, concluding: "I wish all sportsmen taking part the best success in sports as well as in work, studies, and their private lives."

When Romanov finished reading his leader's words, several Soviet athletes were brought forward to respond with similarly grand elocution. High jumper Taisia Chenchik, gymnast Boris Shakhlin, and heavyweight weight lifter Yuri Vlasov expressed "warm feelings of gratitude for the care of the Soviet government and mainly comrade N. S. Khrushchev." In a letter they composed back to him, they wrote:

> *Dear Nikita Sergeyevich,*
>
> *Your greeting is full of concern about peace and the happiness of mankind and it inspired us toward better achievements in sports and other endeavors. We promise the Communist Party and the Soviet people, and you dear Nikita Sergeyevich, that we will represent our Fatherland in the 17th Olympics with a great deal of honor, and we will fight to strengthen the friendships between athletes from all over the world.*

A reporter from *Pravda* reported that Khrushchev's letter swiftly became the talk of the village: "On the street we stopped a dark-haired sportsman who had the word *Italia* on his blue uniform. 'Have you heard about Khrushchev's letter?' The answer was 'Yes, all sportsmen know about it.' "

Like his teammates, Ter-Ovanesyan kept private whatever skepticism he might have felt about Khrushchev's commitment to sports. Nearly a half century later, looking back on that scene, he said, "Khrushchev could care less about sports. He didn't care about sports at all. He was very cool toward sports." In biographies of Khrushchev, the closest he comes to participating in sports is playing shuffleboard. Ter-Ovanesyan recalled a reception at the Kremlin where a Russian skater who had returned from the 1960 Winter Olympics, held in Squaw Valley, California, offered a mild complaint to Khrushchev about the shortage of skating rinks and poor overall sports conditions in the Soviet Union. Khrushchev was coldly dismissive. "Nikita said there were much more important problems in the country, like having a poor woman with ten kids and one herring to feed them," Ter-Ovanesyan said. "He said there were much more important issues to think about than skating rinks." But in the cold war propaganda struggle, perception often trumped reality, and Khrushchev's letter was perceived as a tactical coup for the Soviets. With no Olympic events to write about yet, the message filled a news vacuum and was covered in most of the Italian and European newspapers, receiving enough notice to concern American representatives in Rome. Among officials in the U.S. delegation and at the nearby American embassy, a conversation began about whether President Eisenhower should counter with his own letter to the Olympic athletes.

The Soviet public relations campaign trumped the Americans again that same day when the delegation paid a courtesy call on the U.S. athletes at their quarters. With photographers and journalists recording the scene, officials from the two teams exchanged little flags and diplomatic pleasantries while the athletes mingled on lawn chairs under the breezeway sipping Cokes and munching on potato chips. A few translators were there, but much of the interaction was nonverbal. They smiled, laughed, and traded pins. (The Soviet pin, depicting the world-changing 1957 Sputnik satellite, was the most coveted trinket in the village.) Some athletes were renewing old friendships, like Rafer Johnson and his Russian decathlon rival, Vasily Kuznetsov. Others were connecting for the first time. It was here that Dave Sime first eyed Ter-Ovanesyan and began a conversation they would resume later on the practice field.

Swimmers from the two superpowers had been bumping into one another all week at the Olympic practice pools, where the Soviets trained immediately after the Americans. Bill Mulliken of the U.S.

team regarded his counterparts as "warm and friendly," but he did not feel the same way about the sober Soviet officials supervising the swimmers. The Americans called them KGB. With their "stereotypical trench coats and hats," Mulliken later noted, "they looked like seconds out of an anticommunist B movie. They'd ask us what we'd done for workouts, and we'd tell them the most outrageous stuff, but all they had to do was watch us, and they did." When Anne Warner was talking to women swimmers on the Soviet squad, she thought of it as "just kids talking to each other the way kids do." But the Soviet men appeared much older, she thought, and with their military bearing seemed to come from a different planet than the California schoolgirls with their chlorine-streaked greenish blond hair.

Warner's early encounters with the Soviet swimmers took place in an unlikely setting. The athletes of capitalism and Communism often trained in an indoor pool that had been built expressly for the Fascist dictator Mussolini. Situated inside an athletic compound known as the Foro Italico, which during its early years had been Foro Mussolini, the pool was less than regulation size and had one lane missing, but it was an artistic relic, with elegant columns and mosaic tiles on the floor and walls portraying graceful swimmers and divers. The floor tiles were scuffed to prevent swimmers from slipping when barefoot. The diving board had a hydraulic lift so it would not cover up the wall mosaics. Warner's strongest memory was that the pool was "sanitized with copper that tasted like you were swimming with copper pennies in your mouth."

In preparation for the Olympics, the Italian government had been under pressure to erase or hide physical reminders of the Fascist era, but its effort was half-hearted. Fascist symbols were everywhere at the Foro Italico, most of which had been constructed at Mussolini's directive in hopes of landing the never-to-be-held 1944 Olympics. At the main entrance, visitors encountered an imposing white marble obelisk with *Mussolini Dux* inscribed vertically. How to hide it? The Rome Council had talked about simply yanking it down but decided to leave it as part of history. Beyond the obelisk, walking farther into the Foro Italico toward Stadio Olimpico, *Duce*, meaning "leader," the Italian equivalent of *führer* for Adolf Hitler, was etched into the pavement 264 times. Across from the main stadium and connected to it by an underground tunnel was a smaller outdoor facility, the Stadio dei Marmi. The horseshoe-shaped bowl was rimmed by sixty marble statues of ancient Roman athletes, each looming thirteen feet high, representing Mussolini's visions of the sporting Fascist ideal.

At eight-thirty that morning, long before the Russians paid their visit, Rafer Johnson had walked from the village across the river and down a mile to the Stadio dei Marmi, where he practiced carrying the flag through the connecting tunnel and into Stadio Olimpico, tracing a route he would follow the next afternoon at the Opening Ceremony. On his way to and from the stadium, Johnson passed the obelisk and a set of administration buildings, one containing Mussolini's personal *palestra,* a deluxe gymnasium featuring ornate columns and mobile panel marble walls; a training floor of linoleum and cork; a rectangular block water fountain with mythological figures carved into the cabinet; ropes and punching bags stored on a pulley running along the middle of the high ceiling; and billowy curtains and soft golden light that once projected the bulldog despot's oversized shadow as he practiced fencing and boxing.

An adjacent building housed the Italian National Olympic Committee, known as CONI. Its members and officials of the organizing committee met every morning that August and September in an assembly hall where the front and back walls were covered by green carpet, put there by the U.S. Army after it liberated Rome in June 1944 and transformed the Foro Mussolini into the Fifth Army Rest Center.

Concealed under the green carpet on the front wall, the side that Olympic officials now faced during their daily morning deliberations, was an extraordinary mural, a romantic work of totalitarian iconography so bold and monstrous that it is obvious why the Ameri-

can military covered it up and why Italians would not feel comfortable uncovering it until four decades later. It was titled *The Apotheosis
of Fascism.* Mussolini dominated the mural, standing center stage,
larger than life, delivering a speech, while around Il Duce were his
Blackshirt supporters waving the Fascist flag, and various scenes of
his legions violently beating opponents as the children, mothers, and
fathers of the state huddled together off to the side, with glorious de-
pictions of agriculture and industry across the way, and angels hovering above to protect it all, and representations of the *fascio*—the
hatchet of ancient Rome held together by a bundle of twigs, a sort of
Roman tomahawk—from which the word and symbolism of modern Fascism derived. All of this behind the green carpet, out of
sight and mostly out of mind. It was said that the 1960 Olympics
were sweeping over the city like a fresh breeze of openness, and
Romans felt free and easy, loosened from the dark grip of their recent
past.

A. J. LIEBLING, the acerbic American writer, in Rome to cover the
Games for *The New Yorker,* made his way to St. Peter's Square before
the six o'clock start time and stood near the back of a milling throng
of four thousand people who had assembled to hear an address and
benediction from Pope John XXIII on the eve of the Olympics. The
crowd included a few thousand athletes, representatives from almost
every team, including Jews, Hindus, Muslims, and a small atheist
delegation from the Soviet Union. There were also a few hundred
Catholic youth scouts, some eight hundred members of the Vespa
Club of Europe, who brought their scooters and wore red and yellow
outfits, and various observers like Liebling. "From where I stood, at
the opening of the Piazza, almost diametrically across from the Papal
throne, His Holiness—a blob of white robe topped by a smaller blob
of red cape—looked no bigger than a rabbit's foot," he wrote. Liebling was renowned for his descriptive powers, but in this case his

were no better than those of Wilma Rudolph, star of the Tennessee State Tigerbelles, who was also there, gazing at the Pope from a closer perspective.

"Wilma thought he looked like a jolly, round Santa Claus," her teammate Lucinda Williams recalled. "And we kept saying to her, this is a serious moment, you know? And it was one of the most fantastic moments that I can remember of those days. You really got to see the Pope? But Wilma was young and really didn't understand the whole significance of that. And I can't forget her saying, 'Well, he looks like a jolly, round Santa Claus. And a bowlful of jelly.' And we'd say, 'Girl, you better be quiet, better be quiet.' "

Pope John XXIII had returned to the Vatican that morning from his summer palace at Castel Gandolfo to greet the Olympians. His address was short, six hundred words, and he spoke in Latin. He was seventy-eight years old, and the brutal August heat lingered into early evening, the sun's rays glancing off St. Peter's golden dome, but a reporter from the *Boston Globe* was impressed by "the vigor of his voice and the bell tone clarity of his diction," and Anna Brady of the Baltimore *Sun* noted that "he appeared to be in excellent health and to be thoroughly enjoying himself." As his message boomed over a public address system, he held his script in his left hand, gestured with his right, and stopped short of saying that God was on anyone's particular side. "It is obvious that we cannot wish victory to every team or to each individual athlete," he said. "May the best man win. But this is not an obstacle to our expressing the desire that the contests of these days will be of benefit to you all, and that from them, all without exception will be able to gain some advantage."

When he had finished in Latin, his words were repeated in fourteen languages. Liebling by then was edging his way out, the rabbit's foot disappearing in the distance. "As I walked away, voices cried to me, Who speaks?—Pope? Yes, Pope, I answered, glad to be helpful. I was wrong by that time. It was the voice of an announcer of the Vatican radio station, reading prepared translations of the Supreme

Pontiff's brief speech in English, French, Spanish, [Italian], Portuguese, German, Dutch, Russian, Polish, Hungarian, Rumanian, Chinese, Japanese, and Arabic." In any language, Liebling found the papal words mild if not pedestrian. But "unexceptionable as [they] seemed to a stranger," he noted, "they wildly perturbed the Rome organ of the rival world cult. *L'Unità,* the Communist Party paper, detected in the address an attempt to take over the Olympics." The irony of the situation delighted Liebling, as usual. "The Communists, like the Church, are in a delicate position on the question of the Olympics," he wrote. "They would like to be against them, but the big Communist Party—the one in Moscow—approves of the Games for propaganda purposes."

Liebling was on to something. Beneath the public rhetoric of brotherly love, peace, and sportsmanship offered that day by Nikita Sergeyevich and His Holiness, a fierce propaganda struggle was being waged by partisans from the left and right. The Communist press had begun a relentless attack on the Vatican, accusing the Church and its allies of manipulating the Olympics to political advantage. Even as it praised the Olympic Movement, the Moscow newspaper *Izvestia* accused the Vatican of "provocation, blackmail, roguery, and underground activity against athletes from socialist countries." It claimed that the CIA was in partnership with the Vatican in attempted "poaching." A Polish newspaper reported that priests and nuns in Rome had been assigned to advise athletes about a monastery that would serve as an asylum house for Eastern athletes who wanted to defect, an operation said to be headed by Clemente Cardinal Micara, then an eighty-year-old vicar-general in Rome. *Il Paese,* a local party newspaper, offered further detail about a vast right-wing conspiracy that involved not just the Vatican and the CIA but also the Knights of Malta and "former Fascist exiles from Eastern bloc countries" brought together in the Assembly of Captured European Nations (ACEN), a CIA-funded exile project. After a strategy meeting earlier that summer in Bavaria, this confederation had begun

Operation Rome, run from a safe house at Via Quintino Sella 49, where American agents and Hungarian refugees could debrief potential defectors.

From the other side came conservative press reports and confidential memos detailing similarly nefarious plots hatched by the Communists. Catholic infiltrators at party meetings had reported that nine months before the Games were to begin, thousands of left-wing activists had gathered in Rome to "launch a mass propaganda drive around the Olympics" that would "give sports a rational, modern, nonreligious character shaped by socialist aims." According to files compiled by the American embassy in Rome, the Italian Communist Party then set up "commissions for propaganda related to the Olympics so they can make successful use of the Games in Rome." The party was said to have spent 300 million lire "training activists and printing and distributing leaflets and pamphlets." Activists had been assigned to take foreign athletes on tours of "the ugly side of capitalism" in the Rome slums and suburbs, pay special attention to Asian and African athletes, and make sure that Olympians from the Soviet zone of East Germany did not have "excessive fraternization" with their West German teammates.

On that last goal, separating the socialist German athletes from their capitalist teammates, the early results were unclear. The West German press corps, two hundred strong, had been invited to lunch that very day by Bonn's ambassador to Italy at a restaurant atop a hill called Monte Mario. From that lofty perch, a writer for the *Frankfurter Allgemeine Zeitung* wrote, they savored "the wonderful view on the part of Rome which includes the Olympic Village, the great stadium, and the swimming pools." The luncheon conversation seemed as idyllic as the vista. *Chef de Mission* Gerhard Stoeck told the reporters that he was getting along well with functionaries of the Soviet zone and that the athletes from the two parts of Germany seemed to be mixing even better. "He said that a small-scale reunification was presently being performed in the Olympic Village and at the [practice] venues, which should be taken as an example."

AUGUST 24, the eve of the Olympics, had been a full day for Avery
Brundage. He had started the morning at breakfast with two American generals, veterans of the Italian campaign in World War II, then
granted interviews to reporters from India and the Voice of America
before lunching with the visiting president of Israel. In early evening,
Brundage had been at the front of the Olympic delegation at St. Peter's, and later made his way over to watch the Olympic torch arrive
at the Capitoline steps after its long journey from Greece. Then he
capped off his night by attending a four-hour performance of *Aida*
staged outdoors at the ancient Baths of Caracalla, replete with live
horses and camels and free beer served before the final act.

Between all that, in early afternoon, he and the IOC Executive
Board had met again at the Hotel Excelsior to hear the case against
South Africa. In London that day, the Roman Catholic bishop of
Durban, South Africa, was speaking out against his country's apartheid, calling it "the failure of white South African Christians to apply
their basic rules of behavior to the community in which they lived."
His country's tragedy, the bishop said, represented "the almost perfect example of the immovable object of white supremacy and the irresistible force of African nationalism."

Brundage and his executive board were not yet ready to acknowledge that South Africa had broken the nondiscrimination clause of
the Olympic Charter, even after granting an audience to the Reverend Michael Scott, representing the Campaign Against Race Discrimination in Sport, who had come to Rome to make the case against
South Africa's participation. The myth of white supremacy, Scott argued, was "taught and practiced in schools and universities and even
in many churches. And it extends to the practice of athletics and

games, which must be carried on in separation or apartheid. Under these circumstances, competition under equal conditions becomes impossible." He asked Brundage and the others to imagine what it would be like if the United States Olympic team did not allow Negroes. How would this change world records? How could the South African regime claim that no people of color were good enough to qualify? "The integrity of the whole Olympic Games system of world records is being undermined as long as this absurdity is tolerated of an African country not allowing Africans to represent it . . . This blemish on the ethic of the Olympic Games should be removed here at Rome once and for all."

After hearing Scott, Brundage and his committee called on Reginald Honey, the South African representative on the IOC who had been in the room when Scott made his case. When the meeting ended, IOC chancellor Otto Mayer issued a short statement on *Games of the XVII Olympiad* stationery. It was the belief of the IOC, Mayer asserted, that "the South African Olympic Committee had made every reasonable effort . . . to ensure that no competitor of requisite caliber was excluded from the South African team." The battle against apartheid was deferred, though not stopped.

As Brundage went through his evening rounds, he was given new figures about his vast and growing empire: The Rome Olympics would host a record number of countries and athletes. More than four and a half million tickets were being sold, twice as many as Melbourne. All appeared ready for the start of competition. At venues around Rome, and from Lake Albano, southeast of the city, all the way down to the Bay of Naples, the apparatus of the Olympic enterprise was counted and set in place.

Here is but a small, random sample of what was needed: 12 pole vault uprights, 100 competition hurdles, 384 training hurdles, 40 competition discuses, 165 ash javelins, 40 competition hammers, 138 shots for putting, 96 starting blocks, 110 writing frames for judges, 100 wooden folding chairs, 130 relay batons, 3 mobile luminous indicator boards, 4 special starter pistols, 1,000 metallic torches to fuel the marathon course, 3,000 black competitor numbers on white background for men, 1,500 yellow competitor numbers on black background for women, 300 white competitor numbers on black background for marathon, 110 official basketballs, 60 training balls, 6 backboards, 9 basketball nets, 570 boxing gloves, 580 elastic bandages, 27 speed balls, 47 jump ropes, 4 brass megaphones for rowing, 40 bicycle carrier frames, 318 plastic armlets for cycling, 2 horse slaughter pistols, 100 cockades for horses, 20 electrified blades for sabers, 150 mats for fencing, 480 field hockey balls, 100 sawdust pillows for shooting lines, 60,000 targets for small-bore rifles, 50 water polo balls, 153 water polo caps, 262 weights, 39 steel bars for weights, 40 wrestling whistles, 60 protest flags for Finn Class yachting, 400 floating smoke signals, 340 baskets holding 7,200 pigeons, and a fleet of 288 Fiats, 142 buses, 76 Lambretta motor scooters, and 100 Vespas.

Everything set to go, except the Italian official in charge of those preparations. Virgilio Tommasi, director of technical services for the organizing committee, had been working on the multitude of details needed to stage the Olympics for four years, setting the schedule, securing equipment, finding judges and timekeepers, drawing up regulations, worrying about the weather, making sure every nation had the correct flag and anthem. It was a demanding job that had Tommasi working long hours seven days a week, and on the day before the Opening Ceremony, it became too much for him. As he was driving along Viale Tiziano on his way to his office at the Foro Italico, he lost consciousness, and his car plowed into a tree. His son, Rino Tommasi, a young reporter and boxing promoter who would go on to become a world-renowned tennis writer, was stunned to receive the call saying that his father, having broken several ribs, was being treated at the hospital, where he would remain for the duration of the Games.

Reaching the Olympics along the roads to Rome also proved challenging for the young Italian journalist Gian Paolo Ormezzano. Later honored as the dean of Italian sportswriters, and an Olympics expert for decades thereafter, Ormezzano was a cub reporter for *Tuttosport* in 1960. Like many Italians, he had spent that August on vacation but broke off his holiday in Rimini on the Adriatic Sea to cover his first Olympics. There were no superhighways in Italy then, and he followed the Appenino, a major north-south road, as he drove down to Rome. Exhausted and trying to save money, he pulled to the shoulder and slept in his car. When he awoke, he got out to relieve himself, a gust of wind blew the door shut, and to his dismay he found himself locked out. Here he was bound for his first big assignment, and he might not make it. The prospect of missing his first deadline overwhelmed Ormezzano so much that he broke into tears. No traffic at that predawn hour, no telephones in sight. What could he do?

Out of the morning mist came a busload of Boy Scouts, also on their way to the Olympics. Using a piece of wire on a window that was slightly open, they quickly unlocked his car, and the young writer was back on the road in the scouting caravan, reaching Rome on time, he would say, in the company of angels.

5

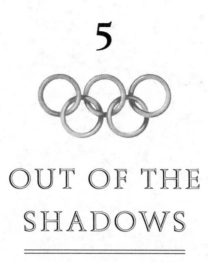

OUT OF THE
SHADOWS

B̲y the time the gates to Stadio Olimpico opened at three on the afternoon of August 25, thousands of athletes and officials from eighty-three delegations had begun the milelong march to get there from the village. Afghans, Bulgarians, Cubans, Danes, Ethiopians, Finns, and on and on, they moved as a human ribbon of exuberant color, crossing the Tiber over the Ponte Milvio and flowing down to the Foro Italico, where they crowded onto the infield grass of the compact Stadio dei Marmi. There, under a blistering summer sun, the temperature soaring toward triple digits, they waited for the start of the Parade of Nations opening the Games of the XVII Olympiad.

Mild complaints were whispered among women on the U.S. team about the impractical burden of their parade uniforms: blue blazers, white wool pleated skirts, red leather pumps, white berets, white stretch gloves, nylon hosiery, and big red purses they had to carry over their right shoulders. They were delighted to be there, but couldn't someone have planned the outfits with a Mediterranean

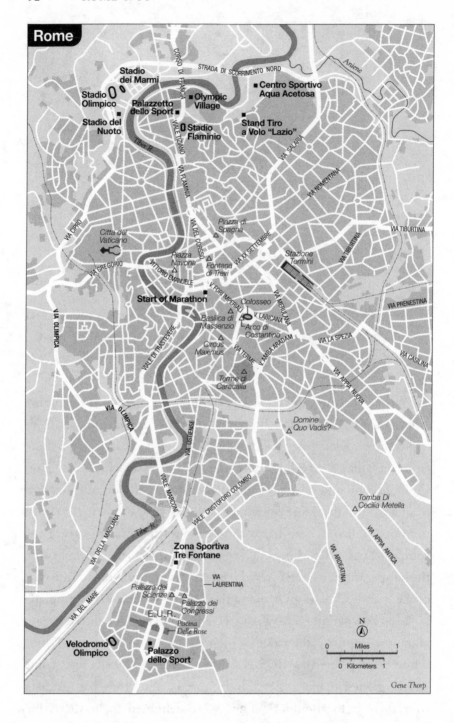

Rome

Stadio dei Marmi

Stadio Olimpico

Palazzetto dello Sport

Stadio del Nuoto

■ Olympic Village

■ Stadio Flaminio

■ Centro Sportivo Aqua Acetosa

■ Stand Tiro a Volo "Lazio"

CORSO DI FRANCIA

STRADA DI SCORRIMENTO NORD

Aniene

VIALE TIZIANO

Tiber R.

VIA FLAMINIA

VIA SALARIA

VIA NOMENTANA

VIA CIPRO

VIA GREGORIO

Citta del Vaticano

Piazza di Spagna

VIA DEL CORSO

Piazza Navona

VITTORIO EMANUELE

Fontana di Trevi

VIA XX SETTEMBRE

Stazione Termini

VIA TIBURTINA

VIA TIBURTINA

V. FORI IMPERIALI

Start of Marathon

Colosseo

V. LABICANA

VIA MERULANA

VIA PRENESTINA

Basilica di Massenzio

Arco di Costantino

VIALE DI TRASTEVERE

Circus Maximus

VIA TERME

V. AMBA ARADAM

VIA LA SPEZIA

VIA CASILINA

Terme di Caracalla

VIA OLIMPICA

VIA OSTIENSE

Domine Quo Vadis?

VIA APPIA NUOVA

VIALE MARCONI

VIALE CRISTOFORO COLOMBO

Tomba Di Cecilia Metella

VIA ARDEATINA

VIA APPIA ANTICA

VIA DELLA MAGLIANA

Tiber R.

Zona Sportiva Tre Fontane

VIA DEL MARE

VIA LAURENTINA

Palazzo dei Scienze

Palazzo dei Congressi

E.U.R.

Piscina Delle Rose

Velodromo Olimpico

■ Palazzo dello Sport

N

0   Miles   1

0   Kilometers   1

Gene Thorp

summer in mind? Most of the Americans had no Olympic experience and knew nothing about marching in formation. It was left to Bo Roberson, the broad jumper from Cornell, a veteran of Army ROTC, to take on the role of drill sergeant in the staging area, at the last minute putting his teammates through the hup-two-three-four paces, hoping they would not embarrass themselves when the world was watching.

The great white bowl of the main stadium filled slowly, but by four o'clock nearly eighty thousand people were inside. In the prime seats at midfield, there was a sudden buzz, and binoculars from above and to the sides focused on a particular row. It was not the queen of Greece who caused the flurry, nor Prince Albert of Belgium, Prince Axel and Princess Margaretha of Denmark, Prince Harald of Norway, or Prince Franz Josef II of Liechtenstein. They seemed Old World; only a reigning monarch in the postwar popular culture could provoke such intense murmuring—movie star Elizabeth Taylor was arriving with singer Eddie Fisher, her husband. When Taylor's entrance caught the attention of the vast cadre of journalists in the press area, they characteristically began a round of double-entendre jokes. It's Elizabeth Taylor in the flesh. A great deal of the same. Liz may have set a new record in neckline plunging at Olympic events.

One distraction replaced by another: a local semistreaker wearing nothing but Bermuda shorts jumped the fence and raced merrily around the oval, dissolving into the throng before the slow-moving security men could nab him. No doubt the Comtesse de Morelos, head of the Olympic fashion police, was horrified by his American-tourist sartorial selection. There was another half hour of anticipation. Then, to the sardonic bemusement of a correspondent from the *Times* of London, a ceremonial band "broke into what was recognized by both British and Italians as a Fascist marching song" to signal the start of the Parade of Nations. The oval track, a rich shade of dark Roman red, offered a vibrant contrast to the green infield and cerulean sky. Carrying the flag for the Greeks was Prince Constantine, a future king and current Dragon Class Olympic yachtsman, who before the fortnight was over would seize a gold medal in the Bay of Naples and receive a congratulatory embrace in the shower from a fully clothed, yacht-cavorting billionaire countryman, Aristotle Onassis.

In line after Greece, honored at the front as the ancient progenitor of the Olympic idea, competitors marched onto the track in alphabetical order based on the Italian spelling of their countries. The Australians, their men outfitted in green jackets, gray trousers, and green hats, were the largest of the first wave of delegations, though more than half of their two hundred athletes—including all swimmers, boxers, and cyclists—remained in the village. Earlier that day, team officials had issued an edict that anyone competing in the first week of the Games should not participate in the Opening Ceremony. The heat and the long march might sap their energy, it was explained. Whatever the reasoning, the order did not sit well with many Aussie athletes, individualists who bristled at the "petty tyranny" of their bureaucratic minders. In the sort of antiestablishment rebelliousness more commonly associated with later years of the sixties decade, those left behind staged a mock ceremony back at the village, the men noisily parading around bare chested with ties drooping from their necks.

Austria, Bahamas, Belgium, Bermuda (more of those dreaded shorts, mustard color), Brazil, Bulgaria (a notably gregarious Iron Curtain contingent, smiling and waving miniature flags, the women in jonquil-colored frocks), Canada (the most sensibly dressed, in short sleeves, without coats), Czechoslovakia, Ceylon. Every team with its own story.

Chile once had planned to send eighty athletes to Rome, but only eight made the trip. The ribbony South American country was still recovering, three months later, from one of the twentieth century's most devastating earthquakes, 9.5 magnitude, and a ferocious tsunami that washed over much of its coastline near Valparaiso. France subsidized travel expenses for three Chilean athletes, other European nations chipped in to fund the rest, and the IOC defrayed all other costs for the team.

Cuba marched in with a dozen athletes—no beards. Nineteen months after Fidel Castro seized power on the island, his athletes were moving noticeably into the orbit of the Soviets, much as his government was doing. In the village, the Russians had sent a contingent to attend the hoisting of the Cuban flag, and reporters from *Pravda* and *Izvestia* were making daily references to Soviet camaraderie with athletes from Cuba and other nascent socialist and anticolonialist governments around the world. As the Cuban Olympians marched into the stadium in Rome, their political delegates were about to walk out of a special meeting of the Organization of American States in San Jose, Costa Rica. An emergency session of the OAS had been convened in an unsuccessful effort to ease growing tension between Castro's Cuba and the United States.

This was more than two years before the Cuban Missile Crisis and eight months before the Bay of Pigs invasion, yet the issues debated in Costa Rica on the same day the Olympics opened in Italy foreshadowed all the difficulties to come. The Eisenhower administration, alarmed by Soviet intrusion into the Western hemisphere, demanded at the OAS conference that the Cubans summarily reject and renounce a recent Kremlin promise to provide Castro with military aid, including missiles. The Cubans refused, calling the Soviets their friends. At the same time, they accused the U.S. of plotting to overthrow the Castro regime, a charge the Americans roundly denied.

Next came Denmark, dressed in scarlet jackets and white slacks, minus the team cyclists who would compete in the first gold medal event of the Olympics the next morning. And now Abebe Bikila and the Ethiopians. Most of them had been alive when Mussolini had last invaded their country. As A. J. Liebling described for readers of *The New Yorker,* "A dozen or so straight, tall, thin men marched past the reviewing stand, and their standard bearer lowered their flag, with its green, yellow, and red stripes, in salute." Liebling could only wonder what they were thinking about. "They were received with polite applause," he determined from his seat in the press section.

Fiji came with five men, the flag bearer draped in a burlap skirt. Scattered applause for the Philippines (spelled with an *F* in Italian) and the blue-clad Finns, and now in marched Taiwan, or Formosa, or so the placard said.

The key political fight of the Olympics was being decided at last. Only hours earlier, the American embassy in Rome had received one last call from the Republic of China's ambassador, who was still hoping that his nation might avoid being called Taiwan or Formosa at the Olympics. "He expressed great appreciation for the efforts made at the American embassy, and he had certain suggestions regarding attentions that might be paid to Mr. Avery Brundage," a State Department memorandum said of the ambassador later that day, not detailing precisely what those "attentions" to the IOC president might entail.

When the embassy's duty officer "asked whether it was necessary to march in the opening parade in order to compete in events," the ambassador replied that he was not sure. The athletes themselves did not want to march, he said, but the delegation's Olympic officials thought they should. To the end, the U.S. was pushing its ally to take the strongest possible political stand. It might be better not to march "even though this risk could prevent later participation," the American embassy official advised, arguing that "the Opening Ceremony would focus attention on names of competing teams, and, second, if the designation was accepted without resistance, it would hurt future battles on that issue."

Yet hours later, with the capacity crowd watching inside the stadium, including several officials from the U.S. embassy, and an exponentially larger potential audience on television and newsreel, here came a banner introducing athletes from Formosa. In a little-noticed gesture of political pride, members of the delegation wore sport coats with insignias that depicted the Nationalist Chinese flag. And as the group moved down the track and passed in front of the official reviewing stand, a team official marching directly behind the country banner unfolded an unmistakable symbol of discontent: a handmade sign that read UNDER PROTEST. He marched with the sign for about a hundred yards before folding it and stuffing it in his pocket.

What reaction did this modest political demonstration inspire? The government-monitored press in Taipei, which had editorialized against participating in the Olympics under any name except the Republic of China, declared that "the people of free China were greatly impressed by the radiophoto picture" of the protest sign. A U.S. diplomatic account from the scene reported glumly that aside from a few cheers in the crowd, the protest was barely perceptible and provoked little comment. It most certainly provoked Avery Brundage, who had been watching from the stands next to the president of the Italian Republic, Giovanni Gronchi. Brundage was "very disagreeably surprised" to see the protest sign, as were all leaders of the Olympic Movement, he said. He considered the gesture "inelegant, political minded, and an offense to the dignity which should prevail in the Olympic Games." Rather than bringing support to the cause, he later wrote in a scalding censure letter to the Taiwanese, "we think that by this way of action you have lost the last sympathy you might have had among the sportsmen of the world."

As the Parade of Nations continued, Brundage's displeasure evaporated with the entrance of the unified German team, outfitted in light gray. Turning to his Italian host, Brundage boasted, "Those are East German athletes and West German athletes in the same uniform marching behind the same leaders and the same flag."

"Impossible," Gronchi said.

The response from Brundage, recounted in an autobiographical manuscript, sounded too perfect to be verbatim, but nonetheless reflected his idealistic, if naive and selective, perspective.

"While it might be impossible politically, in the nonpolitical Olympic Games, such surprising things can happen," he told Gronchi. "Contestants on Olympic fields are individual athletes and not countries. Neither ideologies of different kinds nor political systems are at stake. In the Olympic Games, it is pure sport and sport only. German sport leaders are demonstrating their devotion to the Olympic idea in a way that will make sport history."

Shirley Povich, veteran columnist for the *Washington Post,* thought he observed "a lift in the applause . . . when the two Germanys marched side by side under one flag. Ideologies shelved for this event at least." A Soviet writer detected warm applause as well, noting approvingly that "viewers could not tell the difference among athletes dressed in light gray uniforms which one is from the west and which one from eastern Germany." But the West German press was more measured. The team marched in looking "almost courtly with their neat gray suits," noted the *Frankfurter Allgemeine Zeitung,* saying the drabness of the outfits seemed to match both the personality of the team and the reaction of the crowd. "A bit of the charm and good mood presented by other nations was missing, so the applause remained only friendly."

In other ways, things were less than they appeared. Marching four abreast behind flag carrier Fritz Thiedemann, a bowlegged equestrian champion from West Germany ("I mean, I did ask myself, 'Can't they find a flag carrier prettier than me?' "), the delegation looked larger to observers in the stadium than it was. The Associated Press reported that the Germans entered with the maximum allowable number, 245, but in fact there were far fewer. Most of the track stars, especially from the West, remained in Germany, held back because of the Roman heat wave. At the head of the formation were West German team leaders Gerhard Stoeck and Dr. Max Danz, walking beside their East German counterparts, Heinz Schöbel and Manfred Ewald. All seemed peaceful on the surface, noted a correspondent from *Die Welt,* a West German newspaper, "even though behind the Via Germania, in block 30 [Olympic Village quarters for the German team], political baggage has also been unloaded."

The East Germans were aflame with reports that Hans Grodotzki, a distance runner, had received an anonymous letter in his room in block 30 "urging him to leave the German Democratic Republic forever by not returning there from Rome." An account in *Neues Deutschland* said the "poaching" letter came from "Bonn's henchmen" and included a map "printed by one of the West German revanchist lobby groups." That the effort failed is no doubt why it ever made the East German news. The sender "failed to psychologically destabilize the young runner," according to the report. Grodotzki was said to have given the letter to his team leaders, declaring, "Something like this leaves me completely unshaken."

GREAT BRITAIN arrived in blue blazers and gray trousers, among the largest delegations as always, but fading fast in international sports, much like France. The Brits seemed to boast less talent among the athletes rounding the oval than they could muster up in the press section, where the squad of *Times* of London writers included Roger Bannister, the legendary four-minute miler, and Harold Abrahams, winner of the 100 at the 1924 Olympics in Paris, who would be immortalized two decades later as a main character in the movie *Chariots of Fire*.

Haiti, Hong Kong, India (here were the wrestlers in white and yellow turbans who lifted up little Paolo Pedinelli, plus the dashing middle-distance runner Milkha Singh, known as the Flying Sikh), Indonesia, Iraq (spelled *Irak,* hence the place in line), Iran, Ireland, Iceland, Israel, Yugoslavia, Kenya, Lebanon, Liberia. *Pravda*'s correspondents took note of the African delegations. This was a summer of independence in Africa, and much of the continent had become contested ground in the cold war. Fourteen nations were in the process of being born, and the Congo, with the colonial Belgians leaving at last, was exploding in civil war during the very days of the Olympics. "They exude strength," the Soviet sportswriters Alexei Dykov and Vitali Petrusenko wrote of the Africans. "Together with their nations, the athletes, boxers, and gymnasts of Africa recently fought for independence. Now they march in the Olympics as equals among equals. It is not very important that they have little sports experience. Observers already forecast that the Rome Olympics will reveal many new talents among representatives of the black continent."

The Pakistanis appeared in forest green coats and white turbans, ready to take their difficult geopolitical struggle with India onto the hockey field, where the two neighboring nations dominated a sport taught to them by the imperial British. Panama, Peru, Poland, Portugal, Puerto Rico, Rhodesia, Romania (like the Bulgarians, all friendly, waving handkerchiefs to the crowd), San Marino (the Apennine mountain state, with ten athletes, all pistol shooters and cyclists, out of a populace of fewer than thirty thousand, the highest athlete-per-capita ratio at the Games), Singapore. The Spaniards entered to loud applause.

Eddy Gilmore, covering for the Associated Press, then noticed that "suddenly, a strange quiet came over the vast crowd. Almost before you knew it, it happened."

What happened was a sighting of Rafer Johnson, carrying the U.S. flag, stepping from the shadows of the tunnel at the northeast entrance, marching into view. His movements were rhythmic, precise. In his blue blazer, white pants, red-striped tie, and white straw hat, the decathlete looked cool and calm, but he never felt more nervous, or more alive. Some ceremonial events appear glorious but have no deeper meaning; this one, to Rafer Johnson, was "as important as the competition itself." Never before had a black athlete walked in front as flag carrier for the U.S. Olympic team. Since the moment he reached Rome with the track team after that raucous overnight train ride through the Alps, he had been the most interviewed, most photographed athlete in the village. "Keep in step," he said to himself now. "Don't drop the flag." He cradled it like a baby, one observer thought, like "something fragile that he must not drop." Johnson's life flashed through his mind as he moved along. He thought about his mother watching back home in California and the road he had taken to this moment.

The Johnsons came west from Texas in 1945, when Rafer was nine, and eventually settled in Kingsburg, where his father, Lewis Johnson, found a job with the Southern Pacific Railroad. The San Joaquin Valley town was about as flat, hot, and white as America gets. In the Oak Cliff neighborhood of Dallas, where Rafer came from, he almost never saw a white person. In Kingsburg, the Johnsons were the only black family in town and one of only two in the area. They lived in a small one-story "section house" near the railroad tracks and in the shadows of a local cannery. A legend arose later that they lived in a boxcar—not quite, although the narrow house looked like one. In the summers, Rafer and his siblings worked the fields near the cannery, picking grapes, plums, and peaches. With one exception, he felt very much embraced by the predominantly Swedish farm community, where "everyone knew everyone." That lone exception was the police chief, a racist who reflexively suspected the Johnsons when anything went wrong. "Every time something was taken, something was stolen, a bicycle missing, they came to our house looking for it," Johnson recalled. "We weren't taking anything, and we weren't doing anything." That only stopped after Lewis Johnson had a heated confrontation with the chief.

But the prevailing sensibility in Kingsburg, a community that showered attention on its children, was a boon to Rafer, who excelled in school and in sports. "The parents would build the fields and drive young people back and forth to different competitions [in farm towns scattered around the valley]. They were the coaches. It was a wonderful community for young people." Rafer's best sport was football, but he also starred in basketball and track and field. Much of his athletic skill came from his mother, Alma, who could outrun him until he was a teenager. His mother was also Rafer's role model, the person he most admired. "I can't think of anything I ever did or any place I ever went or any accomplishment I ever had that she was not either there or in my thoughts or we had some conversation about what was happening or going to happen," he said later. "I can't think of a time when she was not a part of what was going on with me." His father, though a hard worker, drank too much and could be hard to handle during his off hours. "There would be weekends when he could start drinking, and the whole weekend would be lost. There were very few Monday mornings when my father was not at work, but there were a lot of weekends when the family suffered because of his drinking problem. At athletic events, sometimes, honestly, he could be a little disruptive. My mother was able to keep him calm for the most part, but there were times when she couldn't control him, and no one else could."

When Rafer was a junior in high school, and the best athlete on the Kingsburg Vikings, track coach Murl Dotson drove him down to watch a decathlon meet in nearby Tulare, the hometown of Olympic decathlon champion Bob Mathias. It was a transformative moment. Mathias was the hero of the valley, someone Rafer aspired to follow. Although there were no decathlons in high school, young Johnson returned from Tulare determined to compete in as many individual events as possible and build up his skills so that someday he might succeed Mathias with the title of the best all-around athlete in the world. Seven years later, here he was in Rome, approaching his dream, leading the Americans into the Stadio Olimpico.

Behind him, after a wedge of team officials, came row after row of American athletes. The walker from Buffalo, the javelin thrower from Newark, the gymnast from Van Nuys, the wrestler from Ponca City, the boxer from Louisville, the equestrian from Camden, the small-bore rifle shooter from Chicago, the fencer from New York, the sprinter from Tuscaloosa, the cyclist from Muskegon, the miler from Portland, the canoeist from Akron, the basketball player from Cabin Creek, the swimmer from Urbana, the weight lifter from Detroit, the shot-putter from Santa Monica. The youngest of the swimmers, Donna de Varona, had just turned thirteen. The oldest of the yachtsmen, Robert Halperin, was going on fifty-three. Track aficionados in the stands looked for familiar faces, Olympic favorites.

Where was the sprinting medical student from Duke, Dave Sime? Back in the village, still recovering from strep throat. "Didn't even watch it on television," Sime recalled. "I was still laid out." Ray Norton, the favorite for gold in the 100, was also back at the dorm, not wanting to aggravate a sore leg by making the long walk on cement from the village to the stadium. Rink Babka, the massive discus thrower, missed it too, though not by choice. Officials had issued him a sport coat far too small for his massive fifty-two-inch chest, and a new one had not arrived in time. But lanky John Thomas was there, the phenom from Boston U., considered a mortal lock for the high jump. And that little guy nearby was Ike Berger, the featherweight weight lifter, all 132 pounds of him, who only that morning in practice had bettered his own world record for the two-hand clean and jerk by hoisting 336½ pounds. There came Cassius Clay, the ebullient light-heavyweight boxer, but many of his teammates in the lower weight classes, who would start competition that night and the next day, stayed back in the village. "They wanted me to march," Nikos Spanakos, the American featherweight, said later, "but I told the coach to go fuck himself and stayed in."

As the athletes streamed from the "tunnel, dark and cold, out into the blazing bright sunlight," Anne Warner, one of the California swimmers, was amazed that they were marching in unison, right foot forward at the same time—Bo Roberson's drilling seemed to have worked. Terry Dischinger, the basketball forward from Purdue, was stunned by the enormous ovation that reverberated through the stadium as the Yanks strode in. "It sounded like thunder coming out of those stands."

American sportswriters traditionally scorned overt signs of emotion in the press box, but few could keep their stoic game faces now.

"When the American flag swept around the far turn of the Olympic stadium, and behind it came marching what had been up to that time the largest delegation that the 100,000 spectators had seen, a great cheer roared out and thousands of people sprang to their feet," Don Maxwell, editor of the *Chicago Tribune,* reported in his daily letter from Rome. "Hats were waved, and I am sure there were tears in many eyes."

More rapture from Fred Russell of the *Nashville Banner,* who described the parade as "the lasting thrill" of the entire Olympics: "When the United States flag came by in the parade of nations, the spine tingle caused a few misty eyes in the press box."

The moment struck Eddy Gilmore as at once moving and politically meaningful, a reaffirmation of America's role in the modern world. "Call it corny, but it brought tears to your eyes. It made your heart beat a wee bit faster. It took your breath away. And all at once, this spontaneous demonstration seemed to justify lend-lease, the Marshall Plan, and all of the millions American taxpayers have poured out on other parts of the world. Sure, Americans love to be liked. And brother, they were liked today."

Among the political and military dignitaries watching the parade that afternoon was General Lauris Norstad of the U.S. Air Force, who now served as supreme commander of NATO forces in Europe. The quintessential cold warrior, Norstad had developed the air defenses for Western Europe against possible Soviet attack. Earlier that afternoon, he had arrived from Paris with his wife and three aides as the guest of Giulio Andreotti, the Italian defense minister and president of the Olympic Organizing Committee. After changing into civilian clothes at the Grand Hotel, the general was escorted to Stadio Olimpico just in time for the Opening Ceremony. The sight of the American delegation marching onto the track to resounding applause, with Rafer Johnson at the lead, struck Norstad as a reassuring political moment.

"What an impressive experience!" he later wrote to his friend, Charles J. V. Murphy, a prolific cold war journalist at *Time* with intelligence community affiliations. "Having heard and read so much criticism of the U.S. and its ways in the last few months, I was surprised and warmed by the enthusiasm for the U.S. which was demonstrated by the . . . spectators in the Olympic Stadium at the opening. By far the greatest and warmest applause was for the American contingent. Our group flag bearer and leader was Rafer Johnson, and he looked magnificent. I discreetly inquired from people of several nationalities about their reaction to this colored boy being in the lead, thinking that there might be some feeling that this was arranged for political purposes, but I found that the case was quite the contrary. It was generally believed that he had been elected by his teammates, but that even if he had been appointed by officials, it was in recognition of the fact that he was a very fine man and perhaps the world's outstanding athlete. The reaction was very good."

Johnson himself was not concerned about why he was chosen. He was proud to represent his country, knew that he had won the respect of his athletic peers, and thought that he could make no stronger statement in support of civil rights and the desegregation of American life than to be the leader of the U.S. delegation at a time when blacks were pushing for equality—and at a time when it remained within the realm of accepted discourse for a white official to refer to him as a "colored boy." The most profound course of action black athletes in his situation could make, he believed, was "showing up, doing their best." His sensibility, he explained later, was that he had to stay positive and keep his focus on what he could achieve. And, for the moment, to focus on carrying the flag. It was a matter of Olympic courtesy for nations to dip the flag when passing the reviewing stand, but the U.S. and the Soviet Union, competing for supremacy in the cold war world, maintained their own uncompromising traditions—never dip. For the Americans, this refusal to gesture had been a matter of law since 1942, when Congress passed the U.S. Flag Code, saying the flag should not be dipped to "any person or thing." Johnson held the Stars and Stripes upright all the way, though he said later that he had not received instructions on how to carry it. "I didn't dip," he explained, "but no one told me not to do it."

In a symmetrical irony, the team entering the stadium behind Rafer Johnson's Americans was the all-white apartheid delegation from South Africa. Sudan, Suriname, Sweden, Switzerland, Thailand, Tunisia, Turkey, Uganda, Hungary (capital *U* no *H*), and then in marched the nation that had crushed the Hungarian revolution only four years earlier.

The Soviet flag bearer was Yuri Vlasov, the heavyweight weight lifter, a national hero in a culture that worshipped strength above other physical attributes. If the Soviets were to defeat their American rivals in the overall medal count, the weight lifters would play an essential role. The U.S. had dominated the sport in the 1950s, but now the Russians thought they had the edge with Vlasov, who had just broken American Paul Anderson's world record, leading the way. "He is a young man, very cultured, very well read," *Pravda* boasted of the engineering student. "Vlasov is the best example of the harmonical physical and mental development of Soviet athletes." That he might have been, but some Americans clucked disapprovingly, calling him a showoff, as he marched into the stadium holding the hammer and sickle stiffly with a single outstretched hand.

Correspondents who choked up at the sight of the American team now transformed themselves into human applause meters to compare crowd reactions. "I suppose I am prejudiced, but I did not think the Russians got half the applause that the crowd gave our contingent," Maxwell surmised for his Chicago readers. Jesse Abramson, the track-and-field expert for the New York *Herald Tribune,* agreed: "To be sure, an American ear detected a far warmer greeting and more decibels of applause when the Stars and Stripes appeared in the arena behind the banner Stati Unit America than when the Hammer and Sickle arrived behind the standard Unione Repubbliche Soviet-iche Socialiste." Fitting the applause differential into a cold war context, an AP report noted that Italy had the largest Communist party in Western Europe, yet the greeting its people gave the Soviets was "polite—but nothing more."

One hears what one wants to hear, as *Pravda*'s Alexei Dyakov and Vitali Petrusenko, stationed not far from their American colleagues, demonstrated in their description of the same scene. The greeting of the Soviet team was effusive, from their perspective, and laden with deeper meaning. "In the Italian clapping of hands we can hear not only the greeting of Soviet athletes but also the excitement for the last achievements of the Soviet Union in opening the cosmos." (Only a week earlier, and three years after Sputnik, they had made another important breakthrough in space by launching into orbit a satellite carrying two dogs, a rat, four mice, and a jar of flies in a cabin de-signed for the future flight of man.) They even found a way to relate the ovation in Stadio Olimpico to the previous day's welcoming letter from their leader back in Moscow. By their interpretation, the recep-tion given the Soviets reflected "warm approval of the peace-loving politics of our government, which found such a bright expression in the greeting of Comrade Khrushchev to the Olympic youth."

From the accounts of American observers, it was not the recent space menagerie or Khrushchev that observers were thinking about when the Soviets marched in, but the unexpected flair of their women athletes. The Western stereotype of the typical Russian woman was unflattering, and a *Los Angeles Times* correspondent repeated that image now by calling them "stalwart." But most of his colleagues presented a decidedly different picture, lurching from the previous ridicule to outright leering. "Their girls looked like Parisian models in white silk dresses with pleated skirts and a most Parisian cut to their necklines," reported Abramson. "Most obviously, the more muscular Amazons had been excused from the parade. Even Yves St. Laurent could not have masked the lines of the lady shot-putters from Russia."

The Associated Press account took the theme even further: "There was a gasp of surprise when the Soviet girls came into the stadium. Shades of Marx, Lenin, Stalin, and Khrushchev. Moscow had sent to Rome something that would not suffer comparison with New York's Rockettes. The Russian gals: (1) Wore red pumps with pointed toes and needle heels two inches tall. (2) Wore billowing white skirts about knee length. (3) A neckline that was not exactly plunging but certainly poised on the diving board ready to jump. (4) They walked as though they had spent ten years of training in the Bolshoi Ballet, sort of floating through the air."

Here was a Soviet variation of Ed Temple's directive to his Tiger-belles at Tennessee State that he wanted "foxes, not oxes." By some accounts, the Soviet transformation was in part in response to a plea from Temple's track-and-field sidekick, Frances Kaszubski, the women's team manager, who had once instructed her Russian coun-terpart, Zoya Romanova, to "send us dolls" when the Soviets first brought a team to the U.S. in 1959 for a dual track meet. For Temple and Kaszubski, the emphasis on appearance was part of a larger ef-fort to gain respect for women athletes and lift them out of the old unfeminine stereotypes. For the Soviets, it seemed part of a concerted public relations offensive in the cold war. A. J. Liebling, always with a fresh take on things, saw it as another sign of the Westernization of the postwar world: "The Russian women were a great deal smarter-looking than they had been at Helsinki, and the men were more re-laxed. When they marched in 1952, their faces were set; they had never before competed in the Games, and were not sure how they would do. Now they were confident and were having a good time . . . We are not getting to look more like the Russians. The Rus-sians are getting to look more like us."

Uruguay, Venezuela, Vietnam. Finally, as the bookend to the

Greeks, here came the Italians, looking *molto bello* in their light blue jackets, white slacks, and white hats. The other delegations had quotas for how many could march, but the hosts entered in full force, nearly three hundred strong, and the roar for the home team was deafening. Livio Berruti, the fleet sprinter from Torino, felt overwhelmed by a spirit of equality and fraternity. As he marched around the stadium, warmed by the shimmering rays of the early evening sun, Berruti said later, it seemed as though all of Europe was walking with him, out of the shadows, away from the past.

6

HEAT

FRIDAY morning was infernally hot in Rome. It was already ninety-three degrees in the shade, where there was shade, by nine o'clock when teams lined up for time-trial road cycling, the first medal event of the Olympics. Leaving every two minutes from a standing start, four-man cycling squads headed out from Viale Oceano Pacifico near the Velodromo for the long ride up and back along Viale Cristoforo Colombo, three laps covering 100 kilometers, or 62.14 miles. Fittingly for the inaugural event, the home Italians were favored, followed by the Germans and Russians, who were moving up fast in the cycling world. The Americans, although not considered medal contenders, were better than many of the event's three dozen teams; if all went smoothly, they could finish in the top third.

The prospect of that was uncertain. One of the U.S. cyclists, Bob Tetzlaff, weakened with inflamed tonsils, had received a shot of penicillin in Rome and was bedridden for most of the thirty-six hours before the race. No sooner had he and his teammates, Bill Freund,

Michael Hiltner, and Wesley Chowen, reached the starting line than they discovered a flat tire on one of the bikes. They changed it quickly enough and were off chasing the Swiss and the Poles, who were at about their talent level.

Racing bikes of that era seem like ancient relics in retrospect. They were ordinary ten-speeds, far from the sophisticated twenty-speeds of the twenty-first century. Commonly made of steel, rather than a lighter frame, they weighed as much as twenty-two pounds—seven pounds more than models of later decades. The brakes were less subtle. If you wanted a responsive bike, you had to go with light tires, which produced more flats. And the seats were an uncomfortable leather. But the machine was virtually the same everywhere; the difference was in the endurance and skill of the rider.

The Danes were among the better teams; not up with the Italians, but competitive with Holland and Sweden in a tier just below. Earlier in the year, they had tied the East Germans at this same hundred klicks, and more recently Knud Enemark Jensen had won the individual Nordic championship. Jensen now was part of his country's time-trial quartet, along with Jorgen B. Jorgensen, Vagn Bangsborg, and Niels Baunsof. With coach Preben Zerland Jensen and a photojournalist from the Danish tabloid *Ekstra Bladet* trailing closely in the escort car, they set off into the coruscating morning swelter. A photograph capturing their start showed them wearing visors but no protection for the backs of their necks.

After a strong first lap, Jorgensen was overcome by sunstroke and was forced to drop out just as his team had started its second lap. Three of four cyclists are required to finish, so his teammates cycled on while Jorgensen, conscious but woozy, was taken by ambulance to a hospital in central Rome. The course layout along Cristoforo Colombo offered little shade, and by now the temperature on the road was well over a hundred degrees. As they reached a short rise in the course, Jensen and Bangsborg "felt stiffness in their legs," according to the account of Lars Bogeskov, writing in the Danish newspaper

Politiken. "Only Niels Baunsof felt strong at that point. He told the other two to get behind him and catch his draft. At a sharp curve near the turning point, a spectator shouted that the Danes were only ten seconds from a bronze medal." With a strong final push, they might catch the Dutch, who were just ahead. They had reached a flat section of the course by then, and Baunsof continued to set the pace for his fatigued partners.

Five miles farther, Jensen shouted, "I'm dizzy!" but kept pedaling. Soon he slowed considerably and was about to tumble, his bike wobbling, when Baunsof grabbed his jersey and kept him upright. Bangsborg came up to steady him from the other side. The photographer in the escort car started snapping pictures, capturing the dramatic struggle of cyclist No. 127. Fearing the heat would claim a second victim and force the Danes from the race, Bangsborg reached over and sprayed Jensen with water. Only teammates could assist one another on the course; help from outside meant automatic elimination. For a moment, it appeared that Jensen had regained his equilibrium. Baunsof, still holding his jersey, asked whether Jensen was OK, and he nodded yes. But Jensen was never good with heat, his brother Paol would say later. He hated to go south, preferring the Scandinavian weather. Anything over eighty degrees, and he suffered. Seconds after Baunsof let go, Jensen fainted, his skull crashing hard into the burning asphalt. He was wearing a light sun cap, not a helmet. He had lost consciousness.

A quarter mile back, the team had passed an ambulance. The escort car now swerved around and sped for help. Minutes later, an emergency medical team lifted the fallen rider onto a gurney and slid it into the back of an ambulance. At that moment, a pack of cyclists from other teams rushed past, including the Americans. Their memories were nothing more than a flash of surprise, something wrong, then gone in an instant, their concentration returning to the struggle ahead. Bob Tetzlaff remembered seeing an ambulance and noticing that the Danish team had stopped at the side of the road. "They were being attended to. I thought at the time maybe they had touched wheels," he said later. "We had no inkling what happened. There were three laps on the course, so we went by them only that once. For sure we weren't going to catch them any other way."

The ambulance took Jensen to a military tent near the finish line. Baunsof and Bangsborg rode behind, completing the race even though their team had been disqualified. Bangsborg was also dizzy, and vomited at the finish. Baunsof, distraught, kept riding until he reached the Olympic Village. Jensen never regained consciousness, and by three-thirty that afternoon he was dead. The wire services reported that he was at a hospital, but in fact he died inside the military tent, which did not have the equipment of a hospital and was overheated, more stifling than the outdoor sun. Prince Axel, the royal highness of Denmark and a member of the IOC, was on his way to the bedside when his countryman died.

Heatstroke seemed the apparent cause, but with the world watching, Italian officials realized the need for a medical inquest. In the cycling world that year, rumors had swirled about racers using amphetamines. Jensen was the first Olympic athlete in modern times to die on the same day he competed. Francisco Lazoro, of Portugal, collapsed during the 1912 marathon and died the next day. What happened to Jensen? The day's grief was accompanied by a nagging unease, a sense that the tragedy was still unfolding. It was a most inauspicious way to start the Games.

AT A SUN-BAKED stadium near the village, at about the same time that Knud Enemark Jensen was keeling onto the asphalt on the other side of the city, the American and Soviet track-and-field teams held an unusual joint practice. When Gavriel Korobkov, coach of the Soviets, suggested that his athletes join their U.S. counterparts that day on the practice field, the Americans readily agreed. It was described as "a friendly gesture reciprocated with equal friendliness." As with most dealings between the superpowers, precisely where collegiality stopped and angling for an edge began was hard to delineate. For decades a keen student of American methods and techniques, Korobkov was always eager for a closer look at the opposition, and the Americans, in turn, seemed to think that a sneak preview of their extraordinary talent might prove psychologically intimidating to the Russians before the official start of the track-and-field competition at Stadio Olimpico, which was still five days away.

Though weak from strep throat, Dave Sime left his sickbed and went to the combined practice along with his roommate, distance runner Jim Beatty. They were quite a pair, Sime too fatigued to undergo his usual regimen of sprints, and Beatty tenderly testing a sprained ligament in his left foot, realizing that the injury likely ruined his medal hopes. At the track, Sime approached the broad-jump area and renewed a discussion with Igor Ter-Ovanesyan. "We kind of bonded," Sime said later. "He was very Westernized. Very American. Spoke English. Looked very American. Crew cut. And I said, 'You know, we'd like to talk to you.' And he said, 'Yeah, I'd like to talk to you.' " Ter-Ovanesyan, who had already had a conversation with Al Cantello, the javelin thrower, very quickly felt "a close relationship" with Sime. When the American suggested that they should leave the village and go out for dinner some night, he readily agreed.

Across the warm-up field, the world's three best decathletes found themselves together in a gathering that defied political imperatives. By any name—Taiwan, Formosa, or the Republic of China—the Soviets refused to acknowledge C. K. Yang's government, their hostility so strong that Russian correspondents wrote as though Taiwanese athletes were not in Rome and did not exist. Yet now here came Vasily Kuznetsov, the Soviet decathlete, with a hearty greeting for Yang, who had come to the practice with his friend and UCLA teammate, Rafer Johnson. "You are very good," Kuznetsov said to Yang, giving him the universal sign of approval: thumbs-up. Johnson had brought a movie camera along to record the scene and handed it to a coach, Bud Winter. "I congratulate you on your record," Kuznetsov said to Johnson, who had obliterated the world mark at the Olympic Trials. "Well, maybe you can improve on it," Johnson replied graciously, as Winter recorded the scene.

But the balance of power had changed since Johnson and Kuznetsov last faced each other at the 1958 dual meet in Moscow. While the Russian snatched the world record briefly and was named the top European athlete of 1959, he came to Rome seeming over-matched by Johnson and Yang even if fully healthy, which he was not. Johnson respected Kuznetsov but now looked upon Yang as his prime competitor. Track experts had virtually awarded the gold medal to Johnson before they left for Rome, and Rafer himself had been quoted as saying that C.K. would finish second. Privately, he was "nowhere near as cocky as that statement suggests." After working out together almost daily for three years, Johnson and Yang knew each other's strengths and weaknesses intimately, as did Ducky Drake, the coach they shared. Drake, who had not been appointed to the U.S. coaching staff, was now in Rome as the official coach for the Taiwanese, but he showed no obvious partiality between his two great decathletes, devoting equal time and attention to each. It had come down to a two-man competition, he told them—one would win gold, the other silver.

As respected as Johnson was by then, his fame in the U.S. could not compare with Yang's status in his island homeland. The frenzy with which the Taiwanese public greeted any news of C.K.'s Roman adventure goes a long way toward explaining his Olympic commit-tee's ultimate decision to stay in the competition even though that meant not marching under the Republic of China banner. In this case, athletic success trumped political defeat. The *China Daily News* was holding a contest offering bicycles, sewing machines, wrist-watches, and fountain pens to entrants who were asked to guess where Yang would place and his scores for each of the ten decathlon events. Taiwan radio already had begun special afternoon and evening broadcasts focused almost entirely on Yang's daily training regimen and his prospects as their only medal hope. C.K. started to feel the pressure. When he arrived in Rome, he thought his countrymen might be satisfied if he placed "fourth or sixth or something like that—then the expectations increased."

With so many stars unlimbering in the practice area, scant attention was paid to Ed Temple and his Tigerbelles. The European press knew next to nothing about them, and American track experts went to Rome predicting that the Australians, led by their "Golden Girl," Betty Cuthbert, who had sprinted to three golds at Melbourne, would dominate again, with the Russians and Germans also in the mix. Doubts about the Tigerbelles persisted. When Frances Kaszubski, the team manager, attended a meeting where officials set the heats for the women's dashes, she could not convince her international colleagues of the accuracy of the world-class sprint times Wilma Rudolph had clocked in the months before the Olympics, so Rudolph was seeded lower than she should have been. Temple was upset when his friend Big K broke the news, realizing this meant that Skeeter's early heats would have more fast runners, making her road to the final more difficult. His task in Rome was to get his women into peak running form without making the strain counterproductive.

At the heart of Temple's sprinting philosophy was the seemingly contradictory yet commonsensical concept of training hard to run easy. As he explained later, "You see some runners, when they run a hundred, near the end they get tight . . . when they get to about eighty meters, you can see them saying, 'Only got twenty yards to go, got to give it everything,' and that is when they lose. What it takes to be a great sprinter, you've got to be relaxed but still moving fast . . . You have that confidence and even flow. And that's something easy to say but hard to do." To teach his Tigerbelles the sensibility of running in a relaxed state, he took them to a hill near the football field at Tennessee State. "I used to have them run up this hill real fast, pumping arms, and then come down the hill dropping the arms and being totally relaxed coming down. And I would tell them, 'I want you to feel that same way coming down the stretch as you feel coming down that hill. Pump it and move forward going up that hill but feeling that same way relaxed as coming down that hill. Then you will know how it feels to be moving fast and relaxing.' "

In another drill, Temple emphasized moving the knees "up and out, up and out" as another way to develop relaxed movement. First the Tigerbelles would walk the drill slowly, then jog on the balls of their feet for fifteen minutes—always with the same motion of their knees—then start sprinting, but with their arms down to ease the tension from their shoulders. You couldn't just talk relaxation, Temple believed, you had to practice it, over and over and over, following that same pattern of walking, jogging, sprinting, knees up and out, creating muscle memory. On Sunday mornings back at Tennessee State, he often took his sprinters into the school's dance studio, where there were large mirrors on the walls, and had them study how their arms popped while they were running. If an arm rose above the nose, it was too high.

Wilma Rudolph sometimes broke that rule, but no one moved faster or with more relaxation once she got going. "Oh, Lord, that skinny little lady, at first we couldn't understand how she could run so fast with her long legs and flailing arms," recalled teammate Lucinda Williams. "Bless her heart, she could seem like the laziest person. We would have to stay on her case. We would beat her out of the starting blocks, but by twenty-five yards she'd done passed us." Tall and fluid in full stride, Rudolph ran with a singular form, at once unorthodox and beautiful. She ran free and easy—as though she were nine years old, flying down the dirt roads of Clarksville, freed at last from the braces she wore during her recovery from childhood polio.

But few were watching Wilma run now. Most American sportswriters were looking elsewhere, their attention focused on the high-jump pit, where John Calvin Thomas was demonstrating how he would soar into history. No athlete, not even Rafer Johnson in the decathlon or Australia's Herb Elliott in the metric mile, was regarded as more golden than Thomas as the Olympics began. A staff of six experts from *Track & Field News,* led by Cordner Nelson, the editor, and his brother, Bert Nelson, the publisher, unanimously picked Thomas to win. *Sports Illustrated,* in its detailed event-by-event assessment on the eve of the Games, wrote of the high jump: "Only question is second place. Thomas is incomparably the best . . ." In the newspaper tribe, Fred Russell's assessment echoed conventional wisdom: "It may be improper to use the phrase best bet in amateur athletics, but among the U.S. entries in track and field, the best bet for a first place gold medal is John Thomas."

In his room at Boston University's Myles Standish dorm, Thomas kept a calendar with one date circled: September 1, 1960, the day of the high-jump final in Rome. He seemed to be aiming for that moment at least since 9:10 on the evening of January 31, 1959, midway through his freshman year, when he exploded into the record books at the Millrose Games in Madison Square Garden by becoming the first person ever to jump seven feet indoors. Jesse Abramson, covering the meet for the *Herald Tribune,* wrote that "in this space age" Thomas's jump was "better than landing a man on the moon"— something that would not happen for another ten years. Track fans in the Garden that night sprang to their feet in a stirring standing ovation, but the least excited person in the arena seemed to be the young athlete himself. "To me it was just another jump," Thomas explained later. "The size and importance of the meet wasn't that much to me. I was just jumping. And I was just seventeen. What was big and enormous to spectators was really just new to me."

The circled date on his calendar was uncharacteristic of Thomas, who was known for his deadpan personality. He would never get too excited, nothing seemed like a big deal to him, for better or worse. This steady attitude no doubt helped him recover from the trauma that came a few weeks after his record leap, when he was working on campus between semesters and got his left foot stuck in the crack between a rising elevator and an approaching floor. The injury, which likely would have been worse had he not been wearing foam-padded desert boots, sent him into Massachusetts Memorial Hospital for several operations over eight weeks. There were three severe tears in his toe joints, and so much tissue was ripped away that a few weeks after putting the leg in a cast, doctors decided to perform a skin graft, taking skin from his left thigh. During the recovery, the patient in the bed next to Thomas happened to be Herb Gallagher, athletic director at a nearby rival, Northeastern University, who marveled at his unflappable attitude. "I'll overcome this," Thomas told Gallagher. "It's only a temporary setback."

Within six months, Thomas was jumping again, and by midsummer 1960 he was better than ever. At the Olympic Trials at Palo Alto, he established a new outdoor world record of 7 feet 3¾ inches, a mark that reverberated around the world. There was nothing innovative about Thomas's technique. He used the traditional straddle roll of that era—seven long strides, a shorter eighth, gather, kick, lift, relax, roll—approaching the bar from the left at a 37-degree angle. But he took full advantage of his lean, dexterous, six-foot-five frame and his uncommon ability to kick his lead right leg straight up into what was called a six o'clock position after takeoff. Not long after Thomas's stunning performance at the Trials, the athletic department at Boston U. received a call from Moscow. An English-speaking correspondent from *Sovietsky Sport* wanted to know the secret of how this young black American could jump so high. Thomas talked to the writer for fifteen minutes but revealed nothing more than that he practiced a lot and had good coaching.

Now, at the joint practice in Rome, he had something more to show the Russians. As a trio of Soviet jumpers approached, all carrying cameras, Thomas was getting into position to make a try at the warm-up height of 6 feet 8 inches. With a silent upward nod of his head, he instructed a U.S. coach to move the bar to seven feet. He cleared the height casually, nonchalantly.

Zamechatelno! the Russians gasped in unison. Wonderful!

Thomas brushed himself off and quickly set himself to clear the height a second time, again with ease. "John is giving them a little psychological handicap to worry about," Bud Winter said softly to a gaggle of American reporters standing nearby. If nothing else, the press corps bought into the gambit. A UPI account declared that "the Russian athletes left the sun-baked stadium sadder but wiser and more convinced than ever that this will be a Stars and Stripes Olympiad." Shirley Povich made the high-jump pit drama the centerpiece of his "This Morning" column in the *Washington Post,* playing off the superpower space race. "The Americans put a man into space yesterday, not very high, only seven feet. But it was important because the Russians may have walked into a propaganda defeat five days before the battle would be joined in Olympic track and field," he wrote. In getting such a close look at Thomas, Povich concluded, "the Russians learned of the futility of any attempt to close the gap in the high jump."

SMALL VICTORIES, even if psychological or ephemeral, were always welcome in the cold war between the Soviets and Americans. Every day, in ways important and irrelevant, the relationship was defined by who had the perceived edge. While John Thomas was provoking whispers of *zamechatelno* at the practice field in Rome, another Bostonian, John F. Kennedy, the Democratic candidate for president, campaigned in Detroit, telling the Veterans of Foreign Wars that the U.S. was falling behind the Soviets in military strength and scientific prowess despite "rosy assurances" to the contrary from his Republican opponent, Vice President Richard M. Nixon. "The missile lag looms larger and larger ahead," Kennedy claimed, arguing that it would take a sharp increase in defense spending, as well as the vigor of a new generation, to close the perceived gap.

At least one American observer in Rome was now seized with a fear that the Soviets were also winning the propaganda war at the Olympics. This was a mysterious character named John V. Grombach, who went by the nickname Frenchy but preferred to be addressed as General Grombach. A 1924 West Point graduate from Louisiana, Grombach had boxed at the academy and fancied himself a world-class athletic figure and renaissance man, though he was also a first-class hustler. He had his fingers in boxing, as an official and promoter in New York state; in television, as a would-be producer who sought unsuccessfully to acquire TV rights to the Rome Games; in fencing, as a member of the sport's international federation; in the modern pentathlon, as an adviser to the U.S. Olympic Committee; in the military, as a retired U.S. Army Reserve brigadier general; and in publishing, as the author of a perfunctory history of the Olympics, a book he persuaded the State Department to buy in bulk and distribute at embassies around the world in the year leading up to Rome.

At the same time, Frenchy was a spook. He had served in military intelligence during World War II and went on to run a secret intelligence branch within the State Department known as the Pond, which operated various business fronts in postwar Europe. In keeping with being a spy, he alternately exaggerated his activities and covered them up. He made many enemies within the shadowy world of American espionage, notably CIA chief Allen Dulles, and had a tendency to assume that those who opposed him were Communist sympathizers. He had a habit of leaking information to Senate and House investigators about people inside the government that he considered security risks.

By the time of the Rome Olympics, Grombach's days as a government spy were over, his Pond long since having lost a power struggle with the Central Intelligence Agency, but he was still working various angles of intrigue as a private investigator and writer. He came to Rome with a writing gig as a columnist for the *Rome Daily American,* an English-language daily partially funded by the CIA, and took it as his mission to expose traitorous misdeeds at the highest levels of the International Olympic Committee. In his first column, appearing on this first full day of Olympic events under the aptly spookish sig "Olympic Lights & Shadows," Grombach unleashed his fury at the IOC's decision to force the anticommunist Republic of China to march under the name of Taiwan or Formosa at the Opening Ceremony the day before. "Unfortunately, this seems to fit the oft-repeated pattern of our abandonment of friends and allies and the U.S. taxpayer," he wrote. "The Republic of China is recognized by forty-five nations including the U.S. and Italy. It is the ally and friend of the U.S. and has been financially supported as such, yet the IOC is allowed to bar its athletes from properly representing their country."

Who to blame for this outrage? Grombach had no love lost for Avery Brundage, the president, who had ignored his efforts to gain the television rights, but his primary target was the IOC's vice president, the Marquess of Exeter, the former Olympic hurdles champ who along with being a lord was also a lifelong conservative and Tory member of the British parliament. It was the marquess, Grombach noted, who "was the prime mover in favor of the USSR motion" to force the name change on the Republic of China. There had to be a nefarious reason for this, and Grombach went into investigative overdrive to sniff it out. First he spread a rumor that IOC leaders had struck a private deal—with the Soviets in on it as well—that Brundage could keep the presidency in 1960 if he would support the Marquess of Exeter for the post in 1964. Then, as Grombach recorded later, he came across "frequent and repeated rumors [in Rome] that the Marquess of Exeter, a very rich and powerful industrialist, was actively engaged and/or his companies were actively engaged in trade with Communist countries and specifically Red China" in the fields of "metals, electronics, and automotive parts." Here was the sort of connection that met Frenchy's conspiratorial imagination. He quickly made plans to stop in London on his way home in September, where he could hire a private investigator to compile a dossier on the British lord.

That night, his affinity for boxing took Grombach out to the glistening new Palazzo dello Sport for the first head-to-head cold war match in Rome between boxers from the U.S. and Soviet Union. It was American featherweight Nikos Spanakos versus Russia's Boris Nikanorov.

Left alone in the dressing room before the match, Spanakos, a tough, smart collegiate boxer from Brooklyn, ruminated about the larger context of the competition. Thoughts about politics or geography are usually the furthest things from an athlete's mind, but Spanakos could not shut them out. He thought about the cold war with the Soviets and how his boxing match against the Russian was an emblematic proxy battle. "I remember saying to myself, 'You know, I'm the champion of America, and he's the champion of Russia, and geographically that's a lot larger piece of land, so he should be better,' " Spanakos recalled later. "And then I laughed at myself and said, 'This is funny.' One of the funny thoughts that came through my head to entertain myself."

Spanakos got off to a fast start, and the boisterous Italian crowd started shouting *"Ni-ko-las! Ni-ko-las!"* Through the first two rounds, he was landing more punches, but the judges penalized him for blows below the belt. They were unintentional, by Spanakos's account. He was five-three, and Nikanorov was five-nine. "I didn't hit him below the belt, I was just weaving down there because he was tall and I was short," he said later. Described by Red Smith as "a game, stumpy, busy little guy who fights from a knee-sprung crouch," the American entered the third and final round thinking he might win. Italian boxing fans were a breed apart from observers at other venues: louder, rougher, more demonstrative, political, and fickle, capable of turning on an athlete or referee at a moment's notice, full-throated choristers and piercing whistlers. They did not seem in-clined to root for the Americans, but on this night they adopted little Ni-ko-las Spanakos and cheered him on. In a final flurry, both box-ers received warnings for head butting, but Spanakos, the aggressor, could not land a knockout punch.

In a unanimous decision that surprised many writers up in the press section, Nikanorov was declared the winner. The *Los Angeles Times* said the decision was "loudly booed." The United Press wire service account described a "mixture of cheers and boos." In *Pravda,* the correspondent claimed that the "clever" Russian had "instantly underlined his mastery" and that his victory "was greeted with warm applause." Spanakos was devastated by the defeat. He was the first American to lose to a Soviet, and he felt that he had let down his side in the proxy war. "I swallowed it reluctantly," he said. "Like I was be-ing ordered to swallow poison."

7

QUICKER THAN
THE EYE

NOT much had gone as planned for Lance Larson before he swam the 100-meter freestyle in Rome. To start with, the event was not his best, but he had failed to qualify in his preferred stroke, the butterfly, at the U.S. Olympic Swimming Trials at Brennan Pools in Detroit, where the water was too cold and he tired in the final lap. Further, Jeff Farrell, who had burned up the 100 free all year, was supposed to be the American favorite, but he was hospitalized for an untimely emergency appendectomy six days before the Trials. In an unforgettable act of courage, Farrell bolted out of his recovery room at Henry Ford Hospital, declaring that he had to earn his Olympic slot like anyone else. Swimming through pain, a five-inch surgical scar covered in tape, he lifted the spirits of the entire U.S. squad by willing his way onto the relay team, but he narrowly lost a qualifying spot in the hundred, leaving Larson as America's best hope for gold.

Soon after arriving in Rome, Larson ate some unwashed fruit that gave him dysentery. He had felt sluggish already from fighting the flu before the team left New York, the same virus that had slowed sprinter Dave Sime and many others. Now he had dropped to 166 pounds, down from his normal 174. At practice, everything about the ornate Italian pool bothered him. He thought the water level was six inches too low, creating a wave that rolled off the side wall. No one wore goggles then, and the backwash irritated his eyes. Several swimmers complained that the pool should have had gutters at the ends to allow water to slop over, but officials at FINA (Fédération Internationale de Natation, the world amateur swimming federation) brushed off the criticism, declaring the venue perfect. Anticipating a furious pace from the favored Australians, Larson tried quickening his stroke, but that threw off his breathing, which he could not get right until two days before the heats, when his college coach at Southern Cal, Peter Daland, not on the Olympic staff, was called in to help.

As a surfer who rode the waves at Huntington Beach, just outside Los Angeles, before he took up competitive swimming at El Monte High, Larson was the quintessential West Coast blond before it became a stereotype. He was the first of the great male swimmers to peroxide his hair, and in that small way helped shape the national imagination about the sun-worshipping Southern California youth culture of the Beach Boys and Jan and Dean. Lance Larson—even the name itself conjured up a Hollywood beach movie. He began using peroxide after worrying that his hair was turning greenish from pool chlorine. "It burned the hell out of my scalp," he said later, but it was a price worth paying for cool white-streaked hair. Along with bleaching his top, Larson had another pre-race ritual that he went through on the eve of the 100-meter freestyle in Rome: a full body shave.

From neck to shin, the process took about an hour and required clippers, an electric shaver, and finally a razor blade as he scraped closer to bare skin. Body shaving was still relatively new then for swimmers, a technique passed along from the Australians, two of whom were his teammates at USC. The conventional wisdom was that removal of hair made you swim faster, but that is not why Larson shaved. "It would rough up the skin; you had more feeling in the water when you were shaved," he explained later. "In my thinking, it was not the drag of hair through the water, it was the muscle sensation from shaving. You had a better feel for how much effort to put out. And it was exhilarating."

Larson was all nerves, far from exhilarated, in the minutes before the 100-meter final, even though he had the best times in the qualifying heats the day before and knew that one of the favorites, Jon Henricks of Australia, the defending Olympic champion, had been eliminated in the semifinals, another athlete slowed by intestinal problems. "There was a lot of tension for me. I was sort of like zoned out. The level of competition, the excitement, just made me very nervous," Larson recalled. "I knew this was *it*. The big race. We had to warm up and then put our sweats back on. The weather was so hot— even though it was night."

More than ten thousand fans filled the outdoor stands at Rome's new aquatic center, the Stadio del Nuoto, on this first Saturday evening of the Olympics, August 27. They had come for the first showdown of men's swimming between the Yanks and the Aussies, who had dominated four years earlier at Melbourne. Watching from the press section was Gian Paolo Ormezzano, the young Italian journalist who had been saved by the Boy Scouts on his drive down to Rome. Now he was covering his first event at his first Olympics, and his writing was as abundant and evocative as the setting:

"Never have so many people gathered around a swimming pool as on that evening, still sultry with the heat of the afternoon. A magic evening, the swimming pool sandwiched between two walls of spectators . . . stacked as high as Tamburlaine's barbarians once stacked so the king, climbing on the hill formed by their bodies, could look into the distance." After his reference to the mythical Scythian conqueror, Ormezzano plunged delightfully deeper into metaphorical waters, first describing the scene as a pagan cult. "The cult of the new man who is making the water his element, every bit as much as the Earth. And now there is a religious silence. Here come the swimmers from another world, those competing in the final of the 100-metre freestyle. Here's Larson, that great ham actor, as bald as Yul Brynner [not quite], Larson who adjusts the laces of his costume a hundred thousand times. Here's Devitt, as grim as Boris Karloff and as huge and fierce as Lon Chaney."

Devitt was John Devitt of Australia, silver medalist in Melbourne, second fastest in the Rome heats, considered Larson's toughest competition, along with Brazil's Manuel dos Santos.

THEY START at 9:10 p.m. A hundred meters, all out, down and back in less than a minute.

"Who is that madman in Lane 6 ahead of everyone else?" Ormezzano wonders. "It's dos Santos, who jerks through the water, moving forward at a slant, as magnificently as a mad hatter."

By the turn, Larson and Devitt catch him.

Larson will remember nothing about the first fifty meters.

"I remember, coming off the turn, I told myself to keep my mouth shut, not to take a breath, or I'd get a mouthful from the wave. I was now thinking straight."

On the home stretch, Ormezzano sees that "Devitt is annihilating the water; if they used a dynamometer we'd find that he's exerting a phenomenal force, wasted, to some extent. Larson, with powerful, priestlike strokes, is still by his side."

Dos Santos exerts himself one last time, then starts to fade.

Devitt pulls into the lead by a foot.

At the seventy-five-meter mark, Larson sees a shadow to his left, slightly ahead, and says to himself, "When are you going to start moving?" And he starts moving.

Twenty meters out, Devitt "is now a poor Christ, his arms flaying with frenzy," Ormezzano writes.

Devitt is in Lane 3. Larson is next to him in Lane 4. The water becomes frothy. Larson worries that he can't see and that his stroke is off. They are straining furiously to the finish, side by side. Larson pulls so hard that Abramson of the New York *Herald Tribune* thinks he might drive right through the wall.

IN THAT ERA, before the introduction of automatic touch pads at the finish wall, competitive swimmers were taught to finish with a big splash. Larson glided the last foot or so, his arm outstretched, and touched underwater, while Devitt made the splash. Or as Ormezzano, with his flourish, described the finish: "As calm as a satiated Roman, Larson slams his hand on the edge of the pool, while Devitt strikes the mosaic furiously, tearing his flesh."

By the account of Arthur Daley in the *New York Times,* they "finished no further apart than the width of a flattened sardine." But Larson was certain that he touched at least six inches ahead. There were three timers leaning over his lane, and three leaning over Devitt's, and from their reaction he believed he had won. So did most people in and around the pool. Photographers rushed over to snap his picture.

"At the end of the race, I thought I was second," Devitt said later, "so I congratulated Lance Larson, climbed out of the pool, and tried not to think about it."

"It all happened so fast," Larson remembered. "I won the race. I threw up my arms and was congratulated by all the other swimmers. I took a victory lap, swam down to the other end and back [a lazy backstroke down and a happy butterfly back], and finally got out of the pool. I was drying off. Guys were running around—and an American official came up to me and said there was a problem."

The three officials hovering over Larson in Lane 4 clocked his time at 55.0, 55.1, and 55.1. According to the rules, if two of the times agree, that is the accepted time. So by the timers, Larson swam the 100 meters in 55.1 seconds.

The three timers over Devitt in Lane 3 clocked his time at 55.2, 55.2, and 55.2. No doubt in that case—the Omega watches showed he swam the 100 meters in 55.2 seconds, one-tenth of a second slower than Larson. Backing up those times, a contraption known as the three-tape finish recorder also listed Larson as the winner; the operator of the device had already congratulated U.S. officials.

So what was the problem? The rules for Olympic competitions were set by the international federations for each event, in this case the Fédération Internationale de Natation, and FINA competitions were decided not by timers or mechanical devices but by judges. While the timers were stationed behind the finish line, leaning over the end wall to observe the finish from a virtually vertical angle, the judges were stationed at either side of the pool, farther away, focusing on the finish from a horizontal angle. There were twenty-four judges in all, twelve on each side seated on four rows of bleachers. Of that group, three were assigned to study each of the eight finishes, so there were three first-place judges, three second-place judges, and on down to three eighth-place judges.

When their results for the hundred were compiled, two of the three first-place judges ruled that Devitt in Lane 3 finished first. One of the first-place judges said that Larson in Lane 4 finished first.

But the second-place judges came up with a different reading. Two of the second-place judges determined that Devitt in Lane 3 *finished second,* while one of the second-place judges said that Larson finished second.

Of those six judges, then, three had Devitt finishing first, three second; and three had Larson finishing first, three second. But after examining the judging results, the chief judge, Hans Runströmmer of Germany, who was not among the twenty-four judges but was standing several yards from the finish line when the race ended, declared Devitt the winner.

The results were posted on the big electronic scoreboard for the crowd to see: 1—Devitt, 2—Larson, 3—dos Santos. The posted times for Devitt and Larson were identical, 55.2.

Larson was shattered. How could they post his time at 55.2 when the timers had him at 55.1—and one timer even had him at 55 flat? It was a matter of illogical logic. Officials could not give him a better time than Devitt if they had declared Devitt the winner.

They rushed the awards ceremony. Devitt was in a daze as he walked over to the victory pedestal. He shook hands warmly with Larson, who had to stand one rung down from Devitt and listen to "God Save the Queen" as the flags were raised. Although he was praised for his good sportsmanship, a photograph caught Larson with a look of disbelief. "I was not feeling so good," he said later. "I felt sick to my stomach, like somebody had just told me my family was wiped out on the freeway."

R. Max Ritter, the U.S. representative on FINA, was equally distraught. Ritter, then seventy-four, was the grand old man of international swimming. A two-time Olympian himself in 1908 and 1912, he was the only remaining founding father of FINA, one of eight men who had established the group and its rules. Now he was confused by his federation's ruling in the first event in Rome. "When I heard the result announced over the loudspeaker, I immediately rushed to the judges' table unbelievingly, as the timers and the finish recorder had clearly indicated first place for Larson," Ritter recalled later. "I wanted to see the judges' cards myself but found that these had been impounded by the FINA secretary and my access to them had been barred."

Ritter demanded to see the FINA secretary, Bertyl Salfors of Sweden, but was told that he was busy with the medals ceremony. Finally, when the ceremony ended, Ritter was granted access to the judges' cards. First they showed him only the first-place cards, which had two votes for Devitt, one for Larson. "I demanded to see the judges' cards for second. Most reluctantly, the chief judge placed those cards on the table, which revealed two votes for Devitt *for second* and one for Larson as second. When I pointed out to the chief judge that this indicated a tie—and that under the rules he would have to submit this tie to a referee, he hesitated and consulted with the FINA secretary, and came back and said that as chief judge he had a vote, and he voted for Devitt; therefore it was not a tie but a clear majority for Devitt."

Ritter, who had helped write the rules, knew of nothing in the rule book that gave Chief Judge Runströmmer a vote. In fact, Ritter had been the chief judge himself at the 1948 Olympics in London and the 1952 Olympics in Helsinki and had never voted.

But the gold medal was already hanging around John Devitt's neck. In the press section, Abramson typed out his opening paragraph for readers in New York: "The hand that is supposed to be quicker than the eye gave the Olympic 100-meter freestyle swimming title to blond Lance Larson of the U.S., but he did not receive the gold medal in the first rhubarb of the Rome Olympics . . ."

Disappointed American officials decided they would have to regroup and plan an appeal. Larson was still feeling empty when he left the pool area and encountered Peter Daland, his college coach. Daland talked tough but had a soft heart. Now he put his arm around the young swimmer and offered the consoling words of a coach. "You shouldn't have made it so close," he said.

WHEN U.S. officials began preparing their appeal of the swimming decision, they turned first to the Olympic studios of the Columbia Broadcasting System, which amounted to a large trailer stationed out at Ciampino Airport. In a later era, the dramatic finish between Larson and Devitt would have been shown over and over again in super-slow-motion replay to the point where millions of viewers would have become judges. But in 1960, not only was there no replay, there was no live television coverage of the Olympics in the United States. The fact that CBS had been able to show the race on its late-night Olympics broadcast hours after the fact, between eleven-fifteen and eleven-thirty that night, was considered in itself a technological wonder. This was still the dawn of the satellite age. By coincidence, an experimental U.S. communications satellite known as Echo I had just been launched into Earth orbit that month and passed over Rome in the evening sky so low and large that it was visible to the eye. But Echo I could only passively reflect radio waves back to Earth; the days of satellites beaming live transmissions from halfway around the world were coming but not quite there. Still, the fact that the Olympics were on television at all, even if delayed, was a breakthrough. These were the first Summer Olympics where broadcast rights were sold commercially and events were televised daily back in the States.

Avery Brundage and the International Olympic Committee had discussed the issue of selling commercial rights since before the Melbourne Games, but they had been so slow and uncertain in handling the issue that by 1960 they had essentially lost control. For the Rome coverage, the Organizing Committee of the XVII Olympiad, run by Italians, not the IOC, made separate deals with CBS, Eurovision, and the Japanese network NHK. Only after endless begging and cajoling was the IOC able to muster a 5 percent cut of the deals. Although Brundage and his cohorts traveled first class and behaved like nobility, which many of them were, in fact, the IOC itself was always haggling for money, like cash-poor upper-class heirs surviving in a threadbare lordly mansion.

The contract with CBS News (there was no CBS Sports then) was negotiated for the Italian organizers through an American ad agency, the Gardner Advertising Corporation, and signed in June 1959 in New York. According to the contract, the base price for exclusive American rights was $420,000, with options for further coverage that lifted the total package to $600,000. At the time, this was thought to be a considerable sum for an athletic event staged on the other side of the Atlantic. In the deal, the Italians said CBS could broadcast up to twenty hours of programming from August 25 to September 11, which averaged about an hour and fifteen minutes per day. The network could cover any event where cameras were stationed (most of the cameras were run by the Italian broadcasting network, RAI) with one exception: it could not show the four-hour opera staged at the Baths of Caracalla.

For its Olympic coverage, CBS News assembled a special production, reporting, and announcing crew totaling about fifty people, most working from the home office in New York. The small team on the scene in Rome was led by executive producer Peter Molnar and three on-air correspondents: Bud Palmer, a former pro basketball player for the New York Knickerbockers who had a distinctive, electric-smooth announcing voice; Bob Richards, known as the "Vaulting Vicar," who was both a past Olympian gold medalist pole vaulter and an ordained minister in Long Beach, California; and Gil Stratton, the CBS sports director at KNXT in Los Angeles. The studio host, stationed in New York, was Jim McKay, a former Baltimore *Sun* police reporter who had moved to Manhattan to host a daytime television drama called *The Verdict Is Yours,* which featured fictitious cases but real defense lawyers, prosecutors, and judges, with McKay as the courthouse reporter host.

Over ensuing decades, McKay would become the face and voice of the Olympics, but this was his first, and he wasn't even there.

After deciding each morning which events to emphasize, a task made harder by their lack of control of most cameras, Molnar and his production crew in Rome mixed microwave feeds of action from various Olympic venues with play-by-play and analysis from the three American commentators. They had three videotape editing machines and film kinescopes in the trailer to put together packages that were sent back to New York along with raw footage of late-breaking events that could not be edited in time. The job was at once technically complicated (they needed a converter to transpose the Italian picture, painted at 625 lines a second, into the standard U.S. picture of 525 lines), and stunningly archaic.

How did the tapes get to New York? They were sent by commercial jet on regularly scheduled transatlantic Alitalia Airlines flights from Ciampino to Idlewild and from there relayed to McKay's crew at a studio at Grand Central Station. The process was as reliable as most air service, which is to say uncertain, depending on such variables as air traffic control, summer thunderstorms, and headwinds. The average flight took nine and a half hours, but Rome's time zone was five hours ahead of New York, a difference that served to CBS's great advantage. If all went right, it was possible for a tape from an event in the morning to make one of the evening shows, occasionally in the prime-time 8:30-to-9:00 time slot but more often on a fifteen-minute or half-hour wrap-up before midnight.

By the first decade of the twenty-first century, television coverage of the Olympics would become such a vast enterprise that the NBC network deployed an army of more than three thousand technicians, producers, directors, researchers, announcers, and reporters to cover the Games. With that in mind, consider Jim McKay's description of what it was like when it all began, after he left his day job at *The Verdict Is Yours* and headed over to the CBS studio to bring viewers the 1960 Rome Olympics.

"What would happen is that I was in New York, and I would be in the tape room waiting for tapes to come in from Rome, and in those days the baggage compartments on airplanes were not heated, and things would freeze," McKay recalled. "I can remember sometimes holding the tape against my body to get body heat to loosen things up. I would stand there, and it was a paste-and-scissors deal. Literally it was razor blades to edit. And I would write my own stuff to go along with it. I did just about all that stuff myself. We didn't have writers. To get information on an athlete, I would go to the *Encyclopedia Britannica* or that sort of thing. There wasn't this stream of information that people are inundated with nowadays. The room I was in was next to the announcer studio, with technical equipment and fairly dim light. And I would stand at the counter and write. The only time I sat down was when I went on the air. I was right in there with the machines."

Critics offered mixed reviews, as usual. John Crosby, whose column ran in the *Boston Globe,* complained that CBS devoted airtime to the "boring" sports of swimming and cycling in the first days and added that he was "not altogether happy about Jim McKay's commentaries, which have a sort of gee-whiz boyishness to them that gets on the nerves and are quite foreign to the CBS tradition of cool professionalism." But in the Baltimore *Sun*, Donald Kirkley called the broadcasts "efficient, effective, and consistently interesting." The Olympics were being handled like a political convention, with "skill and good judgment," Kirkley wrote, saying of McKay: "Quietly, with occasional touches of humor, and engagingly, Mr. McKay is doing very well with his biggest assignment to date." In the *New York Times,* John P. Shanley called McKay a "capable" anchorman and had special praise for Bud Palmer's performance at the Stadio Olimpico during the Opening Ceremony.

Too often in American sports broadcasts, Shanley asserted, commentators ignored events not directly related to the contest on the field "even when they would be of great interest to an audience." His case in point was an anti-Castro rally at a recent New York Yankees baseball game that was not shown on camera and went unmentioned by the announcers. In contrast, Shanley wrote, Bud Palmer "demonstrated an intelligent awareness" that the Olympics represented more than just athletic games. "During the opening day parade of competitors, the cameras caught the delegation from Taiwan, with one member of the group carrying a banner proclaiming that the unit was participating 'Under Protest' because it had not been designated as representing China. Mr. Palmer noted and explained this significant aspect of the parade. In doing so, he was carrying out a comprehensive job of reporting that might serve as an example to some of his colleagues who cover sports for TV and radio in this country."

Palmer's memories of Rome would focus on the technological slowness and heaviness of it all. When he was covering an event, there were no studios to rerecord his play-by-play to make it smoother; it was done once, live, "and, pal, you better get it right because that's your only chance." There was no army of production assistants gathering information, setting up appointments, and shepherding Palmer around, just a single director who would meet him at an event. The cameras were ponderous hulks, weighing more than sixty pounds each, and the broadcast sites were strewn with cables as thick as boa constrictors.

But however archaic the CBS production was, it offered U.S. Olympic officials their best evidence for the Larson-versus-Devitt controversy. Max Ritter gathered up several colleagues and headed out to the airport production trailer certain that television tapes would prove him right. The "worthless" judges, he said, were nothing more than "timid unemployed pussy footers" who operated under the double standard of "America versus the World." Red Smith, the astute columnist, tagged along with Ritter and his crew. "Over and over they ran the pictures," he reported. "There, they would grunt as the racers turned to the finish." Every time they watched, they sounded more certain that Larson had won. When the technicians were able to slow the tape, even the ever-dubious Smith climbed aboard, noting that "one . . . shot in particular seemed so conclusive that at least one unbiased viewer, who hadn't been satisfied watching the monitor, was convinced Larson had won."

"Gentlemen," Ritter declared at the end of the viewing, "does anybody have any doubts?"

None did, though Smith could not resist one last skeptical barb. "Films almost never settle disputes like these," he wrote. "Generally it turns out that at the crucial moment the cameraman was ogling a blonde."

Even if the film was indisputable evidence, and the only blond on camera was the peroxided Larson, it mattered not at all. FINA turned down the American appeal.

THERE WERE no events that Sunday, August 28, a day of rest at the Rome Olympics. Going dark on what could have been a profitable viewer-rich weekend day was yet another indication of how little influence television then had in the world of sports. But just to be able to avoid the stifling heat was reason enough for athletes to be thankful for the early break. Temperatures soared into triple digits, and even though safety concerns had prompted Olympic officials to move some Saturday events out of the brutal midday hours, there had been complaints and difficulties at venues all across town. Hours before the Larson race, before the sun went down, a fan sitting on the sunnier side of the swimming pool had taken out a thermometer and registered a temperature of 108. The fencers at the Palazzo dei Congressi had suffered their own peculiar fate: the heat made them sweat so much that they short-circuited their electric jackets, creating chaos with the automatic touch scoring system.

Now at the Olympic Village, in the languid haze of Sunday morning, Denmark's flag flew at half staff in memory of the fallen cyclist, Knud Enemark Jensen. His grief-stricken cycling teammates had withdrawn from the Olympic Games, but the story was far from over.

News broke that morning that Oluf Jorgensen, the trainer for the Danish cyclists, had told Danish government investigators that he had given Jensen and some other members of the team the drug Roniacol before the race. Roniacol, produced by a Swiss pharmaceutical company, was not an amphetamine but a drug that intensified blood circulation. Used primarily for elderly people who had circulation problems, it was a fast-acting vasodilator that among other side effects could cause flushing and decreased blood pressure. Cyclists might use it to keep their leg muscles at peak strength through a long race, but with that benefit came potential harm to the heart. "I got the prescription from my doctor," Jorgensen told Boerge Jackson, sports editor of *Akfuelt,* a Danish government journal, after appearing at a government inquiry. But a doctor for the Danish team said that before the race he was so alarmed by the potentially dangerous combination of Roniacol and the heat of Rome that he had urged the cyclists not to use it. "I cannot figure that they should ignore the instructions I gave them so clearly," Dr. Gunnar Stenas said.

The report linking Jensen's death to a drug created sensational headlines in Denmark and around the world. "Danish sports have been dragged down into the mud by criminal cheaters in cycling," lamented the *Ekstra Bladet* in Copenhagen. But it did not come as a total shock to other athletes. "There had been rumors about the Europeans; that was why they were so good, because they were taking stuff," recalled Bob Tetzlaff, a member of the U.S. cycling team. His teammate Allen Bell said that doping for a competitive advantage was becoming part of the athletic discussion in 1960. "A doctor cyclist friend of mine said every drug has a side effect and that a lot do worse on them than off them. When I raced, I used to take cough syrup that had caffeine and sugar. Is that dope? It's like someone drinking a few Cokes. The drug use was more common among the Europeans. It came down to they could be rich if they won."

If some Danes were doped before the race, were they the only ones doing it? Not according to a later account from Yuri Vlasov, the Soviet heavyweight weight lifter who had strode onto the Olympic stage at the Opening Ceremony carrying the hammer and sickle in one outstretched hand. "With my own ears in 1959, I heard our senior cycling coach tell the sports minister Romanov that if we didn't have [psychotropic amphetamines], we could expect no victories. Romanov replied that 'the matter could be resolved positively.' Our team received the first packet of tablets before the 1960 Games in Rome."

Vlasov's outing of the cyclists comes with its own context: some weight lifters themselves were said to be using another form of doping in Rome, trying out Dianabol, an anabolic steroid. Amphetamines were the primary concern when it came to drugs and athletes in that era. Steroids were being introduced but were still in an experimental stage where doctors, trainers, and athletes were unclear about the effects, positive or negative.

Suspicions of doping haunted Olympic history. In the modern Games, indications of doping had stretched back several decades, although Olympic officials had been slow to find effective means to limit the practice or monitor athletes. According to a detailed study of IOC minutes undertaken by Wolf Lyberg, former secretary-general of Sweden's Olympic committee, the first mention of doping came during an IOC session in Warsaw in 1937. None other than Lord Burghley, the former world champion hurdler and future marquess, reported on "the practice, the means, and the effects of doping," inspired by concerns that some competitors had used stimulants at the 1936 Berlin Games. In response to Lord Burghley's report, the IOC at its annual session in 1958, in Cairo, adopted its first drug-related resolution: "The use of drugs or artificial stimulants of any kind cannot be too strongly denounced, and anyone receiving or administering dope or artificial stimulants should be excluded from participating in amateur sports or the Olympic Games."

More than two decades later, in advance of Rome, Avery Brundage went public with his concerns. Medical advisers to the IOC, led by Dr. Ludwig Prokop of Austria, had been warning Brundage since the 1952 Helsinki Games that there had been "obvious signs of the reckless use of medicinal substances." At an IOC session in San Francisco in February 1960, according to the official minutes, "Brundage called the attention of . . . members to the use being made of amphetamine sulphates (in pill form) in some sporting disciplines. He stressed the gravity of the problem. The president points out that a product called Amphetamine Sulfate (a so-called pep pill) was nothing else but doping." In response to Brundage's statement, the IOC considered conducting scientific research on the impact and testing of drugs but did not get around to it before the Rome Olympics.

After Knud Enemark Jensen died, his body was taken to the Instituto di Medicina Legale, where three Italian doctors conducted the autopsy. It is perhaps fitting, given the disputatious history of drugs and sports since then, that the Jensen case became shrouded in mystery and uncertainty once the autopsy began. Although the corpse was at the institute for four days before Jensen was embalmed and sent back to Copenhagen for burial, weeks and then months dragged on with no reports from the examiners. With increasing frustration, Brundage and his aides sent one missive after another to officials in Denmark and Rome seeking answers, fearing that they were being stonewalled. Finally, seven months after the fact, on March 25, 1961, an announcement came that defied expectations. The final autopsy report ruled that Jensen died from heatstroke. It said there were no signs of drugs in his system. The full autopsy report itself was not released, was never made public, and subsequently seemed to disappear from official files. Only a partial postmortem report, translated into Danish, was sent to the Danish Public Health Board and police officials in Copenhagen, who expressed satisfaction with the findings.

Decades later, Danish journalist Lars Bogeskov reexamined the case and tracked down one of the doctors, Alvaro Marchiori, who told him, "But of course I remember the investigation of the cyclist who died during the hundred-kilometer race. Because it was the first time at our institute that we had a doping case. And I remember we found traces of several things—among them amphetamine."

The irony is that by then, indeed since the immediate aftermath of the fatality in Rome, the established Olympic history of the Jensen case ignored the Italian autopsy finding and accepted as fact that he died from doping. Marchiori's apparent acknowledgment of this late in his life only reinforced conventional wisdom. Dr. Prokop, a key scientific voice for the IOC in that era, became convinced that Jensen's death was drug related and began citing the case as the impetus for all anti-doping measures that were to follow. The IOC created a medical committee in 1961, issued the first specific list of banned substances (including amphetamines) in 1967, began testing athletes in 1968, and added anabolic steroids to the list in 1976. Imperfect and controversial as it was, a system evolved over the decades for testing Olympic athletes for banned substances they put into their bodies to gain a competitive edge—and that system all traces back to the moment in the hot August sun when Knud Enemark Jensen wobbled on his bike and collapsed to the cement on the Viale Cristoforo Colombo.

AMERICAN DIPLOMATS had been frustrated for days by the seeming propaganda coup the Soviets gained when newspapers around the world reported on the message of peace and friendship that Premier Khrushchev sent to the Olympians in Rome. Now, on the first weekend of the Games, they were upset again. President Eisenhower had written his own letter of greeting, at last, and the White House wanted it to be delivered by Norman C. Armitage, a former Olympic fencer who had carried the U.S. flag at the games in Helsinki and Melbourne. But where was Armitage? U.S. embassy officials in Rome desperately tried to answer that question, with no luck. "In spite of intense and continuous efforts through all available channels, Embassy has been unable so far to locate Armitage," a cable to the State Department reported. It was decided finally to release Eisenhower's statement through Brundage and the IOC.

The message began much like Comrade Khrushchev's, with stilted wording that seemed like it had been translated from Latin. "It is with great pleasure that I, as president of the United States of America, take this occasion to express to the International Olympic Committee and men and women athletes from all parts of the Earth who will participate . . . the sincere and warm wishes of the people of the United States for a most outstanding and successful running of the Seventeenth Olympic Games at Rome, Italy . . ." With its emphasis on respect and peaceful competition, Eisenhower continued, the Olympics "will be an example worthy of admiration and emulation by a world weary with the tensions of international strife and misunderstanding." He concluded with the expressed hope that those who witnessed the events in Rome would "return to their homelands renewed in the experience of fair play, richer in their understanding of other peoples, and with new and inspired insights into the full meaning of the brotherhood of man."

Even though it was released on Sunday, a day of rest at the Olympics, the attention of the press was elsewhere: on the dispute over the Larson decision and the stunning news about Jensen, or looking ahead to the start of track-and-field events later in the week. The American press corps was more than ready to choke up with tears of pride for the Stars and Stripes and Rafer Johnson and his teammates as they marched in the parade of nations at the Opening Ceremony, but unlike their counterparts at *Pravda* and *Izvestia,* they felt no pressure to report on a boilerplate message from Ike. His letter was virtually ignored.

In the meantime, the Soviets staged another set-piece tableau to impress their Italian hosts and the people back home. On Sunday afternoon, just as the Eisenhower letter was being released, a busload of Russian Olympians ventured out to one of Rome's working-class suburbs for an evening of eating, drinking, and politicking with comrades from the heavily Communist Italian labor movement. More than two hundred workers and their families welcomed the athletes in a small courtyard teeming with wine and food on picnic tables covered by red-and-white checkered tablecloths. An elderly workman from the neighborhood glass factory greeted the visitors. "Our countries are far apart, but now we are here together, and we can feel our closeness," he said. There was no escaping the

Khrushchev letter, not even here, at least as *Pravda* quoted an old glass blower: "Khrushchev sends warm regards to sportsmen who met in our city. Send to him, the leading fighter for peace, our warm working-class regards. We are wishing success to your sportsmen and to our brother Soviet workmen."

By *Pravda*'s account, the full complement of Soviet athletes would have attended the proletarian courtyard festival if only there had been enough buses to carry them. One athlete not there was Igor Ter-Ovanesyan, who had accepted an invitation to leave the village and go out to eat with Dave Sime and his wife, Betty, at the Scoglio di Frisio, a restaurant on Via Merulana.

At dinner, the conversation slowly turned toward the future. Here's the deal, Ter-Ovanesyan said. In the Soviet Union, he was taken care of; he had an apartment, a car, a teaching slot at the sports university. "And they give me a lot if I win a medal here," he said.

Sime said he did not know what the United States could offer, except freedom, maybe set him up as a track star out in sunny California, out near the film stars and beautiful people and fast cars. But there was another American in Rome, Sime said, who wanted to talk to Igor. Sime did not mention who this was, but the implication was obvious. It would be a government operative trying to close a defection deal. In fact, Sime barely knew the operative—had met him only once, briefly, and thought he was "kind of slimy; I wouldn't trust that sonofabitch as far as I could throw him"—reservations that he would not pass along to Ter-Ovanesyan. It was a CIA agent who called himself by the fictitious name Mr. Wolf. In an earlier encounter in Rome, Mr. Wolf had urged Sime to put pressure on Ter-Ovanesyan and arrange a meeting.

During their dinner at the Roman restaurant, Ter-Ovanesyan agreed to talk to the other American, but only on one condition: that Sime and his wife were also there. He was frightened, he would say later, but found it all "very interesting."

1

2

On the eve of the Olympics, thousands of athletes assembled at St. Peter's Square for a benediction from Pope John XXIII. In the audience were Christians, Jews, Muslims, Hindus, and a delegation of atheists from the Soviet Union. From across the square, U.S. sprinter Wilma Rudolph thought the pope looked "like a jolly round Santa Claus and a bowlful of jelly."

3

At a conference room in the Foro Italico where Italian Olympic Committee organizers met each day, a green carpet hid a full-wall mural of the dictator Mussolini and his Blackshirt supporters. *The Apotheosis of Fascism* was a work of totalitarian iconography so bold and monstrous the Italian government would not uncover it until the twenty-first century.

4

Opening Ceremony, August 25, 1960. Some rituals appear glorious but have no deeper meaning. This one, to decathlete Rafer Johnson, was "as important as the competition itself." Never before had a black athlete carried the flag at the front of the U.S. delegation.

LEFT: The first political act of the Olympics came when the Nationalist Chinese, ordered to march as Taiwan or Formosa and banned from using any form of the name China, unfurled a banner of dissent. U.S. officials had urged the Nationalist Chinese to boycott the Games altogether rather than accede to the name change, which they said was a concession to Red China.

5

When the Soviet team paraded into view, American writers were shocked by the flair of the Russian women, who had been mocked in the past for their appearance. "Their girls looked like Parisian models in white silk dresses with pleated skirts and a most Parisian cut to their necklines," gasped the *Herald Tribune*.

6

During the first full day of competition, in the midday heat, Danish cyclist Knud Enemark Jensen (center, No. 127) wobbled and collapsed to the pavement. He died hours later. The next day a trainer said that not sunstroke but a drug designed to intensify blood circulation might have led to his death. The tragedy was a turning point in modern athletic history, ushering in the age of drug testing.

BELOW: Lance Larson, prototype of the peroxide-blond Southern California beach boy, thought he had won the 100-meter freestyle race, as did the timers and most witnesses at the Stadio del Nuoto. But the chief judge, out of position at the finish line, ruled Australian John Devitt the winner.

The unexpected star early in the Rome Games was Ingrid Kraemer (above, left) of East Germany, shown here with her coach, Eveline Sibinski. Born in Dresden two years before the city was firebombed by Allied forces in World War II, and known by American sportswriters as the Dresden Doll, Kraemer won both gold medals in women's diving.

10

11

ABOVE: Dispatches from A. J. Liebling informed readers of *The New Yorker* about the events in Rome. With his rapacious wit, Liebling described everything from the marathon to the evening hubbub on the Via Veneto, where the sidewalks were so crowded that "a fair-sized man vainly trying to thread his way . . . has to reverse engines and back out, like a steamship on the upper reaches of a tropical river."

Red Smith, writing in the New York *Herald Tribune,* was a sharp critic of the Olympic establishment, once calling IOC president Avery Brundage "the greatest practicing patsy . . . of this century." But Smith defended the IOC's decision to force Nationalist China to compete under the name Taiwan.

12

The shock of what came to be known as Black Thursday began with the final of the 100-meter dash, where the cocky German sprinter, Armin Hary (far left), beat Dave Sime of the U.S. (far right) in a photo finish. The pre-race favorite, American Ray Norton (to the left of Sime), finished dead last.

13

At race's end, Sime, a medical student at Duke University, lunged forward with such ferocity that he lost his balance, one hand whirling wildly as he struggled to stay on his feet and went flying, literally, reeling and splattering violently crosswise across the track.

The day before the final, Armin Hary (left) rejected a request to meet with the legendary American sprinter Jesse Owens, snapping, "I'm sorry, I haven't time to fool with him." The day after the race, a chastened but victorious Hary visited the American compound and made up with Owens, posing for the photographers.

14

American runners (left to right, Ray Norton, Dave Sime, Frank Budd) console one another after losing the 100-meter dash. This photograph made the cover of *Life* magazine as a symbol of American disappointment.

As hordes of German fans chanted "Hah-ree! Hah-ree! Hah-ree!" at the Stadio Olimpico, silver medalist Sime stood and watched, his face revealing his emotions. For the rest of his life, Sime would replay the photo finish, and each time in his mind's eye he would come closer to beating Armin Hary.

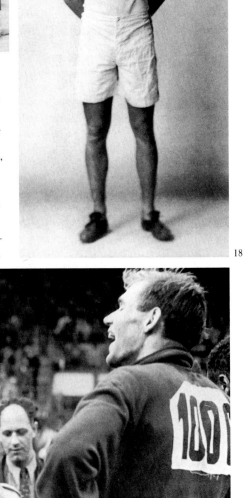

17

In Rome, the pressures of the modern world were closing in on IOC president Avery Brundage. His rules on amateurism were being ridiculed by journalists and tested by athletes. The Soviet bloc sought to replace him and the United States denounced him for the decision on Taiwan. Yet Brundage insisted that "no monarch ever held sway over such a vast domain" of his Olympic Movement.

RIGHT: Brundage had been a trackman at the University of Illinois and a U.S. decathlete at the 1912 Olympics in Stockholm, where he dropped out after eight events, finishing in sixteenth place, far behind winner Jim Thorpe.

18

19

David Burghley, the Marquess of Exeter (second from left), was IOC vice president and head of the International Amateur Athletic Federation. The British lord, a former Olympic champion hurdler, later had a character modeled after him in the movie *Chariots of Fire*. In Rome, he was hounded by an obsessed American spy, General John ("Frenchy") Grombach, a conspiratorialist who thought the conservative marquess was beholden to the Communist Chinese.

Soviet long jumper Igor Ter-Ovanesyan, who studied English and loved jazz and most things Western, was targeted by U.S. intelligence agencies as a potential defector. Dave Sime, the Duke sprinter, was recruited to make contact with Ter-Ovanesyan in Rome. Sime said the effort failed when an American operative who called himself "Mr. Wolf" botched a meeting at a restaurant.

Ralph Boston of Tennessee State won the long jump with an Olympic record leap, holding off Ter-Ovanesyan and teammate Bo Roberson. When Boston's mother got word of her son's gold medal at her home in Mississippi, she said, "I didn't have any idea that my baby's jumping around would ever amount to anything."

When John Thomas, the phenom from Boston University, finished a disappointing third in the high jump, his bronze medal was viewed by U.S. sportswriters as an incomprehensible end to a calamitous day. Not only had he lost, but he was beaten by two Soviets and tied by a third. In the propaganda cold war, they thought, there could be no worse way to lose.

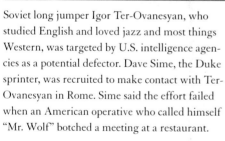

23

Coach Ed Temple (center) built a powerhouse women's track squad at little Tennessee State University, led by Wilma Rudolph (left). "I want foxes, not oxes," he often told his runners. The Tigerbelles were a free-spirited group who chafed at his rules, but followed him to victory, bringing a passel of Olympic medals back to the campus in north Nashville.

24

The gold medal–winning U.S. relay team in Rome—all Tigerbelles (left to right), Wilma Rudolph, Lucinda Williams, Barbara Jones, and Martha Hudson. "Just get me that stick, and we're going to get on that stand," Rudolph said to her teammates before the race.

25

Tall and fluid in full stride, Wilma Rudolph ran with a singular form, at once unorthodox and beautiful. She ran free and easy—as though she were nine years old, flying down the dirt roads of Clarksville, freed at last from the braces she wore during her recovery from childhood polio.

Months after her brilliant performance in Rome, Rudolph was invited to the White House to visit with John F. Kennedy. The new president was so taken by her that he nearly missed his rocking chair as he sat down and then talked to her for an hour, leaving his next appointment waiting outside the Oval Office.

26

27

In another photo finish at the Stadio Olimpico, Lee Calhoun (second from right) edged out teammate Willie May in the 110-meter hurdles, repeating his gold medal performance from four years earlier. Calhoun's amateur status had been restored after officials banned him from competition for a year because he and his wife had accepted gifts for being married on the television show *Bride and Groom*.

28

No race was greeted with more home-country enthusiasm than Livio Berruti's victory in the 200-meter dash. Berruti was among the first sprinters to wear sunglasses during competition; he did so not to look cool, but because he was so short-sighted that without them he could not see the finish tape.

When Otis Davis of the University of Oregon learned that he had broken the world record in the 400 meters, he jumped high into the air in sheer joy. "Something was pushing me out there," Davis said of his remarkable run. "And it wasn't the wind."

Among the most exotic athletes in Rome was Milkha Singh of India, known as the Flying Sikh, who presented a striking image on the track, running in full beard with his long hair tied overhead. Singh felt that he had let his country down by finishing a close fourth in the 400-meter dash, but it was the strongest showing ever for an Asian sprinter.

Track experts knew that Herb Elliott of Australia was the best miler in the world, but nonetheless were awed by the way he pulled away from the field in the 1500 in Rome. When Elliott accelerated in the third lap, U.S. runner Jim Beatty said it was "the most dramatic middle-distance burst" he had ever seen.

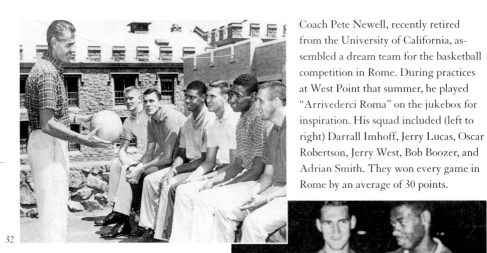

Coach Pete Newell, recently retired from the University of California, assembled a dream team for the basketball competition in Rome. During practices at West Point that summer, he played "Arrivederci Roma" on the jukebox for inspiration. His squad included (left to right) Darrall Imhoff, Jerry Lucas, Oscar Robertson, Jerry West, Bob Boozer, and Adrian Smith. They won every game in Rome by an average of 30 points.

Perhaps the greatest backcourt tandem in history led the Americans to basketball gold, captains Jerry West of West Virginia University and Oscar Robertson of the University of Cincinnati. "One black and one white, with all the troubles that were going on in the country at that time, for [the two of us] to stand there and take that medal for the country, it meant a lot," West said later.

Years before he became Muhammad Ali, an eighteen-year-old boxer from Louisville entered the world stage in Rome as Cassius Marcellus Clay. The talkative star of the U.S. Olympic boxing team was afraid to fly, and his youthful braggadocio did not impress some teammates, but he had no trouble with opponents in the ring on his way to winning a light-heavyweight gold medal.

The three American boxers who won gold medals stand outside their dorm at the Olympic village: Eddie Crook, Cassius Clay, and Wilbert McClure. Clay would not take off his medal even to sleep, or so he claimed. "Fool, go someplace and sit down," Tigerbelle Lucinda Williams chided him, lovingly, when Clay started blabbing about how he was the greatest.

35

A few months after Rome, Ed Temple's wife looked out the window of their home in Nashville and asked if he knew anyone who drove a pink Cadillac. It was Cassius Clay, who had driven down from Louisville in search of Wilma Rudolph, on whom he had a crush. Here they enjoy a jukebox on the Tennessee State campus with gold medal long jumper Ralph Boston.

36

The Palazzo dello Sport was filled to the rafters for the boxing finals, with rabid Italian fans bursting into song "as though every man in the audience was a Caruso," noted British writer Neil Allen. Designed by architect Pier Luigi Nervi, the arena was a modernist dome in which a brilliant shaft of light beamed from the ceiling like the probe light of a flying saucer.

38

After working out together at UCLA for three years, Rafer Johnson and C. K. Yang, the world's best decathletes, knew each other's strengths and weaknesses intimately. While competing for different countries (Yang for Taiwan), they shared the same coach, Ducky Drake. Their spirited blend of admiration and competitiveness pushed them to greater accomplishments together than they might have achieved apart.

39

Darkness had fallen as Rafer Johnson awaited his turn in the penultimate decathlon event, the javelin. A full moon glowed above the stadium. The competition had been intense all of the second day, with Johnson and Yang snatching the lead back and forth.

In the final decathlon event, the 1500 meters, Johnson held enough of a point lead that he only had to finish within ten seconds of Yang to win the gold medal. When Yang looked back, Johnson was right behind him, smiling. It was, wrote *Sports Illustrated*, "the tensest five minutes of the entire Games, and it grew and grew until it seemed like a thin high sound in the stadium."

Rafer Johnson wore a blue coat and tie the next day to receive his gold medal, embraced by two friends and competitors. Silver went to Yang, justifying Taiwan's decision not to boycott the Olympics. Bronze went to Vasily Kuznetsov, the onetime world record holder who had first competed against Johnson at the historic dual meet in Moscow in 1958.

As they came to a stop after the final race, Rafer put his head on C.K.'s shoulder. "I was totally exhilarated that I had won and totally depressed that C.K. had lost," he said. "I had both feelings."

Preliminary field hockey matches were held near the Stadio Olimpico at the smaller Stadio dei Marmi, a horseshoe-shaped bowl that was rimmed by sixty marble statues of ancient Roman athletes, each looming thirteen feet high, representing Mussolini's visions of the sporting Fascist ideal.

BELOW: The wonders of ancient Rome were used to full advantage at the Olympics. Gymnastic events were held outdoors at the Termi di Caracalla and wrestling at the Basilica di Massenzio.

43

No modern marathon since the first one in Athens in 1896 featured more tradition; much of the course was a spectacular tour of ancient Roman history. Yet no modern marathon was more defiant of Olympic tradition. The race began at twilight and proceeded into darkness, the path torch-lit by a thousand sentinels.

"There's one guy we don't have to worry about," American marathoner Gordon McKenzie had muttered at the start when he first saw a "skinny little African guy in bare feet." It was Abebe Bikila of Ethiopia, who as the race wore on pulled away from the pack, the two vertical lines of his No. 11 defining his narrow, bony frame.

47

The street widened as the Arch of Constantine came into view, glowing in the darkness. Abebe Bikila ran on the right side, nearest the bleachers. A shadow cast by a strobe light ran with him, his only competition. The barefoot Ethiopian, running past the monuments of a nation that had once invaded his homeland, reached the finish line with the best time in marathon history, becoming the first black athlete from sub-Saharan Africa to win a gold medal.

The courtship of Igor was a small scene in the cold war drama unfolding in Rome. While the Soviets presented a public image as messengers of brotherhood and peace, when it came to the athletic competition they seized every opportunity to try to rattle the Americans with psychological gamesmanship. That weekend, as the track-and-field events appeared on the horizon, a Soviet athletic planning official, Grigori Kukushkin, told the Western news agency UPI that the Americans were superior in many events only because they had "so many Negroes on the team."

This was not, in itself, an unusual notion. The black press in the U.S. had been pounding away at the same argument. The *Cleveland Call & Post,* in its pre-Olympic issue, listed all the black stars on the American team—John Thomas, Charles Dumas, Rafer Johnson, Ray Norton, Les Carney, Ralph Boston, Lee Calhoun, Hayes Jones, Willie May, Wilma Rudolph, Barbara Jones, Lucinda Williams, Joe Faust [not quite; he was a white high jumper], Oscar Robertson, Walt Bellamy, and Bob Boozer—and concluded: "Without doubt, but for the Negro athlete and his outstanding performances, this nation would have little or no chance in the games to be presented before the eyes of the world."

But any statement related to race was sensitive in the context of the Olympics and the cold war. As the Eisenhower administration tried to make the argument for Western values around the world, it was confronted by the hypocrisy of race relations in the United States. "The central focus of foreign nations on American racial issues centered on the plight of African Americans," a State Department report noted that summer. "Awareness of progress based upon successful desegregation was increasing, but high-profile incidents of racial strife and struggle overshadowed reports of progress. The emotional impact, coupled with sensationalistic press accounts, continued to dominate international discussions of race. The issue weakens the U.S.'s moral position as champion of freedom and democracy and reinforces doubts about the nation's interest in the welfare of others, particularly people of color."

On the very weekend of the UPI interview with Kukushkin in Rome, the news back home included reports of racial strife in Jacksonville, Florida, where blacks had staged sit-ins to end segregation at downtown variety stores. "Angry mobs of club-swinging whites clashed with Negroes in the streets of downtown Jacksonville, setting off a chain reaction that brought more violence and bloodshed," a report in the *Los Angeles Times* began. More than fifty people were hurt, and forty-eight blacks had been arrested, compared to fourteen whites.

The blacks on the U.S. Olympic team knew all about sit-ins and the violent reaction to them. The protests in Jacksonville were part of a movement that was sweeping across the South. Ed Temple and his Tigerbelles had been on the Tennessee State campus that May when white supremacists dynamited the home of a black attorney, Z. Alexander Looby, who was among the leaders of a movement to integrate downtown lunch counters in Nashville. The sit-ins there led to a boycott of downtown department stores that nearly brought Nashville business to a halt. "I mean, when they had the boycott about not buying, nobody went downtown and bought, and there wasn't no doubt about that," Temple remembered. "Everybody participated in that."

In the interview with the wire service in Rome, Kukushkin took it one step further, arguing that blacks had "special physical endowments for sports." Knowing exactly what to do with that potentially explosive quote, the UPI reporter, Tony Austin, walked over to the American compound in the village and read the line to a group of black athletes.

"Oh, sure, John Thomas over there has a third arm," said Bo Roberson, the Cornell-educated long jumper.

"It's nonsense to say there is any physiological difference between Negroes and whites," Thomas said.

Ira Davis, a triple jumper, said track and field was a means to an end.

What is the end? Austin asked.

The group fell silent, until Roberson answered for all of them.

"The end is equality."

8

UPSIDE DOWN

MANFRED EWALD, deputy chief of mission of the unified German team, was seen walking through the Olympic Village with a bouquet of red roses one afternoon during the first week of the Rome Games. That the flowers were for a woman athlete was no big deal. But when, with a formal bow of respect, the East German sports official presented the roses to Wiltrud Urselmann, a silver medalist in the 200-meter breaststroke, his gesture took on a larger meaning. Urselmann was from Krefeld, a city along the Rhine River in West Germany. Winning isn't everything, but success in the Olympics could have a calming effect on East-West tensions within the German delegation in Rome. As a column in the West German newspaper *Die Welt* put it, "Medals reconcile. They make the athletes talkative and even loosen up tense muscles in functionaries' faces."

To a brilliant old crank like A. J. Liebling, the first days of the Olympic fortnight were mostly sideshow. He cared nothing about cycling, and could be stirred neither by Jensen's death nor Larson's

larcenous loss. "To give a technical illusion that Olympic competitions were taking place, they put on preliminaries in various fringe
sports—field hockey, water polo, fencing, and the like—at outlying
Olympic installations," Liebling informed his *New Yorker* readers.
"Of these, swimming was the only one with general international appeal, and there has consequently been more copy filed on the swimming here than on any similar event since the efforts of the *Titanic*
survivors to remain afloat."

Defying the expectations of many experts, a large share of that
early copy was about the Germans, not so much Urselmann's second-
place finish in the breaststroke as the stunning performance of Ingrid
Kraemer in diving. And Kraemer was not just German, she was East
German, the daughter of a Filmosto film factory foreman and party
member from Dresden. Hailed by *Life* magazine as "the first daz-
zling surprise of the games," her success reinforced the conciliatory
power of medals and went a long way toward explaining the rosy
collegiality of Comrade Ewald.

Kraemer was not entirely unknown when she arrived in Rome.
At age seventeen, still in high school, she had emerged from competitions in Europe as someone to watch, especially on the 3-meter
springboard. Her outstanding performance during the tense "exclu-
sion competitions" to determine places on the unified German team
prompted one judge to tell her she could "make it to the top in the
Olympics." But the U.S. divers had never heard of her, and diving
had been their domain for decades. Since the 1924 Olympics in Paris,
of the twenty-one medals available in springboard diving, the Americans had won nineteen—all but a single silver to a Frenchwoman
and a bronze to a Canadian. The dominance in platform diving was
nearly as complete, with U.S. women sweeping all the golds and silvers during that period. Caroline Smith, Elizabeth Becker, Dorothy
Poynton, Helen Meany, Georgia Coleman, Marjorie Gestring, Vicki
Draves, Pat McCormick—these were the golden names of women's
diving, all American.

Kraemer knew less about the Americans than they knew about her. She had never seen them on film, had not been able to study their technique, knew nothing about their prowess. All she knew about diving came from her trainers in Dresden and Leipzig (where she had to go for 10-meter diving; there was no high platform in her hometown) and some Soviet divers. To calm her nerves when she arrived in Rome, she tamped down her own expectations. "I really hadn't dared to hope that I would win," she said later. "I tried not to think about winning. I wanted to do my very best, but I prevented putting myself under the pressure of wanting a medal. I had learned that a wrong movement could easily happen, and tried to leave everything open for myself."

But in her first event, the 3-meter springboard, she made no wrong moves and demolished the American winning streak, nailing jump after jump and amassing a point lead so wide "that she could have jumped into the water with only a little grace in the last round, and she would have won the gold medal," a *Die Welt* account noted. She seemed steady and composed, and she had a certain self-correcting magic to her technique. Whatever minor flaws one of her dives might suggest in midair, Kraemer invariably adjusted and pierced the water cleanly. "We would simply fold together in distorted jumps, which Ingrid manages to get inimitably into the water," said her teammate Ingeborg Busch of Mannheim. The American divers, led by Paula Jean Myers Pope, a bronze medalist in Melbourne, sprang higher off the board and had as much or more grace twisting in midair, but they lacked Kraemer's downward precision and created more splash on entry.

If Kraemer appeared unflappable, her composure came only after a long and difficult struggle against fear. She had first jumped off a low board at age five at a vacation camp run for the children of factory workers, before she even knew how to swim. When she was eleven, she started practicing with the Dresden diving club at a pool that was used by the Soviet Army in the mornings. Three or four times a week, after lunch, she and other young divers gathered at Postplatz Square and rode a tram out to the pool on the outskirts of Dresden, not coming home until evening. Reinhard Kunert, her trainer, noticed immediately that she was unusually flexible and had beautiful foot movements, important characteristics for a championship diver. Yet the very act of sending her body into the water scared her. "I had real problems of fear in my first years," she said later. "I wasn't courageous at all. I had to work hard on it and only bit by bit managed to overcome it. In the beginning the fear was so strong my father made me a special vest of rubber foam so I wouldn't feel the pain hitting the water on my back or my stomach."

Even as the fear diminished, it never went away and followed her all the way to Rome. By then she had come to accept the irony that fear was an important part of her success. Her anxiety about hurting herself in the water forced her to concentrate on the precision of her movements. She went over them again and again in her mind, a form of internal visualization and self-protection. Just as fear helped her, so too, apparently, did a physical defect. It turned out that the extraordinary flexibility that made her movements look so smooth came as a result of her abnormally sensitive soft body tissue. Only decades later would she learn that her condition might have made it unwise for her ever to have taken part in competitive sports.

In the years after the Rome Olympics, propelled by a state-run athletic factory that relied on illicit drugs and hormone treatments, women from East Germany would surge to the front in swimming and other sports, but in 1960 they were still scrappy underdogs. Until Kraemer came along, the only Eastern zone German athletes to win gold medals were boxer Wolfgang Behrendt at Melbourne and speed skater Helga Haase and ski jumper Helmut Recknagel at the 1960 Winter Games in Squaw Valley.

Any medal showing was heralded by the Communist press as an ideological miracle, but Kraemer's performance sent the journalists from East Germany into evocative flourishes that outdid even Gian

Paolo Ormezzano's Fellini-esque depiction of the 100-meter free-style. "Not long ago she was leaning at the fence, her shining turquoise bathrobe completely closed, the hood over her head, hands folded, unconcerned like one of the countless unnamed mermaids who are leaving the water in thousands of pools all over the world, wrapping themselves in a towel," began the *Neues Deutschland* report describing Kraemer's final springboard dive. "But suddenly she threw the bathrobe away, the body in the blue swimsuit became tense, and like a 'dry swimmer' she adumbrated the movements of her jump once, twice, just as she does for every jump."

> *Then she mounted the steps to the three-meter tower. And while seven judges, protected from the blistering sun by colored sunshades, directed their attention to her, while on the large electric scoreboard on the other end of the pool her name shiningly appeared, and while the ten thousand spectators in the light-flooded Stadio del Nuoto held their breaths, she swung into the air.*
>
> *And suddenly she was the one who was ahead of everybody else, she was the superior, the unmatched, the best springboard diver of the world who was about to perform the triumph of her life. Like an arrow she shot into the water, which surface willingly granted her admission, and when her young, fresh face reappeared on the surface, her blonde hair seemed to shine twice as much as usual. The confirmation of the electronic brain was a mere formality. Jubilation in the ranks, the unending chants of overwhelmed camp-followers, had long since announced it: Ingrid Kraemer, the 17-year-old high school girl from the German Democratic Republic, emerged from the water as a golden girl.*

Accounts in the American press inevitably called Kraemer a fräulein and issued her a new nickname, the Dresden Doll. One of her Olympic coaches, Heinz Kitzig, said he expected her to win but knew that Western journalists would be shocked. "The world does not know much about us anymore since what they call the Iron Curtain has cut us off," he said. When one writer asked whether Dresden was in East Germany, Kitzig responded tersely, "It is the German Democratic Republic." Although the U.S. string of gold medals was broken, Paula Jean Myers Pope, who finished second, was not disappointed. "She clearly outdove me on springboard," Pope said later of Kraemer. "I received the silver medal on springboard and was very, very pleased." Part of her satisfaction came in knowing that platform was her better event and that she could recoup the gold there.

GERMANY IN the late summer of 1960 was defined by the cold war but also by the old war—fifteen years after the fall of the Third Reich. Arriving in Berlin that August on a writing tour of Europe's great cities undertaken for the *Sunday Times,* Ian Fleming, the British spy novelist, was struck by the "asphalt-gray" dimness of both the Western and Eastern sectors. He thought the city smelled "of cigars and boiled cabbage." Fifty percent of it had been strafed during the war, he wrote, and even now there were physical reminders everywhere of "the great corporal punishment meted out upon the people who have caused more pain and grief in the world than any other nation in this century." As Fleming drove through the streets of the western sector, he half-expected "at any moment to see the town crumble away again in smoke."

The old rubble fascinated Fleming, who felt a lingering unease about the Germans. He had lost his father in World War I and a younger brother in World War II and said he still had a recurring nightmare of a future German rocket hissing toward London. By his account, there remained 70 million cubic meters of rubble in Berlin piled into Monte Klamotten, rubbish mountains, the entirety known as Hitler's Collected Works.

But what Fleming found most engaging about Berlin was the scent of espionage. Since the publication of *Casino Royale* in 1953,

he had written seven books featuring James Bond, the most illustrious secret agent of twentieth-century pop fiction, and here was a
place teeming with would-be 007s. Berlin was a world-class capital
of intrigue, divided East and West as the country itself was divided,
but with the city's Western half removed from the rest of West Germany, alone and surrounded, a hundred miles inside East German
territory, connected to the West only by the narrow ribbon of an
autobahn.

As he explored the fringes of the Berlin underworld, Fleming,
who spoke fluent German, encountered a spook who told him there
were an estimated ten thousand Communist agents slipping into
West Berlin and an equal number of spies infiltrating the East. Just
the day before the Olympics began in Rome, East Germany announced the arrest of 147 members of an alleged espionage ring "in
the pay of the American secret intelligence service." Once it had been
easy to buy off East German agents with promises of money and freedom, Fleming learned, but now that seemed to be more difficult. In
retrospect, the paths of history can appear obvious, but in the divided
Germany of August 1960, no one knew who would win the cold war.
Some believed the balance was shifting eastward. "They greatly pre-
fer the symmetry of Communism and the planned economy, particularly when the plans seem to be successful," one agent in Berlin's
Western sector said of the Soviet zone. "And the Sputnik and so on
have helped here. They are quite sure they are on the winning side;
that Russia is stronger than the West."

At the White House that summer, within the intelligence community, there was a growing sense that East Germany was "teetering
on the brink of stability," in the words of a National Security Agency
report. A long-held hope of reunifying the German people under a
Western democratic government seemed to be dimming. The Soviet
Union, which oversaw the Eastern zone, was threatening to sign a
separate peace treaty with the German Democratic Republic (a government not recognized by the U.S. or most Western powers). At the

same time, the Soviets also were pushing for the establishment of what they called a "free Berlin"—which the Eisenhower administration saw as another manipulative attempt to bring the entire city under Communist control.

The standoff in Berlin, a city the NSA report described as "one of the most active arenas in the struggle between the Free and Communist worlds," took another turn on the afternoon of Tuesday, August 30. At the same time that Ingrid Kraemer went for her second gold medal at the swimming stadium in Rome, an event cheered on by German fans from both sides of the ideological divide, the East German government announced a decision to prevent West German citizens from entering East Berlin for five days, starting the following day. East German officials said they felt compelled to impose the ban in response to an imminent gathering in Berlin that would stir political unrest: a homecoming of World War II prisoners of war and relatives of the missing. Always eager to blame West German leaders for the nation's Nazi past, the East Germans called the old soldiers' conference "a militaristic and revanchist event of instigation" that could have been conceived by Nazi propaganda minister Joseph Goebbels.

The State Department immediately denounced the border closing, asserting that Berlin was not then and never had been on East German soil. The real purpose of the ban, U.S. officials said, was to further isolate West Berlin. It was also seen as part of the larger effort by the East German GDR to force the Western powers to recognize it.

The Orwellian nature of the five-day ban was obvious. Here the East Germans were trying to prevent West Germans from getting in at the same time that their own people were fleeing in record numbers. More than 100,000 refugees from the East had registered in West Berlin refugee camps in the first eight months of 1960. The number of refugees in August alone exceeded the previous high figure for that month, August 1953, when refugees had flooded over the line in the aftermath of an uprising. During the first five days of the Summer Olympics in Rome, 4,301 people fled East Berlin. Meanwhile, visitors from the West entering East Berlin—visitors, not refugees—declined steadily that year, down 28 percent in July. To explain this drop, East German officials claimed that West Germany had launched a "Close the Gate" campaign.

"Typical Communist propaganda," a West German official responded. "Turning things upside down in the usual way."

Nearly one year later, on the Saturday night of August 12 and Sunday morning of August 13, 1961, the East Germans began constructing the "antifascist protective rampart"—what came to be known as the Berlin Wall, sealing off their side of the city. After that, escape was the only way out.

This was the context of the uneasy show of unity among German Olympians in Rome. A hundred times a day, chief of mission Gerhard Stoeck said, he was asked: How do they live together on the Piazza Grecia, the athletes from East and West? "No incidents," he would say. "They get along well with each other. I am satisfied." Heinz Schöbel, an East German official, was struck by a particular display of unity, when he and his West German counterpart issued a joint criticism of Italian officials in the Olympic Village for showing Leni Riefenstahl's film *Olympia,* which depicted the 1936 Games in Berlin and glorified Hitler and his Nazis. Another symbol of the unified effort came from the athletes themselves, when a four-man kayak relay team, two from East Germany, two from West Germany, won the gold medal and posed for pictures arm in arm, smiling. But none of that compared with the public light shining on the diver from Dresden.

INGRID KRAEMER had also emerged from the rubble of the old war. She was not yet two years old in February 1945, when much of Dresden was destroyed by Allied firebombing. In a massive three-day attack, wave after wave of Avro Lancasters unloaded their incendiary bombs on the civilian population, killing tens of thousands of people and setting the city ablaze in one inescapable ball of fire, an urban hell immortalized by Kurt Vonnegut in his novel *Slaughterhouse-Five*. Kraemer's suburb of Kleinzschachwitz was largely spared, but the film factory where her father worked was leveled. Her earliest memory was going downtown with her mom to pick up her father and walking through "the huge heaps of rubble and debris in the destroyed city." She saw and felt the aftereffects of the firebombing the rest of her childhood. One of her young friends had gray hair before they entered kindergarten. Ingrid herself was haunted by a persistent nightmare in which she was being chased by airplanes, and no matter how fast she ran, she could not escape. For many years after the war, she was so afraid that she slept in her mother's bed. Now, fifteen years after the bombs fell, she had risen to world stardom—out of the fire, into the water.

After winning gold in springboard, her suite at the Olympic Village quickly came to resemble a florist shop, the bathroom so filled with bouquets that she and roommate Gabriele Schoepe could no longer take a bath or shower. A proud German pastry chef at the village cafeteria honored her victory with a special cake soaked in rum (a rich dessert that Ingrid and Gabriele ate on the sly, late at night in their room, away from the watchful eye of trainer Elveline Sibinski, who disliked both the alcohol and the calories). When Ingrid left the village to perform, just the sight of her rounding a corner at the Stadio del Nuoto provoked spontaneous applause from the grandstands. Television, in its Olympic infancy, had not yet discovered the appeal of young female gymnasts—that phenomenon was still a decade away—but in some sense Ingrid Kraemer, flying so gracefully through the air, was a bathing-suited precursor to the agile tumblers.

Not all divers participated in both springboard and the 10-meter platform event, but it had become accepted in the diving community that a gold medal winner in springboard came into platform with a decided edge among the judges, almost like a boxing champ who had to be knocked out or outpointed decisively to lose a crown. Whether that happened on the afternoon of August 30 was open to debate—as it often is when the winner is determined by subjective judges rather than objective statistical measurements. When the results were in, Kraemer had won, and members of the United States Olympic team left the swimming arena feeling once again that the world had un- fairly turned against them, a sour feeling that not even gold medal victories that same day by Carolyn Schuler in the butterfly and Bill Mulliken in the breaststroke could fully erase.

Unlike the springboard competition, where Kraemer seized an early lead and extended it into an insurmountable point spread, in platform diving she held a razor-thin margin over Pope going into their final dives. Kraemer went first, taking the slow-joe, 29-second ride up the glass-enclosed elevator to the diving tower, pausing to hear a last-second instruction shouted up from her coach, letting her blue-green bathrobe float all the way down to the ground floor "like a parachute," stepping to the edge of the tower, turning her back to the water, visualizing every movement in her mind's eye, finding her final foothold, and springing back, whooshing down with two and a half somersaults in 2.1 seconds, and flitting with a quiet snap into the blue pool.

Pope's final effort matched Kraemer's in style, though her legs slapped the water at entry, creating more of a splash. Her dive in any case was ruled slightly less difficult than Kraemer's and brought in fewer points, leaving Kraemer the winner again. The U.S. diving coach, Sammy Lee, was utterly frustrated by that point. Lee, a for- mer Olympic champion who had won platform gold medals in 1948 and 1952 (and was the first Asian-American gold medalist), felt the judges had oversold Kraemer on her last dive, just as they had under- sold Pope on her double-twisting one-and-a-half somersault. Four of the seven judges were from Eastern bloc countries, and Lee believed they were biased against his divers. Horst Gorlitz, a refugee from

East Germany who was in Rome as an Italian coach, said the judges were not only biased but ignorant. "The judges don't even know the sport," he said. Paul Zimmerman, covering the event for the *Los Angeles Times,* talked to a British coach who agreed. "Most of the toughest dives they had to judge are done only in the West, and the judges don't even know what they are seeing when they saw them."

Those frustrations were also shared by American fans in the stadium, who booed, catcalled, and whistled on several occasions when good dives were downgraded. Unlike the springboard, where Pope accepted that she had been beaten, this time she felt that the gold had been taken from her unfairly. "I believed that platform really belonged to me before, during, and after. I have all the films to prove it," she said later.

Was it really another proxy battle in the cold war? Perhaps, but with an unusual twist. When Kraemer was competing to make the unified team, she felt that the West German press was "very unfriendly" to her; at least one journalist, by her account, cursed her because of politics. But now the West Germans were embracing her as a German first, one of their own. The Western newspapers covered her events with obvious national pride, as though there were no separation between East and West. Accounts in *Die Welt* and the *Frankfurter Allgemeine Zeitung* raised no questions about the judging and described the final dives in a way that left no doubt that Kraemer had again outperformed her competition. German fans, who dominated the Stadio del Nuoto audience during her events, cheered long and loud for her every effort. Yet the warmth the West Germans showed Kraemer infuriated the East Germans, who thought the other side was trying to steal her show and diminish the ideological implications of her triumph. Kraemer's victory was no accident, East Germany's *Neues Deutschland* proclaimed. Rather, she owed her success to her "joyful life in the socialism of the German Democratic Republic." The paper also complained that for all the copy Kraemer got in the Western press, it was never mentioned that her father was an official in the SED (*Sozialistische Einheitspartei Deutschlands,* the Socialist Unity Party) and that the young diver herself was a member of the socialist mass youth organization.

The behavior of the West German fans seemed even more irritating to East German observers. "Young people . . . from Bonn unfolded the flag of the Bonn unpeaceful government when Ingrid's triumph had become clear," *Neues Deutschland* complained. "They wanted to pretend to the Romans and all the guests that this woman came from the Adenauer state. But people there know that Ingrid comes from Dresden and was raised in the German Democratic Republic. She stars in Rome under the flag of the overall German team and yet she remains for everyone the Ingrid from the GDR." Cease and desist, the East German paper demanded. "Roll in your flags, renounce the telegrams of your politicians, don't disturb the Olympic peace in Rome."

9

TRACK & FIELD NEWS

R IDING a streetcar from the YMCA hotel in central Rome out to the Stadio Olimpico, Cordner Nelson was worried about pickpockets, so he stuffed his wallet in his track bag and squeezed the bag tightly at his feet. Nelson was accompanied by his wife, three teenage daughters, and younger brother Bert early on the Wednesday morning of August 31—a moment the family had been anticipating for four years. At nine o'clock, with the staging of the first heats in the men's 100-meter dash, plus preliminary rounds in the women's high jump and men's shot put, the track-and-field competition at the 1960 Olympics would begin. *Citius, altius, fortius.* Here were the events at the heart of the games: the running, jumping, and throwing competitions that were called the "queen of athletics" by the Russians and meant at least that much to the Nelsons of Southern California, for whom track and field was work and play, if not religion.

Cord, as editor of *Track & Field News,* and Bert, as publisher, had devoted their lives to the sport for nearly three decades, since their father took them to the 1932 Olympic Games in Los Angeles for Cord's fourteenth birthday. Months before that event, Cord began jotting down times and distances, compiling note cards on various athletes who would come to L.A. to compete. For the rest of his days he would remember the long ride into the city from his small home-town out near Riverside, California, the roaring crowds at the sun-splashed Memorial Coliseum, the electric tension of the 200-meter dash. The scene thrilled him and set him on a path that brought him to Rome as a walking encyclopedia of track-and-field statistics. His magazine office, an eight-by-twelve room in the basement of his home in Stockton, was so stuffed with filing cabinets—five against each wall—that he could barely move, but there was very little down there that he didn't also carry in his head. Bert was the same way, having never witnessed a track meet that he didn't enjoy. "Watching the games is an all-day job for a nut," he explained before leaving for Rome.

When the Nelsons reached the stadium that morning, the broth-ers sat with the rest of the family and nearly two hundred other track nuts who had signed up for the special *T&FN* Olympic tour. Cord made a point of staying away from the press section. He might have been one of the world's leading track authorities, but he was too emo-tionally attached to maintain a journalist's remove. That lesson was brought home to him at the 1952 Olympics in Helsinki when he hol-lered at a U.S. steeplechase runner to slow down before burning out too quickly, an impulsive act that shattered the no-cheering rule in the press box and drew disapproving looks from his colleagues. As Cord and his brood settled into their seats, they began discussing the Nelson Competition, a prefiguring of the fantasy leagues that would preoccupy sports fans in baseball and football many decades later. From depth charts listing the performances of the top fifty athletes in an event, each family member drafted a roster of projected medal winners. A few outsiders joined this speculative competition, including the inimitable McWhirter twins from England, Ross and Norris, authors of the *Guinness Book of Records* and track statisticians on the side.

The media scene in Rome provided barely a hint of what was to come in future Olympics. These were the first commercially televised Summer Games, but studio host Jim McKay was back in the CBS editing room in New York banging out scripts on his little portable typewriter just like anyone else, not yet a household name. Print still ruled, with sports editors and big-city columnists ranking at the top of the press hierarchy. Most of the tribe arrived in Rome after their own grand tours of Europe. Cord Nelson and his family sailed over on the SS *Rotterdam.* Red Smith ventured across France, Germany, Switzerland, and Austria, driving through the Alps and down into Italy in a Peugeot sedan that *Herald Trib* readers would come to know as "Little Becky Trueheart." Fred Russell sent pictures back to the *Nashville Banner* of him posing as a French boulevardier, a Spanish bullfighter, and a Swiss yodeler. Art Rosenbaum, sports editor of the San Francisco *Chronicle,* led a monthlong tour of wealthy lawyers and doctors.

Shirley Povich of the *Washington Post* brought along his wife, Ethyl, and his own aide-de-camp, St. Albans prep school sophomore Donald Graham, son of Katharine Graham and the newspaper's publisher, Philip Graham, who had promised each of his children "one big treat for the summer." While sister Lally, fascinated by politics, accompanied their father to the Democratic National Convention in Los Angeles, where the elder Graham played a behind-the-scenes role in getting Lyndon Johnson on the ticket with JFK, Don, who loved sports, came down to Rome after spending six weeks at a boarding school in Switzerland learning French and German. "As a fifteen-year-old sports fan, I was in heaven," he said later. Along with fetching whatever Povich needed, his job was to take notes at events that his boss couldn't make.

Officially accredited by the Italian organizers and wearing a press badge that could get him into any venue, young Graham spent the first several days at the Stadio del Nuoto (catching a close-hand look at Lance Larson the day after his loss, when he seemed fully composed again), then moved over to the Stadio Olimpico for the start of track and field. When he arrived that first morning, he was surprised to see "lots and lots of empty seats" in the press section. There were 1,239 credentialed journalists in Rome and places for all of them inside the Stadio Olimpico, either at press tables or reserved seats, but many never showed up after the Opening Ceremony, and those who did generally stayed away until the final of an event.

It was a movable feast of observing, writing, eating, drinking, and joking among the U.S. sportswriters, who tended to roam in a pack from event to event, though each writer had his own inimitable style. Red Smith was the acknowledged wit and wordsmith, "a bottomless well of sprightly comment" who "has been all over this city trying to find some Romulus-Remus wolf milk," noted Fred Russell. Not quite two dozen American newspapers sent correspondents to Rome, often a solitary sports editor who could afford to send himself. The wire services, Associated Press and United Press International, dominated the press corps with eighteen journalists each. Then came the contingent from *Sports Illustrated,* including Robert Creamer, who served as the on-scene editor; Tex Maule, who wrote most of the track-and-field stories; and world-class sports photographers John G. Zimmerman, George Silk, Robert Riger, and Jerry Cooke. With several colleagues, they sublet an apartment at the Palazzo Lancelotti, a medieval building situated in the heart of old Rome, not far from the Piazza Navona, with high ceilings and grand windows that pushed open onto an interior courtyard. It was, Creamer would recall, a great place to throw a party, which they did—a memorable event where a gregarious Soviet photographer, a friend of the *SI* shooters, did his part to ease cold war tensions by berating the Germans (*"Bang! Bang!"* he said, explaining that the Nazis had killed his father in World War II), on his way to getting "drunk as a skunk" and urinating into the elegant courtyard below.

Aside from the private parties, the surest place to find scribblers from all over the world each night was on the top four blocks of the Via Veneto district around the Hotel Excelsior, where the sidewalks, as described by A. J. Liebling, were so crowded that "a fair-sized man vainly trying to thread his way . . . has to reverse engines and back out, like a steamship on the upper reaches of a tropical river." The outdoor café tables, Liebling added, were "occupied by visitors to the Games, gasping like stranded sea robins and staring at one another in search of the stigmata of celebrity." One night Liebling pried himself away from the crowd and piled into a taxi. He asked the driver to take him to a showing of *La Dolce Vita,* the Federico Fellini film that had opened earlier that year. He ended up at a cinema in the far reaches of Rome, but Liebling thought the trip was worth it. He saw the movie not so much as a lens into the sweet-sour lives of decadent Italians but more as a new way of looking at modern America. "The actors, an international bunch, speak in their own languages— a novelty Fellini may have picked up from *La Grande Illusion,"* Liebling wrote. "What pleased me was that English, usually with an American accent, has displaced French as the language that, spoken in an Italian film, symbolizes worldly wickedness. Instead of 'Ooh-la-la!' the bad girl now says something like 'I've got news for you.' This marks a change in the Anglo-Saxon place in the international imagination, which is often more important than actuality."

Most foreign correspondents were not exactly living the sweet life during their Olympic stay in Rome. They found housing in inexpensive dormitory-style rooms at the Domus Mariae and Domus Pacis, old church-related residence hotels near the Vatican that also served as press centers. Much like the Olympic Village itself, these quarters brought the world together in all its linguistic diversity, housing correspondents from sixty-three nations—from Gian Paolo Ormezzano, the young Italian writer for *Tuttosport,* to Erdogan Aripinar of Turkey's *Cumhuriyet Gazetesi*; from Federico La Rosa of Peru's *La Prensa* to Sven Johansson of *Dagens Nyheter* in Sweden. To handle this polyglot crowd, the press centers provided a babel of Olivetti desk typewriters: 170 Italian, 140 standard English, 85 German, 60 French, 35 Swedish, 30 Russian, 25 Norwegian, 20 Spanish, 10 Portuguese, 5 Turkish, 5 Hungarian, 5 Dutch, 3 Polish, 2 Romanian, 2 Yugoslav, and 1 Bulgarian.

For the transport of journalists from one venue to another, there were motor scooters, bubble helicopters at the ready, along with sixty little Fiat 500 cars with Italian sailors behind the wheel. Ormezzano, after having locked himself out of his own car on the trip down from holiday in Rimini, was delighted to have a chauffeur in Rome. Olympic authorities even provided a separate car and driver for his mother on the day she came down to visit. All went well until Ormezzano's sailor carried the notion of Olympian liberty a bit far. "The driver liked to use the car to go dancing in the evening," Ormezzano recalled. "But he was found out when he left his uniform in the car while he went to dance, and it was stolen. He was confined to barracks and only allowed out to drive me. I had to telephone the man's superior when we were finished in the evening, and he had twenty minutes to return to post."

DAVE SIME arrived at the stadium that morning "as weak as a kitten." During his time in Rome, he had been more successful with his off-the-books assignment, making friendly contact with Soviet athlete Igor Ter-Ovanesyan, than with his athletic mission, preparing for the 100-meter dash. Still recovering from that ill-advised romp in the bracing Swiss river, he had barely trained since arriving in the village, at least not in the all-out method he preferred. Sime believed

that he improved not by subtly refining technique or slowly rounding into form, but by running and then running some more, one dash
after another until, even though he was exhausted, his limbs felt
looser and ready for the tension of the main event.

This extreme endurance method was rejected in some quarters of
track and field, though the Australian runners believed in it, as did
some high jumpers. Joe Faust, a young high jumper from Culver
City, California, the baby of the U.S. track-and-field team, had radi-
cally rejected the prevailing notion that a jumper had only so many
tries in him. He could jump a hundred times a day to prepare for a
meet rather than the more common fifteen jumps twice a week. The
Soviet high jumpers were practicing the same way, repetitively, not
worrying about whether they were wasting their best leaps in practice. In track and field, as in most sports, the intensity of practice was
part of the endless debate over how to reach peak performance, not
unlike the debate over pitch counts in baseball or full-pads practices
in football.

If running more, rather than less, had always been Sime's way to
strength, could he overcome his fatigue now by running more in the
furnace of Rome? It seemed as though every Olympic delegation entered a sprinter in the 100, sixty-three runners in all, so many that
there were nine heats in the qualifying round. Each nation that
brought a sprinter to Rome was allowed one automatic entry. To enter two or the maximum three runners, they had to meet a time standard set by the International Amateur Athletic Federation, which
for the Rome games was 10.4 seconds. The top-ranked sprinters were
seeded in different heats, so Sime, running in the third heat, faced no
world-class competition. He only had to finish in the top three to
move on, and he did exactly that, finishing third behind runners from
Venezuela and Barbados, but a relaxed three-tenths of a second ahead
of the fourth-place runner. In the heat immediately before his, Sime
had watched the German star, Armin Hary, do the same thing, cruis-
ing to a second-place finish. Ray Norton, the American favorite for

gold, finished first in the sixth heat, but in the slowest field of the nine races.

For the quarterfinal round, starting at four o'clock, there were twenty-seven runners left, placed in four heats. Norton, competing in the first of the four groups, barely improved on his qualifying race but survived, running a 10.6 to tie for second place. Sime and Hary went head-to-head in the second heat. Don Graham, the *Post* copyboy, had been there watching all day, engrossed by the scene. The stadium was noisy if not full, but he was struck by something unusual about the fans. Thousands of them were Germans, all cheering for Armin Hary (pronounced *Hah-ree*) as soon as he appeared, but cheering in a way that Graham had never seen or heard back in the States. These were organized chants, rhythmic, urgent, in unison. E. W. Tipping, an Australian writer, found himself in the standing room area in G Class 4, where he spent "a thousand lire to stand in the boiling sun all day, which not only beat down on us from a cloudless sky but bounced back as its reflections came off the white concrete and marble." He was surrounded by Germans, Tipping noted. "They seem to be the noisiest of the barrackers."

What was it about the Germans? Here was another reminder that World War II remained too close in memory, not just for fans from the Allied nations but also for the Italians. Mussolini might have aligned himself with Hitler, but to the Italian people the Germans still seemed too cold and organized. An editorial in the Italian paper *Il Messaggero* noted, "One might think it is a pity, one might find it ridiculous, but it is a fact that often even now—fifteen years after the last war—that a group of Germans awakes political associations as soon as it reveals the impression of being tightly organized." The reception Germans were getting in Rome did not go unnoticed back home. A columnist in *Die Welt* thought his countrymen were being stereotyped unfairly. "The Germans don't scream and shout more or less than the Italians, Americans, or British," he argued. "The difference: one does not hear the screaming of the Italians,

Americans, or British. They are part of the general background noise. If, however, the Germans start to cheer, everyone looks up and says, 'Aha, the Germans!' "

Aha, the Germans—they were roaring all the way through the second heat of the quarterfinals. Hary and Sime blazed down the track, Hary off to a quick lead and Sime flying closer at the tape. Hary won by a half step, his time of 10.2 setting an Olympic record. Sime closed at 10.3, tying the old record shared by five Americans, including Jesse Owens. But these were just the quarterfinals; Sime and Hary would get two more chances at each other the next day, with the semis and the final, and Ray Norton would get his shot at gold then too. For now the stadium rocked with delirious, metronomic chants from the banner-waving German fans: "Hah-ree! Hah-ree! Hah-ree! *Rah! Rah! Rah! Cha! Cha! Cha!*"

Hary did his own part to intensify any lingering disdain for Germans. At the 1936 Berlin Games, Jesse Owens, the superb athlete from Ohio State, had won four gold medals, defying the racist theories of Hitler and his Nazis. Now a revered elder statesman in track, Owens was in Rome writing a syndicated column for U.S. newspapers. He took particular interest in his own events, including the 100-meter dash, and passed the word that morning through an intermediary, a German newspaperman, that he would love to meet Hary. But Hary abruptly turned him down, snapping, "I'm sorry, I haven't time to fool with him." News of Hary's dismissive attitude toward Owens spread through the Olympics, usually beginning with the phrase "Can you believe it?" One of the lasting myths of the 1936 Berlin Games was that Hitler had snubbed Owens by leaving the stadium before the American was to receive a gold medal. It did not actually happen that way. By the time Owens won, Hitler had been instructed by Olympic officials to shake hands with all winners or none, not just the Germans, and he chose to congratulate none, but the myth endured as an accurate reflection of the Führer's attitude. Nearly a quarter century later, Hary apparently meant no larger insult. In fact, he worshipped Owens and had read a translation of a book about the black runner's 1936 experience "about five hundred times." He was simply a self-centered lone-wolf runner who wanted no distractions—and thought that another runner would certainly understand—but he had unwittingly awakened echoes of Germany's past.

Owens took it in stride. "I've been put off by busier people, buddy, but never by faster ones," he said.

ABOUT THE TIME the cheering died down, the shot-put final began. There was a cold war going on here, it seemed, but it was an all-American cold war. Californian Parry O'Brien, a two-time gold medal winner and the old man of the sport at age twenty-eight, had been feuding for months with Kansan Bill Nieder, who had formed an alliance with the third great thrower, Dallas Long, the nineteen-year-old phenom from Phoenix who had made his name at the 1958 dual meet in Moscow and had won the event at the Olympic Trials at Stanford in July.

Although Nancy Nelson, Cord Nelson's twelve-year-old daughter, had picked Nieder as her man in the Nelson competitions, and her uncle Bert thought it was a wise choice, Nieder was lucky just to be competing. Hampered by a strained right knee, he had finished fourth at the Trials, meaning that he would get to Rome only as an alternate. "I was so heartbroken I was ready to go home and never touch a shot again," he said later. "I wasn't even going to report with the Olympic squad." But O'Brien turned him around, not through encouragement but through a remembered insult. Months earlier, when Nieder had set a new record, O'Brien ridiculed him, saying dismissively, "Nieder is a cow-pasture performer. He only does well in meets when there is no competition." Burning to prove O'Brien wrong, Nieder reported to the Olympic team. He began outdistancing his teammates at the practice meets and forced U.S. track-and-field officials to find a way to get him into the competition, which they did as soon as the third-place finisher at the Trials, the inconsistent Dave Davis, suffered a minor injury.

To Parry O'Brien, shot-putting was part technique, part psychology. As the first athlete to put the shot beyond 60 feet, he had revolutionized the sport, inventing what came to be known as "the O'Brien glide," a new method of throwing where he started with his face directly away from the field and spun 180 degrees, rather than the previous 90 degrees, allowing him to apply the most force for the longest period of time before letting loose. But beyond that, he was a fierce and unyielding competitor who made a point of trying to upset his opponents and shroud himself in mystery. "I always wore two sweatshirts, which I would gradually peel off during warm-ups," he once said. "If I threw long, the opponent would think, 'How can I beat him if he threw that long with two sweatsuits on?' I also took a little white plastic jar to competition and always made it quite visible to competitors. When asked, I would say it's an energy-giving substance. It was clover and honey with water, nothing more, but I wouldn't tell anyone that."

His tactics effectively riled up Nieder, a twenty-five-year-old army lieutenant who had played football at Kansas and was known for his bright smile and hair-trigger temper. If O'Brien tried to show him up, Nieder invariably responded. At the pre-Olympic meet in Switzerland, O'Brien seemed bothered by a photographer standing to his side and ordered the man to relocate behind him. When it was Nieder's turn, he loudly shouted to the photographer, "Come stand in front of me if you want!" It was tit for tat at anything between those two; some teammates speculated that they were competing even on that train down through the Alps to Rome when furniture started flying out of the compartment somewhere in the Swiss night. One writer called them "the Hatfield and McCoy of American shot-putters." Dallas Long, the youngest and quietest of the trio, generally sided with Nieder. "O'Brien was aloof, always aloof," Long said later, recalling how the veteran athlete had not uttered one encouraging word to him in Moscow in 1958, when they had competed together against the Soviets and Long was only seventeen.

Nieder, in a pre-Olympics interview with *Sport* magazine writer Al Stump, said that he and Long encouraged each other to go after O'Brien. "Every time Long and I write to each other, we add the line: Let's whip O'Brien at Rome! It's like a war cry with Long and me. I don't mind telling you that if we can knock O'Brien back to third place in the Olympics, we'll consider it as big a thrill as anything that's happened to us."

But before they reached Rome, Long had become another American victim of unpeeled European fruit. On the train ride from Switzerland, he had vomited uncontrollably, and though he was a Phoenix kid and accustomed to brutal heat, the sun in Rome only further enervated him. After losing eight pounds and some muscle mass, he tried to recover by practicing with the weight lifters, but that proved more troublesome when he strained his back attempting to lift too much. He went into the shot-put final without any expectations of beating O'Brien or Nieder, just hoping to bring home the bronze.

Athletes are accustomed to routines, but the actual day of competition tends to destroy the regimen, especially in an event like the shot put, where, as Long put it, "there is a lot of hurry up and wait. Sit around and wait. Throw and wait. Watch and wait." They started at nine that morning, and it was after six that evening when the competitors came to their final throws. As expected, the three Americans had far outdistanced the rest of the field. Viktor Lipshis of the Soviet Union was in fourth place, more than a foot short of 60 feet, while O'Brien, Nieder, and Long had all shattered the old Olympic mark of 60 feet 11 inches set by O'Brien at Melbourne four years earlier.

One throw left. O'Brien leading with a throw of 62 feet 8½ inches. Would he leave Rome with his third gold medal? The cocky champ paced around with a towel around his neck, flexing his muscles. Nieder's turn. He had felt like "a complete failure" after the Trials, and now he was worried that he would fail again. He wondered whether he had the power of concentration he needed in a tense situation like this. Cord Nelson had noticed that during Nieder's first throw, he seemed shaken by the roar in the stadium for a different event, the 5000-meter run. But Nieder hated to lose to O'Brien. He had his lucky bandage on his right hand, which had long since healed from a year-old injury. He thought about the cow pasture and the war cry. His right leg protected by an elastic brace, he unfurled one last time. He held the sixteen-pound shot in the palm of his hand, unlike the other throwers, who kept it on their fingertips. Nelson chronicled the scene in his notebook: "He bent low. He shoved off, backwards, a little too fast. His left leg swung around a little too far, and he never did get his right leg under him for maximum power. But he was exploding. And the ball rolled up to his fingers, pressing them back as his arm shot forward."

In practice, Nieder had gone past 67 feet. Not quite that now, but good enough—64 feet 6¾ inches. He had whipped O'Brien in Rome. And Cord Nelson's twelve-year-old daughter had the winner.

IN THE CAFETERIAS at the Olympic Village that night there was much talk about the 100. What would happen tomorrow? Could Ray Norton, so disappointing that summer yet still the favorite, fulfill all the predictions and become the world's fastest human? Could Dave Sime redeem his 1956 disappointment? Who was this fleet German? The U.S. coaches knew something about Armin Hary. The year before, he had come to the States in a brief, unsuccessful stint at San Jose State. You have to worry about him, Bud Winter, the coach there, told Paul Zimmerman of the *L.A. Times.* The extraordinary aspect of Hary was his lightning-quick break. In international track circles, they called him the Thief of Starts. It often appeared that he was getting off the mark a split second before the starting gun was fired. During the preliminary heats earlier that day, Arthur Daley of the *New York Times* thought he "rocketed off the mark as if he was so psychic he could sense when the starter's finger was tightening on the trigger."

At an earlier meet in Switzerland where he ran a record ten-flat, the officials were so suspicious they made him run the race again— and he came in with the same time. By then Hary had been fighting the doubters for two years. It all went back to an obscure race in Friedrichshafen, Germany, in September 1958, when he apparently ran a ten-flat for the first time. Track experts from Germany, France, and the U.S. all questioned the time, saying it must have been a mistake on the part of the timers. A track writer for *Suddeutsche Zeitung* wrote that a sudden improvement of two-tenths of a second in the 100 had to be questioned. Marcel Hansenne of *L'Équipe* argued that German starters tended to favor Germans. There was so much pressure to discount the stunning time that officials settled on a way to do it: they ruled that Hary's lane at the Friedrichshafen track was slightly downhill. That decision, according to his sympathetic biographer, Knut Teske, at once fueled Hary's ambition and deepened his distrust of sports functionaries. One thing it did not do was force Hary to change the way he got off the blocks.

How did the Thief of Starts do it? The photographer Robert Riger slipped into a position close to the starting line and took a series of shots. His photographic evidence convinced him that Hary did not leave too soon, even though there were loud shouts of "No!" from fans in the stands when Hary broke in the quarterfinals on his way to the 10.2. German scientists who studied Hary reached the same conclusion. Films showed that his knees were the first part of his body to respond to the sound of the gun, then his toes, then his fingertips, and finally his churning legs. His reactions were three times faster than normal. The average person reacted to sound in twelve-hundredths of a second, Hary reacted in four-hundredths. But it was the combination of mental reaction and physical acceleration that made Hary so dangerous. "It is not something you can learn," he once said. "The mental reaction ends as soon as I make the first movement. It is all body from then on."

In the end, some observers believed the final the next day might come down to the official starter, Ennio Pedrazzini, who had been highly regarded as Italy's top official. The starter used the language of the host country, which would take some getting used to for the Americans: *Aposti . . . Via . . .* and then the gun. And U.S. coaches were concerned that Pedrazzini, like most European officials, fired the gun quickly after the set, in 1 to 1.7 seconds, while most American starters waited a full 2 seconds. The fast gun would help Hary. On the other hand, Pedrazzini had a reputation as a tough starter who would not hesitate to call a false start if the Thief of Starts broke too soon. So it could go either way.

Jesse Owens visited the American sprinters at their dorm rooms in the village that night. First he talked with Norton, who told him that he was still recovering from an old back injury but felt that he would run his best race when it counted the next day. Owens was concerned about Norton's slow times and wondered whether he was ready. Then he went to see Sime, who had sprinted faster each outing that day and had rejuvenated himself after the two preliminary races by running four extra 100-meter dashes on his own at the practice track. He was running his way out of fatigue. The extreme endurance method seemed to be working. Sime was as mad as anyone when he heard about Hary's snub of the immortal American champ, and wanted badly to get back at him. "I almost caught that rabbit, Jesse," he told Owens. "Maybe tomorrow I can."

There was a different aura in the streets of Rome that night. The city had become lively, chaotic, bustling, antsy. Romans had returned in full force in the last hours of August, streaming back by the thousands from their holidays. At dusk, it took nearly three and a half hours to drive from the Stadio Olimpico to the Domus Mariae, near the Vatican. Summer was ending, time to get to work.

10

BLACK THURSDAY

LATE in the afternoon, at a quarter after five, the fastest men in the world emerged from the tunnel at the far end of Stadio Olimpico and strolled casually toward the starting area for the final of the 100-meter dash. It was the second day of track and field, the first of September, and the white bowl of the stadium was filling with spectators for the first time since the Opening Ceremony. Noisy American tour groups filtered in from side trips to Naples and the Amalfi coast. German fans began assembling in cheering squadrons, unfurling their banners. Even the press section was crowded and alert. For the pure distillation of human energy, there was no event like the Olympic 100: crackling anticipation, ten explosive seconds, and it was done.

First onto the track was Armin Hary, age twenty-three, looking less like a world-class runner going for Olympic gold than a Kaufhof department store clerk in Frankfurt boarding the weekend tram out to Stadtwald Park for a picnic in the woods. He was wearing baggy blue cotton pants, a green, gray, and white plaid pullover, and a straw cowboy hat cocked jauntily to one side, matching his smile, which also broke on a wise guy slant. *"Hah-ree! Hah-ree! Hah-ree!"* the Germans chanted upon catching sight of their man. Here was a character only contrarians and fans thirsting for reflected national glory could love; the rest of the world seemed to hate him. Hary was a cocky individualist who cared little about what others thought; all he wanted was to prevail. Growing up in the poor mining town of Gersweiler, not far from Saarbruecken, his young life had been shaped by the unhappiest of childhoods. His father, a German soldier in World War II, came back from three years at a prison camp in Finland to find Armin's mother living with another man. Hary would say later that his mother was not the warmest person, but she taught him self-determination, and he emerged from those early days driven to create "something unique for eternity." While not alone among athletes who came to Rome with movie star ambitions, he had a lock on the role of lead villain. He enjoyed his nickname, the Thief of Starts, as a slightly sinister twist on silent-film idol Rudolph Valentino's Thief of Hearts. His apparent snub of the legendary Jesse Owens the day before had become the talk of the village. Watching him enter the stadium, the writer Marshall Smith, in a cable back to *Life* magazine, wrote: "Armin Hary annoyed everyone by his arrogant air, his cowboy hat . . . His conduct was so overbearing that even his German teammates said they hoped he would lose."

Next came Peter Radford of Great Britain, a coal-haired flash from the West Midlands. Not yet twenty-one, he was heir to a sprinting tradition in the kingdom that traced back to Harold Abrahams, who at the 1924 Olympics in Paris became the first European to wrest the 100-meter gold from the dominant Americans. Radford brought his own inspirational story to the track, much like the great U.S. woman sprinter Wilma Rudolph and her childhood infirmity. Felled by kidney disease at age five, he was wheelchair-bound for three years but overcame that early handicap to become a schoolboy dash champion. In Rome he had won three heats going into the final, and his opponents knew that a year earlier he had run what was then the fastest electronically timed 100 in the world. Though not a favorite, Radford could not be overlooked.

Then there was Enrique Figuerola, wiry and intense. He was the pride of Cuba, a nation that seemed to be turning away from the United States more every day. As Figuerola approached the track for the dash in Rome, his government was announcing that it had seized three more major American corporations in Havana: the tire companies Firestone, Goodyear, and U.S. Rubber Company. Only a dozen Cuban athletes had been sent to the Olympics under the nascent regime of Fidel Castro: a single boxer, wrestler, swimmer, fencer, and weight lifter, two yachtsmen, two gymnasts, and three competitors in track and field. The only ones known on the world stage were the Star-class yachtsmen from the Cardenas family of Havana, remnants from Cuba's society past who had brought the last medal back to the island, a silver from the 1948 Games in London. Figuerola, who had just turned twenty-one, ran well in the heats, tying Radford in the semifinals earlier that day.

In their blue warm-up suits, the Americans walked out of the tunnel as fully half the field, the maximum three—Ray Norton, Dave Sime, and Francis Budd. The youngest of the group at twenty, Budd came to Rome from Jumbo Jim Elliott's renowned track program at Villanova University. In concert with Rudolph and Radford, he featured a personal history that oddly made early physical trauma seem like a predictor of future speed. Budd's variation on the theme: during his childhood in Asbury Park, New Jersey, an illness, probably polio, withered a leg, the right calf two inches thinner than his left. His mother rubbed the leg night after night with goose grease, nutmeg, olive oil, mutton suet, and triple-distilled witch hazel, and— whatever the cause and effect—by high school Budd was excelling in football and track.

While Budd now seemed the healthiest of the U.S. trio, Dave

Sime, looking loose and confident, an orange baseball cap pulled low on his forehead, believed he had regained his strength. After running three heats in a day and a half, plus more practice sprints on the side, the big redhead had sweated his way back to form at last. He had wanted this chance at Olympic gold for more than four years, since the leg injury denied him a trip to Melbourne. That was motivation enough, but the prospect of chasing down the irritating Armin Hary inspired him even more. They had run in two heats together already, including the semifinals that morning, and Sime, four inches taller but with a slower start, had nearly caught Hary at the tape each time, losing by an inch. He had promised Jesse Owens that he would catch that rabbit, and here was the time.

It was also the time for Ray Norton, who had arrived at the Games with star billing alongside Rafer Johnson and high jumper John Thomas. His college coach, Bud Winter of San Jose State, in Rome coaching the Olympic runners, was convinced that his prize student would live up to a promise he had made four years earlier when he first saw Norton race in high school in the Bay Area. Come to San Jose, Winter had said then, and I'll make you the world's fastest human. Only an Olympic gold medal could anoint Norton with that honorific, but he seemed on the verge. Now in his prime at twenty-two, he had set a world record for the slightly shorter 100-*yard* dash, had tied the record for the 200, and had swept the sprints at the Olympic Trials. He had studied the films of Jesse Owens, modeled himself after Owens, and wanted nothing more than to reenact Owens's glory of 1936. *Sports Illustrated* and *Track & Field News* thought he would, predicting a Norton sweep of the dashes and relay in Rome, and the newspapermen repeated the forecast of three gold medals.

With Norton, it was essential that he keep loose. Early in his career, when he failed to make the 1956 team, he developed a reputation for tightening with nerves. But Winter took pride in changing that. The coach was a proponent of the speed paradox: by urging his

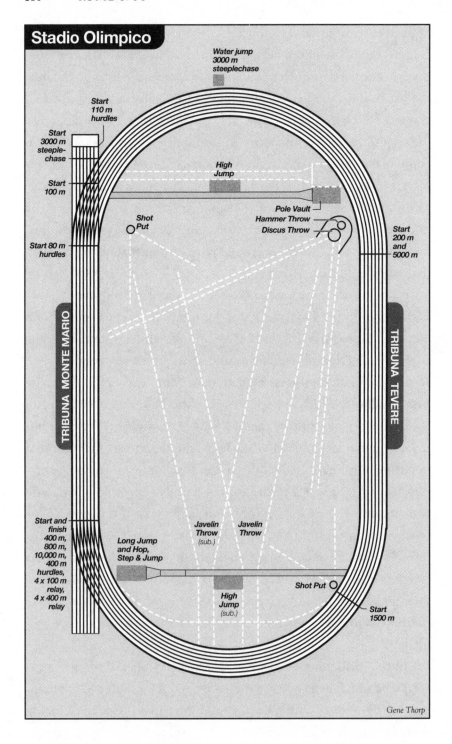

Stadio Olimpico

Water jump
3000 m
steeplechase

Start
110 m
hurdles

Start
3000 m
steeple-
chase

Start
100 m

High
Jump

Pole Vault
Hammer Throw
Discus Throw

Start 80 m
hurdles

Shot
Put

Start
200 m
and
5000 m

TRIBUNA MONTE MARIO

TRIBUNA TEVERE

Start and
finish
400 m,
800 m,
10,000 m,
400 m
hurdles,
4 x 100 m
relay,
4 x 400 m
relay

Long Jump
and Hop,
Step & Jump

Javelin
Throw
(sub.)

Javelin
Throw

Shot Put

High
Jump
(sub.)

Start
1500 m

Gene Thorp

runners to exert slightly less, they would run faster. Run all out, Winter would say, and a sprinter might go thirty yards in three seconds, three times in a row. Now run four-fifths speed, and the time would drop a tenth of a second. Norton seemed to have mastered the technique. He ran with what they called a "loose lip," his mouth open and his teeth not quite clenching, and he also unfisted his hands and ran with his fingers slightly spread. Coming into Rome, one writer went so far as to call him "the most relaxed sprinter in the world."

At the village, away from the track, Norton carried himself with quiet confidence. If Rafer Johnson held a status above the others, more in the company of the gods, Norton was an alpha male among the pack of alphas on the squad. Wilma Rudolph was proof of that. By the first week there, virtually every man in the village had fallen in love with the winsome Tigerbelle. Cassius Clay, the young boxer from Louisville, was dizzy over her. Livio Berruti, the elegant, wavy-haired Italian sprinter, was certain that he could consummate a romantic pairing with her if only they could get some time alone. When Dave Sime ate breakfast one morning at a cafeteria table with the Tigerbelles, one of them teasingly said to him, "Hey, Doc, if you win gold, you can have our whole relay team." Sime laughed and shot back, "Wilma?" But Rudolph only smiled and shook her head no, absolutely not. Even if it was a joke, she was not available, for the same reason that Berruti could never find his opportunity. Rudolph was spending most of her free moments with Ray Norton. They had become the most visible couple in the village, walking hand in hand wherever they went. Even young Clay, so boastful and fearless in the ring, kept his distance. Norton, four years older and more established, intimidated him.

But on the inside, Norton was hounded by worries as he walked into Stadio Olimpico for the hundred final. His mind was not at all loose and relaxed. He had not run a good race since the Olympic Trials, a slump that he attributed to a midsummer incident near the team's temporary training field in Eugene, Oregon. A high jumper—

—either John Thomas or Joe Faust, their recollections differ on that point—found a small garter snake and twirled it close to the sprinter while he was doing stretching exercises. Norton said he jumped in fright and twisted his lower back, an injury that lingered all summer. Sime started beating him race after race. Then came the train ride down from Switzerland in the triple-digit heat, an unsettling passage that Norton believed set him back again. With aspirin as his only pain treatment, he felt uncomfortable in the 100-meter preliminaries, he said later. "I used to drop my hands and look to the sides and coast and do all kinds of funny little things. Well, I tried, but my body wasn't responding."

EVEN IN sprinting, the most elemental sport, there are tools of the trade. Armin Hary carried them in a small black sack: a little hammer, nail spikes, and a starting block. Sprawled on the infield grass, his legs spread wide apart, he took the spikes from the sack one at a time and flicked them nonchalantly into the grass, mumblety-peg style. It seemed all free and easy now for Hary, but in fact he had grown increasingly nervous hour by hour leading up to this moment. He had awakened at six, feeling "well rested and strong," and went to the cafeteria for a breakfast of two small steaks, two slices of dark bread with jam, two glasses of fruit juice, and a glass of milk. On the way out, he snatched a bunch of grapes and popped them into his mouth as he strolled back toward his room. During the walk, for the first time, he began to notice his surroundings. He was struck by the diversity of the athletic congregation and felt "something like the Olympic spirit." After a deep and dreamless afternoon nap, with his teammates protecting his door so he wouldn't be disturbed, he went to a nearby room to play cards. By now he was anxious, unable to eat, feeling a stage fright that would not go away until he entered the stadium and sat in the grass and tossed out his stakes like little knives.

Norton and Sime were now at the starting line, their warm-up suits off, pounding their blocks into place. It was the do-it-yourself ritual of the event: adjust, test, fix, reset, hammer. The Italian starting judge moved into position, holding a shiny chrome starting pistol. Hary edged closer to the track, posture erect, wiggling his loose legs back and forth, then finally flipped his cowboy hat, stripped down to his running gear, and went to work with hammer and block. He was on the outside, Lane 6. Sime had the far inside, Lane 1. Budd was next to Sime, then Norton, Figuerola, and Radford.

In a few minutes, the stadium's crackling nervous hum softened to a cathedral hush as the runners settled into position, one knee touching, head down. Hary swallowed hard, rocking gently side to side. Most eyes were on him, the Thief of Starts. He had jumped the gun once during the semifinals; would he do it again? *Signore* Pedrazzini, the starter, dressed in a fine white summer suit, lifted his chrome pistol skyward.

Aposti. Fingers up, backs curved like frightened cats, heads rising with anticipation.

Via. A split second seemed like an hour now. Sime stared straight ahead but tried to keep track of Hary way out there in his peripheral vision.

The finger tightened on the trigger and . . .

Hary and Sime threw their bodies out before the sound of the gun. False start. The runners decelerated at twenty meters, turned, and ambled slowly back toward the blocks. Norton patted teammate Sime on the rump. There were no yellow flags assigned, meaning the gun jumpers had a freebie, since a second yellow brought disqualification. But the false start only intensified the anxiety. More waiting, legs jiggling, hands through the hair, everyone in position again at last. *Aposti. Via.* And they were off at the gun—but it sounded again, calling them back. Hary was fingered as the lone culprit this time, leaving too soon. From the stands, loud whistles of disapproval shrieked down from the German claques. When the yellow card went to Hary, he felt at once guilty and martyred at the same time, suffering from what he would later call a "culpability complex" that led him to blame himself even when he thought he was innocent. This time he probably did not leave early, photos would later show. But he coolly raised a finger over his lips to shush his jeering fans.

"Hary must feel like someone undergoing torture," Neil Allen, a British sportswriter, muttered to a colleague. Yet when Allen trained his binoculars on the German approaching the blocks a third time, he was surprised that Hary "looked pale but unshaken." What an ice-cold competitor, Allen thought to himself. The arrogance of a winner. A writer from *Die Welt* came to the same conclusion. Through his binoculars, he noticed that Hary "had a distinct wrinkle on his forehead" but seemed "relaxed to the tip of his toes." They were right. Hary would say later that he felt "cold, calm, and fully concentrated." His fans were mostly depressed, worried that the world was conspiring against him and that he could never win without his quick start. Elsewhere in the press box, there was some sense of relief. The prevailing feeling was that now the Thief of Starts would be put to the ultimate test: either play it safe or risk everything.

Observing from the stands, Jesse Owens understood better than anyone the critical importance of a lightning start. Sitting next to journalist Paul G. Neimark, his as-told-to ghostwriter for Scripps Howard News Service. Owens thought back to his own sprints in 1935 and 1936 against Ralph Metcalfe, who "had the greatest finish of any runner who ever lived." They raced fifteen times, Owens recalled, and he was able to hold off Metcalfe ten times. "Each time we met, I'd get away from the blocks faster and have that big yard or so lead going into the stretch. Then Ralph's thunderclap finish would go to work. But even the great Metcalfe couldn't make up that tenth of a second most of the time." In this race, the diffident Hary had the opening burst like Owens, and Sime and Norton were more like Metcalfe. Norton, looking forward to a pro football career, had Metcalfe's strength, and Sime had his precise running style, something he had copied when he taught himself the art of sprinting from books in the Duke library.

It seemed forever before the six sprinters settled in for the third start. Figuerola had trouble with his starting block and kept readjusting it. More anxiety for the runners. Another electric buzz of anticipation for the fans. Could Hary get off to another fast start? In the German section of the press box, they asked the question a different way: would the starter dare to shoot back Hary a second time? Jesse Owens was so concerned that he "had fingers on both hands crossed when Norton and Sime climbed into their starting blocks." Tex Maule of *Sports Illustrated* kept his eyes on Sime as he "set his feet, saw a rough patch in his lane, and reached out and patted it down, hard. The hollow *plop, plop, plop* of his hand against the dusty red track sounded clearly throughout the stadium." It was that deathly quiet, until the gun.

The third start was clean. Norton and Budd broke fast, but by the third step, Hary was striding, loose and relaxed, while the Americans were still short stepping. In his outside lane, closest to the stands, Hary fired clearly into the lead at twenty meters. The German cheering squadrons were chanting. *"Hah-ree! Hah-ree! Hah-ree!"*

Sime had a better than average start, but even with that he was two feet behind Hary after only three strides. At the halfway point he accelerated, the thunderclap of Metcalfe taking hold. He ran tall and erect. The entire stadium was up now, straining to see, organized German chants punctuating the larger roar of the masses. Norton was a meter and a half behind, but still believed in himself.

Between 60 and 70 meters, the Germans started to worry. Where was Hary's looseness? He had completely changed his running style, the Frankfurt correspondent feared. "The elegantly looking powerful pacing of his legs, which make his body nearly weightlessly glide over the running lane, suddenly converted into a stamping and cramped fighting." Hary's thighs cramped, and he was running through pain.

Norton tried to kick into a finishing gear but had nothing. Ed Temple, Wilma Rudolph's coach, noticed Norton's exertion and knew it was over. The young man was trying too hard. Cord Nelson, editor of *Track & Field News,* reached the same conclusion from his seat in the stands, watching the race with his family. "Too tense," he said of Norton. He had seen it many times before. Sprinting, Nelson thought, was "the most violent action your body can take," yet it also required a delicate balance of violence and relaxation.

Norton didn't have it. He dropped to the back like debris thrown off a speeding boat. Budd fell back with him.

At 80 meters the Brits in the press box started pointing. Here came Radford, gaining ground stride by stride, past Norton and Budd and Figuerola! It was one of the best accelerations Neil Allen, Roger Bannister, and Harold Abrahams had ever seen. Radford kept repeating a simple mantra to himself to keep his pistons in sync: push the knee in front, lift the elbow behind.

Hary, arms and legs straining, somehow kept pushing forward. He could not see Radford near his tail but sensed that Sime on the far opposite lane was posing the real threat. "I could feel him like a breath of fire on my shoulders," Hary said later of Sime.

It was now a two-man race, Sime inside, Hary outside. Don Graham, the young copy boy for the *Washington Post,* was exhilarated by the American's rush at Hary. "Suddenly at the finish Dave Sime was just flying at him."

At the end they both leaned at the tape, separated by an inch at most. Sime was pushing so hard that he lost peripheral vision; he could not see Hary. He lunged forward with such ferocity that he lost his balance, one hand whirling wildly as he struggled to stay on his feet and went flying literally, reeling and splattering violently crosswise onto the track. He had given everything, he could run no faster, but was it enough? The judges were not ready to call it. They would wait for evidence from the new Raceend Omega Timer, a photo-finish apparatus from Switzerland that captured both a photograph of the tape and a precise quartz-clock timing down to the nearest hundredth of a second.

But Sime sensed that he had barely lost, and Hary that he had barely won. So had the German fans. Their chants grew louder. *"Ja! Ja! Ja! Hah-ree! Hah-ree! Hah-ree!"* German flags waved in every corner of the stadium. The photographers also sensed the ending, snapping shot after shot of Hary as he retraced his steps back to the starting line, this time walking slowly, feeling strange and alone, allowing only the slightest bent smile to cross his face.

Radford, finishing third, assured of bronze, walked away alone, brokenhearted. Norton and Budd, finishing last and second to last, had watched Sime's desperate splatter and rushed over to him. From the press section, Neil Allen took note as "Norton and Budd lifted Sime off the track, their black bodies like pillars on either side of his tall white frame as they walked him onto the grass."

Sime was less concerned about minor track burns on his arms and legs than the fragile mental state of his teammate, Norton, who had been hyped to win and finished an ignominious last. "I'm sorry," Sime said to Norton. "I'm really and truly sorry."

"And I knew what he meant," Norton said later. "He just meant that I wasn't up to par, and it wasn't there for me, and when he gave me a hug—we hugged each other—I told him, I say, 'Hey, that's the way it goes.' He said, 'You gave your best shot.' I said, 'That's all you can do.' It was a very touching moment."

The official results finally flashed on the electronic scoreboard: Hary first, Sime second, Radford third. The photographs showed Hary breaking the tape an inch ahead of Sime, even though the times for both men were the same: 10.2 seconds, tying the Olympic record. "The young man throws up both arms and finally gives the ten thousand German fans the longed-for pose of victory," reported the *Die Welt* correspondent. "They are screaming, stamping, shouting, and roaring wild chants. They let him know how much they owe him . . . We begin to feel a bit sorry for this young man. They will featherbed him. They will flatter him and schmooze him. They will celebrate him like a gladiator. We begin to worry about him."

For the medals ceremony, Avery Brundage came down from the stands to do the honors. Armin Hary, No. 263, was on the top rung. Dave Sime, No. 397, stood on the second rung, appearing crestfallen as the silver medal was placed around his neck. He could barely look at Hary, who reached down from above to shake his hand. Sime thought he could have won. If only he had been in a lane next to Hary, he would have had a better sense of when to make that final lean, he believed. No excuses, he lost, but it was so close that his knee was the first body part across the line. However, the chest is what counts, and Hary's chest beat his. Sime would replay that final moment for the rest of his life and watch it on film over and over. Every time he watched, as he got older, it seemed that he came closer and closer. But Hary always won. The German flag, with its black, red, and yellow horizontal stripes decorated with the five Olympic rings of East-West compromise, rose above the Stars and Stripes and Union Jack as the band played Beethoven's "Ode to Joy."

Two people unconnected to the race noticed something strange about the world's fastest man as he soaked in applause atop the podium, a gold medal dangling at his neck. They were Adi Dassler, owner of the German shoe company Adidas, and his brother Rudolf, who ran a competing shoe company, Puma. For the race itself, Adi Dassler had been shocked to see Hary come out wearing Puma shoes. Hary always wore the three-stripe Adidas cleats, according to their secret agreement. Now on the medal stand, it was Rudolf Dassler's turn to be surprised. Hary had changed and was wearing Adidas. Werner von Moltke, a Puma official, later told the Dutch writer Barbara Smit that Hary's choice of Puma for the race "was at least partly motivated by a thick brown envelope." In going back to Adidas for the medal ceremony, Smit wrote in her revealing book on the shoe industry, *Pitch Invasion,* "Hary was apparently trying to get paid by both sides." Hary later conceded that was precisely what he was doing, and explained that he had turned away from Adidas when Adi Dassler rejected his request for a job as an Adidas agent and an advance of ten thousand pairs of shoes that he could market.

Brundage, the unmerciful king of amateurism, knew none of this. In fact, his reaction to the results was private gloating about Ray Norton's poor showing. Word had reached him that the American sprinter had agreed to sign a professional contract with the San Francisco 49ers football team when the Olympics were done. This was an affront to Brundage's strict standards of amateurism. He felt it was only fitting for the sinner to finish last.

Norton had left the scene before the ceremony. Out of sight, in the darkness of the tunnel leading from the stadium, he fell into the consoling embrace of Wilma Rudolph, who had better luck on the track that day, winning two preliminary heats in the women's 100. They walked back to the village together and talked into the night.

IN THE Boston area that morning, readers of the *Globe* had awakened to a headline that read "It's Thomas Day in Rome; John Seeks New Mark." By early that evening, across the ocean in the gloaming of Stadio Olimpico, John Thomas, the sensational nineteen-year-old high jumper from Cambridge Rindge Tech and Boston University, seemed to carry the day's last best hopes for his country. For Americans accustomed to dominating Olympic track and field, it was stunning to hear that the dash men had been beaten by a German in the 100. The red, white, and blue had bombed out even worse in the 800 meters, failing to place a runner in the final won in record time by Peter Snell of New Zealand, the first gold medalist half-miler not from the U.S. since 1932. And now three Soviets were challenging Thomas jump for jump in the late going of a contest everyone expected him to win easily.

The high-jump competition was an all-day affair. It started at nine that morning with thirty-two jumpers, and by lunch the field

had narrowed to seventeen who had cleared 6-6¾. American Joe
Faust, with a sore lower back, was the first one out in the afternoon.
After clearing only the relatively low height of 6-8, Charles Dumas,
the gold medalist at Melbourne, was gone, and when Stig Pettersson
of Sweden could not rise above 6-11½, it was down to Thomas, in his
blue USA vest, and the three Soviets: Viktor Bolshov, Valeriy Brumel, and Robert Shavlakadze.

"This is a sensation!" a correspondent for *Izvestia* reported when
the competition narrowed to the final four. "You can hear sports
commentators yelling into their microphones. They didn't expect
this turn of events." The brick-red running track was deserted, done
for the day, all other distractions gone, only high jumping left. The
September sky darkened over the Tiber as floodlights brightened the
high-jump pit with an eerie glow.

Six days earlier, when the U.S. and Soviet teams held a joint practice, Thomas impressed all observers, including American journalists and the Soviet jumpers, by nonchalantly directing his coach to
skip a few heights and move the bar up to seven feet, which he then
cleared easily. *Zamechatelno,* the Soviets said then. Wonderful. More
than wonderful—the sportswriters considered the move psychologically devastating. Just by witnessing that scene, they believed, the
Russians would realize they had no chance. Now, with the height at
6-11½, a height the three Soviets had already cleared, Thomas
tried the same tactic. He passed, saying he would jump again at
the next height, 7 feet and ¼ inch. "Was it gamesmanship?" Jess
Abramson of the *Herald Tribune* wondered from the press box.
Thomas had surpassed seven feet more than any athlete in history,
thirty-seven times, while Bolshov alone among the Soviets had ever
cleared the magic height. Jerry Nason of the *Boston Globe,* who knew
Thomas best, noted that he commonly passed. During the morning
competitions that day, Thomas had disdained the lower heights,
shedding his blue sweat suit only to make the one mandatory qualifying jump.

But Nason was worried about his young hometown hero. A few days earlier, Thomas had confided that he was upset about the landing pits in Rome. There was no sawdust in them, only raw sand, which cut his legs. "The impact is terrible. It's like landing on a rock pile," Thomas had said. Because of the pits, he had not tried jumping seven feet since that practice with the Soviets.

With the bar set at seven feet and a quarter inch, Valeri Brumel was the first to jump. The son of a miner from Siberia, Brumel was a slender teenager, only eighteen, younger even than Thomas, and virtually unknown outside the Soviet Union. It was Brumel who had seemed most awed by Thomas at practice. Shavlakadze, the veteran of the Soviet trio, was concerned that his young teammate might fold under the pressure of his first major international event. But Brumel seemed calm now, and fearless, even as he grazed the bar and watched it fall on his first attempt. Then Bolshov missed too. Had Thomas psyched the Russians again? Here came old man Shavlakadze, already twenty-seven and looking like a nineteenth-century Cossack, with his bowlegs and carefully groomed mustache, white bandages on his right wrist and right calf, and his shoes colorfully mismatched, blue left, red right. The Georgian wasted no time, making a quick approach and easily clearing the bar.

"Now all the pressure was on John Thomas," observed Cord Nelson, taking notes from his seat in the stands. Nelson focused his binoculars on Thomas and saw him drinking an Italian soda and taking his time. By passing at the earlier height, Thomas had been inactive for more than an hour. He set his takeoff position at the 37-degree angle, seven long steps, an eighth shorter one, kick, lift, roll. His lead leg made it over, but his trailing leg dragged and brushed the bar, and it fell. He still had two more tries at that height, but his gold medal task now became exponentially harder. With more misses than Shavlakadze, he would at least have to clear seven and a quarter and the next height to win. Wilfrid Smith, sports editor of the *Chicago Tribune,* sensed that Thomas had become disoriented after the miss. "He was so confused, he wanted to jump right again, even though it was Brumel's turn."

In the second go-round, first Brumel and then Bolshov were successful, each jump greeted with a loud, nervous burst of ovation. *Pravda*'s correspondent, relishing the moment, harkened back to the earlier boasts of his American counterparts in the press box. "The American agency United Press International several days before this competition described a mutual training of Soviet and American athletes and had the temerity to claim that Thomas had gained an incredible psychological advantage that sapped the Soviet strength to fight for victory! And now Thomas was supposed to save the reputation of journalists and experts who could not find one single athlete but him who could aspire for gold. And look . . ."

Thomas cleared on his second attempt, and the bar was raised a notch to seven-one. The night sky grew blacker. Up in the press box, Jess Abramson thought the sequence of jumps was having a stressful cumulative effect on Thomas. "Those Russians kept hammering away at him, one after another clearing the height, with Thomas jumping last." Jerry Nason thought back to an earlier interview he had conducted for the *Globe*. Thomas had revealed that to prevent an upset stomach before a meet, he ate strained baby food fruit from a jar. The only time he got butterflies, he said, was when he failed at a height that he had cleared before. That had already happened this evening. And he certainly seemed nervous out there now. Tex Maule noticed that Thomas's long legs were quivering. Joe Faust, his teammate, who was out near the pit encouraging him, grew worried that sugar from too many Italian sodas was making him sluggish.

At seven-one, Shavlakadze, though lightly brushing the bar, cleared on his first attempt, and Brumel made it on his second. Bolshov missed three times and was out. Thomas failed twice, and had one try left. The stadium fell silent. What was he thinking? First he thought about what he had done wrong with the last jump, concentrating on the mistakes. Then, as he took his position, he tried to erase

everything but the next jump. "There was nothing out of the ordinary I could see happening to me," he said later. "You always have
the attitude that you are going to clear the jump. Never that you are
going to miss."

But the third jump was the worst. He seemed hesitant on the approach, and his chest hit the bar on the way up. For a brief second, he
remained prone in the pit. He was finished. Then he popped up, all
the cameras trained on him, and walked over to shake the winner's
hand. Shavlakadze had the gold, young Brumel the silver, and
Thomas settled for a bronze, which he snatched from Bolshov only
because he had fewer misses.

Jerry Nason left the press section immediately after the medal
ceremony in search of Thomas and found him in the tunnel, "on the
verge of tears." The veteran writer, realizing how vulnerable Thomas
was at that moment, searched for words to buck him up. "I said he
gave them the battle of the games, one against three," Nason reported. "Thomas replied misty eyed. He was proud of the bronze
and would wear it, not keep it in a box." A crowd started forming
around them. Someone asked Thomas whether he was surprised.
"I wasn't too surprised," he said. "I knew Victor Bolshov had jumped
seven feet early in the year, and he wasn't even their best man."
Nason protectively led him out of the tunnel. "I'm going out to eat
with my parents," Thomas said. "I hope they are not too disappointed
in me."

His parents were fine, but the American reporters were a mess.
For them, Thomas's defeat was an incomprehensible end to a calamitous day. Not only had he lost, but he was beaten by two Russians
and tied by a third. In the propaganda cold war, there could be no
worse way to lose. Jesse Abramson started tapping out his opening
for the *Herald Trib*: "The world's highest, most consistent, most un-
ruffled, most unbeatable leaper, the best bet everyone on the face of
the Earth conceded was most likely to win a gold medal here, placed
third." The *Los Angeles Times* called it "the darkest day in United

States track-and-field history." Oscar Fraley of UPI gave it the gloomy label "Black Thursday" and said it was "possibly the most humbling day America ever has suffered in the Olympics." Back in Manhattan, Dick Schaap, the young sports editor of *Newsweek,* took a cable from his correspondent in Rome, Curtis G. Pepper, and slapped on a headline: "Disaster at Rome." Not surprisingly, the Soviet newspaper *Izvestia* went the other way. "Like a dam bursting with torrents of water gushing through, the success of Soviet sportsmen continued to be the center of attention, and let us note, in sports where foreign observers did not foresee our success . . ."

As it happened, Armin Hary blitzkrieged his way to gold on the anniversary of an event far more troubling than the temporary loss of prestige for the American track-and-field team. Precisely twenty-one years earlier, on September 1, 1939, Adolf Hitler had ordered his army into Poland for the start of World War II. And now, at the same hour that Soviet high jumpers outperformed the American John Thomas, Nikita Khrushchev was bringing more tension to cold war politics by declaring that he would travel to New York for the opening of the 15th General Assembly session of the United Nations. It was another aggressive move, seizing the initiative from the United States. Khrushchev's announcement provoked immediate concern in Washington. In a memorandum to President Eisenhower, Secretary of State Christian A. Herter surmised that Khrushchev, who said his aim in New York was to inspire a worldwide disarmament conference, in truth had a different goal in mind: "to turn the UN General Assembly session into a spectacular propaganda circus." The Soviet premier was to sail for America two days before the end of the Rome Olympics.

THE STORY LINE of American humiliation was too strong to let contradictory evidence intrude. Black Thursday in reality was not bleak for the U.S. in sports beyond the floodlights of track and field.

The American swimmers had their finest day at the Stadio del Nuoto. Chris von Saltza, at age sixteen the leader of the "sweethearts" from Santa Clara Swim Club, won the 400-meter freestyle, shattering the world record and at the same time gaining revenge on her friendly nemesis, Australia's Dawn Fraser, who had beaten her in the 100 but this time finished fifth. And the U.S. men won both relays. Lance Larson, swimming a strong butterfly in the third leg of the 400-meter medley, finally earned the gold medal that had been denied him unfairly in the 100 free. Most impressive was the performance of Jeff Farrell, the irrepressible Kansan who had overcome a bad shoulder injury in college and made the Olympic team by swimming in the Trials days after having his appendix removed. With the medley relay and 800 freestyle relay set only an hour and ten minutes apart, Farrell had the strength to swim the anchor leg in both, each time leading the U.S. to Olympic and world records. The medley, an Olympic event for the first time, was particularly satisfying. After Frank McKinney led off with the backstroke and Paul Hait followed with the breaststroke, Larson hit the water for the third leg holding a slim lead and widened it to 7 meters with his blistering butterfly. Then Farrell, who had failed to qualify for the 100 in the Trials, swam the fastest freestyle of the games, kicking farther and farther away from the second-place Australians and winning by seven seconds, or 15 meters.

At the Palazzetto dello Sport, the graceful little Pier Luigi Nervi–designed arena within walking distance of the Olympic Village, the U.S. basketball team spent that supposedly disastrous day trouncing Yugoslavia. The final score, 104–42, made the game look closer than it was. In the tradition of all nervous coaches, Pete Newell had worried beforehand. His squad, with Oscar Robertson, Jerry West, and Jerry Lucas leading the way, had been thrashing the opposition all week, with a scoring average of 107 points and a victory margin of 45 points in wins over Italy, Japan, and Hungary. But Newell warned his players that he had seen Yugoslavia, and they "were really good."

Terry Dischinger, the gunning forward from Purdue who was the team's fourth or fifth scoring option, poured in 12 points in the opening minutes, and the rout was on. The Yugoslavs started squabbling among themselves. Newell thought they gave up. "They knew they couldn't beat us, and they didn't care." Their indifferent play reflected an interesting political twist that Newell noticed in other Eastern bloc teams. They seemed to be saving energy for the Soviets, whom they truly despised. The score was 40–7 when the starters were pulled. Newell was an inveterate talker with an endless supply of inspirational gimmicks. During pre-Olympic training at West Point, when the team broke for lunch at an Italian restaurant, he kept punching the same song on the jukebox: Mario Lanza singing "Arrivederci Roma"—an unsubtle reminder of their mission. But now his team had played Newell into silence. "At halftime I didn't know what to say other than kind of talk about the weather or something like that," he recalled. "What can you say when you're ahead that much?" The Soviets were next, and Newell would have plenty to say about them.

Across the city, in the larger Palazzo dello Sport, an arena filled to the rafters with rabid Italian boxing fans, Cassius Clay took on the Soviet surge alone that day. His opponent in a quarterfinal bout was Gennady Shatkov, a veteran Olympian who had won a gold medal in Melbourne as a middleweight but had moved up to fight as a light heavyweight in Rome. Clay had won one bout already, stopping a muscular Belgian named Yvon Becaus with a left hook and right cross with 1:10 remaining in the second round of the three-round match. Becaus was "the strongest man I've met, but he was crude," Clay had declared afterward.

Shatkov was anything but crude. A scholar outside the ring who would go on to receive a law degree, he was a keen student of the sweet science who had fought hundreds of matches in his career and had a punch that one Soviet journalist said "you felt first and saw later." Jules Menendez of San Jose State, the U.S. Olympic boxing coach, thought Shatkov was a prime example of Soviet strengths: age and experience. In Moscow alone, Menendez told *Ring* magazine, there were six thousand amateur boxers and one hundred twenty trainers. The average age of the Russians competing in Rome was twenty-six or twenty-seven, whereas the American boys were eighteen and nineteen. Clay knew nothing about Shatkov, but the Soviets had carefully observed him. Their scouting report: "He is tall, magnificently built, moves lightly, and has an excellent sense of distance."

Although only eighteen, Clay did not lack experience. He learned how to box when he was eleven, and by the time he reached Rome, he had fought in 128 official amateur bouts, nearly half ending in knockouts. Early in his career, he exhibited an urgency to be in the spotlight that made him at once charming and irritating. Nikos Spanakos, his teammate on the Olympic team, would always remember the time he and his brother, Pete, another boxer, were getting off a plane with Clay after a Golden Gloves meet in Chicago. "As we were coming off, photographers came out to take our pictures, and Cassius actually pushed us aside and got in the middle so he could be the center of attention," Spanakos said. "That was Cassius."

Traditionalists thought his style in the ring could be obnoxious as well. On April 28, 1959, at the Pan American Games Trials at the old tan sandstone and red-roofed UW Field House in Madison, Wisconsin, Clay approached John Walsh, the University of Wisconsin's veteran coach. Clay boasted about his first match victory over Leroy Bogar of Minneapolis, during which he had danced and jabbed and at times seemed to taunt his opponent before knocking him out in 1:42 of the second round. Had Walsh seen it? Clay asked. "I couldn't stand it," Walsh replied, according to the boxing writer Jim Doherty. "I got up and left." The next day, Clay suffered a rare loss, eliminated from the Pan Am team by a tall left-handed marine named Amos Johnson. Clay, stunned, said he had a hard time figuring out the lefty. Spanakos, who was also there, recalled that Clay had eaten "six plates of spaghetti" the night before at a local restaurant, "and the guy hit him in the belly, and he didn't make it." The loss did nothing to diminish Clay's expectations. He boasted on his way out of Madison that he would make the Olympic team the next year and win a gold medal.

The Olympic Trials, a three-day tournament that began on May 19, 1960, were held at the Cow Palace in San Francisco. Scores of amateur boxers were there, champions from the army, navy, air force, marines, AAU, NCAA, and eastern and western Golden Gloves tournaments. Only ten would make it to Rome. Clay's first opponent was another tough marine, Henry Hooper, who fought him to a draw until the middle of the third round, when Clay landed a devastating right that knocked Hooper down for the ten count. In the semifinals, he beat the air force champ, Fred Lewis. Jack Fiske, the expert boxing writer for the San Francisco *Chronicle*, was ringside and noted that Clay had not endeared himself to the Cow Palace aficionados. "The crowd booed cocky Cassius Clay's clear cut decision . . ." Fiske reported. "The fans were displeased because of the eighteen-year-old high school student's clowning tactics against the wild swinging Lewis. The loser, from Phoenix, packed plenty of power and was willing enough but was no match for Clay's ramrod left jabs and right smashes to the head."

In the final against Allen Hudson, a soldier from New York City, Clay was leading early in the third round when he was floored by a wild left elbow. The referee ruled it a knockdown, infuriating Clay. He came back with two quick rights to the chin, and Hudson fell against the ropes and collapsed to the mat, spitting blood, looking dazed. Referee Vern Bybee moved in to examine Hudson, who signaled that he wanted to keep fighting. Then came another ferocious Clay right, and Bybee stopped it. Hudson could not believe the match was over, Fiske reported. He "leaped into the air in a rage and threw himself to the canvas and nearly went berserk while appealing to his corner and the referee."

Now, three and a half months later, inside the noisy arena in Rome, Clay found himself up against a fighter who in many ways was a smaller, older, Russian version of himself. Gennady Shatkov, like Clay, preferred to work at a distance, using quick, powerful jabs and fast footwork to keep opponents off balance. But precisely because he was much smaller than Clay, Shatkov was frustrated. "The main thing was that I could not find the right plan for the fight," he said later. "Clay works at the same distance in the same way as I did when I boxed at my own weight, but now, however, I had to go inside myself. That is, do exactly what Clay expected me to do." Keeping Shatkov at a distance, Clay scored with single punches, while Shatkov could not reach him.

"At the break my coach told me to work close in and attack," Shatkov recalled. " 'Easier said than done,' I thought. Fifteen centimeters height advantage certainly makes a difference." The second round went much like the first, and by the third round Shatkov realized that he would be unable to penetrate Clay's defenses and did not have the power to mount an attack. "I lost like a middleweight to an excellent light heavyweight," he said. "I shook Clay's hand. It was no disgrace to lose to a boxer like that."

Here was an athlete who seemed to have a wiser perspective on losing than most sportswriters. Shatkov's defeat was no different than John Thomas's in the high jump, or Dave Sime's and Ray Norton's in the 100-meter dash. It would be hard for outsiders to accept, but athletes understood. Usually you lose because someone else is better that day.

Interlude

DESCENDING
WITH GRATITUDE

IT could be said that Joe Faust failed at the Rome Olympics, coming up short after working toward a single moment for seven years, but his disappointment was not written into the larger drama of the U.S. men's track-and-field team on what came to be known as Black Thursday. Few had heard of Faust before or after September 1, 1960, and he was virtually invisible at the competition, withdrawing after the preliminary round in the high jump. He barely dragged his pained body over the bar at 6-4¾, then bowed out, finishing in seventeenth place, which was far worse than he might have done but better than fourteen other jumpers from Tunisia to Iceland. That is how most Olympic athletes finish, unknown and unseen, away from the glare of media hype and patriotic hope. Like any of them, Faust would have been delighted to win a gold medal at the Stadio Olimpico, but he understood that in the larger scheme of things it would not have mattered, and the scheme of things is what he was all about.

There had been a touch of fame in the family before his athletic career. His father, Louis (Bob) Faust, was an actor who played a villain in several John Wayne movies, including the 1947 *Angel and the Badman*. Bob assumed the role of bad man in the family, too, leaving his pregnant wife and seven children. Joe was five when his parents separated, and spent much of his childhood with a foster family in Culver City. He was a normal kid except in two respects: he had wondrous spring in his legs and religious curiosity in his heart. By age ten he was a precocious Catholic, searching for the spiritual essence of life.

His junior high track coach noticed Joe's exuberant bounce and quickly steered him toward the high jump. It was 1953, and together they developed an ambitious long-term plan to get to the 1960 Olympics. One out of a million chance, perhaps. "But I believed him," Faust said of his coach. "And we started working." His first jump was 3-foot-7, but by the end of that year he was at five-eight and moving higher by the week. He did the straddle jump, like most jumpers of that era, approaching the bar from a left angle and kicking up and over with his lead arm and leg. "I loved seeing the bar as I went over it," he said, something no high jumper would do in later decades after Dick Fosbury introduced the revolutionary Fosbury Flop, going over shoulders first, torso and head skyward. At fifteen Faust cleared the bar at 6-8, setting a new standard for his age group, and as he approached age seventeen he was recruited to jump at UCLA.

Faust lasted a month there, dropped out, and transferred to nearby Occidental College. He had been valedictorian of his high school class, but school now was all confusion to him. The seven-year plan to reach the Olympics still drove him, and he worked out twice a day, all the while feeling pangs of guilt about "the achievement complex." Jumping was his ambition and salvation; he infused it with religious symbolism.

Each jump had its own ritual; what he called the cycle of repair. He looked at the crossbar and saw the crucifix. As he approached, he imagined jumping into the arms of a loving God. He rose with penance, sorry for his sins, and descended with gratitude, thankful for love and forgiveness. Over and over again, penance and gratitude, sin and redemption, repairing himself inside and out, jumping a hundred times a day. It was all deeply personal and private. He never talked about it to others, never boasted that God was on his side. His heavenly thanks were not for how high he jumped, but simply for the act of jumping at all.

By July 1, 1960, Faust was exceptional enough to compete at the Olympic Trials at Stanford. Everything felt right that day. He was struck by the beautiful care with which Payton Jordan, the Stanford track coach, had prepared the stadium. The grass was a velvet cut of green, the track smooth and flawless, the takeoff area with just the right bounce, the landing pit soft and inviting. Hours before the competition, Faust went off by himself to meditate, visualizing his jumps. There were thirteen competitors, led by John Thomas, the amazing leaper from Boston U., and Charley Dumas, the defending Olympic champ. All the attention was on Thomas, as he set a new world record, but there was a lively contest for the other two Olympic slots. When the height reached 6-9, seven jumpers were still around. Faust nicked the crossbar on his first two jumps and was on the verge of elimination. "I started visualizing the prayer part," he said later of his preparations for the third try. "I dedicated the next jump to all the people who might be on crutches around the world. But it was not a trade-off with God. It was a feeling of, Why leave anyone behind?"

He cleared the bar with ease. And then 6-10, and 6-11, and finally he soared over 7 feet for the first time in his life and clinched a spot on the team.

It turned out that his father was in the stadium that day. Angel and the badman. When Joe soared over the bar at seven feet, Bob Faust rushed to the edge of the track at the north end, closest to the high-jump pit. A security officer held him back, until he shouted,

"That's my son!" Joe came over to greet him. He had never seen his dad so full of joy.

That moment, as it turned out, was the Olympic peak for jumping Joe Faust. A few days later he strained a disc in his lower back. Determined to fulfill the seven-year plan, he gutted it out at practice meets in Oregon and Switzerland, wincing in pain but showing just enough to keep his place on the team. He was still only seventeen when he reached Rome, the youngest man on the track-and-field squad, and he soaked it all in, joining the throngs who saw Pope John XXIII at the Vatican, mixing with foreign athletes, even coming to the aid of Leif Kvist, a young man from Sweden who had lost all his money and had been standing outside the gates of the village, broke and starving, until Joe brought him food from the bounteous Olympic cafeteria.

Then came the day of competition, the anticlimax, a jump of 6-4¾ and no more.

Athletes can spend the rest of their lives with regret, wondering what might have been. Joe Faust went back to California and wanted to become a Trappist monk. He fasted outside the gates of the Abbey of New Clairvaux up near Vina for three days and asked to be called Zachary, but he could not clear his mind of images of a woman he had fallen in love with and decided the monastic calling was not for him, not exactly. Over the years, he married, had children, got divorced, and struggled with questions he could not answer. He wondered what purpose God could invest in a molecule two thousand feet underground. What part did that molecule play in the scheme of life? It was a hole in his theological construct that remained unfilled for years, until it came to him that a single molecule had its own graceful movement, with its neutrons and electrons, and was connected to all other movement in the universe. "That lonely molecule is not so lonely," he decided.

Nearly a half century after his moment in Rome, Faust, in his mid-sixties, lived a monastic life alone in a cramped room in a cottage nestled on the side of a scrubby tan hill just off the 710 Freeway not far from Cal State, Los Angeles. Inside his room, he had a table, a filing cabinet (folders on new high-jump landing pit designs, trash technology, mind and spirit notes), a shelf of books (*The Joy of Mathematics, The Sistine Chapel, The Child's Creation of a Pictorial World*), another shelf of food (cereal, bananas, seven-grain bread, grapes, oranges), a small refrigerator, a sofa bed, and a computer. There were makeshift shelves and a grill out near the side door. It seemed all he needed. He was like a single molecule of Olympic history buried deep underground, alone, but still moving, and in his movement connected to everything else. Once he knew Rafer Johnson, Wilma Rudolph, Cassius Clay.

The backyard had the markings of a scavenger, a cluttered junkyard of collected planks of oak, sheets of plywood, scraps of iron, chunks of cement, bricks, stones, all arranged in a haphazard yet loving array. Down at the bottom third of the yard there was a clearing with an old mattress on the ground, and a further look showed two poles rising at either end, a bamboo crossbar nearby, and a worn path in the dirt coming from the left toward the tattered mattress. With no one watching, Joe Faust was high-jumping still, with a sore knee but bounce in his step, practicing his cycle of repair, rising with penance, clearing the crucifix, absolving his sins, descending with gratitude.

11

THE WIND
AT HER BACK

E~D TEMPLE~ was so worried about forgetting some minor detail that he barely slept at night in his dormitory room at the Olympic Village. Preparing for a race made him more anxious than the competition itself. He had ten runners in his charge, seven of them Tiger-belles, each with her own idiosyncrasies and different schedule of heats. Some coaches simply told their athletes when to show up and met them there, but Temple was not that relaxed. He waited outside the women's gate at the village every day and peppered them with questions before they boarded the shuttle bus to the event. Do you have your shoes with you? Are you wearing your USA uniform? Do you have your official number vest? Did you remember your starting blocks? On the bus to the practice area at the Stadio dei Marmi, he was still talking, usually as a diversion, except to those few who preferred silence. "Those who didn't want to talk, I wouldn't talk to because they were concentrating. Others wanted to run their mouth. People act in different ways. Then at the practice area I would stand on the field while they were warming up. I might have a conversation with them: Have you written home? Have you heard anything from home? Have you seen so-and-so? Just to get their mind off it."

Wilma Rudolph, his star sprinter, could have had several troubling things on her mind when they reached the practice field on Friday afternoon, September 2. First, there were concerns about her physical condition. During a training jog with the Tigerbelles a few days earlier, she had stepped in a sprinkling hole and twisted her left ankle. It happened during a warm down, four laps around the field at the end of practice, part of the Coach Temple routine. "She was talking and trying to jog at the same time, and wasn't looking where she was going, and she put her foot in this hole, and she fell down. We got her up and everything, and she was able to walk on one foot a little, but limping, and we got her to the trainer, and the trainer taped it and iced her down. We waited until the next morning, and it was a little sore, but she was able to run with the ankle taped up." The night before the race, Temple had taken Wilma and the Tigerbelles to watch Cassius Clay and the other American boxers compete at the Palazzo dello Sport. When her ankle seemed to be swelling again during the matches, he had made a trip to the refreshment stand and bought a Coca-Cola "just to get the ice, and sat there holding it on her ankle."

Along with lingering concern about the sore ankle, which seemed better that morning, there was the mental anguish of watching her close companion Ray Norton—billed as the next Jesse Owens—finish dead last in the men's 100 the day before, sending the American press corps to the thesaurus in search of hyperbolic Armageddon metaphors. In consoling Norton after his defeat, the "heartsick" Rudolph had vowed to win a gold medal in his honor. But would that promise burden her with too much pressure now in the final of the women's 100, not her best event? As Armin Hary had demonstrated, the start could be crucial, and with her long legs, Wilma was no better than average getting out of the blocks.

Much to worry about, but that was not her inclination. Wilma Rudolph was thriving in Rome. With her endearing smile, playful manner, and the entrancing eyes of a forest fawn, she drew men and women to her side with unadorned charm, a demeanor that an observer once called "of a natural delicacy and sweetness as true as good weather." If all the guys in the village were crazy about her, she managed to handle it without making other women jealous. It was said that if you told Wilma you liked her dress, she would give it to you then and there, even though she only had two dresses in college; the one she was wearing and the other one at the cleaners. Worldly things meant little to her, nor did prizes and fame. Her will to win came from another impulse, to prove herself worthy. Her carefree disposition made it difficult to imagine the trauma she had endured in the first twenty years of her life.

As a child, Wilma was underweight and sickly, and also special and spoiled—not an easy circumstance in the boisterous family of railroad man Ed Rudolph and his wife, Blanche, who together brought home less than $2,500 year and lived without indoor plumbing in a dusty red-frame house at 644 Kellogg Street in Clarksville. The neighborhood was poor and black, tucked into the undulating hills up Kraft Street from the Red River on the back edge of then all-white Austin Peay State University. The Rudolphs had twenty-two children between them, although only eight together and rarely more than that number living with them at one time. Wilma was the fifth of the final group of eight. Her siblings, competing for attention in the cacophony of the overstretched household, did not begrudge her the time and care she needed, though they groused that she never had to do the dishes and teased her for being a crybaby.

During the worst years of Wilma's childhood infirmity, they took turns carrying her from room to room. They massaged her polio-crippled left leg four times a day and were part of the troupe accompanying her down to Meharry Medical College in Nashville, the nation's leading training hospital for black physicians, for heat and water therapy on the one day a week that their mother, a maid, did not have to work in the large homes on the white side of town. "The trips to Nashville, we would always go to the Greyhound bus station and get on this huge, big bus, and it seemed like such a long ride to Nashville because of all the stops in between," recalled Yvonne Rudolph, her older sister. "We would get to the hospital, and it seemed like a huge building, so different from anything in Clarksville. Wilma was shy, and sometimes she would just cry because she didn't like it at all. But we kept telling her that it would make her better and she would feel better, and she would not always have to wear the brace. I think that's what really kept her going, because she knew one day she would not have to wear it."

As Wilma later described her early childhood, she was depressed and lonely at first, especially when she had to watch her brothers and sisters run off to school while she stayed home, burdened with the dead weight of the heavy braces. She felt rejected, she said, and would close her eyes "and just drift off into a sinking feeling, going down, down, down." Soon her loneliness turned to anger. She hated the fact that her peers always teased her. She didn't like any of her supposed friends. She wondered whether living just meant being sick all the time, and told herself it had to be more than that, and she started fighting back, determined to beat the illness.

By age eight she would ditch her leg braces when her parents were not looking, but she was still the last kid chosen in outdoor games, which amounted to the Rudolph brood's version of the Olympics: who could jump the highest, run the fastest, throw the farthest. Then one day her father, who did the shopping in the family, came home with regular shoes for Wilma, marking a dramatic change in her life. As Yvonne remembered the scene: "They were no longer the high-top shoes that she had to have with the braces. And my mother took her into a room all by herself; she didn't even let us know she had these shoes. And they put them on her, and she came out of the room, and she was beaming all over. It was like she was a whole new little girl. And after that it was like she knew she was no different, and it gave her more confidence at that point." On special days, the Rudolph girls would be expected to deliver speeches at their church. It was Wilma's turn soon after she got her new shoes. "And when she got up, you didn't hear her braces," Yvonne said. "And she went up on stage, and she said her speech very loud and very proud, and she took a bow. And everybody in the church cheered for her. And she was just very, very happy."

It was around that time that her brother Westley put up a peach basket in the backyard, and Wilma, without braces and barefoot, began to play ball with him. She seemed obsessed with the sport, her mother thought, as though she were making up for lost time. She would shoot baskets soon after she awoke in the morning and before she was called in for dinner at night. Within a few years she was playing for Coach Clinton C. Gray's squad at Burt High. That is where Ed Temple, who also moonlighted as a high school basketball referee, first spotted her. He was so struck by the way this freshman phenom, the lanky girl nicknamed Skeeter, breezed down the court on the fast break that he invited her to attend his track camp at Tennessee State in the summer of 1955.

She almost gave up at first. Temple's boot-camp training regimen, including daily three-mile and one-mile cross-country runs through the potholed and snake-infested pastures next to the college farm, discouraged her, but even more she felt outclassed by the older Tigerbelles, who consistently drubbed her in the sprints. But Temple saw something. Greatness was what he wanted for his girls, but it was the one thing he couldn't teach. He believed you were born with it. He couldn't make you run fast. What he could do was help you run faster. "Stretch out!" he would yell at Wilma. "Stop digging postholes! Stop pounding. Stride! No clenched fists! Open palms!" She stuck with it, and by the next fall, barely sixteen, she was running a leg with the Tigerbelles on the bronze-winning relay team in Melbourne.

Heriwentha (Mae) Faggs, the first of Temple's great Tigerbelles, was eight years older than Wilma and served as her big sister during those early days in track. They were opposites in many ways: Faggs was loud and fiery, a confident woman from Bayside, Queens, who barely stood five feet; Wilma was a shy country girl who towered nearly a foot above her mentor. But Faggs fully empathized with the teenager's situation. She had been only sixteen herself at the 1948 Olympics in London. Now she was so protective of the other Tigerbelles that they called her Mother Mae. "Skeeter, you do everything I do. Mae will take care of you," Faggs told her when she joined the relay team. Rudolph readily agreed and followed Faggs around, copying her every move. When it came time to run the 200-meter final at the 1956 Olympic Trials, Faggs instructed her, "We'll run around the turn, and by the time we get off the turn, we'll start kicking. I'm gonna holler, you hear?" "All right, Mae," Rudolph responded. In an oral history, Faggs recalled what happened next:

"Just like I said, because she was just a lane over from me, I turned my head to say, 'Come on, Skeeter.' And she said, 'OK, Mae, I'm coming.' We were coming down the straightaway when I turned my head back, but Skeeter was about a stride in *front* of me. She looked, and it shocked her so, she slowed down. I said, 'Oh, buddy, you did the wrong thing. Never slow down for Mae.' I kicked off. After the race, I told her, 'I said do everything I do, but I didn't tell you to beat me!' "

When the Tigerbelles returned from Australia with bronze medals, a young reporter for the Nashville *Tennessean* named David Halberstam was assigned to write a feature story about them. The Melbourne Olympics represented an end and a beginning: the last race in the fine career of Faggs, and a promising debut for the high school phenom Rudolph, who had run the crucial third leg. Halberstam, only twenty-two himself, was of their generation, and track had been his best sport at Roosevelt High in Yonkers, New York. A young writer of great enthusiasms, he was thrilled by the opportunity to talk to the local Olympians and recount their story. For the rest of his life, he could remember driving over to the Tennessee State campus and meeting Coach Temple and the Tigerbelles, but what would stick most clearly in his mind was an unsettling exchange after he returned to the newsroom. Born and reared in the Northeast, barely a year out of editing the *Harvard Crimson,* Halberstam was still discovering the racist assumptions embedded deep into the cultural geology of the South. He considered the *Tennessean* a progressive paper, mostly on the good side of the civil rights struggle, yet here was a veteran desk editor scratching a word out of his copy. Halberstam had called the college runners "coeds." Years later, some women might object to the word for sounding sexist, but in this time and place the editor had a different problem. *Coeds* is a term reserved for white girls, Halberstam was told. "You can't call these colored girls coeds."

For the next year, Wilma was the most famous student at Burt High: world-class sprinter and star basketball player on one of the fastest, highest-scoring teams in Tennessee. As a junior, Skeeter led her team to the State Negro Basketball Tournament in Nashville, averaging more than thirty-two points a game, and gained renown for her furious fast breaks and unblockable hook shot. In her senior year, she and her boyfriend, Robert Eldridge, discovered that she was pregnant. "I was mortified," she said later. "Pregnant? I couldn't understand it. Robert and I had just started to get involved in sex, and here I was pregnant. We were both innocent about sex, didn't know anything about birth control or about contraceptives." Coach Temple feared that her running career might be over prematurely. He thought it would be difficult for her to recover from the harsh disapproval of her community. "She was a hero with them, and when they found out she was pregnant, they just said, 'Well, she done threw away all of her opportunity.' And everyone knew that I had a rule then that we didn't want any expectant mothers, or didn't want any runners with children. This was the fifties, and times were different then. She graduated and was expecting, and walked across the stage six or seven months pregnant and got her diploma."

Later that summer, after spending a day with Wilma and her parents in Clarksville, Temple realized that her determination was stronger than his no-babies rule. Polio, racism, teenage mother-hood—no single obstacle could stop her. "She wanted to prove to the community that she didn't let them down, and I think that's what gave her the extra push, the extra determination to want to win."

Now, on this Friday afternoon two years later in Rome, her moment of proof neared. It was time to enter the Stadio Olimpico for the finals of the 100-meter dash. Temple was so nervous that he was "about to climb the fence." Then he looked across the stadium's training room to the rubdown table. What worries? Most of his runners were "really fidgety" in that situation, but not Wilma. She had fallen fast asleep.

UNTIL WILMA RUDOLPH awoke from her nap, the Olympic talk all day had been about the hell of the afternoon before. Arthur Daley had descended into the underworld of Dante's "Inferno" to describe the "Stygian gloom" of America's loss for readers in the *New York Times.* It seemed that "ancient Roman gods had reached through the centuries to deliver a hex on the barbarians from across the sea." Or maybe there was a baser explanation, one more commonplace in accounts of the fall of man. Could it all be explained by the banner on the front page of the *Detroit Times?*

"Wine, Women Blamed for U.S. Olympic Flop" ran the headline over a UPI dispatch containing all the essential ingredients of Olympian melodrama. First the writer dredged up the "wine, women, and song" trope, then he combined it mixed-metaphorically with a reference to "yesterday's Pearl Harbor performance by the U.S. team." Next he rounded up an unidentified U.S. official to squeal on the off-field behavior of the losing athletes. "The boys have been living it up too high," said the official. "Just the other night I got back to the village at two in the morning. A taxi with about six members of the track team came in right behind me." And as a clincher, the nightlife of the carousing Americans was set in stark contrast with the training propriety of the otherwise evil Soviets: "You can't catch any Russians out dancing after ten!" the official harrumphed.

As odds-on favorites who lost badly, Ray Norton and John Thomas were the main targets of criticism. Both found the charges ridiculous. "I've been going to bed early—too early," Norton said. "Anyone who says I've been staying out late is a big liar." His coach, Bud Winter, slept down the hall in the men's dorm, he added. "The coach says good night to me every night. They're trying to make excuses for my bad time yesterday, and that is no excuse." For his part, Thomas, who had been accused of "spending too much time on Rome's glittering Via Veneto, the street of a thousand tables and gaiety," said that most of his visits there were with his parents and younger sister and brother, who were enjoying their first trip abroad. "I was all eyes; I never got tired," Thomas said later, adding that his parents got him back to his dorm even earlier than the Russians. There was plenty of horsing around, but nothing unusual for robust athletes buzzing with sexual energy. The dance floor at the village was always hopping. Lance Larson and a few swimming pals borrowed a pack of village motorbikes for a few hours to tool around the ancient piazzas, young women clinging to their backs. And as it turned out, a taxi stuffed with frolicking Americans had indeed pulled up to the village gates at two one morning, but its occupants included shot-putters who had already competed and some discus men and pole-vaulters whose events were still days away. As for wine, the alcohol consumption of journalists and Olympic officials was oceanic compared to the small pond of furtive drinking among some athletes.

There was something about Thomas's personality, the way he

reacted to loss, that played into the frustrations of those journalists and officials who expected him to win. They wanted him to be angry and expressive, to show some fight in his battle with the Soviets. Instead he reacted like it was just another day, no big deal. As he explained later, his thinking was, he missed the jump, what else was there to say? "It was not like the world was going to end and everything come crashing down. Either you make it or you don't." But after he missed, he could sense immediately that people looked at him differently. He thought they were projecting and fantasizing about how they would feel in that situation, and wanted him to feel the same way. "All the stories the reporters wrote were concocted by them. It had nothing to do with me," he said. He sensed their aggression, sometimes bordering on hostility. What happened? Were you partying too much on the Via Veneto? Were you wearing the wrong shoes? Were you not getting enough sleep? They had to have explanations. And the intensity was only greater because he had lost to the Russians.

Even the Soviet press seemed to be piling on. Two radio commentators from Moscow and a correspondent from *Pravda* tracked down Thomas near his dorm room in the village that Friday afternoon.

"Tell us about yesterday," one of them began.

"What do you want me to say?" he answered.

"What do you think of the Russian jumpers?"

"I think anyone who jumps seven feet is good."

When the Soviets turned to leave, Eddy Gilmore of the Associated Press followed them. The Olympic competition was as much mental as physical, they told him, and Thomas was the victim of a psychological defeat. They were laughing when they said it.

As much as Thomas tried to convince himself that it was over and he could move on, he started to discover on the first day after Black Thursday that his image was forever stuck in the floodlights of the high-jump pit at the moment he failed to clear 7-1. *The important thing in the Olympics is not winning, but taking part; the essential thing in life is not conquering but fighting well.* That was the creation myth of the modern Games, the Olympic Creed that founder Pierre de Coubertin first uttered in 1908. In his own phlegmatic way, Thomas tried to live by those words, but the outside world would not let him, especially in the vitriolic context of the cold war. It was much easier to enjoy the taking part and to endure the losing with no one paying attention, without expectations, like his high-jump teammate Joe Faust. For the great John Thomas, though, what followed were days of questions, years of hate mail, constant reminders that he had lost— and a persistent nagging feeling that life would have been so much easier with a gold medal in Rome.

Winning, rather than just taking part, was by no means only an American obsession. Word also spread that Friday about a Greco-Roman wrestler from Bulgaria who threw a match to help a Russian win the gold medal. The gesture of Iron Curtain submissiveness happened amid the glorious fourth-century ruins of the Basilica di Massenzio, which the Italian hosts had ingeniously transformed into a three-mat wrestling venue, replete with floodlights, outdoor grandstands, and a row of twenty telephone booths for deadline journalists. Late in a semifinal match between Dimitro Stoyanov of Bulgaria and Avtandil Koridze of the Soviet Union, with the score tied and both wrestlers facing elimination from gold medal contention if it ended in a draw, Stoyanov suddenly seemed to lose his fighting will. His dive allowed Koridze to win and kept the gold medal away from Branislav Martinovic of Yugoslavia. Almost alone among Eastern Europeans, the Bulgarians were thought to be loyal to the Soviets to the point of athletic obedience. Yugoslavia and Hungary, by contrast, took pride in beating the Big Reds. Only four years earlier, at the 1956 Melbourne Games, Hungary defeated the USSR 4-0 in water polo just after the Soviets had crushed the Hungarian revolution. That confrontation was the stuff of legend, contested with such ferocity that it became known thereafter as the "Blood in the Water" match.

The Russians now denied a wrestling fix. "Any such suspicion is completely unfounded," declared their Olympic spokesman, Nikolai Lubomirov. But René Coulon of France, the president of the International Wrestling Association, had little doubt about what had occurred. "I was personally at the match when the two men were wrestling. They fought magnificently for eleven minutes. Then I saw the Bulgarian take a look at the clock. A few seconds later he let himself fall on his back. I immediately stopped the match and had the international technical committee meet on the case. They decided to disqualify the Bulgarian and give one penalty point to the Russian." They could not disqualify the Russian, who went on to win gold, Coulon said, because they could not prove that the Soviets were complicit in the scheme. Emrc Vehei, a Turkish wrestling official, agreed, though he believed the Russians were in on it. "This is a real slap in the face of true sportsmanship," he said. "Nobody can be absolutely sure, but our past experience has taught us that the Bulgarians and Russians have performed such things in past international matches."

The Olympic spirit was also under assault in the boxing world that Friday. Loud protests night after night from a few countries—especially Great Britain, which thought it had unfairly lost several bouts—finally prompted the International Amateur Boxing Association to announce the sacking of fifteen Olympic judges for incompetence. The Brits had threatened to pull their boxers unless action was taken. In a peculiarly Italian compromise, the fired officials were allowed to stay on the scene, to avoid embarrassment, but would not work. The ring controversy was of great interest to A. J. Liebling, a boxing expert whose *New Yorker* essays on the sport had been collected in his legendary 1956 book, *The Sweet Science*. From Liebling's perspective, while the Brits and Americans had complaints, the real victims were boxers from Asia and Africa. "Olympic referees form a solid European Bund, accustomed to officiating in each other's countries and to doing favors for each other's nationals in trouble," he wrote from Rome. "They are solemn, histrionic gentlemen who constantly interfere with the boxers, and the new 'wild men' (from third world), having no referees of their own in the combine, constantly get the worst of it. These unfortunates are in the position of politicians who want patronage but have no votes to trade."

Collusion among Olympic boxing officials was nothing new. None other than Avery Brundage himself, when he headed the American Olympic Committee in 1936, sent a post-Olympic report to the IOC in Lausanne lambasting the officiating in Berlin. Even Brundage's antipathy toward American factions that had urged the U.S. to boycott the Olympics in Nazi Germany that year, and even his belief that America could learn a thing or two from Hitler, in this instance could not repress a complaint about inequities in the boxing ring. "No set of officials could have been as ignorant of boxing and boxing rules as the decisions indicated. Collusion, therefore, must be the interpretation of such ghastly decisions," his report asserted. Four days into the boxing competition that year, the Brits and Americans were so upset they threatened to withdraw. But they kept boxing, "and both lived to regret it," the report stated. "Great Britain and the U.S., the world's oldest boxing nations, failed to win a single gold medal between them, while Germany had four boxers in the finals, twice as many as any other nation . . . We doubt any of the four would have reached the semis had the bouts been held in any other country."

Once again, the Germans. But in Rome on this Friday, the day after rhythmic shouts of *"Hah-ree! Hah-ree! Hah-ree!"* echoed throughout the Stadio Olimpico, there was one small gesture of atonement connecting 1936 and 1960. At the request of Gerhard Stoeck, chief of mission of the German team, Hary sought out Jesse Owens and apologized for declining to visit with him before the 100-meter dash. "We thought he should go see Owens," Stoeck explained. "The incident had given the boy a black eye, so we asked him to make the visit, and he agreed. He is a strange boy sometimes." Strange he could be, yet Hary was now the rage of Germany after defeating the Americans. "Everybody asks for Hary," wrote a columnist in *Die*

Welt. "Hary occupies everybody's mind. Hary dominates every con-versation. Hary came out of each telephone receiver. Hary on the subway. Hary in the office. Hary on the screen. Hary in the kitchen. Hary, Hary, above all."

Tipped off beforehand, American photographers and writers were waiting at the U.S. sector of the village when Hary approached with a bustling retinue of Germans. Hary and Owens shook hands and exchanged pleasantries with the help of an interpreter. The young champ noticed a pack of cigarettes in the old champ's shirt pocket. "You smoke? That's no good. No good!" Hary said. "I'm old now. It's all right," Owens responded. He asked the interpreter to tell Hary that he was a great champion with a wonderful start. Then, in street clothes, on a patch of grass outside the men's dorm, the Ameri-can and the German dropped into the sprinter's stance, right knee touching, knuckles down. Ready, set—but no gun, only the click and whir of cameras.

WILMA RUDOLPH was just waking from her afternoon nap when the American comeback began on the Stadio Olimpico track. It came, appropriately, in a demanding event, the 400-meter hurdles, and leading the way was one of the most respected yet least celebrated athletes on the U.S. squad, Glenn Davis. For journalists and sports fans who took an interest in track and field only once every four years because of the Olympics, Glenn Davis was far down the list of celeb-rity attractions, but to track nuts like the Nelson brothers of *Track & Field News* and teammates like Rafer Johnson, he was up near the top. Davis was a winner, he just rarely talked about it. He had won the gold medal in the 400 hurdles at Melbourne. In 1958, when he received the James E. Sullivan Award as the best amateur athlete in the U.S., he had won the NCAA finals and then gone on to defeat the Russians at the tense dual track meet in Moscow. Yet his finest per-formance, he would insist, came at none of those high-profile venues but at a meet in Stockholm where he had swept four competitions: the 400, the 400 hurdles, the 100, and the 200, running world-class times in all of them.

It was that versatility, and his relentlessness, that made Davis like a brother to the decathlete Rafer Johnson, who worked out with him often in Rome as they prepared for their separate events. "Glenn Davis turned out to be one of my best friends" on the team, Johnson said later. "He was tough as nails. One of the toughest athletes I'd ever been around. I worked out with him, and he was a load to keep up with. He would run these repeat two-twenties or three-thirties or quarter miles, again and again. He would run you into the ground." The friendship of the white runner from Ohio State and the black decathlete from UCLA extended beyond the track. "We had a lot of common interests. I really got to know him," Davis recalled. "We ran around together and talked about poetry. I liked to read poetry, and he wrote his own." The connection is what counted, Johnson said later, not the poetry, which was forgettable. "We made it up. We made this stuff up. I never wrote anything down. It was about where we were and what we were doing and who said what. We had rap before rap was here."

Like Johnson, and also much like Dave Sime, Glenn Davis's future in track seemed uncertain a year before Rome. Slowed by the recurrence of an old football injury, his conditioning suffered, and so did his nerves. There was a brief period when every hurdle seemed insurmountable. But like Johnson and Sime, he persevered. His speed returned just in time for the Olympics, along with his supreme confidence. He was the world's leading student of his event, breaking it into segments and knowing the maximum speed of his opponents for each segment and precisely how fast he had to run to win. No one could beat him, he said—and no one did.

In the 400 hurdles, a runner must push himself at sprinter speed for about as long as the human body can endure, all the while clearing ten intermediate hurdles three feet high and spaced 35 meters apart. It requires a unique combination of speed, stamina, and timing. At the final in Rome, Davis cleared the first hurdle smoothly, but he bumped the second and fell off-stride, disturbing his timing all the way through the sixth hurdle. He was near the rear of the six runners then—"running scared," he would later say—but regained form over the seventh hurdle, closed the gap, and burst into the lead in the final straightaway before throwing himself across the finish line and spilling onto the track. Not only did Davis win another gold with a time of 49.3 seconds, but he led an American sweep, with teammates Cliff Cushman and Dick Howard winning silver and bronze.

At the awards ceremony, the medals were placed around the necks of the three Yanks by a distinguished British gentleman of late middle age who walked with a stoop as he approached the podium. It was Lord David Burghley, the sixth Marquess of Exeter, vice president of the IOC, and winner of this very event at the 1928 Olympics in Amsterdam. Red Smith watched from the press section as "the self-possessed Davis, Olympic and world champion, bent low to let England's old Olympian hang the gold medal around his neck, waved to the crowd, grabbed Lord David's elbow with a companionable clutch, and shook hands. Cushman grinned like a blond billiken getting his silver bauble. Hands folded in prayer, Howard bowed his neck as though for the guillotine."

Many members of the press held a fondness for the marquess, extolling his athletic grit, sense of humor, and belief in fair play. They recalled the time he finished second in a U.S. race but adamantly refused first prize when the winner was disqualified on a technicality, saying that he would have none of it and that he was beaten by a better hurdler. When asked once why someone of his refinement would concentrate on such a demanding event as the 400 hurdles, his Lordship smiled and said, "I won the bloody race at the Penn Relays one year, and from then on I was stuck with it." In his upper-class way, he was a full-effort man—without his work, the Olympics would not have been in war-ravaged London in 1948—who carried himself with a classic air of self-importance softened by self-deprecation. In a letter to a friend in the IOC revealing his elevation to marquess in 1956, he had written: "My father has unfortunately died during the past few days, and as a result I now become the Marquess of Exeter. I shudder to think of the effect of this in the sphere of international sport. I can see a long vista of suspicious enquiries as to who the devil this chap 'Exeter' is, and when they hear the answer I am quite certain they won't believe it. However, rather like a pet dog who answers to 'You b——!' I shall also answer to either Burghley or Exeter!"

It seemed fitting that the old Olympian, answering the call in Rome, had been bathed in warm applause as he approached the podium to bemedal the American hurdlers. Good feeling all around, except for one observer who took in the scene with some measure of consternation: the conspiracy-minded Frenchy Grombach.

When not extolling the virtues of his favorite sports, fencing, the modern pentathlon, and boxing, Grombach had been using his column in the *Rome Daily American*—a two-week sinecure secured for him by friends in the CIA—to attack Lord Burghley for his role in forcing Taiwan to compete as Taiwan or Formosa rather than the Republic of China. The former State Department spy had become obsessed with Burghley, convinced that the old Tory was in league with the Red Chinese. An inveterate spook in a city now crawling with them, he spent his Roman evenings trawling hotel bars and cocktail hours trying to haul in fresh gossip on the marquess. It was Grombach's nature to insert himself into any situation where he saw red. Earlier in 1960, he had been on the case of Yves Montand and Simone Signoret, the French acting couple with leftist political beliefs who had applied for admission into the U.S. so that Signoret could pick up her Academy Award for best actress in the film *Room at the Top*. In a letter to the U.S. embassy in Paris, Grombach had warned: "Some individuals may mistakenly believe that leniency toward people like Montand will improve our relationship with France and win friends for the USA, but any weakening of this nature will be more harmful than advantageous."

Grombach wanted no weakening with the Marquess of Exeter, either, though he seemed darkly pleased to note that the slouched figure down there awarding the medals was "badly crippled with arthritis and needs a cane to get around."

As Lord Burghley hobbled away, the long-jump final was nearing an end at the far side of the stadium. The preliminaries had started early that morning, with the stands barely a third full, and by late afternoon the unwieldy forty-nine-man field had been culled down to the final efforts of Ralph Boston and Bo Roberson of the U.S., Manfred Steinbach of Germany, and Igor Ter-Ovanesyan of the Soviet Union. In the now-crowded stadium sat Jesse Owens, looking cool in a yellow short-sleeve polo shirt and racing cap, and besieged by autograph hounds, who had also surrounded crooner Bing Crosby, seated nearby. Even as he signed his name, Owens kept his eyes focused on the jumpers. Of all the Olympic track-and-field records, his broad-jump mark set at the 1936 Berlin Games had endured the longest. As he approached his forty-seventh birthday in Rome, Owens said he felt "like a father who has come back to watch his successful children."

In the family of athletes, Ralph Boston was like the big brother of Wilma Rudolph and her teammates, the lone male Olympian from Tennessee State. He played cards with the Tigerbelles, teased them, worked out with them, and rooted for them. Coming out of the rural South, reared in the lumber mill town of Laurel in southeast Mississippi as the youngest of ten siblings, Boston taught himself long-jump techniques by studying films of the 1956 Olympic champ, mimicking the way Greg Bell kicked into the air and jackknifed his legs before bringing them close together at the finish. His first desire was to be a decathlete like Rafer Johnson, but at 164 pounds he lacked the upper-body strength for the weight events. Going into 1960, his aim was simply to make the U.S. Olympic team in the long jump, but now he was the favorite. With a stunning leap of 26 feet 11 inches at a warm-up meet in California earlier that summer, he had already broken Owens's world record, and now he was expected to set the Olympic record as well. But going into his last jump, Boston was not even certain of winning a medal. Overcome by nerves, he had to find an official to escort him back to the bathroom under the stands.

Returning to the infield, he took his position at the end of the runway, 100 feet from the takeoff point. He had already fixed his spots precisely with the steel tape measure. One deep breath, relax, four loping strides—free and loose to unlimber his body—and then he was at full speed, trying to clear his head of all but a few key thoughts. First the starting mark. He had to spring into the air as close as possible behind it, but not go over into the narrow putty forestrip and get disqualified. Speeding down the runway for this final jump in Rome, he felt something slightly amiss and had to adjust his stride just before takeoff. Once airborne, he tried to concentrate on bringing his feet back within 10 or 12 inches of each other for the landing. Not perfect—he knew he could do better—but when officials marked his distance at 26 feet 7¾ inches, Boston had seized the Olympic record. Even then, a medal was not assured, with three rivals still to go.

Next came Ter-Ovanesyan the jazz-loving, Voice of America–listening newfound friend of Dave Sime, who had grown up in Kiev worshiping Jesse Owens. When Igor was an eighteen-year-old at Melbourne and again in the dual meet with the U.S. in Moscow in 1958, he had inwardly feared the American athletes and did not believe he could beat them. In Rome he was still not sure that he was better than Boston and Roberson, but he no longer viewed them as invincible. One day shortly after arriving in the village, he had visited the U.S. compound and happened to be weighing himself on a scale in the landing just as Boston was coming down the stairs. "Hello, Ralph, I'm Igor," he said. Boston's reaction was: Who is this guy? He vaguely knew the name, not the face, but thought Ter-Ovanesyan must be nice if he knew English. Igor sensed the beginning of a rivalry. He thought they acted "like two dogs walking around sniffing each other."

In his dreams, Ter-Ovanesyan sometimes found himself flying. It was such a pleasant feeling, he thought, floating lightly above the ground. He tried to re-create that feeling in the long jump, but knew that if he put together all the jumps of his life, his total time in the air would be only a minute or two. Broad jumping was not so much pleasant as strenuous. He thought it was "like you are stuffed in a cannon and pushed and fly forward with a lot of force. The sense of flying comes only in dreams. It is just a slow gliding in dreams, but in reality it is a tough push kind of feeling."

His father, Aram Aveticiovich Ter-Ovanesyan, a professor of sports theory in Kiev, had made it to Rome for the Games and was there to watch as Igor flew down the runway and into the air on his final jump, landing at 26 feet 4½ inches. It was just short of Boston, but moved him ahead of the others. Manfred Steinbach, a sprinter and long jumper who had fled from East Germany to West Germany only a year earlier, went next and also surpassed 26 feet, but he was marked a few inches short of Ter-Ovanesyan.

All that remained was the final jump of Bo Roberson. The all-sports star from Cornell was "dead tired." He had not been able to practice much since hurting a leg earlier in the summer, but this was his last chance, and the other jumpers knew that he was a fearless competitor. "Continental sports crowds have a way of sensing moments of drama en masse, and now the thousands in the seats by the long jump hushed each other into stillness," British journalist Neil Allen wrote in his diary. "The muscular Roberson stood at the beginning of the runway, looking at the cinder path he would have to travel. His dark face was impassive, but I wondered at that moment if he thought with a sudden disquiet of the serious hamstring injury which caused his left leg to be bandaged. Suddenly he crouched and then sprinted for the board that would relieve him of this unbearable tension. He hit it sweetly, rose high, and then landed in a shower of sand."

Boston stood nearby. Had gold been snatched from him at the last minute? "My heart was really pounding as they measured that last jump of Roberson's," he said later. The electronic scoreboard put up the distance: 26-7¼. Boston had won by a half inch. Silver for Roberson, bronze for Ter-Ovanesyan. In the stands, Jesse Owens felt only a twinge of disappointment about losing his record, then consoled himself by saying that these were his boys, Boston and Roberson, and they carried on his tradition. Ter-Ovanesyan felt badly only for a moment, too, then was overwhelmed by a new sense of confidence. He had jumped within inches of the Americans, and someday soon, he felt, he would fly past them. Down in Laurel, Mississippi, Boston's mother broke into tears when told by a local reporter that her son had won gold in Rome. She was so excited that she had to sit down and drink a glass of milk. "I didn't have any idea that my baby's jumping around would ever amount to anything," Eulalia Boston said.

Inside the Stadio Olimpico, for a fleeting moment, Boston looked across the infield and caught the eye of Wilma Rudolph. Quite a day for little Tennessee State.

Only twenty minutes earlier, Rudolph had been awakened by the sound of Coach Temple's voice. "Time to wake up, Wilma. Time to run! Time to run!" She got up, yawned, and said "OK, I'm ready," and slowly put on her shoes, taking her time as though nothing in the world awaited her. Finally she grabbed her starting blocks and strolled outside. No one should ever be in a hurry, Wilma thought, unless they hear the gun, and the footrace is on. Now here she was, preparing for the 100, No. 17 on her back. From a distance, she seemed all legs and hips in her uniform of short white shorts and blue shirt with red trim. She was the only American in the final six. The defending champion, Betty Cuthbert of Australia, had pulled up lame in the preliminaries, but Rudolph still had to beat Maria It-kina of the Soviet Union, Giuseppina Leone of Italy, Dorothy Hy-man and Jennifer Smart of Great Britain, and Catherine Capdevielle of France.

From his vantage point at the opening of the tunnel, Temple could see only part of the track—the starting blocks and about the first thirty meters. Just get on the stand, he said to himself as Rudolph unlimbered in Lane 3. Just get up there on the stand.

Aposti. Via. And the gun. She started slowly. At 30 meters, when she disappeared from Temple's view, he wasn't sure but had a good feeling. At the halfway point, Fred Russell, the hometown colum-nist, noticed that Wilma was breaking free with "her long stride and blazing speed." Red Smith scribbled "leggy doll" and "syrupy stride." No one ran quite like the high-waisted Skeeter: loose, light, with beautiful form. She broke the tape a full three strides and three-tenths of a second ahead of Hyman, who finished second, and Leone, a close third. As Rudolph slowed down past the finish, the slightest remnant of a limp was evident from the twisted ankle. She stopped abruptly, turned around, and walked back toward the start, hands on hips, catching her breath, as Hyman and Leone rushed over for quick congratulations.

"Wilma won! Wilma won!" someone shouted to Temple in the tunnel. "You're joking," he said. Then he stepped into the golden late afternoon sunlight, and "they flashed it on the big scoreboard and put the time, the new Olympic record, 'Wilma Rudolph USA,' and I said, 'Hot Dog!'"

The time was 11 flat, the fastest ever, crushing Cuthbert's 11.4 in Melbourne and her own 11.3 in the Rome semifinals. It would have been a world and Olympic record, but there was too much wind pushing her for the record to count, officials said. The breeze was blowing at 4.75 miles per hour, exceeding the allowable 4.473. Half-way down the track on her return to the starting blocks, she began running again, a happy lope. She jumped into the arms of Earlene

Brown, the dancing shot-putter (between throws of her competition, on the way to winning a bronze), then found a spot on a bench in the shade to rest and soak it in. Her teammate Barbara Jones, who had been eliminated by a narrow margin in the semifinals, came over with a brush and comb and helped Wilma compose herself. Foxes not oxes.

Out came Avery Brundage, with his gray suit and wet lips, for the medals ceremony. With a single long step, the champion Tigerbelle climbed from behind the podium to stand on the top rung. Wearing her blue sweat suit and holding a straw USA hat, she bowed to receive the gold medal. The crowd was hers, roaring. The American flag rose high, the "Star-Spangled Banner" played, and Wilma Rudolph waved, stepped off the podium, and ran away, her medal bouncing against her chest, the wind gently blowing in her face.

12

LIBERATION

WHAT a *bella festa* the Rome Olympics are, thought Gian Paolo Ormezzano, the young journalist covering his first Games for *Tuttosport*. There was work to be done, but in the atmosphere of a wonderful party. The city was sultry and enchanting. The organizing committee was so efficient that even the Germans could not complain. Despite the political tensions of the cold war, there seemed to be a prevailing spirit of hope and freedom. Venues were accessible, athletes approachable, restaurants and bars abundant, stories everywhere. Each day seemed an affirmation to Ormezzano that the people of the world could coexist: Americans and Soviets, East Germans and West Germans, Indians and Pakistanis. Conflict outside the Olympic bubble might appear irresolvable, but here he even saw Israeli and Arab athletes walking arm in arm. One day he pursued a report that a woman police officer had been attacked in the male section of the Olympic Village, but it proved to be unsubstantiated rumor. Aside from the usual complaints about biased judges, the biggest misunderstanding he witnessed was when a well-known Norwegian journalist got so drunk that he cabled his article to the wrong newspaper, which recognized his famous byline and puckishly published his dispatch on its front page.

Ormezzano's assignment was to cover the swimming competition, but on the Saturday afternoon of September 3 he took a seat in the Stadio Olimpico to watch the final of the men's 200-meter dash. A field of seventy-one runners had been narrowed to six, and the surviving runner who drew him to the event was Livio Berruti, a fellow Italian and close family friend from Torino who had attended the same school and was in his brother's class.

Berruti was another of those Olympians like Wilma Rudolph, Peter Radford, and Frank Budd who underwent the metamorphosis from sickly child to world-class sprinter. It was not polio in his case, but severe allergies and bronchitis. Now he was the Torino Express, a tall, pale, strong-legged twenty-one-year-old whose image was already familiar at the Olympics and worldwide, largely due to an unforgettable wirephoto that ran in hundreds of newspapers showing him rounding the curve in a preliminary heat just as a pigeon took flight a yard away on the inside lane. A few pigeons had been loitering around the stadium for more than a week, since their release at the Opening Ceremony. "It was an unusual photo," British writer Neil Allen jotted down in his diary, "but the flutter of the gentle bird's wings and the silken stride of the sprinter go together. Grace, swiftness, fluency are words that I find synonymous with Berruti."

There was one other thing about Berruti that made him stand out: he ran in sunglasses. Decades later, shades would become the trademark of sprinter cool (as well as a form of profitable sponsorship), but Berruti was ahead of his time. And though he looked jazzy, that is not why he wore them. He wore glasses—regular indoors, tinted in the sun—because he needed them. Without them he was so shortsighted that he could see neither other runners nor the finish line. The sunglasses he brought to the track were the ones he wore every day, "nothing special for competing," he later explained.

Nearly an hour before the 200 final, the other five sprinters arrived at the track to warm up, but Berruti stayed behind in the cool of the dressing room. He had run the best race of his life in the semifinals earlier that day, recording such a fast time that he became concerned about exhausting his energy and good karma. Alone and out of the heat, he made a point of "doing nothing" for a half hour, before finally emerging to hammer in his blocks and practice his starts. In the minutes just before the race, the air around the track sparked with compressed tension and gamesmanship. Was Berruti so sure of winning that he didn't have to go through the warm-up routine with his fellow runners? Was he trying to psyche out the others, or was he too detached, overconfident? Had the Americans lost their cockiness, if not their nerve?

Three of the six runners wore USA uniforms. Ray Norton was there, seeking redemption, along with teammates Les Carney and Stone Johnson. The 200 had always been Dave Sime's best event, but he had failed to qualify at the Olympic Trials and was nowhere near the Stadio Olimpico on this Saturday afternoon. He and Jim Beatty, the injured distance runner who had bombed out in the heats for the 5000, had escaped with their wives down to Sorrento and Capri for the weekend. The head track coach, Larry Snyder, had instructed Sime to stay in Rome, but Dave rarely listened to the coaches. "Snyder was a real prick," he said later. "I didn't like him at all. He was arrogant. And he didn't like me. I was older and very independent, and he told me, 'I won't run you if I catch you being out late.'" Rather than get to bed late, Sime decided it would be better not to go to bed at all.

With Sime gone to the coast and Armin Hary also skipping the 200 to concentrate on the 4 x 100 relay later in the week, Ray Norton had convinced himself that he could win. He knew Berruti from

competing against him on the Scandinavian circuit in 1959. Although
Norton would later say that they were pals and recall how they taught
each other words of English and Italian, the American would not
acknowledge that past friendship before the race. When Berruti
walked over to shake hands with Norton, Carney, and Johnson, they
quickly brushed him off and huddled among themselves, turning in-
ward as though to escape the pressure. "Usually the Americans were
relaxed and friendly, but they were upset about losing the hundred
meters, and were tense and closed," Berruti recalled.

Perhaps because it was a Saturday, and many tourists were on side
trips to the coast, the bowl of Stadio Olimpico was less than two-
thirds full. The German choristers were missing, replaced by Italians
cheering their local favorite as he prepared to enter the blocks. *Ber-
ru-ti! Ber-ru-ti! Ber-ru-ti!* From their row in the stands, Cord Nelson
of *Track & Field News* and his family found the sound joyful, for some
reason so much less threatening than German chants for Hary. Even
the soda vendor in their section got into the spirit of the moment and
charmed young Nancy Nelson by calling out "Coca-Cola! *Acqua
minerale!* Ber-ru-ti!" Then silence until the gun.

In Lane 4, Berruti got a good jump. He was ahead at 70 meters,
and stretched out as he approached the curve. "Berruti runs the curve
better than anyone else," Neil Allen recorded in his diary. Shouts of
"Italia! Italia! Ber-ru-ti! Ber-ru-ti!" echoed through the stadium. Berruti remembered that during the semifinals, he had eased up after
the turn and told himself not to do that again. He had to lengthen his
stride and keep himself under control. In the press box, the Italian
journalists were overwrought. One collapsed in a faint. In the final
stretch, Norton faded. Stone Johnson fell back with him. Abdoulaye
Seye, a Senegalese running under the flag of France, kicked past
Marian Foik of Poland. Les Carney came up on the outside. Berruti
blocked out the roar of the crowd, but his ears were keenly sensitive
as he listened for footfalls behind him. He approached the finish line
knowing that he still held the lead, and threw himself at it, sprawling

onto the dark red track, overcome "with that kind of liberation you feel when you've faced a difficult test and managed to pass it."

With a new Olympic record of 20.5 seconds, tying the world mark, Berruti won gold, with Carney taking silver and Seye bronze. Berruti, his knees and elbows slightly bruised but his sunglasses unharmed by the fall, bounded up and was hugged by Seye, who had run over to congratulate him. "He was very simpatico," Berruti said of Seye. The Americans seemingly were not. They stayed to themselves, crestfallen, as the celebration erupted around them. The exhilaration of the Italians in the stands was unforgettable, a moment remembered by Don Graham, the *Post* copyboy. "They just exploded. It was unlike anything I had ever experienced," he said. Cord Nelson was sitting amid a battalion of Italians who made torches from newspapers and waved their firebrands as they shouted "Ber-ru-ti! Ber-ru-ti! Ber-ru-ti!" again and again for five minutes until three young Italian women carried out the medals for the presentation by Prince Axel of Denmark. The one carrying Berruti's gold medal wept. The band played "Fidelia Italia," with gusto.

Ormezzano was so overcome that he hopped the fence, scuttled across the small dry moat, and scampered onto the field to hug his friend. The journalist was in tears, but the sprinter seemed serene, almost cold. "The problem is that I'm very shy, and when I won, I didn't know what to do," Berruti said later. "I wasn't 'cold,' I was embarrassed by the acclaim." He was a national hero now. Officials escorted him to the field box holding Italian dignitaries. One after another they kissed him on both cheeks.

Off to the side stood Ray Norton chewing on a piece of fruit. Two races, two last-place finishes. Jesse Owens he was not. He had tried as hard as he could—too hard, he now thought. It made him "tied up again like a knot." As he stood talking to Les Carney, Rafer Johnson approached, patted Norton on the back, and said, "You'll get 'em next time, champ." Norton turned and saw a wide smile on Johnson's face, and it temporarily lifted him out of his funk. "Rafer is carrying his own load," Norton thought. He's got C. K. Yang waiting on him. But he's the team leader, like a big brother to everyone, and just his presence and a few words of support were inspirational.

"There were a lot of reasons I did that," Johnson explained later. "First of all, I was the captain, and I felt I needed to do that. And in particular I had to do it in his case. Wilma was a really good friend of mine, and Wilma was very close with Ray. And from what I went through in 1956, all of my teammates who had performances that were less than expected, for the most part I knew how they felt. I wanted to reach out because I had that experience in fifty-six. There's not a whole lot to be said. I just wanted to touch him and let him know there would be other days when he would have the opportunity to show the world what he could do, and this just wasn't the time. I went over to him and physically wanted to put my hands on him and let him know that I understood. You know you can just have a bad day. A bad twenty seconds. And sometimes it turns into an hour, turns into a day, into two days. Once you start spiraling down that road, it is hard to reverse it. Just so hard, and it becomes so hard because you try too hard. And it starts affecting everything. How you think and how you talk and how you move, and pretty soon you are messed up."

On the way out of the stadium, Norton was met in the tunnel again by Wilma Rudolph. Raymond Johnson of the Nashville *Tennessean,* working on a column about the Tigerbelle, stood nearby.

"Don't worry, honey, you did all right," Rudolph said.

Norton threw his track shoes in disgust and collapsed onto a bench next to her. "I did awful. I just can't explain it. I just don't know what's the matter."

The crowd backed away, giving them privacy. Looking for some way to console her friend, Rudolph offered to give him the gold medal she had won the day before. No thanks, he said. She might need it some day to prove that she had really won the 100. But that was the kind of person she was, Norton thought to himself. She thought of others so much that she would even give away her gold medal.

As they rose from the bench, Rudolph reminded him to pick up his shoes.

"I don't want the shoes," Norton said. "I never want to see them again."

Livio Berruti was leaving the stadium at about that time. He did not comprehend the meaning of his victory until then, when he was surrounded by a phalanx of *carabinieri*. What did he need with these officers? The answer became obvious when he stepped outside the gates. Hundreds of Italian fans pushed forward, clamoring to shake his hand or just catch a glimpse of the Torino Express.

EARLY THAT evening at the Palazzetto dello Sport, a sellout crowd gathered for the most anticipated basketball match of the Games, the United States versus the Soviet Union. Tickets were so tight that James D. Zellerbach, the U.S. ambassador to Rome, had to make a personal plea to Avery Brundage to secure seats for his family. The little arena was so overflowing, noted Braven Dyer of the *Los Angeles Times,* that "if you took a deep breath, you were apt to shove somebody off the next seat. Rabid fans jammed the aisles and occupied every inch of standing room." Some of the best views in the house ended up belonging to Bill Nieder and Dallas Long, gold and bronze medalists in the shot put, who had arrived without tickets but were corralled by Pete Newell, given USA warm-up suits, and placed down at the end of the bench. Newell was not expecting trouble, but it never hurt to have two musclemen nearby.

The United States, where basketball was invented in 1891, had dominated Olympic competition going back to the 1904 Olympics in St. Louis, when the Buffalo Germans, a team of six young men from a YMCA on the east side of Buffalo, won the championship. With basketball in its infancy and most countries still learning the rules, the St. Louis contests were merely exhibitions. The sport became an official Olympic event at the 1936 games in Berlin, where the USA won the gold medal by defeating Canada 19–8 on an outdoor packed-dirt court that turned muddy in a rainstorm. The Americans had never lost an Olympic match since, but going into Rome some observers said their basketball dynasty could be vulnerable, especially against the Russians.

Stepan Spandarian, the short, gray-haired Soviet coach, had issued a warning earlier that summer. "We can beat the Americans at the game they invented," he said. He thought he had reasons to be optimistic. At the world championship in Santiago, Chile, in 1959, a U.S. team had lost to both the Soviet Union and Brazil, an unprecedented failure that was described in the *New York Times* as a "propaganda defeat of the first magnitude." If U.S. prestige suffered from the Santiago fiasco, the losses there did not necessarily foreshadow long-term collapse. Construction delays in Chile had postponed the world championship for several months, and by the time they were held, the Americans were preoccupied with other responsibilities. Not an all-star team but a mediocre air force squad was finally sent, with predictable results. Spandarian was further encouraged when the Soviets toured the U.S. as part of the US-USSR Exchange Agreement and held their own against the best AAU teams. He knew the skills of Bob Boozer, Burdette Haldorson, Lester Lane, and Allen Kelley, all U.S. Olympians from the AAU ranks, but had no scouting reports on the American collegians. Of Oscar Robertson, he said, "He is only six-five. He cannot worry us as much as Bill Russell did at Melbourne." The Soviets were taller and faster than ever, Spandarian claimed, and could run and shoot in the style of the West. One Soviet journalist, sharing the coach's confidence, went so far as to bet an American writer a bottle of vodka on the outcome.

In preparing his team for the game, Newell played up Spandarian's boast. They think they're going to beat us, he told his players. They say we *invented* the game, one of the few things they'll acknowledge we invented. Guys, this is more than a game. We're talking about a way of life.

Only basketball, yet the symbolism was unavoidably greater. Newell showed no reluctance to emphasize the cold war stakes. Before the game, he invited an American official into the locker room to talk to the team about the Soviets, their political system, their propaganda machine, and the importance of beating them. Jerry West— West, the perfect name for the situation—absorbed the larger meaning of the confrontation. The consequences of East-West tensions had come home to his family years earlier, on a June morning in 1951 when word reached Cheylan, West Virginia, that David West, his revered older brother, had been killed by an artillery shell in Korea. Since then, Jerry had been haunted by war and "the incredible pain and devastation it brings not only people but countries." All the talk of nuclear holocaust scared him. He would do anything to serve his country, but he didn't want to go into the military and get killed like David. This was his contribution, on the basketball court. "This was not about the USA beating the world, it was about beating Russia," he said later. "The differences in our countries were so enormous, it was like two boxers that had hate for each other. Everyone was afraid of each other. We heard about all the big guys they had and how physical they were. It was almost like you were driven by fear."

Meaning comes from life experience. The cold war talk meant less to Oscar Robertson. Growing up in the inner city of Indianapolis, he worried about poverty, about being beaten up, about his grades. There were a lot of things more important than worrying about the Russians.

After West scored the first basket of the game with his efficient, perfectly squared-up jumper, the only thing the Americans had to worry about were the referees, Bozhidar Takez of Bulgaria and Roger Weber of Switzerland. The Soviets could not keep up with the U.S. fast break, but the refs kept calling what Newell called "ticky tacky" fouls and violations. Newell thought one ref was blowing his whistle at every opportunity because he was overly sensitive to the cold war tension and wanted to control the game like a political mediator. "This one official was from Switzerland, and the only thing he would ever see is the three-second violation. He caught Oscar one time dribbling through the three-second area and called a three-second violation!" After several calls, Newell pointed at his watch and tried to say "one thousand one, one thousand two, one thousand three" in Italian. "The ref looked at me and said, 'Oh, that's a very nice watch'—as though I was trying to sell it to him," Newell joked later.

Although Spandarian had spoken dismissively of Robertson beforehand, the Soviet game plan seemed to focus on him. They double-teamed him with the small guard Valdis Muiznieks and six-six Yuri Korneyev, and at times surrounded him with three players. Displaying the extraordinary all-around skills he would take to the National Basketball Association later that year, Robertson merely turned from being a scoring big man to a stunningly effective point guard, constantly feeding West with precise passes for open shots. "The floor play of the Big O was something to pop eyeballs," noted Braven Dyer. Newell pulled him from the game twice in the first half—once after a technical foul—and with Robertson, West, and Jerry Lucas all on the bench late in the half, the Soviets made a run, narrowing what had been a seventeen-point deficit down to 35–28 at the break.

In the locker room at halftime, Newell told his team that they could not trust the officiating. "We're going to have to just go out in the first five minutes and put them away," he said. The players responded with what he later called "the greatest press defense I ever saw." Robertson and West—a combination for the ages—pressured the Soviets from baseline to baseline, stealing the ball time after time before it reached midcourt. After a spurt that widened the lead to thirty points, Newell backed off, took out his starters and began substituting so that all twelve players got in the game, everyone except the two shot-putters down at the end, who had warm-up suits but no trunks. West sat down as the leading scorer with nineteen points. Robertson, held to only two points in the first half, finished with sixteen but wished that he could have stayed in longer and pounded the Soviets even more. "They didn't know who we were," Robertson said of the Soviets. "They miscalculated our ability level." One imagines the Big O never had to utter those words again in his career.

When questioned after the game about his officiating, the Bulgarian referee said the Soviets played a cleaner style and that he didn't like the way the Americans threw their elbows. Jerry Lucas, who finished with twelve points, disagreed, saying the Russians were "getting away with murder under the boards." Perhaps the Americans were treated unfairly by the refs, but the foul totals contradict that perception. The Soviets were called for thirty fouls; the U.S., twenty-eight. Robertson, Lucas, and Les Lane had four fouls each, and only Terry Dischinger fouled out. On the Soviet side, two starters had four fouls, and two fouled out, including Viktor Zubkov, their leading scorer, who had been in the violent rebound battle with Lucas and Walter Bellamy all night. No matter, the final score was the hardest elbow of all in the cold war struggle: US 81, USSR 57. No one could come close to the Americans, not yet, though reserve center Darrall Imhoff astutely predicted that the world would catch up someday soon.

More than three decades later, after the IOC had dropped its last pretensions of amateurism, and after American prestige in the international game had indeed slipped, the U.S. sent to the 1992 Barcelona Olympics a group of NBA superstars who came to be known as the "Dream Team." Michael Jordan, Magic Johnson, Larry Bird, Charles Barkley, Karl Malone, John Stockton, Scottie Pippen, Patrick Ewing, David Robinson, Clyde Drexler, Chris Mullin—wave after wave of basketball wonder. But that squad of multimillionaires essentially represented an attempt at restoration, a mercenary effort to return to the greatness that once was, to repeat the untarnished brilliance of the original dream team in Rome led by the college stars Oscar Robertson and Jerry West and Jerry Lucas and Walt Bellamy, all of whom would later join Coach Newell in basketball's Hall of Fame.

As they left the Palazzetto dello Sport, the American players knew that two games remained, against Italy and Brazil, before gold was theirs, but beating the Russians was what mattered. Pete Newell made that clear when he gave them three days off and encouraged them to visit Venice or Paris. He didn't need the jukebox now for motivation. Arrivederci, Roma.

ANOTHER AMERICAN sports dynasty was challenged that Saturday evening, with far different results. This happened on Lake Albano, twenty miles southeast of Rome, where the heavyweight crew final was held. The setting seemed almost too achingly beautiful to disturb, even with the clean glide of sculls and graceful sweep of oars. The smooth blue-black waters of Lake Albano reached depths of nearly six hundred feet, filling the five-mile oval bowl of a primordial crater embraced by rich green slopes on the south, sunburned brown hills on the east and north, and a vast landscaped terrace on the west leading up to Castel Gandolfo, summer palace of the Pope. A correspondent for the *Times* of London described his surprise while approaching the lake: "Those who row are so used to going down to rivers that it comes as a curious sensation to climb steeply up a mountainside and find oneself nine hundred feet above the neighboring airport and rowing at a height at which one is usually asked to fasten one's belt ready for landing. A tunnel cut through rock suddenly brings one out on the inner edge of an extinct volcano."

The eight-man crews came out late Saturday for the heavyweight showdown after four days of racing on the rowing course, which cut on a diagonal 2,000 meters across the currentless lake. It was an event long dominated by the United States, which had won every gold

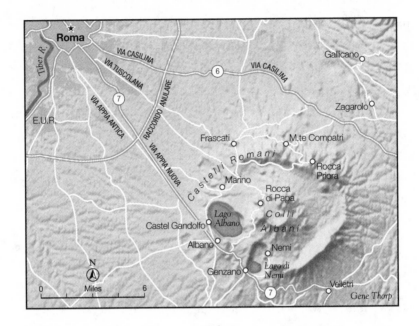

Gene Thorp

medal since 1920. In that era, the U.S. team was the winner of an Olympic Trials regatta contested by the best college and club crews, not an all-star team of rowers plucked from various crews, a policy adopted in later decades. From 1920 through 1956, the University of California had represented the U.S. team three times; Yale and Navy, twice; and the University of Washington, once. To the surprise of many experts, the Naval Academy prevailed again in 1960 and made it to Rome.

It had been a trying year for the Midshipmen. When their long-time varsity coach, Rusty Callow, retired before the season because of deteriorating health, it was widely assumed that he would be replaced by Paul Quinn, the plebe coach, who had led the Navy freshmen to four national championships, was beloved by his oarsmen, and was well regarded within the Eastern rowing establishment. Other programs in the East had such esteem for Quinn that no other coaches applied when the job came open, assuming he deserved it. But the Navy athletic director thought Quinn was too closely aligned with Coach Callow, wanted a break from the past, and brought in

Lou Lindsey, a former Cal coxswain who was the club coach at Stanford. It was a challenging situation for Lindsey. The crew that awaited him was talented and experienced, losing only the number seven man from the year before, but the rowers were also disappointed about Quinn's being passed over and reluctant to embrace the new coach. Appearances did not help: Lindsey was short and unprepossessing, in stark contrast to the commanding, six-four Quinn.

"Human nature is such that you slowly get used to anything," Peter Bos, the senior captain of the Navy crew, said later—and he and his teammates slowly adjusted to Lindsey. "We never said, 'God, this guy is the greatest,' but we took direction. And we started out rowing well." Early in the spring, they scored an important win, defeating Syracuse University and Cornell for the championship of the Goes Cup regatta over a wind-shortened course at Onondaga Lake near Syracuse. Midway through the season, they hit a rough patch, finishing last behind the University of Pennsylvania and Harvard University on the Schuylkill River in Philadelphia, then losing to California but defeating Wisconsin in a three-way race in Madison over a 1¾-mile course on Lake Monona (moved from the usual Lake Mendota because of choppy waters). Cal was considered the top team in the country then, and Navy kept pace, finishing only a seat-length behind. When they returned to Onondaga Lake for the traditional season-ending Intercollegiate Rowing Association Regatta, the Middies again lost to Cal in a close finish.

While training for the Olympic Trials, they ended a long workout by fooling around inside the boathouse at Annapolis, tossing guys in the air, and the stroke man, Joe Baldwin, hurt his wrist in the horseplay. The mishap sidelined Baldwin for several days, but what seemed like misfortune gave the team a needed spark. The stroke man sits first in line, facing the coxswain, and sets the rhythm and pacing of the crew. It is a crucial assignment, requiring ease and precision. With Baldwin out temporarily, Coach Lindsey put another member of the crew, Lyman Perry, in the stroke man's seat, and the team responded positively. Suddenly, they said, they felt like they were flying. When Baldwin recovered, he was placed in another seat and Perry kept on as stroke man.

Even with that, at the Olympic Trials they barely made it out of the semifinals. An official started the race prematurely, oblivious to the fact that the Navy coxswain had raised his hand to indicate he was not ready. The shell was not lined up properly, facing at an angle toward another boat instead of straight ahead. In the frenzy to straighten out and catch up, one of the Navy rowers "caught a crab," meaning he could not lift his oar from the water at the end of a stroke. He dropped his oar handle temporarily, losing a stroke or two, and Navy had to put on a furious sprint through rough waters the rest of the way to finish second, collapsing in exhaustion at the end.

It was a brutal way to qualify, but they got what they wanted: a third chance at California. The final turned out to be Lou Lindsey's finest moment. Using his familiarity with the opposition as a former Cal man himself, he gathered his squad the night before the race and set the strategy: at a thousand meters, Cal would try to break away, using what was called a Power 20—meaning twenty strokes with extra exertion, a vigorous sprint within the middle of the long race. Rowing is as much psychological as physical, and Cal would use its Power 20 at a point where they thought they could break the will of the opposition. Lindsey told his men to listen carefully to the Cal coxswain, and as soon as he went into the Power 20, Navy was to follow suit.

"The idea was that if you hold them for their Power 20, you're going to gain the upper hand. If they don't gain a thing, it is inherently demotivating for them," Peter Bos recalled. "And that's exactly what happened the next day. At a thousand meters we were even with Cal, and when Cal took the Power 20, we took ours. At the end of the twenty we were still even with them. And five strokes later we were four seats out front. Why does that happen? Both crews did the same thing. But in their minds they lost, and in our minds we won.

And the adrenaline you get from winning, and realizing what you had done, makes a helluva difference in your performance. We spurted to that four-seat lead and ended up winning by a full boat length."

Other than the Navy crew itself, few were thrilled about the outcome. Most experts at the Trials shared the feelings of the Syracuse coach, Loren Schoel, who complained afterward: "I'm not convinced that Navy is the best U.S. crew or that it will win in Rome." Clifford (Tip) Goes, the chairman of the U.S. Olympic Rowing Committee, a Syracuse man himself, was so lukewarm about Lindsey that he orchestrated a move to keep Lindsey from being named coach of the entire Olympic rowing team, an honor that traditionally went to the heavyweight coach. Instead, rowing officials split the coaching, placing Lindsey in charge of only his own crew.

Once the rowers reached Italy, the prospects grew no brighter. Several members of the Navy crew joined the ranks of U.S. athletes weakened by dysentery. During training on Lake Albano, they had lost badly to a makeshift eight made up of American teammates from the two four-man shells. Then they barely survived the preliminary rounds of Olympic competition and went into the final with few experts thinking they could retain the championship. But the U.S. tradition was strong, and its crews had fired back from underdog situations before. At Amsterdam in 1928, the then-not-so-old soldier Douglas MacArthur, a sports addict who headed the American Olympic Committee, exhorted the Cal crew to an upset victory from the backseat of his limousine as his driver eased down a riverside roadway closely paralleling the rowing course.

Inspiration in heavyweight rowing now seemed the domain of the Germans. Their coach, Karl Adam, had become the talk of the sport for his innovative designs, astute race tactics, and rigorous training methods, including weight lifting to build shoulder muscles, which the Italian press, wary of German power and efficiency, dismissed as "Teutonic eagerness." The brawny physics teacher from

Ratzeburg came to Lake Albano with a veteran crew combining rowers mostly from Ratzeburg and Kiel who were skilled in the use of an unorthodox oar variously described as a tulip, a coal shovel, or a spoon. All three images accurately evoked a scooped-out rather than flat blade that was difficult to master but provided advantages if handled with proficiency, which demanded strong wrists because of greater water resistance. When working their tulip blades perfectly, the heavyweight eight—Klaus Bittner, Karl Hopp, Hans Lenk (who went on to become a world-renowned philosopher), Manfred Rulffs, Frank Schepke, Kraft Schepke, Walter Schroers, and Karl von Groddeck—presented an odd but hypnotizing sight. In another Adam innovation, the number four and five oarsmen pulled from the same starboard side to prevent veering, while all eight sat up straighter and stroked faster than other crews as little coxswain Willi Padge urged them onward.

Since arriving from Germany, the Ratzeburg-Kiel men had found a daily routine as comfortable as their stroke, leaving the Olympic Village at dawn, driving to Lake Albano, training until noon, pausing for lunch at a nearby abbey, resting in the shade for a few hours, training again until sundown, and returning to Rome late at night. When a correspondent for *Die Welt* asked Lou Lindsey what he thought of the Germans, he said they would have to prove it on the water. But when the subject of their oars came up, the "slim, energetic" U.S. coach said he had tried to introduce the "coal shovels" in American rowing but faced much skepticism. If the Germans had success on Lake Albano, it would become easier for him to make his case, Lindsey added with a smile, "though they don't really have to win the gold medal."

For his part, after a week on the lake, German coach Adam concluded that the stiffest test of his crew would come not from the U.S. but Canada. He had watched the Canadians carefully in two earlier races and determined that they rowed each time precisely the same way, speeding up at 1,000 and 1,750 meters. On the eve of the final, he presented a race plan to his men that was a variation of the strategy Navy had used at the U.S. Trials. Germany would allow the Canadians to come as close as a half-length of the lead after one of their power pushes, enticing them into believing that they could succeed, Adam said. Then, just as the Canadians thought they could grab the lead, the Germans would speed up to forty-five beats a minute with a counterattack. The result would be psychologically devastating, he predicted, sending the Canadians into a shock that would amount to a half-boat push for the German side.

The race went exactly as Adam planned. With calm waters and a slight tailwind, Germany seized a quick lead, with Canada second and the U.S. near the back of the six-boat field. At the halfway point, the Germans were ahead by one and a half lengths, followed by Canada, France, and Czechoslovakia. In the U.S. boat, the oarsmen came to the realization then that they had no chance at gold. "Gold was the only thing we had in mind, not bronze or silver," Bos recalled. "But halfway through, we just knew that practically we could not win gold. It just affects your performance when you see what is not possible. Like with the Power 20, when you expect to do something and don't do it on the water, it quickly affects your strength and performance. The chemistry changes. The second half of the race we rowed hard, knowing the best we could do is maybe take third, and it affected our rowing." Up at the front, at the 1,750-meter mark, the Canadians put on a power rush, just as the German coach had predicted, almost snatching the lead until the Germans, waiting patiently for that moment, went into a ferocious forty-five-beat counterattack and powered across the finish line nearly a boat length ahead, shattering the Olympic record by 5.2 seconds.

Bynum Shaw of the Baltimore *Sun* had been monitoring coverage of the Olympics from his bureau in Germany. He was particularly interested in East German television, which he could pick up in Berlin. When Dresden's Ingrid Kraemer won the diving events, Shaw noted, her victories were "hailed as an example of the rewards of clean socialist living." When West German Armin Hary won the 100, no correlation was made between politics and athletic success. And now, at the finish of the heavyweight eights, with a crew from West Germany about to win gold, the East German announcers seemed to be looking desperately for a socialist hook. They found it back in third place. As Shaw reported: "The East German commentary ran like this, starting in a small disapproving voice and ending in a wild frenzy—'That's the German team coming in now, with Canada not far behind. But look, here come the Czechs in a great finish! There they go, in magnificent coordination! What a thrill! Czechoslovakia wins the bronze medal!' "

At least the Czechs were in the picture, more than could be said of the Americans.

At the end of the race, the U.S. oarsmen stopped dead in the water and slumped—exhausted, silent, disappointed. They had made no mistakes, they had raced as fast as they were capable that day, but it was not sufficient. The Germans were an average five years older, twenty-six to twenty-one, at the physical peak for an endurance sport, and were obviously superior. Now the Americans had to stay far from shore and watch the crews from Canada and Czechoslovakia row dockside and receive silver and bronze while still seated in their shells, and then witness the German eight clamber merrily out of their boat and stand tall on the dock as Avery Brundage placed gold medals around every neck; and then listen as not the "Star-Spangled Banner" but after forty years something else—Beethoven's "Ode to Joy"—rang out across the deep lacquered waters. Finally the Yanks could row in, to polite clapping, with dusk settling over the mountain, and start what Peter Bos called "the process of 'Life goes on.' "

THAT NIGHT, Dave Sime and Jim Beatty and their wives made their way back from Sorrento. It had been a long, full day, with a boat ride to Capri, and the couples were exhausted as they boarded the train for Rome. Sime had a fever again, and his face was swelling in reaction to prednisone that Doc Hanley had given him ten days earlier. He needed to alter the corticosteroid dosage to stop the swelling before he ran in the relay, and he also wanted to look presentable for dinner the next night with the American agent "Mr. Wolf" and Igor Ter-Ovanesyan. The couples rode third-class in a car that throbbed with Italian life: old men, families, babies crying, chickens cackling.

When they reached the Termini station in Rome, the streets were raucous, people everywhere exuding a spirit of liberation. It was not just a Saturday night but a night of national triumph. Adding to the glory of Berruti's victory in the 200, the Italians had won gold in water polo, coming from behind to tie the defending champion Hungarians 3–3 in a final match that, in a sense, was meaningless, since they had already clinched the championship. Yet it sent the sixteen thousand partisans at Stadio del Nuoto into delirium. The Italian team had entered the Olympics with such modest expectations, said one of its stars, Eraldo Pizzo, that "if someone had offered us a bronze medal before the Games started, we'd have taken it." Now they were celebrating on the Via Veneto, walking the street wearing their gold medals, surrounded by loving throngs, people buying them drinks all around, as the chants echoed late into the night, "Ber-ru-ti! Ber-ru-ti! Ber-ru-ti! Italia! Italia! Italia!"

13

THE RUSSIANS
ARE COMING

T HE second Sunday of the Olympics was another day off, and at midmorning a line of buses pulled away from the village carrying Soviet officials and dozens of athletes on an all-day outing into the Italian countryside. The caravan traveled southeast down the Appia Nuova in the direction of Lake Albano and turned off to Genzano di Roma, where it was said the scalding sidewalks outside the town hall were so crowded with celebrants of Italian-Soviet Friendship Day that it "was almost impossible to walk." The mayor led the welcoming party and greeted his guests with a long speech, the first of many.

The Soviets were invited to stay for a fireworks display later but politely declined, leaving after lunch for an hour-and-a-half drive around the eastern rim of Rome and up to the town of Monterotondo, where another celebration in their honor awaited, this time at the local stadium. A festive band of drums and horns led them into the center of town playing the "Inno di Garibaldi" hymn. That evening they finished the tour with a stop at the suburb of Torpignattara, where the local Communist Party wanted to honor them. "The town was decorated with lights, flowers, little flags, the streets were flooded with people, balconies were full, there were hundreds of faces and waving arms in windows," reported a correspondent from *Pravda,* who accompanied the delegation. "One can hear from everywhere slogans being chanted. Peace. Friendship. Long live the Soviet Union. An Italian roofer, Fernando Dedolini, found an interpreter and took him to a group of our athletes and said, 'Soviet athletes achieved the greatest glory in Rome. When you go back home, please tell your workers that the Italian people admire the grand foreign policy of your government and its endless fight for peace.' "

Another day of propaganda in the cold war—and not a bad day for the Soviets who stayed back in the village, either. They played chess, watched television, jitterbugged to American rock and roll, and tossed another verbal grenade down the street at their super-power adversaries. This time it was Yuri Litovev, coach of the USSR hurdlers, offering a critical appraisal of the U.S. team, saying they were chokers. "The Americans came here expecting to defeat every-one," Litovev declared. "When they could not do it, they became afraid." His case in point was poor Ray Norton, taking it from all quarters now. Litovev said that when he saw Norton run at the dual meet in Philadelphia in 1959, he ran "free and smooth," far from the runner who finished last in both the 100 and 200 in the heat of Rome. "Here I see a different man, one I do not recognize," Litovev said. "He is tense and runs as if he is tied up."

To say that an opponent choked is perhaps the worst insult in the world of sports, and it was not well taken when Litovev's quotes were read back to officials and athletes relaxing in the quiet Sunday sun outside their dorms in the U.S. sector. Dave Sime, back from Sor-rento, called it "a lot of hogwash. No nationality or race of people has a lien on championships." Bud Winter, the Olympic assistant and Norton's head coach at San Jose State, responded in a bitter tit for tat, saying "there's never been a bigger choke-up than the Russians at

Melbourne." And head coach Larry Snyder dismissed it as political pap: "The Olympics provide a big propaganda sounding board. Let them make hay out of it while they can. We all know it is absolutely ridiculous."

The Soviets were asserting themselves like never before in Rome, and their confidence was a source of consternation for the Americans. If the Olympic stage was a proxy battleground in the cold war, U.S. officials felt increasingly frustrated that they were in an unfair fight, with the two sides playing by different rules. Ever since the Soviet Olympic Committee was recognized by the IOC in 1951, the essential question had been the same: Did their state-sponsored system—in which they claimed to have no professionals, even as their star athletes were treated as elites and provided with jobs and housing and living stipends—comply with Olympic amateur regulations? Western nations were not beyond reproach in terms of under-the-table payments to supposed amateurs, but those flaws were considered less pervasive. In its own way, the amateur debate was a smaller version of the larger struggle between communism and capitalism.

The American press and public began paying more attention to the issue after the summer of 1954, when Avery Brundage, in his second year as president of the IOC, paid a visit to the USSR. The head of the Soviet Olympic Committee had sent Brundage a cablegram inviting him to attend, at its expense, the annual sports parade in Moscow. Brundage accepted but decided to pay his own way. He expected to stay three days in Moscow and ended up touring the country for three weeks, from Moscow to Leningrad to Kiev to Tbilisi and Odessa. His reaction to what he saw there in some ways mirrored his response two decades earlier to his encounters with Nazi Germany.

The glory of sports superseded politics. He was greatly impressed by the organization and the emphasis on physical culture, starting with the sports parade in the capital, an event that overwhelmed him. "The sports parade I was invited to was fantastic," he said later. "It wasn't really a parade at all. It was a huge demonstration of physical culture and gymnastics. I'd never seen anything that approached it in magnitude and beauty. There were Uzbeks and Tajiks and Cossacks and Armenians and Georgians; each delegation included four hundred to three thousand boys and girls, more than thirty-four thousand participants." The colorful costumes and immensity of the production made Brundage think it was something out of *The Arabian Nights.*

After the young athletes paraded around the field, he watched them one after another give demonstrations with wands, balls, hoops, and ribbons. He was amazed to see one group swiftly set up seventy horizontal bars on a vast green carpet covering the stadium infield, where an equal number of girl gymnasts performed to classical music. The stands on the far side of the stadium were filled with thousands of people holding blue, yellow, or green cards, switching colors in unison like a card section at an American football game. As the colors changed behind them, portable water fountains spurted high in the air, and loudspeakers played the music of Tchaikovsky, Rimsky-Korsakov, and Borodin. Ideological banners were woven into the scene. "Ready for Labor and Defense." "Glory to the Fatherland." "Hail Lenin and Stalin." "Three Million Bales of Cotton for the Nation." "Peace—Peace—Peace." All the propaganda for peace was particularly striking to Brundage. He thought the Russians had "stolen the ball" from the Americans, at least in the appropriation of language.

For decades, Brundage had been proselytizing with religious fervor his belief that physical education and competitive sports made for better citizens—and, if need be, better soldiers as well. He now found it ironic that his philosophy was met with ambivalence in the U.S. but embraced by the Soviets. "The USSR has adopted such a program on a national scale never before attempted (except by the Germans in the thirties and their 'Kraft durch Freude') and have placed all the power of the state behind it," Brundage concluded. "As

I watched those thousands of husky, healthy Soviet boys and girls parading enthusiastically, I thought of Army rejections of 47 percent in the United States. In those countries behind the Iron Curtain, life is grim, and sports fills a vacuum. Their champions are given the title of Master of Sports, and they occupy respected positions in their world, idolized by the youth of the country."

But did their system contradict the Olympic ideal of amateurism? In Moscow, at meetings with top sports officials, Brundage brought a briefcase full of clippings from the Western press detailing how the USSR violated various Olympic rules. In an account of his trip later published in the *Saturday Evening Post* and ghostwritten by Will Grimsley, a wire-service feature writer, Brundage said, "These newspaper stories alleged that the Communists took athletes away from their work and studies and put them into training camps for many weeks at a time; that they gave athletes special allowances and favors, as well as cash prizes; that they included political agents on their teams; and that they used sport for political purposes, propaganda, and national aggrandizement."

Not surprisingly, the Soviets denied the charges. Nikolai Romanov, chairman of the Committee on Physical Culture, told Brundage that the Soviet Union had no professional athletes and that there were "no special inducements or material rewards" for athletes. At one time, they would get cash prizes for outstanding performances, Romanov said, but that practice had been discontinued. Their policy on training camps was no different than that of the Americans, he argued, never more than fourteen days at a time, just like the U.S. Trials. And their approach to winning was also the same as it was in the West, he asserted.

"We want to win. You don't criticize us for that, do you?" he asked.

"No," Brundage replied. "So long as you follow the rules."

Brundage then showed Romanov several articles written by Soviet defectors who said they were placed in training camps for months and were paid full salaries by the state to do nothing but compete. As the IOC president later recounted the scene, Romanov responded coldly, "These men are deserters, traitors. Would you attach any truth to their statements if they had been Americans and turned against your country?"

This was the same Nikolai Romanov who six years later led the Soviet delegation to Rome and headed the Olympic entourage on the Sunday tour of the Italian countryside.

THE DOMUS Mariae, headquarters for foreign correspondents, was bathed in sunshine that Sunday afternoon, with typewriters clacking away, Neil Allen wrote in his diary. "As journalists will at nearly any given hour, we talked shop"—mostly about what was in the other papers. It was all fairly bleak for the Brits. Christopher Basher, sports editor of the *Observer,* asserted that Great Britain's mediocre Olympic showing was attributable in part to poor planning. Officials failed to prepare properly for the "gippy tummy" caused by the heat, he said, and ignored all advice on how best to adjust to late summer in Rome. Gordon Pirie, a highly touted 5000-meter man who failed to make it out of the qualifying round, was quoted as saying that the runners needed two weeks to acclimatize themselves but instead were flown to Italy only four days before the competition began. Basher agreed and said the delay was for no good reason. "There was too much talk of the athletes getting bored if they were here for any length of time. Anyone who gets bored in Rome, with every facility from a track to the opera on his doorstep, has not the temperament to win anyhow." In the *Times* of London, the sporting insignificance of the Brits was seen as yet another sign of a lost empire: "Modern sport was given birth in Britain in the nineteenth century, but this is no reason to think that our methods are still the best. Anyone watching these Olympics must be aware that a sporting revolution is upon us . . . Britain seems no longer to be a great power . . ."

British gloom had nothing on French despair. One silver in rowing, a bronze each for a wrestler and a runner, and that was it so far for their team. There was hand-wringing in the National Assembly, calls for an investigation, laments everywhere for what was being called *"L'Affaire Olympique."* When a visiting Italian dignitary presented French President Charles de Gaulle with an honorary gold medal that weekend, satire became irresistible. A Paris cartoon showed de Gaulle bounding off to compete in Rome himself, harrumphing "Nothing gets done in this country unless I do it."

The German press, when not worrying about whether Armin Hary would get too big a head from his victory in the 100, focused again on the apparent vulnerability of the United States. "Rome is puzzled. What's wrong with the Americans?" asked a columnist in *Die Welt.* "After ten days, the end result becomes visible: America, the apparently invincible colossus of the Olympic Games, is the big, sensational loser of the games. Never before have we looked into so many disappointed faces, never before have we seen the American self-confidence shattered in such a way."

But was it really? *Times* reporter Arthur Daley left the press compound for a stroll through the athletic village that afternoon. To his surprise, he found the Americans "very much alive in the blazing sunshine. Not one had committed hara-kiri. The shock of unexpected defeats had worn off ever so slightly. At least the numbness had faded away, and toppled demigods were able to smile again." Back home, American pride was especially strong in Nashville that Sunday, where an editorial in the *Tennessean* boasted, "A & I Athletes Show the Way at Rome." "After a series of gloomy failures, America's Olympic team surged forward in the athletic battle in Rome with some spectacular performances, of which all America is proud," the editorial stated. "Particularly gratifying to Tennessee were the outstanding performances of Tennessee A&I's Wilma Rudolph and Ralph Boston. These are tremendous athletes, and it should be noted that both are excellent students at A&I. Tennessee and the country congratulate these performers, their coaching staff, and the state university."

Correspondents for *Pravda,* those who avoided the bus tour, seemed to be feeling the most upbeat as they perused Italian journals in search of positive mentions of the Soviets. In Rome's *Il Messaggero,* they found a column extolling Russian modesty "such that you forget you are standing next to famous world champions." But modesty takes you only so far in the propaganda war; not nearly as far as winning. Combing through Milan's *Corriere della Sera,* they passed quickly over some critical paragraphs "in which are mentioned many stupidities" and focused on the depiction of Soviets as winners who "from Olympics to Olympics become more and more competitive and frightening."

ROME TEEMED with spies that weekend. One among them was Imants Lešinskis, who traveled to the Olympics ostensibly to cover the games for *Dzimtenes Balss (Homeland Voice)*, a biweekly newsletter in Riga, Latvia. His name does not appear on the official list of accredited journalists, indicating he might not have needed a press pass, or, more likely, that he used one of his many aliases. His true mission was not to cover athletic events in any case. He was an agent for the KGB, the Soviet security and intelligence operation, and *Dzimtenes Balss* was a KGB propaganda tool attached to Riga's Communist Party paper, *Cina.* At the time, the newsletter did not circulate back home but was intended to spread the good news about Soviet-controlled Latvia to readers abroad.

Lešinskis came to Rome both well trained by the Soviet state and privately disenchanted with it. As a child in Latvia, he had learned Communist Party ideology from his mother, a party member who was said to be one of the few citizens in her neighborhood welcoming the Soviet tanks when they first rolled into the Baltics. An excellent student, he was sent to Russia's elite Institute of Foreign

Relations on the recommendation of Eduards Berklavs, a powerful Latvian Communist leader. But Berklavs, who believed in "socialism with a human face" and opposed the "Russification" of Latvia, was eventually denounced as a nationalist and purged from his position as deputy chairman of the Latvian Soviet Socialist Republic's Council of Ministers. This happened in 1959, shortly after Lešinskis graduated summa cum laude from the institute, and—according to accounts he later told his daughter—his connections to Berklavs put him in jeopardy. He was given the choice of "working for the KGB or having his promising future in shambles."

Soviet agents in Rome took on various missions. Konstantin Gyanov, the KGB's head of sports security, was in charge of monitoring the athletes, watching where they went and to whom they talked. It was not as overt as in Melbourne, when security officers were stationed in every apartment suite, and the athletes could go out for a walk only if there were five or six of them together, but still the athletes knew at all times that they might be under surveillance. Other agents kept an eye on the Vatican and various exile groups to track defection activities from the other end. Lešinskis did some of both; his assignment was to ingratiate himself with Latvian exiles on the Australian Olympic team and try to persuade them that all was well in the homeland and that they could come back and visit. But in fact, he told his family later, he could no longer abide the government for which he was spying. His "belief system was shaken"—first by the crushing repression of the Hungarian revolution, then by the ousting of his patron Berklavs.

So overwhelming was his disillusionment that, even though he had a wife and young daughter, Ieva, back in Riga, Lešinskis took a break from his work with the Australians and walked into the U.S. embassy on the Via Veneto to seek political asylum. His anxiety about defecting was intensified by the fact that he knew little English then, though he was fluent in French and German. The duty officer had to find a political colleague who spoke French, so that nuances would not be missed in the delicate and potentially dangerous conversation. After debriefing Lešinskis, the Americans made a counteroffer: don't defect, but return to your job, only as a double agent. They talked about the "little daughter" that he might never see again if he defected, and argued further that a defection would not be as beneficial to his native Latvia as remaining with the KGB and working his way up to positions where he could glean the inner workings of the Soviet system. Lešinskis agreed, and left the embassy a double man—same job, different mission.

While the traveling busloads from the Soviet delegation were still on their mission to the Italian countryside that Sunday night, September 4, Igor Ter-Ovanesyan slipped out of the village to have dinner with Dave Sime and his wife Betty at the Scoglio di Frisio on Via Merulana. There were KGB agents circling around the team, Ter-Ovanesyan realized. He was polite when they were around but felt that he had little in common with them and tried to "keep them at arm's reach." He could never be sure that they were not following him and considered the pressure of being watched "awful—the worst thing that can be imagined in the world."

Sime did not know what to expect this time. At their previous dinner, Igor had talked about how much he loved Americans and their freedom, but he felt that he had a bright future in the Soviet Union—especially if he won a medal in Rome. Now a medal was his, not gold but bronze, which was still more than his coaches expected of him. And Sime already had an uneasy feeling about the American agent, the pseudonymous Mr. Wolf, who was supposed to close the deal.

Ter-Ovanesyan arrived at the restaurant "kind of excited about this whole moment of meeting with the Americans." He was not thinking of politics so much—not like Imants Lešinskis—but about the contrasts of freedom and security. Here was that rare chance to "look into a different window," he thought. He entered into an easy conversation with Sime, enjoying the moment, not taking it too seriously. Then the American agent appeared. Sime watched the scene unfold, or unravel, from there:

"And here comes this guy, Mr. Wolf. He comes up. I say, 'Mr. Wolf, this is my friend . . . ' He says, 'Yeah, yeah' . . . and he starts immediately. He didn't even look at me or my wife. He goes right to Igor and starts speaking to him in the Russian dialect from where [Igor's] from. And I can see Igor panic. Really panic."

Mr. Wolf asked the couple to leave so that he could talk to Ter-Ovanesyan alone. This only heightened Igor's alarm. "I don't want to talk to you alone. I'm leaving with them," he told the agent, and he got up and walked out with Dave and Betty. Sime recalled what happened next: "When we were walking out, he says, 'David, I don't know if this guy's a double agent or not, but I don't really want to talk to him. I'm too scared.' And that was it. It ended. The CIA blew it."

Ter-Ovanesyan remembered the incident much the same way and said that seeing the American agent in person frightened him, though that alone did not keep him from defecting. His mind had not approached the tipping point, he said. He imagined what would happen to his relatives—nothing good. And on a practical athletic level, he compared the two systems in terms of how they treated track-and-field stars. In the Soviet Union he was "more or less" a professional athlete. He was getting support in terms of his career, with stipends, special considerations, good coaches. He had a clear picture of where he was going and what he was doing and how the Communist state would treat him as a world-class athlete. America was all unknowns. Track stars there told him they had little to look forward to in their sport after the Olympics. Wasn't it true that his friend Dave Sime couldn't even play bush league summer baseball in South Dakota?

. . .

IN THE capital of the Free World, five blocks from the White House, came another lesson that Sunday in the contradictions of the United States in 1960. The American Contract Bridge League was holding a regional tournament at the Mayflower Hotel, with five hundred players at the tables, but when Frank Tucker and Roberto Seymour of Newark, New Jersey, and Kenneth Cox and Kenneth Shorter of New York arrived at the registration desk, they were told that they could not compete because of the color of their skin. The affiliate bridge organizations in Maryland, the District of Columbia, Virginia, North Carolina, and South Carolina had whites-only charters. Over the objections of the regional president, who said he did not want any distractions, the four black men eventually were allowed into the ballroom to watch, though not play, and many sympathetic participants directed them to the best matches.

Here again was precisely the sort of racism the U.S. State Department could not rationalize in its cold war propaganda battle with the Soviets but desperately hoped to overshadow in Rome through the triumphant achievements of black athletes. The key figure in that enterprise, the American flag bearer Rafer Johnson, was just now preparing to take the world stage.

Johnson had spent much of that Sunday evening relaxing in a lounge chair under the pillars of his dorm in the Olympic Village, listening to jazz on a little portable radio. His time was coming, the two-day decathlon competition started in the morning, and now he wanted to clear his mind. He found it "really inspiring to have that kind of pulse, if you listen to music and just go with the sound and the beat, and empty your mind of any other thoughts that you possibly can, and just go with how the music makes you feel. Not the pressure of going into the decathlon tomorrow, or something that Coach Drake told you to remember, or the defeat in fifty-six, and do I have the juice to do it this time? 'Kuznetsov is here, but now I got a tougher guy in C. K. Yang; a lot tougher now than Kuznetsov. What am I going to do?' Instead of going through all that, it's all of that but none of that. It is just music. 'That is all I am listening to, and all that is on my mind is music.' It just clears you out. So then when you finally start thinking about what you need to do, it is fresh. It is motivating, clean. It pushes you."

14

THE GREATEST

ROME awoke to a different world Monday morning. Gone was the high blue sky, as a brisk wind blew in the first gray clouds since before the Opening Ceremony. The Germans said it was a hot-winded sirocco that had swept across the choppy sea from North Africa; local meteorologists simply noted that a low-pressure system had settled heavily over the capital region. The temperature dropped only slightly, into the eighties, still a relative relief, and while Olympic officials considered the possibility of a weather delay, Italian farmers looked heavenward at the prospect of the first rain in two months.

The dense sky was familiar to Rafer Johnson. It reminded him of late-summer mornings back in Kingsburg when he and his younger brother Jimmy rose at dawn to go fishing. He was up just as early now on this fifth of September in Rome, stirring from an anxious sleep, butterflies fluttering in his stomach. The nerves were natural, he believed. Experience had taught him that if he ever found himself without that feeling on competition morning, it would not be a good day. You had to have butterflies to be ready, he thought; without them you were in trouble.

After a breakfast of steak and eggs, Johnson, in a dark blue track-suit, boarded the bus at the village gate and reached the Stadio Olimpico an hour early to warm up for the first day of five decathlon events. His friend, schoolmate, and rival, C. K. Yang, in a tracksuit gleaming white, arrived with him, buoyed by a message he had just received from his mother back home in Taiwan. "Misun, I know you will win. God bless you," she had said. *Misun* was her pet name for C.K. It meant lovely child. The intensity of the imminent showdown left Johnson, Yang, and the Soviet Vasily Kuznetsov less eager than usual to talk to one another. When Johnson stepped onto the track, his nerves settled, overtaken by a jolt of adrenaline. He felt loose and "prepared at any cost" to win.

It would be a busy day inside the stadium, with most of the key events scheduled for the afternoon, and only irrepressible track fans were scattered around the stands when the morning competition began at nine. The press section filled slowly. Some in the high-spirited corps of American sports columnists, who became track experts once every four years, arrived with an uncharacteristic ho-hum attitude; none more so than Red Smith. Literate and deftly sarcastic, Smith was never at a loss for an opinion. He was always absorbing, and usually right, but he might have had a blind spot when it came to the decathlon. To track-and-field experts like Cord and Bert Nelson, who had taken their usual seats among the fans that morning, the decathlon was the sport's ultimate challenge, but to Smith it was a grinding bore.

He had forced himself to the track, Smith groused, for the day when "the world's greatest athletes" would begin "the world's dullest competition." In his opinion, the decathlon amounted to "a quadrennial chance for guys who can't do anything very well to win

interplanetary renown by doing many things in a great blaze of mediocrity." The complex scoring system, in which competitors accumulated points based not on whether they won an event but how
their best effort rated against an established standard, also frustrated
Smith, while at the same time providing him with comic material. In
the decathlon, he said, "victory is achieved by mathematics, and the
chief scorer is an IBM electronic brain with the classical Greek name
Ramac. Medals are awarded on the basis of a point score which runs
into the thousands and which isn't going to be explained here for the
fairly sound reason that it's already been explained in a booklet containing seventy-eight pages of arithmetic tables." Shirley Povich was
no kinder. He called the decathletes "the peasants of the games" and
noted that "years back"—but wasn't it just then, from the lips of his
colleague Smith?—"one fellow was unkind enough to suggest that
the decathlon is a haven for mediocrity."

In theory, these provocative judgments could be defended, even
championed, but in Rome they were proved wrong. There was nothing lowly about the best decathletes, even though their work was exhausting and merciless. To put mediocrity and Rafer Johnson in the
same sentence seemed preposterous. He was universally regarded as
the athletic royalty of the Games. Yang held the same status in Taiwan, and Kuznetsov in the Soviet Union. As for dullness, with thirty-
one athletes competing in ten events, there were bound to be long dry
spells, but Smith would be silenced by the time the two-day contest
ended, his prediction overtaken by crackling tension on the track.

Although a test of endurance, the decathlon begins at a sprint.
The first event is the 100-meter dash. Kuznetsov was in the first
of the five heats along with David Edstrom, the young decathlete
from the University of Oregon who had burst onto the international
scene with his strong third-place finish at the US-USSR dual track
meet in Moscow two years earlier.

Like Joe Faust in the high jump, Jim Beatty in the metric mile, and hundreds of other competitors, Edstrom arrived in Rome realizing that he had no real chance at a medal—in his case because of a lingering groin injury that had slowed him since midsummer. Just to compete in the Olympics was a notable achievement in itself, but now he faced the outer limits of an athletic dream he had nurtured since his childhood growing up on his parents' dwarf-fruit-tree farm in Sherwood, Oregon, about twenty miles from Portland. Inspired by the 1954 movie *The Bob Mathias Story,* in which Mathias, the handsome two-time (1948 and 1952) gold medal winner, played himself, young Edstrom became obsessed with the notion of being an Olympic decathlete. On a patch of vacant land inside the hundred-acre nursery behind their house, he and his father constructed a makeshift decathlon practice field, including a three-hundred-yard oval track, handmade hurdles, and a sawdust high-jump and pole-vault pit. Throughout his teenage years, almost every day in the summer and after school in the fall and spring, Edstrom worked on his lonesome backyard mission, keeping a diary of his progress. He became proficient enough to earn a track scholarship from the legendary coach Bill Bowerman at Oregon; then to team up with his second track-and-field hero, Rafer Johnson, in Moscow in 1958; and finally to join Johnson again in Rome. But he entered the Stadio Olimpico on the morning of September 5 with a groin pull, an injury he had never had before, and though he was not certain how his body would respond to the 100-meter dash, he had a feeling that it would not respond well.

The first heat went well for no one, as it turned out. Edstrom survived the race without further injury, but his time of 11.4 seconds put him in a deep hole, giving him 768 points in an event where a good score rose to the 950-to-1000 range. Kuznetsov outran Edstrom but was too slow himself, coming in at 11.1 seconds for only 870 points. The experts at *Track & Field News* concluded from that first dash that the Soviet star had lost a step from his peak showings in 1958 and 1959 and would not be a threat to Johnson and Yang now. "Kuznetsov and Edstrom showed right off that they would not be a factor for the gold medal," the magazine noted. The Soviet journalists might have reached the same conclusion, but they were under orders not to mention Yang, who had obviously surpassed Kuznetsov. In their dispatches, they would keep noting that Kuznetsov held the second-best score in history—utterly ignoring Yang's showing in the Trials—and compare their man only to the American, not the unrecognized Formosan.

"You have to do it on that day. You have to do it when they fire the gun." Those words from Ducky Drake echoed again in Rafer Johnson's brain as he lined up for his heat of the dash, No. 447 on his back. He knew how important it was to get off to a good start on the first event. But what if the gun goes off again and again and again? There were three false starts in Johnson's heat, and the third was called so late that Rafer had sprinted 40 meters before he heard the recall gun. No excuses, but in a stamina-testing event where successful competitors need to conserve energy whenever possible. Johnson, through no fault of his own, had expended too much too early. On the fourth try, he came in with a 10.9, three-tenths of a second behind his best showings. When Yang, in the last of the five heats, got off on the first gun and broke the tape at 10.7, he left the track with 1034 points and an 86-point lead on Johnson.

With one man dropping out already, the tribe of thirty all-around athletes moved into the infield at midmorning for the second event, the long jump. Once again the luck of the draw seemed in Yang's favor. He was the last to jump, giving him the advantage of knowing what marks he had to reach. Once this had been Johnson's favorite event—he was good enough at it to qualify for the broad jump in Melbourne—but he ran into a stiff headwind on his first leap and managed only 23 feet 7½ inches. Yang topped that on his first jump, going 24-5¾. That turned out to be C.K.'s best jump, while Rafer on his third and final try came closer to him, at 24 feet ⅝ inches. Still, Yang increased his lead, and went to the noon break ahead by 130 points.

ACROSS THE TIBER at the Olympic Village that lunch hour, cyclist Jack Simes (rhyming with *dimes,* not to be confused with sprinter Dave Sime, as in *rim*) sat down at a cafeteria table near the same young boxer he had eaten next to the day before. Simes, who had bombed out in his own Olympic competitions and was struggling with his place in sports, had never seen anyone quite like Cassius Clay. At the first dining encounter, he had been "amazed at this guy's confidence," he recorded in his diary. Clay had boasted that he was so fast nobody could hit him and that he would win a gold medal and soon everybody would know his name. Now Simes saw Clay at the table again, this time staring down at a plate of steaks stacked high like pancakes. "What kind of lunch is that?" Simes asked, laughing. A trainer with the boxing squad, sitting nearby, shook his head with a smile. Clay explained that he was readying for competition and needed the steaks for strength.

The boxer was about to dig in when he noticed a caravan of convertibles easing along the village roadway outside the cafeteria window. Who's that? he asked. Simes said he thought it was Belinda Lee and some English movie star, and that he had heard that Bing Crosby and Grace Kelly were also supposed to be visiting the athletes sometime soon. He had read about it in the village newsletter that morning—all these film stars were coming. "With that he bolts from the chair and heads straight for the door without saying a word," Simes wrote of Clay in his diary. "The trainer yells, 'Come back here! You haven't touched your food! That Polack's gonna beat the hell out of you!' Then, raising his voice, adds, 'He's the European champ, you know!' This has no effect either. The boxer never looked back, the trainer left, and I ate lunch by myself."

After lunch, the clouds over Rome dropped the first rain. "You have to be in Rome on a rainy day to know what real sadness is," wrote Edouard Seidler, correspondent for France's national sports newspaper, *L'Équipe*. "Rome is lugubrious during a storm. It is only made for sunny days." This first spray of rain was not enough to disrupt outdoor Olympic events, but it served as a warning of things to come. Yet if the dreary sky enveloped the ancient city with a mood of sorrow and heaviness, as Seidler said, that sensibility did not seem to make it into the stadium.

It was almost three o'clock when Rafer Johnson returned to the infield "determined to make up for lost ground" in the shot put, one of his best events. While it would be unfair to characterize him as primarily a strongman, it was indisputable that his decathlon prowess was built around the throwing events: shot put, discus, and javelin. Unlike most throwers, his legs were surprisingly spindly—"they are legs of a runner rather than a muscle man," noted Fred Russell— but he had a powerful upper body. A few seconds of exertion followed by long spells of sit-around-and-wait is the usual frustration of shot-putters, and with so many competitors, the down time was more frustrating than ever now, especially after Johnson disappointed himself with a poor first throw. Red Smith, if he was paying attention, must have felt reassured by the tedium. But when Johnson's turn came around again, he heaved the shot 51 feet 10¾ inches, worth 976 points and surpassing Yang's best effort by more than 8 feet. This brought a dramatic turnaround in the overall scoring; from 130 points down, Rafer now, with that single showing, grabbed the lead by 143 points. He felt he would need every bit of that cushion going into the fourth event of the day, his worst, the high jump.

The shot put turned out to be the end for David Edstrom. The pain in his groin was too much for him now, and there was nothing he could do about it. All those hours on the makeshift decathlon course out at his Oregon tree farm had come to this—after three events in Rome, he had to drop out.

As a morning-to-night enterprise, the decathlon had to fit around a busy schedule of other events inside Stadio Olimpico, some that drew more attention that day. By a quarter to five the stadium was nearing capacity in anticipation of two major races: first the men's 110-meter hurdles, then the women's 200. The throaty German hordes had returned in full force for the hurdles, there to support Martin Lauer, who had set the world record at 13.2 seconds earlier that year, a mark matched by American Lee Calhoun during the pre-Olympic meet in Bern. In the Olympic final, those two were joined by Willie May and Hayes Jones of the U.S. team along with Keith Gardner of the West Indies and Valentin Chistiakov of the Soviet Union.

Calhoun, the defending gold medalist had spent the summer convinced that he could set a new world mark of 13.1. All of his training had been geared toward that record time. He was supremely confident about his form clearing the hurdles and felt that his only concern was speed. His amazing race in Switzerland, he told his wife, Gwen, who accompanied him to Rome, could have been even a tenth of a second faster, and in any case was just a warm-up for what he would do now.

Gwendolyn Bannister Calhoun certainly hoped that her husband was ready. As a spouse, it was natural for her to root hard for him, but in her case the race in Rome had a stronger personal meaning, a matter of the couple's redemption. They had been college sweethearts since meeting at a school dance at North Carolina College at Durham (later renamed North Carolina Central University), a predominantly black school with a first-rate track program led by the brilliant coach LeRoy T. Walker, who in later years would serve as both president of the university and the first African-American head of the U.S. Olympic Committee. After a few years together, when Lee was graduating, he and Gwen decided to get married. They had no money for a wedding or honeymoon, even though Lee had reached international stardom by then with his gold medal in Melbourne. According to Gwen, Coach Walker one day mentioned to

her that they should try to get on *Bride and Groom,* a daytime television show where young couples were married on the air and given
various gifts and a free honeymoon. "LeRoy said this might be something good for you. He showed me what you had to do to be on the
show. If they enjoyed your letter, they would put you on the show.
Mine must have been a humdinger," Gwen said later. "I didn't tell
Lee about it until I knew for sure. He thought it was wonderful. We
knew we didn't have anything; didn't even have a job. [But] it was
my choice. Lee didn't have anything to do with it."

Gwen and Lee were scheduled to appear on *Bride and Groom* on
Friday, August 9, 1958. Eight days before the wedding, Dan Ferris,
head of the Amateur Athletic Union, heard about the program and
declared that Calhoun would lose his amateur status if he got married on the show and accepted any gifts. Then Ferris revised his position to make it even stronger: Calhoun would lose his amateur status
even if he went on the show but did *not* take gifts. Using the same
argument he made in telling Rafer Johnson that he could not take an
acting role in the movie *Spartacus,* Ferris argued that Calhoun was
unduly benefiting from his status as an athlete and that the couple
would not have been invited on *Bride and Groom* had he not been a
track star.

Calhoun desperately wanted to maintain his amateur status—he
was already pointing toward the 1960 Olympics—but he thought
Ferris's ruling was unfair. Anyone could be on the TV show, not just
athletes, he said. And everyone enjoyed the right to get married in
the style they wanted and to accept gifts for the wedding. What if
friends wanted to give a wedding gift of money for a honeymoon?
Would that be illegal?

When Gwen heard about the AAU announcement, she tried to
talk Lee out of going through with the television show. "I didn't want
him suspended. I thought about just getting married on my parents'
lawn," she recalled. But by then Calhoun was adamant, and Roger
Gimbel, the producer of *Bride and Groom,* had come to his defense,

bringing in NBC lawyers to make an appeal to the track officials. "The main argument [we] made I think was telling at the time," Gimbel remembered. "This is a free country, and you should be able to get married any way you want to—it's your business and not the Olympic Committee's business. Also, [we made] the argument that it was the bride, not the groom, who received the presents. It was just a shocking decision. I felt it was really embarrassing. I felt like, 'this poor guy!' "

After meeting with Calhoun and NBC's lawyers, Ferris remained unmoved. He called the whole show a "publicity stunt." Calhoun, in an interview with the *Chicago Defender,* a black newspaper, said he would not back down either. "I will appear on the show regardless of what the outcome will be," he said. "I feel my decision is right, and I will appeal the case if Ferris goes through with the threatened revocation."

In front of a national television audience, the Calhouns were married as planned on August 9. Lee's stepfather, a minister, performed the ceremony. Gwen got to choose her own gown ("It was gorgeous," she said later). A few friends and family were there, along with a famous stranger, someone who had never met Lee or Gwen, yet came to support them. It was none other than Jackie Robinson, the trailblazing black baseball player who had broken the national pastime's color barrier in 1947. Now retired, he worked for Chock full o'Nuts, a popular New York City lunch-counter coffee chain. Lee did most of the talking on the air, answering questions about their lives and romance. Then came the gifts: silverware, china, a sewing machine, gold watches, a freezer full of frozen foods, perfume, a vacuum cleaner, a carpet, plane tickets and traveler's checks for the honeymoon in Paris, and an aboveground swimming pool that they had no room or use for and donated to the Boys Club of America.

Dan Ferris threw in the additional present of standing by his threat and revoking the hurdler's amateur track status. After the Calhouns' time in Paris, where a photographer from *Ebony* followed them around, the couple moved to Cleveland, where Lee took a job in the city recreation department working with tough juveniles. If money was at the root of his problem, it was also the way out, as it happened. Midwestern chapters of the AAU were so upset with the decision that they threatened to withhold contributions to the national headquarters unless Calhoun was given another chance. In December 1958 his indefinite suspension was cut to one year. He returned to training and by the summer of 1959 was back on the track that led him to this wet and overcast Monday afternoon inside Stadio Olimpico—where he had a chance to become the first 110-meter hurdler to win consecutive gold medals, and certainly the first to overcome the obstacle of being a television groom.

Rome's new red track was soft and slow from the earlier rain, and a strong wind blew directly into the faces of the hurdlers as they took their marks. Calhoun had been pointing toward a record time, but there was little chance of that now. He and teammate Willie May lined up side by side in the two inside lanes. At the gun, Calhoun took the lead, then hit the first hurdle, something he rarely did, and was thrown slightly off stride. Lauer knocked the same hurdle, and then the fourth and fifth as well, and was in fourth place as they reached the homestretch, the German barrackers in the stands chanting his name in vain. May, a lanky six-three, had caught Calhoun and was running even with him as they neared the tape. In Melbourne, the race had been a photo finish, with Calhoun winning because of his lean at the tape. Now it came down to a lean again. Watching in the stands, Bert Nelson noted that May's long lean reminded him of the one Calhoun had used in Melbourne. Almost, but not quite. "Calhoun, who possibly more than any other man has popularized and improved the lean, was not to be outdone at his own game," Nelson wrote. "Bending until his upper body was almost horizontal, Calhoun actually took the string with his head. But heads don't count, and the judges had to view the photos."

Gwen Calhoun was a wreck watching the finish. "Whenever I

watched him run, I was nervous. I remember when he hit the tape, he fell, rolled over, and got up. He doesn't remember it because it was so quick. I asked if he had hurt himself, but he was up so fast he didn't remember." And she was more nervous waiting for the results. "We had to wait so long to find out who had won"—five minutes in that situation seeming like forever. "I just remember I kept looking up at the scoreboard. They had everyone else up there but Lee and Willie May." Hayes Jones had finished third, winning bronze, barely edging out Lauer. Finally the scoreboard flashed the first two places. Calhoun first, May second. The time was way off, 13.8, but that was explainable by the poor conditions.

Two Olympics, two photo finishes, two gold medals.

Gwen started jumping up and down with joy. On the track, Lee felt flushed with vindication. "Winning in Melbourne meant a lot, but winning in Rome was a special achievement since no one else had ever won consecutive gold medals in high hurdles," Calhoun said later. "I was out to prove I could do it, and with going through the suspension hassle, it gave me an especially good feeling."

EARLIER IN the competition, Ed Temple's greatest hope was just to get one of his runners on the medal stand. A bronze would do. But in the four days since Wilma Rudolph won gold in the 100, all of that had changed. From a relative unknown, Rudolph had risen to international stardom, belle of the Olympics, the favorite in anything she did. Even some of the Soviets said she was the most amazing figure, male or female, in the Games. It was not just the way she ran, so lean and flowing, but the combination of her physical skills, her biography, and the way she presented herself. Long before it became commonplace for the media to build Olympic coverage around a personality, much attention in Rome was being paid to the Wilma Rudolph story.

Wherever she went in the village or on the streets of Rome, she was quickly surrounded by adoring fans. "I'm afraid to go out in the morning," she confessed to reporters one day. "They recognize me everywhere, whether I'm wearing a dress or my sweat suit." And everywhere the fans wanted the same thing: a photograph with *"la Gazella Nera"*—the Black Gazelle. For a self-described lazybones who never wanted to exert more energy than the situation required, all the hoopla could have been too much. It had always been hard to get her to eat, and when she did eat it was usually some junk food, a hamburger and soda. Her mother, Coach Clinton Gray at Burt High, Coach Temple—all had tried to improve her eating habits, with little success, and now she was eating even less than usual. Her weight dropped from 140 down into the low 130s. Coach Temple kept urging her to "stay off those feet," but there was always someplace to go and someone else who wanted to talk to her. Despite all that, Rudolph had the right disposition to handle the outside demands, as well as the added stress of watching her close friend Ray Norton fail so painfully on the track. It seemed that nothing could faze her.

As the Olympics progressed, it became apparent that Rudolph had grown into more than just a winning athlete with a winning personality. Her success had taken on a larger meaning, as a woman who had overcome the odds, and in that sense she was now an important symbol to her women teammates and all females in sports. Anne Warner, one of the "sweethearts" from the Santa Clara Swim Club who combined to win six gold medals among them (three for Chris von Saltza, two for Lynn Burke, and one for Warner), said that all the swimmers looked up to Rudolph and considered her an inspiration. They had read the stories about her life and watched her with reverence as she moved around the Olympic Village.

The sprinter's childhood malady had a special meaning to them, Warner recalled later. "I had read the stories about her fight against polio and what she had done. She was really a hero for a lot of us. It didn't matter that it was a different sport. She was just such a beautiful runner. And I think that polio was such a part of our lives then, too, because we were swimmers. A lot of times your parents were nervous about going to swimming pools in that era. And there was no Salk vaccine yet when we were starting out. So the fact that she had polio meant something special to us."

Each swimmer seemed to have a personal story that deepened the connection to Rudolph. The great von Saltza's father was a polio survivor who had trouble walking the rest of his life. His disability led to his daughter's gold medals, in a sense: Chris first headed over to the local swimming pool as a youngster one summer when her father could not take the family on its annual vacation. Warner remembered facing her first polio threat before she entered kindergarten, when there was a widespread belief that the disease spread in swimming pools. "I think when I was five, I went swimming at a local pool and got a high fever, which was a sinus infection, and my mother rushed me to the doctor because they were having a polio scare in 1951. My pediatrician's wife had been taken to the hospital that day to an iron lung from which she never came out. So that whole polio thing was personal for me, and the fact that Wilma Rudolph had overcome polio and become such a magnificent runner was remarkable."

Soon after the 110-meter-hurdle results were announced, resolving the photo finish between Calhoun and May, Rudolph and her five competitors stepped out onto the slow track for the 200. Coach Temple had a good feeling now. "I felt after she won the hundred that she had a good chance to win the two hundred because she was a better two hundred runner," he said later. "She could just run the curve so well, plus when she hit the straightaway, she could open up with her long legs and her fluid stride and . . . she was going to be awesome." The 200 had been the source of Rudolph's teenage disappointment, when she failed to survive the preliminary heats in Melbourne. But it had been her best race ever since. Before the qualifying heat in Rome, she was so confident that she asked Temple if it would be OK for her "to just loaf" if she had a good lead. Give it your all for 150 meters,

Temple told her, then look around, and if you have a good lead, go ahead and coast. That is exactly what Wilma did, and it so happened that she coasted to an Olympic record time (23.2 seconds)—once again proving Temple's maxim that you have to ease off to speed up.

For the final, she faced not only a slow track against a swirling wind, with ominous storm clouds forming overhead, but also was handicapped by being slotted in the far inside lane, where the curve in the 200 is tighter and more difficult for a long-limbed runner to negotiate. At the gun, she was slow out of the blocks but surged past the field at the curve and lengthened her lead with every stride down the straightaway. In the press section, the Brit, Neil Allen, had his binoculars trained on countrywoman Dorothy Hyman, who would finish third, but he was thrilled seeing Rudolph as she "went majestically away from the field." Even the German fans, as they watched their own blond-haired Jutta Heine race for the silver in Lane 3, joined in the roar for the American.

The time was ordinary, 24 seconds, but the victory was historic. From that crowded little red house in Clarksville, out of an extended family of twenty-two kids, from a childhood of illness and leg braces, out of a small historically black college that had no scholarships, from a country where she could be hailed as a heroine and yet denied lunch at a counter, Skeeter had become golden, sweeping the sprints in Rome. When Raymond Johnson of the *Tennessean* went looking for her after the race, she was typically modest, saying she was glad it was over and that she had not run her best. "I meant to run faster in the finals," she said. "But somehow when the race started, I just couldn't get going any harder." The joke was that she ran harder an hour later as she made her way back to the village with her Tiger-belle teammates Lucinda Williams, Barbara Jones, and Martha Hudson. As they approached the gates, a mob spotted Wilma and started toward her. But she had done enough for one day, and it looked like an electrical storm was about to hit, and she and her buddies just took off, sprinting away toward their dorm at record speed. They easily outdistanced everybody, Johnson noted, "including the rain, which they beat by fifteen yards."

By then the conditions inside Stadio Olimpico were a mess. First the sky grew dark, then papers started flying everywhere, thunder rumbled over the hills, lightning flashed, and in a rush down came the rain. It was about six o'clock, and the decathletes were set to begin their fourth event of the long day, the high jump. Perhaps Red Smith viewed this as welcome relief from his assignment covering the blasted event—he certainly seemed energized describing the "swooshing, pounding cataracts" of rain before skipping out with most of his colleagues and heading across town for the boxing finals. The stands cleared of all but the bravest souls. In their section, the last ones holding out were the *Track & Field* Nelson clan, covering their heads with rain gear and umbrellas. Young Nancy Nelson looked around and was shocked to see "the stadium was empty." Her sister Rebecca took advantage of the emptiness by dashing all the way up the steps to the Olympic flame. Had it gone out? She thought so. Finally, Cord Nelson rounded up his brood and took them under cover below the stands, where they waited around with the few other diehards for the decathlon competition to resume.

In a dank and crowded training room nearby, Rafer Johnson took shelter from the storm, surrounded by fellow decathletes, some of whom had thrown blankets on the floor. Rafer was exhausted already, and the high jump was his worst event, and now he had no idea when they would send him back out there. But he had trained mentally for moments like this, just as he had trained his body. Since that disappointment in Melbourne in 1956, he had thought a lot about the unexpected, about what he could control and what he could not control. "You better be prepared for something other than what you expect the situation to be," he recalled. "And don't be surprised if it very seldom turns out the way you think it's going to. Whatever it turns out to be, if you are ready to deal with those changes, whatever they are, it can make you very tough. It can make you a very good competitor, because pretty soon it gets to be that whatever happens, you can deal with it. At that time, I didn't have things in total control. But I was very tough."

THE RAINS continued, Rafer and C.K. waited, darkness fell on Rome, and the action moved across the city to the Palazzo dello Sport for the finals of the Olympic boxing matches. The new arena was a cylindrical marvel of modernist design, with every seat offering a clear view of the action and a brilliant shaft of light filtering down on the ring from the apex of the ceiling like a probing beam from a flying saucer about to land. But it could have been held in a cave, and it would have felt the same on this night; the joint was jumping, packed to the rafters with a standing-room-only crowd of more than eighteen thousand raucous boxing fans. Prized tickets were going for 6,000 lire (about $9.60 then), a price steeper than any ticket after the Opening Ceremony. There were smatterings of supporters for every country represented in the finals, but by far the dominant claque was Italian—loud, vociferous, on edge, ready at any time to burst into a chorus of joyous song ("as if every man in the audience was a Caruso," noted the Englishman Neil Allen) or to unleash a volley of whistles and boos. They had come to cheer on the home squad, which had no fewer than six men going for gold out of ten classifications from flyweight to heavyweight. Czechoslovakia, Hungary, Ghana, and South Africa had one boxer apiece remaining, while the Soviets had three, the Poles four, and the U.S. three.

"Those Italian fans are really rabid, especially in the boxing," recalled Jerry Armstrong, the American bantamweight, who had already lost in the quarterfinals. Armstrong and teammate Nikos Spanakos, the featherweight who had been outpointed by a Russian ten days earlier, reached the arena that night on a bus carrying a troupe of already-beaten fighters from all over the world. Their shuttle from the village turned out to be as contentious as some of the sparring they would witness later. As Spanakos later remembered the scene, the bus driver took "a long, circuitous route" before eventually coming to a stop and announcing that he would go no farther unless they paid more money. "The Greeks said 'No way, let's jump him!' They subsided and even offered to pay for me in the end, but they did not want to be ripped off. It was a long bus ride to get out there."

In the first five bouts, the Italian boxers won once and lost twice, and the partisan crowd was growing anxious. Then, in the welterweight match (148 pounds), Giovanni Benvenuti, already the European champ and considered the best hit man on the Italian team, scored the first knockdown of the night, flooring the Russian Yuri Radonyak in the first round. Radonyak got up and survived the full three rounds, eventually losing a 4–1 decision, but by then the crowd was delirious about Benvenuti. The arena still resounded with songs and loud cheers when the first American boxer, light middleweight Wilbert McClure, stepped into the ring to face another Italian, Carmelo Bossi of Milan. McClure was taller and had a longer reach than his opponent, but he started cautiously, letting the Italian land a few body punches in the first round. In the second round, Bossi could only get inside for clinches, constantly drawing the attention of the referee. In a freewheeling final round, McClure came out swinging and never stopped, landing a combination right-left that sent Bossi against the ropes, his knees buckling. Bossi flailed back until the final bell, most of his swings missing wildly, the crowd on its feet in a ceaseless roar. The gold medal went to McClure on a 4–1 decision, a resolution that the Italian crowd found hard to dispute but disliked intensely nonetheless, fouling the mood.

That was the situation when another American, Eddie Crook, an army sergeant based at Fort Campbell, Kentucky, entered the ring to face Poland's Tadeusz Walasek. In the stands, Pete Newell, the U.S. basketball coach who had come to support the Yanks, sensed a "lot of anti-American feeling" bubbling up in the crowd. To Newell, it

seemed rooted in ideology. He sensed there were many Italian Communists in the arena. "For some reason, they seemed to have a bigger
audience in boxing of the radical element than they did at basketball
or even track," Newell said. Whether it was politics or merely boxing's combustible mix of mob psychology and controlled violence,
the Crook bout left no doubt as to the anti-American sentiments in
the stands.

Even more than McClure before him, Crook started his fight cautiously. He used what one boxing writer called a "sneaky left" to keep
Walasek away while dodging the Pole's occasional errant swings.
From his press seat near ringside, Neil Allen was impressed by
Crook's style. "I thought Crook produced the best boxing of the evening, winning the first two rounds with crisp left jabbing and hooking and perhaps having to share the third when Walasek threw
everything into a desperate counterattack." Other impartial observers, while less effusive in their praise of Crook, thought he outfought
Walasek and were not surprised when he was declared the winner.
But the Italian crowd, which had been rooting loudly for the Pole—
or against the American—and did not appreciate Crook's deliberate
style, erupted when the decision was announced, booing, whistling,
throwing programs, stomping their feet. As the minutes dragged on,
the disagreement turned into something more resembling a protest.
When Crook stepped up to accept his medal from U.S. ambassador
Zellerbach, he looked around in astonishment as the audience kept
booing and hissing and cursing while the American flag rose to the
rafters and the "Star-Spangled Banner" began playing. "The rotten
demonstration went on for seven minutes, according to the clocking," noted Shirley Povich, "and mostly it was the Italian fans making the foul noises."

Pete Newell feared a riot. The Americans in the audience, with
that unifying us-against-the-world sensibility of feeling proud, outnumbered, and misunderstood, rose and sang the national anthem
with vigor. Povich captured the moment, focusing on the loudest

singer. "A visitor in Rome named Bing Crosby who gets big fees singing got up on his feet . . . and belted out a song for free at the summit
of his voice. It was an old number called the 'Star-Spangled Banner,'
and this was no time for soft tones, because the American flag was in
trouble. It was being booed at the Olympic boxing finals, and Crosby
unloaded with a fierce Ethel Merman bust-down-the-roof vigor that
could get him thrown out of the crooner's union. Every other American in the big Palazzo dello Sport was singing, too, because they
wanted to make themselves heard in reply to the catcalls and rude
bums who didn't like the U.S. flag there at the top of the Olympic
pole."

Cassius Clay heard the commotion from his dressing room. He
was next up for the Americans, coming out to face another Pole,
Zbigniew Pietrzykowski, for the light-heavyweight title. The booing strengthened Clay's resolve as he made his way to the ring. He
knew that he would have to "leave no doubts" in his match.

Over an eleven-day period there had been 280 bouts with boxers
from fifty-four countries, and Nat Fleischer, the veteran editor of
Ring magazine, claimed that he had watched them all. The Olympics had featured "above par" sparring, better than at Melbourne, but
unacceptably bad officiating, he believed. From his perspective, the
bias tilted away from the U.S. and toward the Communist bloc. At
least three of the Americans who lost in earlier rounds—Humberto
Barrera, Jerry Armstrong, and Quincy Daniels—were eliminated on
what Fleischer called "raw decisions." All, he thought, were victims
of the sporting politics of the cold war. Now here came the last America versus Iron Curtain boxing match of the Games—the eighteen-
year-old kid from Louisville versus the experienced left-handed Pole.
Pietrzykowski had been the European champ three times, took home
a bronze medal from Melbourne, and had lost only 13 times in 233
fights going into the match. He was well known to Fleischer, whose
journalistic objectivity did not prevent him from giving advice to

Clay in the holding room beforehand in the presence of Jules Menen-dez, the coach, and Ben Becker, the team manager. "Having seen the Pole in action several times, I told [Clay] that if the fight went beyond two rounds, he had to go all out to win." Clay listened and agreed. "I'll do that," he said.

All on the American side knew that Clay was their best fighter, but his weight class was also the most talented. In an earlier bout, he had struggled against the American-trained Tony Madigan of Aus-tralia, who was cool and experienced just like the Pole. The an-nouncer Bud Palmer, covering the fight for CBS, in fact believed that Madigan might have beaten Clay. Pietrzykowski presented the ad-ditional problem of being a tall lefty. The most difficult loss of Clay's young career had been against a tall lefty, Amos Johnson, at the Uni-versity of Wisconsin Field House at the Pan American trials a year earlier. How would he handle one now?

The first two rounds were uneventful. Pietrzykowski stayed back, trying to find openings for his long reach. Clay was so quick that he could dodge the Pole's left even with his gloves down. His footwork was on display, dancing left, skipping right, hands down, then in for a punch. Most of his lefts were landing just short. Both rounds were close. The boxing writers talked about what a showman Clay was but questioned whether he could really take a punch. Neil Allen thought Pietrzykowski won the first "in which there was some neat defensive work by both." Povich agreed, recording that Clay "was taking a beating from Ziggy." The judges and most observers thought otherwise and gave the round barely to Clay. In the second round, a furious attack in the last thirty seconds gave that round also to the American, but going into the final round, it was still too close for comfort. Fleischer's warning registered in Clay's corner. You have to go out there and get him now. Get him is precisely what Clay did.

"The whole picture changed in the third and last round," Allen recorded in his diary. Clay came to life "and began to put his punches together in combination clusters instead of merely whipping out a left jab. He pummeled Pietrzykowski about the ring, blood came from the nose and mouth of the Pole, and only great courage kept this triple European champion on his feet." Povich, who thought Clay could only "salvage the fight" with a knockout or something close, watched as "all of a sudden Ziggy had a bloody nose, and it seemed that Clay could hit harder than it appeared [a common theme throughout his later career] . . . and then Ziggy's whole face was a bloody mask. Clay was throwing punches from angles that were new, and he had the Pole ripe for a knockout, but in his eagerness and greenness he could not put his opponent away." Still, in the opinion of *Ring*'s Fleischer, "Clay's last-round assault on Pietrzykowski was the outstanding hitting of the tournament." It was, Fleischer said, "an exhibition of perfect hitting by the Kentucky schoolboy."

By the time it was over, even the Italians in the arena were on Clay's side. One of them was Rino Tommasi, a young boxing promoter and writer whose father, Virgilio, the technical director of the Olympics, had been watching the events from his hospital bed since his injury in a traffic accident on the eve of the Opening Ceremony. "It was a great night," Rino Tommasi said later of the boxing finals— an evening punctuated by the victories of three Italians and the unforgettable performance of the American light heavyweight. Clay was both an attractive boxer and a great actor, Tommasi said, two characteristics equally admired by the Italians. Years later, as a prominent sportswriter in Italy, Tommasi would interview Pietrzykowski, who told him that despite his success in Europe, he knew before entering the ring that Clay would beat him and that he was simply glad he lasted three rounds.

There were no hisses or whistles when Clay was announced the unanimous winner. Lute Mason, the sports director at the CBS station in San Diego, who was in Rome with a tour group but spent his days helping with the network's coverage, sat ringside at the fight and was assigned to get Clay up to the broadcast booth for an interview with Bud Palmer. "That was my last amateur fight. I'm turning pro," Clay said. "But I don't know exactly how. I want a good contract." He had intended to keep the USA trunks he wore in Rome as a souvenir, he said, but "now look at them!" They were streaked with the Pole's blood.

AS THE LOUD night of boxing drew to an end on the other side of Rome, Rafer Johnson and C. K. Yang were trudging out of Stadio Olimpico. Their competition had resumed after a rain delay of an hour and ten minutes. It was cold and dreary, the stadium lit eerily by floodlights, when the decathletes had returned to the field along with judges and timers wearing rain slickers. Olympic rules said that five events had to be completed each day; postponements were not part of the equation for this all-around contest. But no one said fans had to stay and watch, and few did. The Nelsons were among a band of fewer than a thousand who huddled in the giant stadium to witness the high jump and 400-meter run. Johnson did no better than usual in the high jump, barely clearing 6 feet, and Yang drew closer going into the quarter-mile first-day finale. Johnson always considered the 400 the toughest event in the decathlon. Here it was the end of an exhausting day—more tiring than usual because of the rain—with four events already draining your system, and now you had to run all out for as long as you could. At first Rafer hated the 400, but over the years he had grown to love it, and so did C.K. Late at night, on a soggy track, worn, chilled, and weary, they ran in the same heat. Johnson got off fast, C.K. passed him on the curve and started to pull away, then Rafer came storming back and nearly caught him at the end. It was another 1005 points for Yang, but a strong 985 for Johnson, who now led by a mere 55 points.

Would it be enough? At the Trials in Oregon, Johnson remembered, he had led by 200 points at the break and was barely able to hang on. But now he was almost too tired to worry—and too hungry. He slumped in his seat on the shuttle bus back to the village, then headed straight to the cafeteria for his first meal since steak and eggs at breakfast. It was past one in the morning when he reached his bed. The biggest athletic day of his life was but a few short hours away.

15

THE LAST LAPS

EVERYONE seemed up and about early Tuesday morning. Cassius Clay paraded through the village before breakfast, gold medal dangling from his neck. "I got to show this thing off!" he kept boasting. His coach said Clay had slept with the medal, or at least gone to bed with it. The young boxer was too excited to sleep; visions of his future flashed in his mind. He was on his way to signing a professional contract, earning serious money, and becoming even more famous as the heavyweight champion of the world. "Fool, go someplace and sit down," Lucinda Williams chided him lovingly, like a big sister, when he approached the Tigerbelles and started blabbing on about how he was the greatest. Dallas Long, the bronze medalist shot-putter, said nothing when he came across Clay that morning, but thought to himself: "This guy is such a jerk. He's never going to amount to anything."

Earl Ruby of Louisville's *Courier-Journal* visited the village first thing to get material for a column on the hometown hero. Clay told him that he hoped to be home by Friday, but first he had to stop in New York for television and radio interviews. While they were talking, Clay spotted Floyd Patterson, the heavyweight champion of the world, and himself a 1952 Olympic gold medalist, walking through the village. "Good Lord, there's the champ!" Clay shouted, running toward him. As Ruby later recounted the scene:

"Patterson said, 'Hi, boy. How's your dad?' Clay and his father had gone to Indianapolis three years earlier to meet Patterson at an exhibition. Clay loomed over Patterson. 'Look, I'm three inches taller than him,' he told reporters. 'When I fill out, I'll be bigger all around. That's something good to know. You see, I may have to fight him some day.' "

From the sprinter Dave Sime came another story of Clay encountering Patterson that morning of September 6. As Sime remembered it, he was sitting at the breakfast table in the cafeteria with Clay and a group of black American runners and boxers. "We were kidding around in this huge Quonset hut of a dining facility, and Floyd was coming toward us. Cassius said, 'Watch this, I'm going to get this guy. Watch this!' And as Floyd is walking by, he jumps up on the table with his knife and fork and says, 'I'm having you next! I'm having you for dinner!' Patterson walked by and chuckled. Floyd took it as a joke. He was laughing. Floyd dismissed him as a kid. We were all cracking up."

Ed Temple had yet another story. He remembered sitting on a stoop outside the cafeteria with Clay when a bunch of people ran by after spotting Patterson in the distance. When Temple asked Clay whether he wanted to follow them, Clay said no, "I ain't going to see no Floyd Patterson, because I'm going to be heavyweight champ myself some day." Temple could only shake his head at the kid's audacity.

Several photographs were taken that day showing Clay posing with Patterson, so that much is established fact. If other details in the various accounts conflicted, they also fit a pattern. Throughout his life as Cassius Clay, and later as Muhammad Ali, it would require literal vigilance to separate the real from the apocryphal in stories about him. Many he would concoct himself, some would be enhanced by others, but all were in service of the mythology of a self-invented character who became everything his vivid imagination could dream of and more. And all of it flowed from his inaugural performance on the world stage in Rome, where his actions were not yet infused with much larger symbolic meaning but seemed more a source of mild annoyance or comic relief.

Rafer Johnson was also up early. He had slept fitfully, his mind racing with his shortcomings in the first day of the decathlon and his expectations for the second. On the bus to the stadium, Johnson felt anxious, under more pressure than he had ever faced. His stomach was upset, not just from nerves but also from the huge meal he had eaten at midnight. His muscles were sore from the fourteen-hour day ending with the merciless 400-meter dash in the late evening chill. "The four hundred really takes you down," Johnson explained later. "You've got to recover from that, and you don't eat right and you don't sleep. And you come back the next morning . . ."

It was humid by the time he reached the track, with a draining early heat. Far from top form, Johnson made a tactical mistake before the opening event, the 110-meter high hurdles, in failing to stretch adequately. "I have a routine that I always do, and it can be a hundred twenty degrees out or freezing, and I still do that routine," he recalled. "But because I was so tired from all the stuff that happened the day before, the length of the day and no sleep, I underdid my warm-ups, and I wasn't ready to run that race." Hurdling was one of Johnson's specialties, an event he relied on to build his second-day cushion. But everything went wrong this time. He got off to a slow start, was thrown off his stride, nicked the second hurdle, stumbled and nearly fell, and was struggling to hang in there for the rest of the race. He finished with his worst time since before Melbourne, 15.3 seconds, nearly a second slower than his fastest efforts. Yang had no troubles in his heat, clearing the hurdles with excellent form and busting the tape at 14.6 seconds. The result was a swing of 183 points, putting C.K. in front by 128. The stoic Johnson thrived on pressure, but this was pushing him to the brink. Leaving the track, he walked toward his coach's seat in the stands. "Don't worry," Ducky Drake told him, "it's not over. You've got your best events coming."

The seventh event, the discus, was scheduled to get under way at 10:10, but the qualifying throws for the regular discus competition were taking place then, so the decathletes had to wait until those were done. When Johnson's turn finally arrived, his timing was off on his first throw, and again on his second. Invigorated with a sudden surge of energy for his final effort, he flung the discus 159 feet 1 inch. It was not his longest throw ever, but given the pressure he was under, he considered it one of the most competitive moments of his career. Yang could not reach 132 feet, and with another swing in momentum, Johnson was back in the lead by 144 points with three events to go after the lunch break: pole vault, javelin, and 1500 meters.

Few Olympic athletes knew one another as thoroughly as Rafer Johnson and C. K. Yang. It was not just that both had trained at UCLA for the same event under the same coaches. A deeper sensibility seemed at work in their symbiotic relationship, a spirited blend of admiration and competitiveness that pushed them to greater accomplishments together than they might have achieved apart. When Yang arrived in Los Angeles from Taiwan three years earlier, he spoke little English and was intimidated by Johnson, who had been his hero. "Are you the right C. K. Yang?" the school's assistant track coach, Craig Dixon, asked when first catching sight of him. "How come you're so skinny?" At Dixon's urging, C.K. started building his body at a downtown gym, working out with Jack LaLanne. Johnson embraced him from the start. "When I got there I had no friends," Yang recalled. "Rafer took me under his wing. He even took me home to Kingsburg, where I met his family." Their bond transcended the language barrier. Johnson later remembered that when C.K. arrived, "he handled English like I handled Chinese. Breakfast, lunch, and dinner, all he wanted to eat was beefsteak!"

Rafer was the mentor in their relationship, yet he insisted that he learned as much from C.K. as the other way around. He considered it a "blessing" that Yang came to UCLA, he said later. "C.K. was the most knowledgeable athlete at what he did. I always had an extra coach there with him. We talked about almost every event. I did more questioning of him than he of me." But the ordeal of Rome, years of work narrowing down to a final three events, tested the generous nature of their friendship. Rafer had no interest in talking to C.K. that morning, nor did C.K. want to talk to Rafer. All through lunch they kept apart. "It was just so intense, we had to get a little distance," Johnson remembered.

Until, that is, the pole vault, an event at which Yang excelled and Johnson struggled. In previous competitions, Yang regularly beat Johnson by a foot or more. Now Rafer needed all the help he could get. First to his aid was the Soviet star, Kuznetsov, resigned to third place but scoring strongly in second-day events, who whispered some advice to the American about how to move his hands up the pole during the approach. Then Yang broke the silence and huddled with Johnson briefly, going over the best speed for his run and most effective posture for planting the pole. They were mostly their own coaches during the Olympic competition; Ducky Drake was allowed no closer than a front row seat, and they could not stop themselves from coaching each other even now. Johnson, certain that his gold medal dream was on the line, pushed his body to a personal best of 13 feet 5⅜ inches. This was before the era of springy fiberglass poles that sent pole-vault heights into a loftier dimension. After clearing just over 14-1, Yang ordered the crossbar moved up to 14-9, hoping to pull away with a personal best of his own. His powerful approach sent him up high enough, but his body brushed the bar on the way over—and he had to settle for the lower score. There are so many what-ifs in the decathlon, and here was another: What if Yang had cleared that height? He would have seized the lead yet again and virtually clinched the gold. Instead, Johnson's best-ever vault kept him in front, though by a mere 24 points.

APART FROM the relays, scheduled for Thursday, this was the final afternoon of running competition on the track, and two premier events remained: the 400-meter dash and the 1500 meters. It was about 3:20 that afternoon when the six finalists for the 400 settled into the blocks for their staggered start. The sextet was stellar, led by Carl Kaufmann of Germany, who was assigned the inside lane. Otis Davis of the U.S. stood two lanes over in Lane 3, Malcolm Spence of South Africa next to Davis, and then Milkha Singh of India in Lane 5.

Of that group, the most exotic certainly was Singh. Part of it was his wondrous nickname, the Flying Sikh. Then there was his striking image on the track—running in full beard with his long hair, normally covered in a turban, instead "tied overhead in a topknot with a small chiffon handkerchief." And finally, his uncommon speed came with a moving life story. If the Olympic Movement idealized the notion that all people could live and compete in harmony, here was another lesson in the real-world obstacles to that vision. Singh was only eleven years old in 1947, when he witnessed the worst that man can do to man. He was living with his parents and other Sikh relatives in a city then known as Lyallpur inside the boundaries of the new nation of Pakistan. During the bloodletting that accompanied the partition of India and Pakistan, he watched as his parents were killed by Pakistani Muslims. With no adults to help him, he joined the desperate migration of Sikhs across the border into India, making the final leg of the journey by clinging to the side of a refugee-packed train rolling into Delhi.

From that difficult childhood, Singh had risen to star status in India, a country not known for its track prowess. After feeling outclassed as a novice twenty-year-old sprinter at the Melbourne Games, he began studying the techniques and workout schedules of American 400-meter runners and trained under a U.S. coach who had been sent to India by the State Department. Year by year he improved his times, taking first place in the 400 at both the Asian Games and the Commonwealth Games in 1958 and snatching several victories on the European tour in 1960. The Flying Sikh arrived in Rome as a favorite of the world press. "We can't automatically assume that the admirable Indian runner, Milkha Singh, will be beaten," wrote Edouard Seidler of France's *L'Équipe*. "We're continually impressed by his training and the consummate art of his running. Is he capable of running in a near world record time? Yes!" The *Washington Post*'s Shirley Povich was another believer, writing that "Milkha could be the first bearded winner of the 400 meters in Olympic history."

As he entered the stadium for the final, Singh felt "quite relaxed," but by the time he lined up for the start, his nerves were eating at him. He realized that he had never run in a field this strong. He had beaten the South African Spence in the Commonwealth Games, but both Davis and Kaufmann had coasted to wins ahead of him in the preliminary heats in Rome, and they seemed capable of more—blasting through the 400 faster than the bearded one had dreamed of running. Kaufmann had his legion of German fans chanting his name now, but Davis was the runner Singh feared most. The scariest thing about Otis Crandall Davis was that at the relatively ancient age of twenty-eight, perhaps because he had come to running so late in his career, he seemed only now to be reaching his peak.

Davis came from Bill Bowerman's renowned track program at the University of Oregon, but he was not a typical Bowerman product. At a school that specialized in white distance runners, Davis was a black sprinter who had taken up the sport very late. He grew up in Tuscaloosa, in the shadows of the University of Alabama (a school that he could not attend because of the color of his skin), joined the air force for four years out of high school in the early 1950s, and from there ended up in California, playing basketball at Los Angeles City College and cleaning toilets at an aeronautics plant. A skinny six-one rebounder who could run forever on the fast break, Davis was offered a scholarship to play basketball at Oregon, but he never adapted to the conservative style of play there and ended up on the track team. Kenny Moore, who grew up in Eugene and went on to become a world-class marathoner and writer, remembered how as adolescents he and his pals were all attracted to the newcomer. "We instantly adored this gentle, bemused black man, the first most of us had been anywhere near, save for some gospel singers who came through at church."

In fact, Davis was burning inside and did not feel so gentle or bemused, though he would never show that to the local kids. As Bowerman told the story later, the basketball coach, frustrated by Davis's play, urged the track coach to take a look at him. Davis would later insist that this was myth and that he decided on his own to go out for track. Whatever the case, Bowerman tried "Ote"—as he called Davis—first in the high jump, then the 100, then the 200. "I didn't know how to start, but I seemed to be a good finisher," Davis recalled, and that characteristic eventually led him to the longest sprint, the 400. His first year at that distance was "trial and error." At the NCAA tournament at Indiana University he ran too fast, burned out in the homestretch, and was passed by the entire field. "Then I went to an AAU race in Colorado, and they said I ran too slow. I just had to figure things out."

At the Olympic Trials at Stanford, he finished third, barely making the team, but from there he got stronger week by week, his times dropping steadily during the warm-up meets in California, Oregon, and Switzerland. Bowerman was mostly preoccupied with his milers, Dyrol Burleson and Jim Grelle, both of whom had also made the Olympic squad. His advice to Davis was to stay with the pack for the first 200, coast the third 100, and then burn his way home. Davis listened but felt that he was finding a rhythm on his own. "Each week I was learning, so the timing of Rome was just right," he said. Walking out toward the track from the Stadio Olimpico tunnel for the final, a feeling washed over him that he had never felt before. It was a sensation of "sheer concentration, singleness of purpose." If Milkha Singh was suddenly overtaken by nerves as he knelt at the starting blocks, Davis felt just the opposite, a supreme confidence. Whoever was going to win would have to come by me first, he said to himself.

At the gun, Singh and Spence set the early pace while Davis got off to his usual slow start. "I saw the Indian guy in the corner of my eye," Davis said later. "He was outside of me. I knew the pace had to be fast." Spence and Singh were clocked nearly a half-second ahead at the 200-meter mark as they approached the curve. "Then Davis accelerated so violently and so irresistibly" that he flashed into the lead, Neil Allen noted in his diary. The stadium erupted in a roar, electrified by Davis's charge. The Flying Sikh looked to his side to gauge his position, thinking the pace was too fast and that he had better slow down. At that very moment, Davis passed him, followed by Kaufmann. "That fraction of a second decided my fate," Singh reflected later. With 100 meters left, he had dropped from the front to near the back. Davis was now ahead. Watching in the stands, Coach Bowerman was worried that Davis had surged too soon. Had he? The lead was almost seven yards, then five, then three, and two. Kaufmann was closing ferociously, making up ground as they neared the tape. But Davis, thinking only of reaching the end, blocking out the fatigue, refused to fade.

Davis ran upright—"swayback," he called it—with his hands in front of him, while the German leaned far forward at the end, his head low, his hands winging behind him as though he were preparing to dive into a pool. Kaufmann splattered into hard cinder instead, sprawling onto the track. Davis felt the tape break at his chest and knew that he had won, but the judges were not sure. It looked too close to call, another photo finish. Paralleling Kaufmann's closing surge on Davis, Singh had narrowed the gap on Spence, the space between them so narrow that they, too, had to wait for a final ruling. Every second feels like an hour in a situation like that. This wait was nearly fifteen minutes, an eternity. Finally the names flashed on the electronic scoreboard: 1—Davis, 2—Kaufmann, 3—Spence, 4—Singh. All four had broken the Olympic record, and Davis had smashed the world record, coming in at 44.9, the first ever to run under the 45-second mark.

When Davis learned of the results, he jumped high into the air in sheer joy, legs wide apart, arms high above his head. Then he dropped his track suit, picked it up, waved his hands all around, grabbed his face in disbelief, overcome with emotion, shook hands with a straw-hatted judge, and twirled around, two 360-degree turns, hands over his eyes. His U.S. teammates rushed over to congratulate him as American fans in the stands, some wearing rain slickers, stood to cheer. "Something was pushing me out there," he said. "And it wasn't the wind."

The Flying Sikh had been the first to shake Davis's hand. Singh was heartbroken, feeling that he had disappointed his country, but in fact his showing was hailed back home. "He clocked his best," wrote the columnist for the *Times of India*, "but that wasn't good enough and one might venture to say that, all in all, no athlete could have done better under the circumstances. It is the Perfect Failure, and long after tiresome persons have finished lamenting that he did not secure even a bronze medal shall we remember the long months of preparation, the gradual improvement, and the great moment and the best performance of our versatile athlete. If Milkha Singh failed, it is a lesson to all athletic-minded people in this country of how much it takes to produce a world best. Shabash"—well done—"Milkha Singh!"

The photo-finish call on the 400 had taken so long that a loud hum was still reverberating inside the stadium in the aftermath of

Davis's record run when the 1500 field began to assemble on the track. Here was an impressive assortment of sub-four-minute men from Sweden, Norway, Romania, Hungary, the U.S., and France, but one among them seemed in a world of his own. Herb Elliott of Australia was the clear favorite. He had been blessed by none other than the godfather of milers, Roger Bannister, who described Elliott as if he were some primordial species born in the wilderness and bred for running. "To match his hawk nose and the gaunt, Viking manliness of his face, he has a lean body and a smooth stride, lithe and steady, about as gentle as a panther," Bannister wrote in the *Sunday Times*. "At his coach [Percy] Cerutty's Portsea training camp, he runs wild and barefoot along the beach, over sand dunes, seeking to replenish primitive energy sapped by the artificiality of track training. When running, he seems to achieve instinctive and unfettered expression of all his potentialities. Though he may very well have a racing brain, too, the refinement, pace, judgment, and tactics have so far been superfluous . . . Like so many Australians, he has a sense of freedom and is unafraid of enjoying his successes and making the most of them."

While revealing in some respects, Bannister's rendering of Elliott mostly underscored the mix of condescension and envy with which many Brits viewed their stereotypically untamed younger brothers from Down Under. Mature beyond his years at twenty-two, already a husband and father, Elliott might have been a natural-born runner, but it was a combination of will, brainpower, and rigorous training that brought him to Rome as a gold medal favorite. Far from a mindless creature, he was an aesthete who loved poetry and looked for the beauty in life. After an early high school career as a runner in Perth, he briefly abandoned the sport altogether, taking up the teenage pursuits of smoking and drinking beer, until he started a comeback under the tutelage of Cerutty, the brilliant but oddest of odd ducks. That Cerutty had been booted from a room in the Olympic Village because of his busybody ways was a surprise to no one. Even Elliott had a love-hate relationship with his iconoclastic coach, viewing him as equal parts guru and pest. Still, he believed deeply in the sixty-three-year-old goateed vegetarian and knew that without the program of careful diet, bodybuilding, swimming, and running up eight-story sand dunes, he would not be where he was now.

Elliott and Cerutty made a lasting impression wherever they went. In 1958 they had flown to California for a series of track meets and stayed at Cordner Nelson's home in Stockton. Now, two years later, as the Nelsons sat in the stands of Stadio Olimpico for the 1500 final, they thought back to that unforgettable visit. The girls all developed huge crushes on the dashing Elliott, who could play the piano, read, and talk at the same time, but it was Cerutty who dominated the scene. "Cerutty was opinionated. He was saying a lot of things and always thought he was right," Cord Nelson recalled. "Like no one else knew how to train an athlete. At our house he was talking about foot planting. How you put your foot down on the track when you run. How Paavo Nurmi [the great Finnish distance runner from the 1920s] ran heel first. He had Elliott run across our living room toes first. And after dinner, Mrs. Nelson served ice cream and got chewed out by Cerutty, who ranted about its unhealthiness. The next morning he and Elliott ate raw Quaker Oats with fruit and nuts, part of their training. We all started eating raw oats after they left."

After his own raw oats breakfast on the morning of the Olympic final, Elliott, who was allowed to take a room outside the village with his wife, Anne, visited a Catholic cathedral, praying and easing his mind, then paced around before heading over to the track hours ahead of time. He and Cerutty consulted again, reaffirming the tactics they had decided upon the night before. Cerutty would be seated in the stands near the first turn, a fourth of the way around the track. Elliott was to look for him there on the last lap. If the coach waved his towel up and down, that meant someone was closing from behind. If he waved it in a circle, that meant Elliott had victory assured but was on pace to break the world record.

At the race's start, Elliott, in white shorts and shirt with a gold and black diagonal stripe, lined up on the inside lane but was quickly passed by several runners and found himself boxed in near the middle of the pack. From the stands, it appeared that he was loping along easily, but in fact he felt tired and was worried about a heavy feeling in his legs. He was in fourth place after the first lap and stayed in that position the second time around. Then, after the first turn of the third lap, he glided easily to the front, running a few yards ahead of Michel Bernard of France and Hungary's Istvan Rozsavolgyi. He coasted out front for a half lap before suddenly breaking away as though propelled by a booster rocket. As Neil Allen viewed it from the press section, "he struck unanswerably, struck with complete disregard for what was happening behind him among his courtiers." Track experts knew Elliott was superb, but nonetheless they were awed by how gracefully he separated himself from an excellent field. It seemed to Roger Bannister that "no other athlete in Rome commanded such superiority over his rivals." The American runner Jim Beatty, watching in the stands, thought it was "the most dramatic middle-distance burst" he had ever seen. Elliott's hands seemed weightless, his body perfectly erect, his feet barely touching the ground.

Rounding into the bell lap, he felt the wind blowing into his face and worried about fading just as he approached the prearranged signal point.

"Time to give him a rev-up," Cerutty muttered to a nearby radio reporter in the stands. Concerned that Elliott might not spot him in the crowd, the coach bolted from his seat, ran down the aisle, hopped a railing, and landed in the dry moat that separated the stands from the track. Cerutty had never been one for protocol and was willing to test any rule, break any barrier, to help a gifted runner. Here he was nearing the edge of the track, wildly waving not a towel but his yellow T-shirt in a wide circle. There was no way Elliott could miss it. "I got the circle signal and cut loose," the runner said later. He increased the lead from 10 meters to 12 to 15 to 20. "It just seemed superhuman," recalled Don Graham, the young copyboy for the *Washington Post*. "It was so beautiful to watch, you could hardly believe it." To the *Times* of London, it was "as if he had donned some crown and was followed only by camp followers."

The Australian writer E. W. Tipping, from his seat in the stands behind the crooner Bing Crosby, cast his gaze away from Elliott back to a commotion in the moat. "Two Italian policemen had pounced on Percy, and there was quite a brawl until [they] managed to push him back across the moat . . . And poor Percy we fear never did see his protégé breast the tape . . . He had to keep one eye on his stopwatch and one eye on Elliott and one eye on the cops. He didn't care what they did to him after he got his signal across to Herb."

Pulsing down the homestretch, Elliott finally struggled against fatigue. Dealing with pain is the unavoidable fate of a miler. The way Elliott saw it, "it's when you stick to it that you show you're the superior man." He stuck to it now, running through the pain, his 3:35.6 shattering the old Olympic record set by Ireland's Ron Delany in Melbourne in 1956 by nearly 6 seconds. The pace was so swift that five runners trailing far behind him also broke the old mark.

Tipping tapped out a column in the form of a letter to his two boys, Paul and Tony, "and all the other schoolboy Herb Elliott fans" in Australia. They were correct, he began. "He *is* the greatest runner of all. Greatest middle distance runner, anyway. There's only one way to describe how he won the derby of the Olympics this afternoon. He won like Phar Lap"—the greatest racehorse in Australian history. After the race, Tipping noted, "Herb was cool, calm, and collected, as if he'd just finished one of those interclub miles we've seen him run at Olympic Park [in Melbourne] on a Saturday afternoon. But we noticed he had a good squint at the gold medal as soon as he stepped off the stand after the victory ceremony. A group of Australians sitting underneath a results board tried to start 'Waltzing

Matilda,' but it petered out. Someone shouted 'Coo-eee,' the call of the Australian kangaroo."

Much like the socialist commentators earlier in the Games who went wild over Czechoslovakia's third-place finish in the eight-man heavyweight crew while virtually ignoring the stunning victory of the Germans, the French press now kissed off Elliott's amazing performance to concentrate instead on the surprising second-place finish of their Michel Jazy. French medals were so few and far between in Rome that Jazy's showing, punctuated by a burst nearly as strong as Elliott's in the last lap, immediately became the stuff of Gallic legend. "Neither the French who were in Rome nor those who were in front of their TV screen will forget this extraordinary 1500 meter race, because Michel Jazy, the small typographer . . . achieved an historical feat," wrote a columnist for *Le Miroir des Sports*. "Michel Jazy satisfied all who believed in him against all hope. As a result of a fantastic effort, he won the silver medal, destroying the French record in the process. The little guy was thus rewarded for the terrible sacrifices that he had made, the long and difficult training sessions that he had endured. With Michel Jazy, France also had her stadium god." At last, Charles de Gaulle might no longer feel the need to do it all himself.

Cordner Nelson, who assigned himself the metric-mile coverage for *Track & Field News,* caught up with his former houseguest Elliott after the event "swigging an Italian beer." Was it a modest act of rebellion against his coach's strict diet? No, ice cream was far worse than beer. Cerutty had wanted a faster pace during the race, but that would have been counterproductive, Elliott said. "If it had been any faster, I could hardly have finished." Having escaped the clutches of the Italian police, Cerutty was now mingling with the press corps, rejoicing in the victory. He felt giddy enough even to make fun of the great Roger Bannister. "Here is how you run," he said to Bannister and then proceeded to waddle with what Tex Maule of *Sports Illustrated* called "all the grace of a spavined plow horse, a travesty of Bannister's style." The Brit replied dryly that he felt compelled to say he found himself hard to recognize in old Percy. So did everyone, it seemed, except the one with the gold medal, Herb Elliott.

DARKNESS HAD fallen by the time Rafer Johnson and C. K. Yang got around to their final javelin throws. A full moon glowed above the stadium. C.K., his body chilled by the night air, wrapped his shoulders in a blanket. Rafer knelt patiently, chewing a wad of gum in rhythmic circles. The competition had been intense all of this second long day. First Yang had snatched the lead after the high hurdles, then Johnson had taken it back with the discus, then he had watched his margin shrink with the high jump. "That was the kind of day it was. Dramatic, going back and forth," recalled Don Graham. "What was fabulous about it was that it lasts two days, and both guys were on top of their games, pushing each other." The javelin, the penultimate event, was usually Johnson's safety cushion, where he amassed enough points to withstand any charge in the closing 1500-meter run. He tried to relax, to turn off his mind and just perform, but he could not stop himself from brooding about the situation. His approach on the final effort was too slow, he felt sluggish, and his distance was the shortest of his three throws. He would have to settle for just under 230 feet, still 6 feet better than Yang, but not enough to make him feel comfortable.

Here came the 1500, and Johnson was now leading Yang by only 67 points. As fate would have it, they were scheduled to run in the same heat, the last one. Fluent in the arcane scoring system of the decathlon, both men swiftly calculated that if Yang won by 10 seconds or more, the gold medal was his. This was far from an improbable task. C.K.'s best time in the event was 4:36.9, while Johnson's best was nearly 13 seconds slower.

In the front row of the stands near the 330-meter mark sat Ducky Drake. The UCLA coach's words had always been crucial to Johnson. It was a letter from Ducky that had reassured Rafer and inspired him on the way to his groundbreaking victory in Moscow two years earlier: "Remember you're the champion. You're the one they have to beat, so let them worry. Go about your work with a quiet confidence that cannot be shaken."

Johnson's confidence was not shaken now, but he needed more advice, so he approached his coach at the edge of the stands. How should he run this most important race of his life? Drake had already thought it through. "The key thing is that when C.K. tries to pull away—and he will try—you have to stay with him. At some point C.K. will look back to see where you are, and you have to be there. If he opens up, you have to go with him. You cannot let him build that yardage."

Easier for Drake to say than for Johnson to do, but still it was a sound plan, perhaps the only plan that could save him. Rafer nodded in agreement and walked back toward the track. About halfway there, he turned and saw none other than C.K. approaching the same spot at the edge of the stands. Ducky, after all, was his coach too.

"Ducky said to me, 'C.K., you run as fast as you can. Rafer cannot keep up with you!'" Yang later recalled.

At that moment, Drake was like a master chess player competing against himself. He saw the whole board and was making the best moves for both sides.

But C.K. was not convinced. He trained with Rafer every day. He knew how competitive his old teammate was. Even if Yang was so much better at this distance, he felt uneasy. What if he tried to pull away and got a cramp like he did at the Trials in Oregon?

It was twenty minutes after nine by the time they approached the starting line. "The pressure was on. I don't know if I've ever felt more pressure than I felt starting that race," Johnson recalled. "Most times I compete, and it's like I have a little bit of control. In that event, it wasn't like I lost control, but I was so excited and felt the pressure so much that it's like I'm going to lose my breath. Like I couldn't breathe. You don't really have trouble breathing; it's not like you're going to faint. But breathing becomes a chore. And it was a chore for me to breathe before that race. So I knew it was going to be tough. This is pressure time."

There were four other runners in the race, but they were inconsequential, like ghosts, not there. All that mattered were Johnson and Yang; all eyes in the stadium were trained on them. After a late workout, Pete Newell and some of his players on the American basketball team took seats near Ducky Drake to watch the climax. They became totally engaged in what Newell called the "greatest single sports event I've ever seen." Most of the Tigerbelles were there, too, rooting hard for Johnson. Lucinda Williams said she and her teammates had crushes on Rafer, their captain. "But he was too focused to look at anybody. He was the greatest, greater than Cassius. He was such a gracious man." The darkening night and the nip in the air, a sense of autumn coming, something ending, added to the tension. As the race got under way, Tex Maule jotted down the impressionistic scene: "His strong, cold face impassive, the big man pounded steadily through the dank chill of the Roman night. Two steps in front of him, Formosa's Chuan-Kwang Yang moved easily. In the gap between them lay the Olympic decathlon championship."

Johnson ran the first two laps with determination. "I stuck to him like a shadow, dogging his footsteps stride for stride." Midway through the race, C.K. picked up the pace, but Rafer stayed with him, moving his position from Yang's inside shoulder to his right shoulder. He wanted to be fully visible when C.K. turned around. Just as Coach Drake had predicted, C.K. did indeed turn around. And he was stunned to see Rafer at his right shoulder, running faster than he anticipated. Not only that, "he looked like he was smiling or something," Yang recalled.

Johnson was smiling, but it was pure acting. "I figured he was expecting to look back and see me dragging, with my head down, looking as though I were ready to die. That's what he thought he would see, and I just wanted to be sure to let him know that this was going to be different. I didn't feel any different. I could have had my head down and dragging because I was feeling that kind of fatigue and pressure, but I didn't want to show him that. So I smiled as big a smile as I could get."

By the final lap, troublesome memories of Oregon seeped into Yang's head. He worried that he might cramp again. But how could he shake the big guy? He felt he had no choice but to steel himself for one more acceleration, one final push to break into the clear. It seemed to work for a short time, but then Yang felt his body weakening. Coming around the turn, he looked back again, and there was Johnson, clinging, only three yards behind.

Johnson tried not to think about the clock, or how fast the pace was, or the pain in his legs. He was "struggling so hard," noted Neil Allen, "that we in the stands could almost feel his pain." But he kept telling himself that he had one crucial advantage over C.K. "My huge advantage was this was the last time I was going to do this. It didn't matter. This was the last time. And C.K., he had several more times; this was not his last race. I probably made that to my advantage more than it properly was. I kept saying to myself, 'I don't have to do this again! I don't have to do this again!' That was one of the positive things that was going through my mind, and just carrying that thought, to me, was very helpful. It wasn't anything I spoke or verbalized to anyone, but just to myself. I said, 'This is it. Just this one more time. I can do this one as good as I've done it.' You sort of talk yourself into feelings sometimes that you use in the most positive way, and that was definitely what I was doing. I would never run the fifteen hundred again. Never. Never. More important, I would never run it at the end of doing nine other events. 'You don't have to do this again. And you don't have to do the decathlon, either.' "

Tex Maule called it "the tensest five minutes of the entire Games. And it grew and grew until it seemed like a thin high sound in the stadium." Down the homestretch, Yang was bobbing and struggling,

Johnson was moving mechanically, sheer will propelling him forward. They crossed the line only 1.2 seconds apart, Yang at 4:48.5, Johnson at 4:49.7. It was Johnson's best time ever. Yang had finished ahead but knew he had lost. A few steps after finishing, Rafer caught up to C.K., his close friend and tenacious foe. He felt at once jubilant and sad. "I never in my whole life but that once competed against someone where I had a little bit of ambivalence about beating him," he would explain later. "I mean, I wanted to win. I didn't want to lose to him, and I wanted to beat him and all that, but I just had ambivalence. I was exhilarated that I won and totally depressed that C.K. lost. I had both feelings."

As they came to a stop, Rafer put his head on C.K.'s shoulder. Yang bent down to catch his breath, and Johnson bent with him, hands on knees, as officials and photographers rushed toward them in the artificial light of the stadium. Johnson straightened and walked around, arms akimbo, smiling and shaking hands with well-wishers, utterly out of breath. Yang slipped over to a bench and put his head in his hands in despair. He had wanted to win and thought he would win. But Rafer Johnson was still a god to him, and a friend, and he would have other chances. (Yang in fact would go on to set the world record in 1963.) He got up, jacket around his shoulders, head bowed, and found a Taiwanese official who hugged him and patted him on the back.

A few seconds later, Yang was bending down again when Johnson appeared, lifted him up, and stood with him arm in arm. "It was a moment of such beauty," Neil Allen wrote in his diary, "that I was not surprised to see one friend in the press box with tears in his eyes, and I for one, for the first time in my life, found that my hands were trembling too much to type." To Don Graham, "that fantastic moment when Yang turned to Rafer and hugged him, that seemed like what the Olympics were all about." The special vacation that his father had arranged for him now gave Graham this unforgettable memory. He left the stadium thinking that he wanted to be a decathlete.

Being a decathlete was now the last thing on Rafer Johnson's mind. He had pushed himself to the finish line by telling himself this was the last time, and now he told the world. "I never want to go through that again—never," he said in the dressing room. "I'm awfully tired . . . I don't even want to think of another decathlon. All I want to do is get back to the Olympic Village, walk around by myself, look at the moon, and think."

After back-to-back fourteen-hour days, ten events, draining humidity, evening chill, rain delays, unbearable tension, and the accumulation of an Olympic record 8392 points (by the scoring system used in 1960), Rafer Johnson left the Stadio Olimpico for the last time at eleven o'clock that night, retracing the steps he had taken nearly two weeks earlier as the captain and flag bearer for the U.S. Olympic team. As he trudged, relieved and exhausted, along the moonlit Tiber and over the bridge, C. K. Yang, now just a friend, no longer a competitor, walked once again at his side.

JOHNSON'S VICTORY was a cause for celebration. Not only was he immensely popular among his teammates, but his starring role in Rome was a relief to U.S. officials who saw the Olympics as an important propaganda battle in the cold war. With racial confrontations and overt acts of segregation rocking the South, from Florida to Washington, DC, during the very days of the Games, and the Soviets spreading stories about the inequities of American life at every opportunity, Rafer Johnson, the person and the athlete, was viewed as a powerful antidote to the otherwise irrefutable poison of American racism. And while other controversies swirled around the U.S. team—Did some athletes choke? Were they partying too much? Could they be counted on to say the right thing?—Johnson was a rock of stability. No one could question his sense of purpose or his goodwill. The Soviets admired him as much as anyone else. In the dressing room after the meet, Kuznetsov, who had been unable to mount a charge for gold but finished with the decathlon bronze, embraced Johnson with a bear hug and kissed him on both cheeks. The Soviet press did the same, figuratively, prominently noting Johnson's achievement and harkening back to his glorious performance earlier in Moscow.

What the Soviets and their Eastern bloc allies would not acknowledge was the silver medal winner. *Pravda*'s account of the decathlon took note of who came in first, third (Kuznetsov), and fourth (Soviet Yuri Kutenko), but said nothing about second place, as though C. K. Yang did not exist, an ideological extension of their refusal to acknowledge Taiwan, by any name. At the American legation in Budapest, Hungary, U.S. diplomat Nicholas Feld took note of this omission in a dispatch to Washington. In reading the Olympic coverage in the Hungarian sports magazine *Kepes Sport,* he said, "although Rafer Johnson and Vasily Kuznetsov, his longtime Russian rival, are carefully covered, the magazine made no mention of the California collegian Yang, a Nationalist Chinese . . . In this respect, the Hungarian press followed the Soviet technique of relegating the Nationalist Chinese to the *memory hole* by expunging Yang from the pages of sports history."

In Taipei, it was already morning when the decathlon ended. The local papers had waited overnight for the results and hit the streets with extra editions. Yang's silver medal was the top story, his photograph on the front page of every paper. The Chinese Track and Field Association sent two trucks into the streets with loudspeakers blaring the news. Volunteers roamed block to block with pamphlets extolling the exploits of "the Iron Man of Asia." Top officials made their way from the capital city to rural Taitung County to pay their respects to C.K.'s parents. They announced that since "the Chinese Communists will not permit the enslaved millions to know the glory of their countryman," plans were under way to direct broadcast transmissions to the mainland. President and Madame Chiang, who had been given periodic reports on the decathlon, were said to have "smiled happily when told of the results." Among other things, the decathlon story had at least temporarily overwhelmed accounts of Chiang's repression of leading democratic dissidents. Keeping the track team in Rome, rather than boycotting the Games as the Americans suggested, now seemed fully justified in Taipei with the news that Chuan-Kwang Yang was bringing home the island's first and only Olympic medal.

16

NEW WORLDS

BEFORE President Eisenhower held a press conference on the Wednesday morning of September 7, White House advisers prepared a memo detailing his suggested answers to possible questions. The issues of the day included a water dispute involving India and Pakistan; the role of religion in the general election campaign between Vice President Nixon and Senator Kennedy, whose Catholicism had emerged as a significant issue; the latest on the bloody revolt in the Congo; Khrushchev's impending visit to New York for the opening session of the United Nations; and the cold war propaganda battle going on at the Olympics in Rome.

One question Eisenhower's staff thought he might get was along these lines: "Mr. President, would you comment on the U.S.-Soviet rivalry at the Olympic Games, which are now taking place in Rome, Italy?"

The proposed answer read as though IOC president Avery Brundage had scripted it:

"The Olympic spirit emphasizes individual competition, good sportsmanship, and international friendship," Eisenhower was to say. "It is, therefore, a mistake to consider the Olympics as a competition between two large nations. Olympic champions come from both large and small nations. All the Olympic champions, whatever their race or national origin, merit the admiration of sports followers everywhere. The Olympic creed states that 'the important thing in the Olympic Games is not winning but taking part.' "

As it turned out, no variation of that response was uttered aloud by Eisenhower when he met the press in the Executive Office Building that morning, because no correspondent raised the question. But if the press would not broach the subject of cold war sports rivalries, others would. There was growing concern among American officials in Rome that the U.S. was not being aggressive enough in counteracting propaganda from the Soviets and was particularly vulnerable on issues of race. The competition at the Summer Games extended beyond the athletic arenas, their thinking went, and it seemed naive not to acknowledge it. The Olympic gathering was not just another sporting event but one of those rare occasions when the wide world was watching and paying attention, and when it was important to deal with perceptions as much as reality. At about the same time that Eisenhower held his press conference in Washington, Arthur Lentz, press chief of the U.S. Olympic Committee, visited the U.S. embassy in Rome to push that argument—"informally asking" diplomats there to persuade the president to make another public gesture before the Olympics ended.

Ambassador Zellerbach agreed and drafted a dispatch to the State Department in the compressed grammar of diplomatic cablespeak: "Especially in view some press allegations individual misbehavior, and Communist taunt that U.S. relies on Negro leadership in games while discrimination exists against Negroes at home, message congratulating team composed of 'Representative Americans' on sportsmanlike competition in best Olympic tradition would be useful."

The embassy message made its way to the White House with strong backing from foreign policy analysts. "The Department also believes it important to team morale and national and international opinion that the president extend congratulations to the team on its athletic performance," asserted a State Department memo to the White House. Enclosed was a draft of what Eisenhower could say. Echoing the phrasing of Zellerbach, the last line of the draft stated, "All citizens take pride in the gallant performance of *these representative Americans* in the face of stiff competition." It took another week for White House aides to edit that sentence and release it under Eisenhower's signature. By that time, the Olympics were over, the athletes, journalists, and propagandists of the world were dispersed, and the statement ended up gathering dust in the files of U.S. Olympic Committee president Tug Wilson at his office on North LaSalle Street in Chicago. And in the final draft, the phrase "these representative Americans"—wording that Olympic and State Department officials thought would best emphasize that black and white athletes were equally American—was changed to read ". . . in the gallant performance of *their representatives* in the face of stiff competition." The meaning was lost, along with the message.

One question reporters did ask Eisenhower at the Wednesday morning press conference concerned his age. In little more than a month, Ike would celebrate his seventieth birthday and become the oldest president in American history, passing Andrew Jackson. The president cut short a query about how he "maintained good health" at that advanced age with a baseball analogy: "First of all, when a pitcher has a no-hitter going, no one reminds him of it." But in fact Eisenhower did seem old that September, and it was not just because Kennedy, rich and handsome and forty-three, was going around the country talking about vigor and youth and getting America moving again. Life was changing noticeably during those final months of 1960; the world seemed on the cusp not just of a new decade but of a new cultural era. No one could say precisely what the future would bring, but some hints, good and bad, could be gleaned from the Olympics in Rome.

Hours before Eisenhower met the press in Washington, Rafer Johnson appeared on the infield at the Stadio Olimpico for the last time. He was out of uniform, dressed in a white shirt and sharp dark suit and tie, as he stepped onto the platform to receive the gold medal he had earned the night before. "Weeks to train, a day to compete, and a lifetime to remember"—that was the Ducky Drake motto that helped drive Rafer toward his goal. He would have the ultimate memory now, and the realization brought tears flowing down his face, but the decathlon champ and first black ever to carry the American flag at the Opening Ceremony was far more than a bit of sporting nostalgia. What could be said of Cassius Clay, with his irrepressible sense of self, and even more of Wilma Rudolph, with her unconquerable grace, was most applicable to Rafer Johnson, with his universal class and cool. All of them to varying degrees were not so much "representative Americans"—as the diplomats would have it—but groundbreaking figures, pushing forward.

ALSO BREAKING ground was Ljudmila Shevtsova-Lysenko of the Soviet Union. In the women's 800-meter run that Wednesday afternoon, Shevtsova tied her own world record of 2:04.3 while barely edging out Brenda Jones of Australia, but the excellent time was not the most noteworthy aspect of the event. The history came in the running of the race at all. While Wilma Rudolph's magical victories in the sprints drew far more attention, and the CBS Olympic coverage of Rudolph blazing to the tape proved inspirational to a generation of girls in the United States, the 800-meter race marked another important step in the long push for recognition of women in sports.

Progress in the modern Olympics might have moved slightly ahead of society at large, but still it came fitfully. The women's 800 had been run once before, in 1928, and then was banned for thirty-two years because the males who controlled track and field thought women were incapable of running such a long distance. Most of the old guard never wanted it to return. When a proposal to reinstitute the race was made at the IOC session in Munich in 1959, John J. Garland, a U.S. representative, voted against it. The minutes of that meeting state that he was "opposed on account of the fact that, in Amsterdam in 1928, he was shocked by this women's race which figured on the program." Men collapsed during or at the end of races quite often, but the sight of women so fatigued was too much for Garland. Avery Brundage felt the same way. "I can still see the contestants [in 1928] falling from exhaustion and collapsing all over the track," he said as a way of explaining his opposition. But the IOC vice president under Brundage, the Marquess of Exeter, the former British hurdler, pushed for the return of the women's 800, saying that the IOC "must go with the times." The Australians also supported it, along with the Soviets and most of the Eastern bloc countries—just enough for the measure to pass by a close 26-to-22 vote.

That women were participating in the Olympics at all challenged the original concept of Pierre de Coubertin, founding father of the modern Games (or more precisely, not the first modern Games but the first modern version that succeeded). Although de Coubertin envisioned his Olympics as a revival of the ancient Greek Games, in which women were not allowed, his sexism was more personal than historical. He said he was disturbed by the very notion of women competing in sports, often citing how upset he once was to see women whooshing down a snowy hill on sleds. In his writings, though he grudgingly approved of women taking part in a few athletic endeavors, he did not think they should compete in public. Despite his disapproval, women participated in some Olympic sports, starting in 1900 with tennis and golf. Archery was added four years later, then gymnastics and figure skating (a Summer Games event in that era), followed by fencing in 1924, but still not track and field. Led by the dynamic French activist Alice Milliat, women athletes formed their own track-and-field organization to counter the men, and staged their own small-scale version of the Games in Paris in 1922 and in Sweden in 1926. They finally forced the IOC to include women's track and field in 1928, but the backlash after the running of the 800-meter race in Amsterdam was so intense that it led to a temporary step backward. In 1929 the IOC voted to remove the entire women's track-and-field program from the Games. This ban was overturned two years later with the help of some male officials, led by Gustavus Kirby, the U.S. representative on the International Amateur Athletic Federation, who said that if women could not compete, the American men might boycott the 1932 Games.

But the misperceptions persisted for decades, and so did the barriers. Chris McKenzie, the wife of U.S. marathoner Gordon McKenzie, and herself a distance runner from England, often trained with her husband in the Bronx in the two years leading up to the Rome Olympics, but she found herself on the outside when it came to events, banned from running in 5-kilometer and 10-kilometer races because she was a woman. Since Chris is a name used by both sexes, she often entered events under her real name, hoping the sponsors would not discover that she was a woman until it was too late. At least once she was chased down the street by an outraged judge. At a race in Washington, DC, she ran carrying a sign that read: "If I Can Carry a Baby for Nine Months, I Can Run 10 Miles."

The restoration of the women's 800 was a long time coming, and even now there were objections. As Shevtsova-Lysenko and her competitors gathered on the Stadio Olimpico track, Don Graham overheard a British journalist muttering to Shirley Povich about how it was "unconscionable—they should never allow women to run so far." The harrumphing continued during the race, especially when a runner who was leading after the first lap, Dixie Willis of Australia, veered off the track and collapsed before the end. Braven Dyer of the *Los Angeles Times* said the event left him "cold," then described the scene much as the old-line journalists had back in Amsterdam, saying "the sight of exhausted ladies bent over double in the middle of the track at the finish of the 800 meters is something I won't forget for a long time." But this time there was no long-term overreaction, and the rise of women in track and field continued, slowly. Twelve years later, at the 1972 Munich Olympics, women would run the 1500, and after another dozen years they finally could run as far as the men, undertaking the marathon at the 1984 Games in Los Angeles.

In a later study of women and the Olympics, Bridget Mary Handley identified five obstacles they faced. The first was psychological, "the assumption that females are not tough enough psychologically to stand the stress of competition." Second was sociological, based on the historic "connection between sports and war" and the notion that physical competition was "not compatible with society's stereotyped image of what the female should be." Third was physiological, "the fear of becoming heavily muscled and unfeminine in appearance." The final barriers had to do with two of the defining biological characteristics of women: menstruation and pregnancy. As women increased their participation in the Olympics, Handley said, all five factors were shown to be based on "misconceptions, hearsay, male chauvinism, old wives' tales, and sparseness of biological, medical, psychological, and sociological data." Women were not as fragile as commonly assumed and were no more susceptible to stress than men. Medical science established that strenuous sports did not damage the reproductive organs, and studies showed that menstruation had no effect or minimal effect on performance. Handley cited a study of women at a track-and-field meet held in Prague in 1930. Performances dropped during menstruation in only 8 percent of the cases; in 63 percent there was no change; and 29 percent of the women had their best performances while menstruating.

Shevtsova-Lysenko and the twenty-six other women who finished the 800 meters in Rome were among a record 611 female athletes at the 1960 Games, up from 376 at Melbourne four years earlier.

They competed in thirty-nine events, also a record, double the number they were given in Berlin in 1936. Ten events were in track and field, nine in swimming and diving, six in gymnastics, five in equestrian, five yachting, two fencing, and two canoeing. There was a complicated cold war aspect to the involvement of women in international athletics. Where could one draw the line between a belief in gender equality and raw propaganda opportunity? Did the Soviets support the increased role of women out of an advanced sensibility or a realization that their women could help them win more medals than the United States? With U.S. officials, was it a matter of principle or a fear of failure—as was evident at that first dual track meet with the Soviets in 1958, when concern about losing a combined point count led some American officials to consider not bringing Ed Temple and his women's team to Moscow? In questions of gender as well as race, cold war politics pressed hard on athletic deliberations, eventually forcing change.

EIGHT LONG days and nights had passed since the first throwers assembled at the Stadio Olimpico. The shot-put final on August 31 turned out to be a sweep for the U.S. team. Now, after being shut out in the hammer throw, it was time to see if the Americans could bookend the shot-put accomplishment by dominating the discus. They came in with the defending Olympic champion, Al Oerter, a purchasing agent for a Long Island aircraft company, who felt renewed by a new diet, a weight-lifting program, and "a philosophy of life that concentrated on his health, his family, and himself." A Polish thrower, Edmund Piatkowski, was highly regarded, and the Russians had talked about winning a medal, but the rest of the field seemed unthreatening; the home favorite, Italy's Adolfo Consolini, the 1948 winner who had delivered the athlete's oath at the Rome Games' Opening Ceremony, was now an ancient relic competing in his fourth Olympics and was eliminated in the qualifying rounds.

Oerter's strongest competition promised to come from teammates Dick Cochran, the NCAA champ from Missouri, and Rink Babka, the Southern Cal grad who had tied the world record earlier that year and arrived in Rome confident he could win gold.

On that first day of track-and-field events eight days earlier, Babka was in the Olympic Village cafeteria, chatting with a group of teammates and drinking iced tea. He had been winging the discus over 200 feet in practice and never felt better, yet day after day he had watched various teammates falling sick. What was going on? Now he knew one reason. "The tea was OK, but the ice they were putting into it was chopped off blocks on the floor," Babka recalled. That night, he felt too miserable to sleep. "I was losing my stomach in the bathtub." At three in the morning, he staggered over to the infirmary for treatment, and spent the rest of the night talking with another ailing athlete, swimmer Paul Hait. Over the next week, as his competition approached, Babka could barely practice. Dogged by the heat and his upset stomach, he lost 14 pounds, from 265 down to 251, and was still trying to regain his strength as he sauntered toward the stadium's discus area for the September 7 final.

Among the people watching the throwers in Rome was the person perhaps most responsible for Babka's athletic career. This was thirty-two-year-old Otis Chandler, a strapping six-three "California redwood," as he once was described, who had been a shot-put star at Stanford and whose self-described "biggest disappointment in life" to that point had come when a wrist injury prevented him from competing for the 1952 U.S. Olympic team. Chandler was better known as the publisher of the *Los Angeles Times,* a job his father, Norman Chandler, had bestowed upon him a few months before the Rome Games. Like Don Maxwell, editor of the *Chicago Tribune,* Chandler felt obliged to file a story or two while watching the Olympics. He had been among the American mourners after Black Thursday, particularly bemoaning the U.S. losses in women's diving events and the men's high jump. While the Europeans had obviously improved their techniques over the years, some American athletes seemed list-less in Rome, he had written. "Whatever the cause, we are no longer invincible, for the rest of the world has caught up to us."

Nearly ten years earlier, when Rink Babka was in junior high at Palo Alto, a self-described cowboy hick whose family had recently moved from Wyoming, the boys in his school were called to the gymnasium for a speech and special presentation by the great shot-putter with the famous Chandler name who attended college at nearby Stanford. "When he walked into the gym and our coach introduced him, Otis looked like Adonis; he was gorgeous," Babka recalled. "In my mind, I went, 'Jeez, look at a man that size.' And he spoke so well. He talked about weight lifting, athletics, don't smoke, don't drink, go to college, get a degree. The typical rah-rah presentation. Then he asked—we were all squatting on the floor—'Anybody want to learn to throw the shot put?' " Babka's hand shot up reflexively, and after the speech he found himself heading out to the school field with Chandler and six classmates. When Babka's turn came to try the shot, Chandler complimented him. "He said, 'You have some potential here, young man.' That is all he had to say for me. From then on, I always said the man who gave me a little bit of a nudge was Otis Chandler."

Although Babka also excelled in basketball and football, and was recruited to Southern Cal primarily to play basketball, he eventually concentrated on the track-and-field throwing events, and narrowed that down to the discus because of a knee injury that made the violent plant-and-pound stress of the shot put difficult. He emerged as a world-class discus man at USC, trouncing most collegiate competitors and winning first place for the U.S. at the historic first dual meet with the Soviets in Moscow. After graduating in 1959, he landed a job with the Deutsch Company, an electronics firm in the Los Angeles area, that allowed him to slip out at three every afternoon to train at Southern Cal in preparation for the Olympics.

Throwing the discus required twisting, but not pounding, and

Babka came to think of it as the most difficult and graceful of throwing events. Rotating around one and a half times, pivoting with the left foot, and landing in the middle of the ring with the right—there was a graceful flow, a magical groove, that made it sometimes seem that the less a discus thrower exerted himself, the farther the saucer flew. "You have to control yourself and put yourself in a relaxed mode," Babka explained. "It's just like the backswing in golf; you can't go back too far and too fast, or you tie yourself up. You go back soft, and instead of full, you take it back three-quarters. The same when you wind up for the discus, you don't take a full swing back." Everyone was searching for that groove in Rome, and Oerter was the first to find it. Hal Bateman, the reporter covering the event for *Track & Field News,* kept his eyes on Oerter as he "walked into the ring, spun around, and let the discus fly. The throw was so effortless that it didn't look like it could go very far, but it did, and it landed two feet beyond the world record." Unfortunately for Oerter, that throw came during warm-ups, and did not count.

The discus final dragged on for hours in a slow-motion fashion that required as much mental stamina as physical endurance. Babka, going sixth out of the group, got off a throw of 190 feet 4¼ inches on his first try. Oerter, lacking the smoothness of his warm-up fling, slipped slightly in the ring and could not match Babka, reaching 189 feet 1¼ inches the first time. In the second through fourth rounds, Babka felt the energy drain from his body and failed to surpass his first throw. But no one else could either. "I ran out of gas," he said later. "And when I realized that, I was just hoping I could hang on." But like C. K. Yang and Vasily Kuznetsov providing advice to Rafer Johnson before the pole-vault competition in the decathlon, Babka could not resist giving tips to his teammates. "I started talking to Dick and Al about what they were doing wrong—they were in trouble," Babka recalled. He noticed that Oerter was "dropping his arm too low, so low that when he came around, his parabola was too high because the body was off." Oerter would say later that he was never

more nervous in his life, but on his fifth attempt, he leveled his motion and threw the discus an Olympic record 194 feet 2 inches, clinch-
ing gold for a second straight time. Babka finished second, and
Cochran came in third, completing the sweep. In the discus and shot
put, at least, Otis Chandler could rest assured that the Americans remained invincible. Oerter would go on to win again in 1964 and become known as the greatest discus thrower of all time. Babka receded,
unable to beat Oerter in the big matches, but he consoled himself
with this thought: "I always tell people I am the best discus coach in
the world. I coached gold, silver, and bronze in one Olympics."

Not far from the discus ring on the Tribuna Tevere side of Stadio
Olimpico, the pole-vault competition continued into the darkness of
that Wednesday night. There were thirteen men in the final, but the
floodlights beamed on one among them, Donald Bragg of the United
States. Bragg was the Cassius Clay of track and field, all acting all the
time. Like Clay, Bragg came to Rome with one goal in mind: to become a professional. But if Clay's mission was to turn a boxing gold
medal into a lucrative pro boxing career, and to use his acting skills to
enhance his image, Bragg could find no parallel path. There was no
serious money to be made in pole-vaulting; his goal was to vault his
way into acting.

Everyone in the Olympic Village knew the role to which Bragg
aspired. Day and night for two weeks, they had heard him beating
his chest and bleating the high, curdling yell of Tarzan. *Life* magazine played along, running a photo essay that depicted him barefoot
and bare chested, wearing nothing but a loincloth, stalking the ancient Roman ruins as though he were hunting jungle beasts. Bragg
had been pretending he was Tarzan since he was ten years old in
Penns Grove, New Jersey, when he tied long ropes from tall oak trees
so that he could swing from limb to limb. "His biggest Tarzan problem is his voice, which he feels is too high pitched," *Life* reported. "As
a student at Villanova, he joined the choir to reduce his register to a
lower key. But he still wants more coaching so that when he sum-

mons Jane and Boy, his other jungle friends will be suitably impressed." As part of his voice training in Rome, Bragg sang for his dinner at the village cafeteria—whether anyone wanted to hear him or not—joining the Italian waiters in renditions of "O Sole Mio."

At a hulking six-three and two hundred pounds, Bragg was if nothing else the last of his kind. After the 1960 Olympics, his event would undergo a transformation with the introduction of fiberglass poles that, with their extraordinary spring and flexibility, completely changed the technique of pole-vaulting, greatly increased the heights that could be reached, and as a result required different skills from the athletes. Bragg was all power and speed, with burly shoulders and arms; in the fiberglass era to come, pole-vaulters would need to be more agile and acrobatic. Bragg's type would be rendered obsolete. In so many realms, these Rome Olympics represented either the end of something or the start, and here was another small example in track and field.

Records should be appreciated within the context of the times, and usually on the continuum of progress evoked by the Olympic motto—faster, higher, stronger—as athletes improve decade by decade from advances in nutrition, training, technique, and equipment. Few events show a record gap over the years as striking as the pole vault. More than three and a half decades after Rome, the brilliant Sergei Bubka of the Soviet Union would vault higher than 20 feet, but going into 1960 no vaulter had cleared 15 feet at the Olympics. Bob Richards, one of the three correspondents in Rome for CBS, had set the Olympic mark of 14 feet 11½ inches at Melbourne. By seven-thirty that Wednesday night at Stadio Olimpico, Bragg and his teammate Ron Morris had already broken Richards's record, each clearing the bar at 15 feet 1⅛ inches. Bragg topped it first, and when Morris cleared it as well, Bragg helped him out of the pit. What looked like a gesture of friendly teamwork came with an ulterior motive. "So I'm thinking, Ronnie is a little technician who can sneak out an inch at a time, but if we jump the crossbar up four or five inches, he'll be vulnerable," Bragg recalled in an oral interview. After helping Morris out of the pit, Bragg said to him, "Hey, Ronnie, it's great we just beat the Russians and Germans and everyone; now let's go for the world record."

That was too much of a bump-up for Morris, but he did agree to move the bar up to 15 feet 5 inches, a height both of them had achieved previously, though not in Olympic competition. It was too high for Morris; he couldn't come close on three tries. Bragg nonchalantly rested flat on his back on a bench, using his warm-up jacket as a blanket in the evening chill. When his turn came, he went through his usual routine, loosening his arms on the pole, but nothing seemed routine now. His right leg and knee had been hurting since the Olympic Trials, so sore that he had vaulted only once between July and Rome and had skipped as many heights as possible all day to limit the pounding on his body. But the pressure was getting to Bragg. He felt his career as Tarzan depended on this moment. The crowd expected him to win. When he had missed earlier at a lower height, he heard whistles and boos from the stands. Even his uniform was bothering him. The shirt was made of wool, and his number— No. 431—felt too heavy and drooped when he ran. But as he stood at the end of the runway, he said to himself, "Your leg is bothering you, but what in hell are you saving it for? This is it. Go get the son of a bitch." And he did. His shirt barely brushed the bar on the way over, but nothing moved. Tarzan Bragg, the gold medal his, bounded from the pit, walked back toward the bench, shook his fist in triumph, cupped his hands over his mouth, and let loose: *"Aaayyyaaahhhh! Aaaayyyaahhh!"*

ONE MORE day of track and field, except for the marathon, noted Arthur Daley of the *New York Times*. Black Thursday seemed like a long time ago. In the cold war rivalry of which the American president would not speak, the Soviets were gobbling up medals in gymnastics (twenty-six medals, ten gold), kayaking (four medals, three gold), fencing (seven medals, three gold), shooting (seven medals, two gold), and Greco-Roman wrestling (five medals, three gold), and perhaps their strongest sport, weight lifting, was just getting under way. But most of those sports—even gymnastics in that era—were considered obscure and unimportant in the United States. The U.S. squads had prevailed so far in track and field, basketball, boxing, and swimming, the prototypical American events. "Despite some failures," Daley wrote, "the United States will emerge from this carnival in rather handsome shape after all."

At his press conference in Washington that day, Eisenhower had been asked by David Kraslow, a correspondent for Knight Newspapers, how he would define "our national purpose" and whether he thought the American people were losing sight of it. In response, Eisenhower said that he had heard "a lot of talk" about the national purpose recently. "I am not concerned about America losing its sense of purpose," he added. "We might not be articulate about it, and we may not give daily the kind of thought to it that we should, but I believe America wants to live first in freedom, and the kind of liberty that is guaranteed to us through our founding documents; and secondly, they want to live at peace with all their neighbors, so that we may jointly find a better life for humanity as we go forward. This, to me, is the simple purpose of the United States."

That night in Moscow, U.S. ambassador Llewellyn E. Thompson was buttonholed by Nikita Khrushchev at a diplomatic reception for the United Arab Republic. The Soviet leader was still preoccupied with the U-2 spying incident that had heated up the cold war since early May, when Francis Gary Powers's spy plane was shot down over Soviet territory. Whose idea was it to send that reconnaissance plane into our airspace? Khrushchev asked Thompson. In the chaotic days after the incident, Eisenhower had asserted publicly that he knew all about the spy plane and that it was his decision, but Khrushchev could not believe it. From the beginning, he had hoped that

Eisenhower would say he knew nothing about it and that it was a rogue CIA operation. That would have given both leaders a way to ease the tensions. Now Khrushchev would have to take his case to the United Nations. Wary of the setting that evening, with "the entire diplomatic corps . . . crowded around us," Thompson suggested that perhaps that was "not the place nor occasion for a discussion."

The next morning, Khrushchev summoned Thompson to the Kremlin to continue the conversation in private. After more complaints about the U-2 incident, Khrushchev changed course and said that he wanted to speak "personally, frankly, and confidentially." Thompson stopped taking notes but committed the conversation to memory. "In explaining why the Soviet Union did not intend war and believed the world would eventually go Communist, and our grandchildren would live under communism, he said this was because the Soviet system was better, and when this was demonstrated even we would adopt it," Thompson reported in a cable to the State Department. Khrushchev then launched into a "long harangue" about steel production and how the U.S. was producing at only half capacity, a fatal handicap that could never happen in the USSR. And about U.S. agriculture surpluses and what the Soviets could do with such surpluses. And finally, Thompson reported, Khrushchev brought the one-way conversation around to the subject of freedom. "He observed that we often spoke of freedom under our system, but I surely had been able to see the extent to which people enjoyed freedom in the Soviet Union. He started to say I was free to go anywhere I liked, but then corrected this to say Moscow and its environs. He exuded confidence, and it was impossible not to be convinced that he genuinely believed what he was saying."

The show was all prelude, rehearsal for what was to come. Early the next evening, Khrushchev would set sail for the New World and his historic appearance at the U.N. General Assembly in New York.

17

THE SOFT LIFE

O<small>NLY</small> three days of competition remained, and the sense of things coming to an end was palpable. As cool autumn weather nestled into the Roman hills, A. J. Liebling described "a childish sadness ... Like leaving a school where one has been happy, and knowing that the school will never reopen." It was in that atmosphere that Avery Brundage, who looked like nothing if not a stern principal, strode into the ballroom of the Grand Hotel at one o'clock on the Thursday afternoon of September 8 as the guest speaker at the first fall meeting of the American Club of Rome.

On the go from dawn to midnight, Brundage had been everywhere during these Olympics: to the Bay of Naples to watch the yachting; to Lake Albano for the rowing; to the opera, the ballet, and the art museum; to meetings with countesses and princes and presidents; to interviews with the *Times of India* and Voice of America; to Dutch dinners and Soviet receptions and German dances. Yet he always seemed to be around in early evening at the Stadio Olimpico to drape gold medals around the necks of track-and-field champions. Safe to say he was not besieged by well-wishers as he made his rounds. The *Rome Daily American* aptly described him as "more or less an international voodoo doll, with critics left and right sticking pins in him." But, the paper added, "he doesn't seem to mind." Now, in front of a relatively friendly audience made up of expatriate businessmen, retired military officers, foreign service personnel, and a sprinkling of spies and writers, Brundage reached into his suit pocket and took out a stack of New York Athletic Club note cards on which he had jotted down the themes for this luncheon address. The opening words on the first note card asked the question "What is this all about?"

This meant the Olympic Movement, his favorite subject, one he returned to at every opportunity. Brundage repeated his mantra: The Olympics brought together people from all over the world, of every race, religion, color, and political belief—all joined in a demonstration of goodwill. In their modern form, they had survived for sixty-four years with no army, little money, only volunteers and the strength of a powerful idea. In a notation on the side of the note card making this point, he had written in block letters: CONTRAST BOORISH BELLOWING U.N. It was a given to Avery Brundage that his world body was far superior to the other one that was about to meet in New York.

But the success of the Olympic Movement had brought with it serious problems, Brundage added. The Games had become too large and expensive. He fretted, as his note cards put it, about "excessive nationalism US v USSR, hymns, flags, point scores." And then there was what he saw as the greatest threat: the erosion of pristine amateurism. "We are in a perpetual battle to keep our games pure and clean and honest," he said.

The despoiling of amateurism was Brundage's longest riff. In his note cards, the irregular stanzas that followed the capitalized AMATEURISM could be read like a free-verse poem from the Brundage chapbook, a hypnotic, romantic longing for his imagined innocence of times past:

> *Thing of spirit diff[icult] to define*
> *Philosophy of life dedicated to task not to reward*
> *No great working for money*
> *Painter and musician*
> *Don't even know amounts of great cathedrals etc.*
> *Many acts of religious devotion*
> *In business Ford & Edison*
> *Politics Washington Jefferson*

The modern world was seducing and commercializing and corrupting athletes, body and soul, in the United States as much as anywhere, just as surely as lobbyist gifts corrupted the political system:

> *Subsidy no good*
> *College athletic scholarships*
> *Commercialization*
> *Pacific Coast conf[erence]*
> *H.S. boy athlete 50 offers*
> *We ask mink coats, under table money*
> *Symptom same disease*
> *Life too soft, many lazy, don't like work*

It wasn't always this way, Brundage said. Our forefathers built up the United States with hard work, intelligence, and skill to create the highest standard of living enjoyed by people anywhere at any point in history. But look where we are now. Even our Olympic team is soft, struggling to hold its own against the world.

> *Can't get something for nothing*
> *Better get back to fundamentals*

Victims of our own prosperity
I have seen other countries
800,000 gymnasts [in USSR]
We should change entire education process
Phys ed more about mental above all
Change thinking teach children self discipline

Red Smith of the *Herald Tribune* had slipped into the ballroom and was listening as Brundage talked about America becoming too soft and how there were eight hundred thousand gymnasts in the USSR. Smith could concoct a delicious column out of even the most mundane sporting ingredients, but here was a tasty recipe for him. What a rich contrast he could see between the old man's lofty ideal and the reality of his existence.

"Avery Brundage, who always goes first-class, got up on his hind legs in Rome's luxurious Grand Hotel, fixed the well-fed members of the American Club with a glittering stare, and delivered himself of a stirring panegyric on the Spartan way of life," Smith wrote. "Fast living, the president of the IOC warned, wagging a manicured finger, was threatening to reduce the United States to a second-class power . . . Sipping their espresso and gumming their dolce, his listeners heard the words of doom . . ."

There was, as it turned out, far more to the contradiction than even Red Smith could discern. Twenty years later, after Brundage's death, an investigation by *Sports Illustrated* would uncover his personal duplicity. The man who harrumphed about "teaching children self-discipline" in fact had two children out of wedlock at the time of the Rome Games—two sons born in 1951 and 1952 to his Finnish mistress, Lilian Linnea Dresden. His name was left off the birth certificates, he acknowledged in a private notation, because "showing my name . . . as the father may cause undue and adverse publicity in view of my present marital status." At the time, he had been married since 1927 to his wife Elizabeth Dunlap Brundage, with whom he was childless. His affair with the Finnish mistress, who lived in a house he bought for her in Redwood City, California, was only one of hundreds for the upright moralist.

"SLAVERY AVERY," some athletes called Brundage. The derisive nickname evoked their hostility toward the IOC's rules of amateurism, but also reflected a larger disdain for the holier-than-thou attitude of those in power. It came across as a bit too easy for the Chicago millionaire and his upper-crust associates to talk about the virtues of sport for sport's sake. Their notion of the amateur ideal seemed naive if not miserly, concocted for the lifestyles of the already wealthy. The whole notion of the gentleman amateur was nothing more than a late-nineteenth-century boarding school convention that somehow was imposed on the rest of the athletic world. What, for example, could the Marquess of Exeter know about the daily financial struggle of poor or middle-class athletes who had to train constantly to retain their world-class edge? In a letter to Brundage before the Olympics, the British lord had commiserated with him about how so many athletes were grousing about their restrictions to journalists, who seemed more interested in stories of hardship than the glories of amateurism. "There is an angle which I find depressing, namely that in the old days when people were really hard up and had to make sacrifices for their sport, they had far more idealism than now, when they are three or four times as well off and expect everything to be found for them," he wrote. "One might have thought that it worked the other way around. This is not confined to sport only."

Many athletes had individual stories about what they thought were the unfair or nit-picking intrusions of the Olympic hierarchy. We have already seen how Lee Calhoun endured a one-year suspension for getting married on *Bride and Groom,* and how Dave Sime had to find his way back from Pierre, South Dakota, after being told he couldn't play semipro baseball, and how Rafer Johnson was warned that a role in *Spartacus* would doom his gold medal hopes. And there were many more: Bob Mathias, who had been contemplating a comeback attempt as a decathlete earlier in the year, had been told that he was definitely ineligible because "his television and movie contracts depended upon his athletic reputation." Abie and Muriel Grossfeld, the young married couple of U.S. gymnastics, were threatened with being "turned in" to the U.S. Olympic Committee for working during the summers at a gymnastics camp near Traverse City, Michigan, run by their coach at the University of Illinois, where they earned "something like thirty bucks a week." Pat Smythe, a British equestrian, was told by the IOC that she could not participate in Rome if she worked as a part-time journalist for the *Daily Express*.

For all of these known cases, far more was going on below the surface. Some of the as-yet undetected situations were serious breaches of the amateur code. There was Armin Hary's financial connection to German shoe companies, for example, and the common practice in Sweden of promoters paying track stars to appear at meets there. Most were of a pettier nature, part of the grist of the sporting life. Nikos Spanakos, the U.S. boxer, who grew up poor in Brooklyn before boxing collegiately in Idaho, said later that financial boosters were an implicit factor in the amateur boxing world. "We called them sugar daddies in those days," Spanakos recalled, saying the boosters could come as often from a local Elks Club as from a gambling parlor. "It was under the table. Everything under the table. Sometimes after a fight, an amateur fight, you got a watch or fifteen or twenty dollars." The American weight lifters, who worked out at the York Barbell Company gym in York, Pennsylvania, were taken care of by the company owner, Bob Hoffman, who was also their coach. They received free housing and food and a weekly stipend ostensibly for working in his factory. "We could go to any restaurant in town, and he'd pick up the tab," said Ike Berger, the featherweight lifter. James Bradford, the heavyweight, when asked about the subsidies, responded, "Right. But it had to be done very, very quietly." He made a hand gesture of money being passed under a table.

Brundage and his men could not prove it, but they suspected something fishy was going on with some Italian athletes in 1960. The IOC chancellor, Otto Mayer, went public with the accusation that Italy had persuaded its best soccer players and boxers to postpone going professional until after the Olympics so they could help the home country have a stronger showing in Rome. The implication—and fear—was that they were already being paid, but on a deferred basis. This touched on the huge political side to the amateur issue that divided East from West. How could state-subsidized athletes from the socialist nations be called amateurs? Brundage had been facing that question since his visit to the Soviet Union in 1954, but to some in the West he seemed less than vigilant in enforcing the amateur code on Eastern bloc delegations. Don Graham, the *Washington Post* copyboy, remembered listening to long lectures in Rome from big-city daily track-and-field writers "on how our guys were amateurs and the Soviets were all products of the sports machine."

It was a common perception among journalists in Rome that Brundage's fight on the amateur issue was at once draconian and illogical. "Brundage had a misguided notion of athletics and amateurism," said Rino Tommasi, the Italian sportswriter. "You can't do a sport well if you don't do only that. He was old-fashioned—and in a way too tough. There is an old saying that the only difference between an amateur and a pro is that a pro pays taxes." Hours after the Opening Ceremony, when a group of reporters retreated to a hotel bar, a colleague turned to Neil Allen and scoffed as he recalled the moment when Adolfo Consolini, the Italian discus thrower, had emerged from the throng of athletes gathered on the Stadio Olimpico infield to recite the oath of amateurism. "It's all pretty hypocritical, isn't it? That chappie getting up there and swearing away to be good amateurs. Lot of rot, really."

Brundage's view of amateurism could not be separated from his utter contempt for professional sports and their feeder programs, especially in football. In the early 1950s, he wrote a memo to himself declaring that it was a mistake even to put *pro* and *sports* in the same phrase. Eighty percent of newspaper sports sections, he lamented, was "devoted to professional baseball, football, boxing, horseracing, etc., WHICH ARE NOT SPORT AT ALL. It is a question of nomenclature. Professional sport is a branch . . . of the entertainment business." College football, he believed, was not far behind—"so thoroughly commercialized that it can hardly be called a sport. There is no reason why our institutions of higher learning should be football factories and farms for professional leagues." College football had become "a national scandal" whose abuses were "poisoning our entire amateur program." He saw in football the creeping professionalism that he so desperately wanted to keep out of the Olympics.

But could he ever win his "perpetual battle to keep our games pure and clean and honest?" The IOC had been engaged in that battle since at least 1937, when it adopted a report on amateurism at its session in Warsaw that prohibited athletes from receiving gifts for competing or taking jobs that capitalized on their notoriety, and declared that a professional in one sport would be considered a professional in all sports. Olympic Rule 26 defined an amateur like this: "An amateur is one who participates and always has participated in sport solely for pleasure and for the physical, mental, or social benefits he derives therefrom, and to whom participation in sport is nothing more than recreation without material gain of any kind, direct or indirect."

But maintaining strict amateur standards over the years seemed more and more a losing cause. An essay in *Sports Illustrated* on the eve of the Olympics declared that Rome "will see the last amateur Olympics." Led by delegate Albert Mayer of Switzerland, some Olympic officials had concluded by 1960 that the line between amateurism and professionalism was so jagged they should draw the line somewhere else. They shared the practical opinion of Gaston Meyer, chief editor of France's influential *L'Équipe,* who had concluded a series of articles on amateurism with the line "Do not forbid what you cannot prevent." Albert Mayer proposed a novel solution: ignore what it means to be an amateur and instead only define professionalism. To deal with "a public and world scandal," Emile Birnbaum noted in *L'Echo Illustré* of Geneva, Mayer had "the courage to say publicly what everyone thinks privately, and to want to open the wound. He says we must accept at the games not only amateur athletes but also athletes who are not amateurs, who receive bonuses and draw a profit from their athletic activities. According to him, the only ones that should be excluded are the true professionals, those who live predominantly off their sports earnings . . . The line will no longer be drawn between amateurs and nonamateurs, but between nonprofessionals and professionals. It will no longer be the profit that will exclude, but the fact that the profit is the principal income."

Brundage had managed to quash that idea, for the time being, when it was brought up at the IOC meeting at the Excelsior Hotel on the eve of the Olympics. His alternative was to propose holding a competition "for the purpose of awarding a prize for the best article published in the press in defense of a better understanding of amateurism." As he later told the luncheon gathering of the American Club of Rome, according to his note cards:

> *The other day a journalist said why bother—you fight*
> *A losing battle . . . everyone wants to make money—*
> *No more amateurs but fortunately there are still a few idealists.*

For the athletes from Germany's Eastern zone, Thursday had begun in mourning as news spread through the village of the death of their president, eighty-four-year-old Wilhelm Pieck, who had seen them off to Rome only a few weeks earlier. Pieck was a former carpenter who had fled Germany with the rise of Hitler and oversaw a resistance movement from Moscow during the war. There he became close to Soviet Premier Joseph Stalin. In 1949 he returned to his homeland to become the first president of the Soviet Zone's fledgling satellite regime, the German Democratic Republic. In the socialist system, his title had been largely honorific; the real power rested with Communist Party boss Walter Ulbricht, but Pieck was a symbolic father figure in the East, a connection to the anti-Nazi past. "Everyone could see our athletes standing around talking, being strongly moved," reported the East German newspaper *Neues Deutschland.* "And when the news had spread in the village, many of the Soviet athletes came to express their condolences, along with the Hungarians, the Poles, the Czechs, Romanians, and Bulgarians."

At the final day of track-and-field events at Stadio Olimpico, the Eastern zone athletes arrived wearing black ribbons in honor of Pieck. They also performed surprisingly well, with Hans Grodotszi of Menterode finishing second in the 10,000-meter run and Walter Kreuger of Hohendorf taking second place in the javelin. With those two silver medals, and the Olympics nearing an end, journalists from the Eastern zone dropped all pretenses of considering this a unified German team. There had been one modest but important political separation all along. In its daily scoreboard, *Neues Deutschland* had denoted an athlete from the East with the designation GDR, the initials of the government entity, but identified an athlete from the West as WD, meaning West Germany, rather than by the parallel government designation, BRD, the initials for the Federal Republic of Germany, or *Bundesrepublik Deutschland.* This was a not-so-subtle way of trumpeting the legitimacy of the Eastern zone government, which was still unrecognized by most countries in the West. Now, in the final days in Rome, the socialist newspaper even started counting medals separately from the West and boasted of how athletes from the GDR could "pride themselves in having conquered sixth rank of all the participating countries." It was left unsaid that by those standards, the West German athletes had accumulated even more medals.

But journalists from West Germany had also fallen into a less accommodating mood. A columnist from *Die Welt,* echoing the ideology-tinged explanations that more often emanated from East Berlin, now gave a political reason for the disappointing showings of three Eastern zone athletes: Siegfried Valentin in the metric mile, Manfred Matuschewski in the 800, and Hermann Buhl in the steeplechase. "They failed when it really mattered. They lagged far behind their personal records and at the same time nearly collapsed when they crossed the finish line," the columnist wrote. "A mediocre performance resulted in complete exhaustion. It was not physical but mental and psychic exhaustion. They were not independent but were indebted to their state, their functionaries, and their own promise to give everything in their power to the praise and fame of their state. Rome has demonstrated that an athlete exposed to this kind of burden will rarely manage to achieve top results which lead to Olympic medals." The temptation to link sports success to ideology was always a slippery slope: How then to explain the overall success of the Soviet team, and the unburdened victories of Poland's Jozef Schmidt in the hop, step, and jump, and Zdzislaw Krzyszkowiak in the steeplechase?

The friction within the German community in Rome reflected the growing tensions playing out back home. The five-day ban on West Germans trying to enter East Berlin had been lifted (1,061 Westerners had been sent back from the border during that period, according to the Interior Ministry in Bonn), but now the Soviet zone government was attempting to permanently tighten the border. Starting midnight Friday, special permission would be required for any West German seeking entry into East Berlin. The *Frankfurter Allgemeine Zeitung* described this as a hostile act and predicted that it was "the first step of a conversion of the sector border into the national border of the GDR." It was also seen as part of a broader strategic effort by the Soviets and East Germans to press the Western powers on the status of Berlin in the run-up to Khrushchev's visit to the United Nations. A communiqué from the Soviet zone news agency said the new policy was nothing more than a precaution against "Western provocations."

The German hordes in Rome had returned to the Stadio Olimpico one last time Thursday afternoon to chant in unison for the men's and women's relay teams. In all three of the final races, the Germans were considered strong medal contenders, going head-to-head with the Americans.

First up was the men's 4 X 400. A light rain had dampened the track by four-thirty, when the six teams took their positions, the Germans in Lane 2, the Americans in Lane 4. American Jack Yerman seized an early lead in the first leg, then young German star Manfred Kinder blitzed back in the second, so that only a tenth of a second separated the two teams. The stadium was in full roar by the time Glenn Davis, the all-round U.S. star who had already won gold in the 400 hurdles, took the baton on the third leg. He picked up two crucial yards on the exchange, pounded steadily down the track, and when Johannes Kaiser tried to pull even with him as they rounded the curve toward the backstretch, the American found another gear. "I took it easy so he would use up his strength catching me on the backstretch," Davis recalled. "When he came up, I carried him wide. Then when he relaxed, I kicked and opened up the lead I wanted."

He was four yards in front when he handed the baton to the anchor, his fellow gold medalist, Otis Davis. Now came a rematch of the exhilarating 400 final, with the American again trying to hold off Carl Kaufmann. Davis, the former basketball player, was still considered a novice in the running world, but he was at his peak in Rome, and his tactical skills were now catching up to his raw talent. He knew that Kaufmann had a terrific closing burst and gauged his own race accordingly. "I just learned how to run in the last couple of races," he told *Track & Field News*'s Cord Nelson later. "I accelerated a little to make Kaufmann use his strength to catch me, then I floated. When he came up again, I'd accelerate, then float again. I figured he'd use up his power trying to catch me each time, then I'd turn on the kick and walk away." This was, in its own way, a variation on the tactic that Karl Adam had devised successfully for his German heavyweight crew on Lake Albano. Kaufmann could not close the gap, and this time there was no need to wait fifteen minutes to determine the photo finish. In bringing the Americans to the tape in an Olympic and world record time of 3:02.2, a full five-tenths of a second ahead of the Germans, Glenn Davis and Otis Davis had both secured their second gold medals in Rome. Tex Maule went so far as to call it "the most intelligently run, aesthetically satisfying race of the Olympics."

AT SIX that morning, back in Nashville, Charlie B. Temple was getting her day under way. After feeding her two young children, she took four-year-old Edwina to a babysitter and seven-year-old Bernard to school, then drove over to Tennessee State and began her routine at the school's post office. She knew that this was the last big day in Rome for her husband and his Tigerbelles, who would take the track in a few hours, given the time difference. Martha Hudson, Barbara Jones, Lucinda Williams, and Wilma Rudolph were her girls too. Her presence in their lives might go unnoticed to the rest of the world, but Mother Temple was as important to them as Coach Temple. She fed them, baked cakes for their birthdays, and listened to their problems when they felt uncomfortable talking about certain subjects with the coach. When they did something crazy to upset him, she was the one to make peace. When they weren't practicing, they often came into her cramped office and helped her sort the mail. Tennessee State might turn out the best runners around, but it was no track factory, just a tight little family.

The family dynamics had changed considerably since the Tiger-

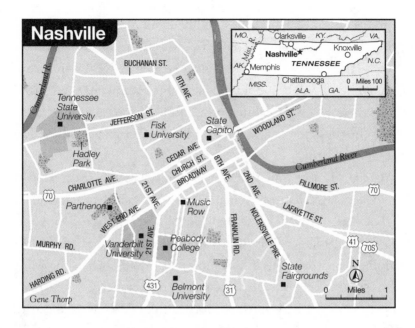

Gene Thorp

belles reached Rome. The runners still thought of one another as sisters, but Wilma Rudolph's transcendent performances in the 100 and 200 had made her alone world famous. She was the star, mobbed everywhere, while the others hovered in the background. Unavoidably, given human nature, there was a tinge of envy among some of her teammates. "There was possibly some jealousy from one or two of our members—a feeling that she was getting all the accolades and all the attention," recalled Lucinda Williams. "But it's a team effort, and sometimes that's hard for individuals to understand. I always accepted Wilma for her worth and dignity, not only in running but in her personality and her caring." Rudolph was sensitive enough to appreciate the situation and saw only one remedy: get them all gold.

"The race that I think she wanted more than anything else was the four by hundred," Ed Temple remembered. "She had two medals, but the other girls were down because they didn't get to the finals in the hundred and two hundred and didn't win any medals, and this was the only chance they were going to get, and she was determined that they were going to win a gold medal." In the warm-up room before the race, the Tigerbelles huddled and prayed together. "Just get me that stick," Rudolph, who would run the anchor leg, said at the end. "Just get me that stick, and we're going to get on that stand. We're going to win that gold medal!" Her teammates could barely contain themselves; no jealousy now, just fire burning inside. They'd get her the stick, they said. They'd beat the Germans, and the Russians, and the Brits.

Martha Hudson ran the first leg. She was the shrimp of the Tigerbelles, a five-foot-one dynamo from McRae, Georgia, who had caught Coach Temple's eye in high school when she beat some Tigerbelles at the Tuskegee Relays, and arrived at Tennessee State in 1957. Hudson, who worked as a dormitory receptionist when she wasn't training or studying, was always competitive but rarely won in major competitions. She had finished fourth in the 60-meter dash at the 1959 Pan American Games in Chicago, then qualified for the 100 in Rome but failed to reach the semifinal round, her time more than a second slower than Rudolph's. With her quick start, she kept the Tigerbelles competitive now, her short legs carrying her down the track in the lead pack with the runners from Germany and Great Britain. As she handed the baton off—and up—to the five-seven-and-a-half Barbara Jones, Hudson joked later, she thought to herself, "I doubt if ever before so much depended on so little."

Jones was the most experienced Tigerbelle. She had first competed in the Olympics at age fifteen at Helsinki in 1952, began her college career at Marquette University in Milwaukee, then transferred to Tennessee State, arriving in time to lead the women's team at the dual meet in Moscow in 1958. She had been slowed by a lingering thigh injury most of the year and was heartbroken to finish fourth in the 100-meter semifinals in Rome, where she had hoped to join Rudolph on the medal stand. Now she faced a world-class field in the second leg, going against Maria Itkina of the Soviet Union and Dorothy Hyman of Great Britain, both of whom had made the 100 final ahead of her. This time no one could outrun her, and she handed the baton off to Lucinda Williams with the Tigerbelles barely in second place.

Coach Temple, watching from the warm-up area, could not see the first two legs, but he caught sight of his team just as the stick moved from Jones to Williams. When he saw Williams so close to the lead, he felt good about their chances, knowing that she could "run the curve" as well as anyone. The Savannah native was the other twenty-three-year-old veteran in the group, one of the bronze medalists on the relay team at Melbourne and a winner in the 200 at the dual meet in Moscow. Married and already a graduate of Tennessee State by 1960, Williams had stayed in Nashville and continued to run with the Tigerbelles while studying for a master's in physical education. In Rome she competed in the 200 but finished a disappointing fifth in her semifinal heat. This was her last chance, her last race, and she had something to prove. She had never felt the adrenaline going through her so fast. She blazed around the curve even with the Germans and reached out to hand the baton to Rudolph.

Fred Russell, the hometown Nashville columnist, was watching in the press section. "One of the least appreciated moments is the passing of the baton in an Olympic sprint relay," he noted. "One runner, finishing at full speed, tries to hand the stick to another who's starting as fast as she can within the prescribed zone of twenty-two yards." Except now, Rudolph had started and then stopped. It seemed almost as though the speed with which Williams came at her took her by surprise. She stuck back her hand, but the rhythm was off. "Get me the stick," she had said. But where was it? For years thereafter, Williams would be blamed for the slight bobble that left Rudolph standing there empty-handed for a split second until the transfer was secured. But it was not her fault. Williams just came in too fast, and Rudolph was at first too jumpy and then a trifle slow. Rather than risk dropping the baton or running beyond the handoff zone and being disqualified, Wilma stopped to make sure the baton was in her hand. "When she missed the first time, I said, 'Oh my goodness,'"

Temple said later. "But when it got in there the second time, let me tell you something . . ." The handoff delay had cost Rudolph two or three yards on the opposition. And she had every reason to be tired; this was her tenth race, counting qualifying heats, of the Games, as many as any athlete had run.

But Williams and her teammates were not the least concerned. "We knew that once she got that baton, it didn't matter who was ahead. She was going to catch them, and she did." Coach Temple moved closer to watch the final dash. "When she got the stick, in seventy-five yards she caught the whole pack, and from then on it was a matter of by how far she was going to win," he recalled. "She won the thing by five yards going away. I never seen nobody . . ." His voice trailed off before picking up again. "I wish I had a stopwatch on her those first seventy-five yards. I mean she moved. She had a mission to accomplish, and she did it. When she crossed that tape, and the other three ran and grabbed her and they had a dance on the track, they were so happy."

The foreign press corps, which had fallen for Wilma just as so many of the male athletes had, swooned at the sight of her breezing across the line, far ahead for a third time. *"La Gazelle, naturellement,"* a French photographer was heard to shout, when someone asked who won. *"La Chattanooga Choo-Choo."* Clarksville, actually, but close enough. The scene even brightened the outlook of the grumpy male chauvinist A. J. Liebling: "All these runners were colored, and Wilma Rudolph, our last runner, made the women in the other lanes look like members of a third athletic sex—perhaps junior misses. She runs the hundred in time that would have won dual meets between men's university teams when I went to college. I am on principle opposed to the serious consideration of women's track events in Olympic Games, but if they are to be taken seriously, American women may as well win them . . . In any case, Miss Rudolph is a joy to behold, even when standing still."

In watching Rudolph, Tex Maule remarked that her graceful,

straight-up stride reminded him of the way Dave Sime ran. Now here came Sime and his teammates on the men's 4 X 100 relay team, preparing for a final showdown with the Germans in the last race on the Stadio Olimpico track. It was just past six o'clock. Dusk filtered the fall sky. The light rain had stopped. Sime gathered with his talented squad: Frank Budd, Stone Johnson, and Ray Norton, who entered the stadium with the burden of a goat, perhaps the biggest disappointment of the Olympics, a would-be champion who had finished dead last in both the 100 and 200. While Dave Sime went to Naples and back and worked on his mission with Igor Ter-Ovanesyan in recent days, Norton kept running, trying to work his way out of a slump that he believed had been caused by injury, not by choking under pressure. Was he ready? The coaches, uncertain, switched the lineup, placing Norton second and giving the anchor leg to Sime.

Nearby were the Germans: Bernd Cullmann, Walter Mahlendorf, Martin Lauer, and Armin Hary, the imperturbable antagonist who now, with his victory in the 100, strode the track as "the fastest man in the world." Also, it seemed, the haughtiest. If this was the dawn of a new sporting age, when a sense of entitlement came with being an athletic star, Hary was leading the way. Some viewed him as a misunderstood iconoclast who hated bourgeois convention; others just considered him rude and self-centered. "Since he has become an Olympic champion, Armin Hary has been acting like Maria Callas," wrote a columnist for the French *Le Miroir des Sports,* comparing him to the opera diva. "He puts on airs, strikes an attitude, poses for effect, and treats his court seriously. With the journalists, he is casual and evasive, not hiding the fact that he takes pleasure in being begged, and showing by his whole attitude that henceforth, Mr. Armin Hary has specific times for holding court . . . that, moreover, he only respects that which seems good to him. The new god of the stadium is anxious to accomplish feats beyond the world of sports. 'He is not bad,' the Germans say. 'He is just pigheaded and volatile. He has a bad personality. But it is better to have a bad personality than no personality.' "

Hary, pigheaded or not, had made one decision already that had pleased his coaches and teammates. Unlike Norton, he had decided to forgo the 200-meter dash, for which he had also qualified, in order to save his energy for the relay. The Frankfurt newspaper called it "a good decision," noting that the centrifugal force of the curve on the 200 could be physically wearing for "fragile, sensitive runners" like Hary, and that running the relay without him "would be meaning-less" for the Germans. For the final, they put Hary in the second spot, running against Norton, while Sime in the anchor leg would face Lauer. The Germans ran from the fifth lane, near the outside, while the Americans had the inside lane, their starting blocks lined up around what the old railbird Red Smith called "the clubhouse turn."

What happened in this relay? From the stands, as on the track, it was all in the perspective. "What a race!" began the account in the *Allgemeine Zeitung*. "This was a race which surpassed everything else which the spectators cheered about previously. Whoever saw Hary in this race . . . will not have the slightest doubt anymore about his world record as a sprinter." With their fans chanting effusively in unison, the German journalists watched as "Cullmann stamped en-ergetically through the curve, and the exchange with Hary was per-formed just like out of a sprinter's textbook. The man from Frankfurt stormed full of energy along the straightaway, leaving no chance to any of his adversaries. Again the stick exchange worked perfectly, and Mahlendorf boomed along the curve. In the inner part, though, Johnson [Stone Johnson of the U.S.] gained some ground. The ex-change then between Mahlendorf and Lauer was also performed wonderfully, and then the man from Cologne and Dave Sime stormed side by side over the homestretch. Sime was, there is no doubt about that, slightly ahead. But . . ."

And quite a *but* it was, but first consider the beginning of that last sentence. Even this boosterish account of German glory had to point out that Sime was slightly ahead. That meant he crossed the finish line first. His anchor leg was one of the greatest 100s he had ever run. When he took the baton, he was three strides behind Lauer. The stadium crowd was on its feet, in full roar, watching as Sime blazed down the track with his ferocious upright style and beat the Germans. He was thinking about nothing else but getting to the tape. He had made it. He had been perhaps the greatest sprinter never to win gold, denied his chance in Melbourne by an injury, barely nosed out by Hary in the 100 a week earlier. Now the big redhead crossed the finish line first, but—turned around, looked back, and saw that something was amiss. The Italian judges were standing at the spot where Frank Budd handed off to Ray Norton, and were waving a bright flag.

Ray Norton had worried all week about the timing of the second leg. As an anchor runner, he had been accustomed to taking the handoff from Stone Johnson, but now he had to adjust to Frank Budd. Watching from the stands, Bud Winter, Johnson's coach, could see trouble as Budd approached the transfer point. "Frank tightened up a bit and slowed coming into the exchange. I knew it because I could see his head go back. That was enough to throw Ray off," Winter reported later. This was the wrong moment to slow up approaching Norton, who was too anxious, running too fast. Norton said he felt stronger than he had in months. "When Budd hit the mark, I took off, and I just absolutely flew, and he couldn't catch me." As Budd realized that Norton was nearing the end of the 22-foot zone, he yelled for his teammate to stop. Norton slowed almost to a complete stop to take the blind handoff. Pincus Sober, the manager of the U.S. track team, had a perfect view of the handoff and realized immediately that "Norton definitely went out of his zone." The judges realized it as well.

Aside from Budd, who was in the vicinity of the judges, his work done, the American runners seemed the last to know. They were focused entirely on the race ahead, intent on defeating the Germans. Sime hit the tape in record time, 39.4 seconds, a tenth of a second ahead of Lauer. But he would say later that he never felt so bad in his life as the moment when he looked back, saw the commotion of the Italian judges halfway around the track, and realized what had happened behind him. So much work for nothing. He was inconsolable, "more angry than disappointed," and after letting off a little steam with Norton, he walked off by himself, wanting only to be alone, and far away. Norton was equally devastated. When he lost the 200, he threw his shoes against a wall. Now he never wanted to wear them again. "It was like a total nightmare for me. I had worked so hard . . . but it just wasn't for me."

Just as the disqualification was being announced, Wilma Rudolph and the Tennessee State relay team approached the stadium infield in preparation for their gold medal ceremony. For Rudolph, it was a moment of contradictory emotions: jubilation for the Tigerbelles, who would go home to Nashville with six gold medals—one each for Jones, Williams, and Hudson; three for Rudolph—but excruciating pain for her close friend Ray Norton, who would go home with none. When a CBS interviewer assembled the Tigerbelles for an interview, Rudolph seemed subdued. So was A. J. Liebling, who noted that "with few exceptions, the citizens of the short-lived stadium republic mourned for Norton." The exceptions were the German fans who, as one of their writers noted, "blustered as if they were in Berlin, Cologne, Frankfurt, or Hamburg, but not in the Italian capital. Waving happily, the German relay team thanked the applauding spectators block after block, while the Americans virtually sneaked back into their booths."

ALMOST EVERY night since August 31, the Nelson brothers had hosted what they called a celebrity banquet at the downtown YMCA or the Agib Hotel, where most of the two hundred self-described track nuts from the *Track & Field News* tour group were staying. Guest speakers at the banquets included the colorful Australian coach Percy Cerutty; the Flying Sikh, Milkha Singh; modest Peter Snell, the New Zealander who won the 800; and the boisterous shot-put winner, Bill Nieder. After the relays, with all track events done and accounted for except Saturday's closing marathon, the Nelsons' final guests were the U.S. coaches, Larry Snyder and George Eastment, along with Soviet coach Gavriel Korobkov and his assistants. It was a peculiar cold war athletic gathering. Even though the U.S. men's team clearly had outperformed the Soviets, winning twenty-two medals and nine golds to the Soviets' thirteen medals and five golds, the Soviet coaches arrived at the banquet like conquerors, and the prevailing interpretation was that the Americans had been disappointing. The disqualification of the men's relay team because of the handoff to Ray Norton brought back all the trauma of Black Thursday, when both Norton and John Thomas had suffered unexpected losses.

John Lucas, an assistant track coach at the University of Maryland, sat at the head table near Korobkov and later remembered the Soviet coach opening their table conversation by saying, "My friend John, thank you very much." For what? Lucas asked. "And the Russian coach said, 'Everything we know about track and field in the Soviet Union, we learned from you people. We were barbaric, but we read all of the American track-and-field books.'" The person Korobkov had learned from most, Payton Jordan, now the track coach at Stanford, was in the audience. They had met for the first time two years earlier at the dual track meet in Moscow, but Korobkov had been studying Jordan's running techniques since he had written the Russian an advice letter when Jordan was a sprinter at Southern Cal in the 1940s. Now it was Jordan seeking answers from his former pen pal during the question period of the banquet. The Americans had come to Rome with a suitcase full of world records and enormous expectations, Jordan noted. What had happened to change the fortunes of the two teams? "I answered, half-jokingly, 'We didn't want any miracles on the eve of the Olympics,' " Korobkov recalled. "So we tried to plan our training so these miracles would occur during the Games themselves."

After Snyder spoke to the demanding crowd, Korobkov put his hand on the American coach's shoulder and said, "Take it easy, it's only a game!"

"Yes, it is just a game," Snyder responded. "But haven't the stakes got too high recently?"

18

"SUCCESSFUL COMPLETION OF THE JOB"

Hᴉꜱᴛᴏʀʏ is replete with moments that ache with misplaced optimism, and that seemed true of the period of the 1960 Summer Olympics, even as signs of a troubled world riddled those days of late August and early September. The Games were bookended by the Soviet spy trial of American U-2 pilot Francis Gary Powers and Khrushchev's threat to stir up things at the UN, while in between came increasing tension in divided Berlin and violence in the rebellious Congo. Whatever Avery Brundage's wishes, the Olympics were in no way isolated from the eruptions and disruptions of the modern world. Rome had its share of spies and propagandists looking to turn every situation to their advantage. Yet those days in Rome were infused with a golden hue nonetheless. The shimmering was literal—emanating from the autumnal sun; the ancient coloration of the streets, walls, and piazzas; the warm angles of refracted light—but it was also figurative, an illumining that comes with a moment of historical transition, when one era is dying and another is being born. It was in that glow that India and Pakistan met to determine the gold medal in field hockey on the last Friday afternoon of the Games.

They competed for the world championship thirteen years after Pakistan's painful birth and three days after an apparent settlement of water rights for the bordering nations in the Indus River Valley, an accord that President Eisenhower cited as "one bright spot" in a troubled world. Perhaps, said the president, this would prefigure a broader rapprochement between predominantly Hindu India and predominantly Muslim Pakistan, including resolution of the larger territorial dispute over the Kashmir region. How could he foresee a future in which the two nations would be at war five years later and on the brink of nuclear exchange thereafter?

India versus Pakistan on the field hockey pitch in Rome melded the old world with the new. The popularity of the sport in both nations was a remnant of colonialism, a game taught them by "British sahibs long, long ago," as Robert Daley noted in the *Times*. But like cricket, the other peculiarly British export, hockey was not thrown off with the yoke of imperialism. After independence, it remained the national game of both India and Pakistan. While relegated to the status of a girls' prep school enterprise in the United States, field hockey made claim to being the second most popular team sport across the globe—not in terms of spectators or participants, but in the number of countries where it was played, behind only soccer. And at the highest levels, it was a decidedly male and rough sport at that, a ferocious ancestor of its better-known winter relative, ice hockey, played in more of a soccer format. Seventy minutes of nonstop action in two thirty-five minute halves, no timeouts or substitutions, eleven players per side, with shin-scraping sticks, frenetic scrums, and a hard pellet of a ball. Among the sixteen nations that qualified for Olympic competition, none was in the lofty realm of India, which won its previous games by a cumulative score of 24–1, and Pakistan with a 19–1 margin. India was not just the defending champion but a field hockey dynasty that had held onto the gold medal for thirty-two years, since grabbing its first title at Amsterdam in 1928.

It was fitting that Kashmir, the flashpoint in the India-Pakistan political dispute, also held a special place in their national game. In the fertile plains of that region, below the grand Himalaya Mountains, stood large groves of mulberry trees, their wood almost unbreakable and yet malleable, perfect for the shaping of curved field hockey sticks. While most sticks were still manufactured in England then, the wood came from the mulberry trees of Kashmir. Just as much of the territory was claimed by both sides, so too were many of the players. Several members of the Pakistani team had been born in various Indian cities—Bhopal, Delhi, Amritsar, Lucknow—and transmigrated to Pakistan with their families after the political-religious division in 1947. Indeed, one of the most revered players in field hockey annals, Feroze Khan, a center-forward who helped lead India to its historic gold medal in 1928, eventually left for Pakistan, where by 1960 he was a national icon as coach and team selector. There was a similar crossover on the Indian team, with players born in Multan and Bannu in Pakistan.

Anyone interested in field hockey could have found a cheap ticket to the title match, held across town from the Stadio Olimpico on the smaller Velodromo field not far from the Palazzo dello Sport. With Germany eliminated in the quarterfinals and no other major competitions on the national agenda, legions of German fans were motoring north already, clogging the Italian border in retreat, and American tourists who remained in Rome found other things to do. The considerably fewer Indians and Pakistanis in Rome comprised virtually all of the five thousand spectators who filled about a fourth of the seats in the sparsely populated stadium that Friday afternoon. They made up in spirit what they lacked in numbers, to say nothing of the colorful display of turbans, handlebar mustaches, and gold and purple saris. But even with the small stadium crowd, the game was watched by more people than any field hockey contest in history. It was televised live throughout Europe on Eurovision, and highlights were shown the next day on CBS after the tapes reached New York. The fans living in Delhi and Lahore, Calcutta and Rawalpindi, were the only ones left out. With no live coverage back home on radio or television, crowds gathered outside news offices in the major cities, waiting for word from the Teletype machines.

Each team had an intimate knowledge of the other—the particular skill of individual players, the rhythm and tactics of the eleven—and that familiarity, along with a soggy field, made it a tight defensive game with few scoring opportunities. Eleven minutes into the first half, Ahmad Naseer, on the left wing for Pakistan, displayed perfect control of a swift pass from the right, moved into the scoring circle "with brilliant footwork and speed," as the correspondent for the *Pakistan Times* reported, and flicked home a goal. After that, according to the *Times of India* account, "neither team could do anything except for a few individual demonstrations of expert use of the hockey stick, rapid moves, and superb dribbling." It was noted that India's right wing, amid all the cleats and clatter, played barefoot, and that its center-forward, wearing his long hair in a chignon, was remarkable in the way he could stop a fast-moving ball and flip it nonchalantly in front of him as though he were turning a fried egg over easy. In other words, there was no more scoring, and Pakistan won, 1–0, ending the long reign of India.

In Karachi, vast crowds that had been waiting in anxious silence outside the wire offices erupted in exuberant cheers and shouts at the news. Reports of the historic upset provoked an impromptu *bhangra* in Lahore, with thousands of men dancing to drumbeats in the city streets. There had not been that much excitement, one reporter declared, "since Pakistan defeated Britain in cricket six years earlier." Homeland pride surged through Pakistani neighborhoods in London, where thousands of émigrés had been able to catch the second half on the BBC. In Rome, A. B. Awan, the Pakistani chief of mission for the Olympic delegation, rushed to the embassy and sent a cable to President Ayub Khan: "On behalf of the hockey team, I report successful completion of the job. Pakistan has won the gold medal."

Hours later, back at the Olympic Village, members of the hockey squad gathered with the rest of the Pakistani athletes and began dancing to the chant *"Ut-Suta-ta! Ut-Suta-ta! Pak-i-stan! Pak-i-stan! Ut-Suta-ta! Ut-Suta-ta! Pak-i-stan! Pak-i-stan!"* The essence of Pakistan at this moment had nothing to do with politics, religion, or territory, but only of an overlooked people rejoicing—a variation of "Hip! Hip! Hooray!"—at being the best at something, reminding the world that not everything revolved around the big boys of the United States and the Soviet Union and Europe.

THE EXHILARATION of the Pakistani delegation recharged a global assembly whose crowded energy had diminished late that week as athletes whose events had ended packed up and left the Olympic Village for home. In the U.S. delegation, among the first to depart were the boxers and women swimmers. The men swimmers extended their European tour with competitions around the continent, while the women, led by multiple gold medalist Chris von Saltza and her lucky toy frog, flew directly back to New York. All was not lightness and joy for the "sweethearts" from Santa Clara, California, on their flight west across the Atlantic, even though they had performed better than expected at the Stadio del Nuoto, far outpacing the Australians, Germans, and Brits by winning five gold medals and three silvers out of nine total events. "We get on the plane, and we're halfway home, and our chaperone says, 'Oh, well, girls, it's so nice we are going home now,' " remembered Anne Warner, who earned gold in the relay. Warner and her teammates in fact were not so eager to go home. They wished they had been given the option of continuing the European tour, like the men, especially considering how few competitive swimming opportunities awaited them in the States. It did not help when the chaperone revealed the reason for their return: she had to get home herself, and there was no one else to chaperone them. In the hierarchy of sports of that era, few had less say-so than the bright young women swimmers, so back they went.

The boxers returned at the same time, but far more eagerly, none more purposeful than Cassius Clay. On the flight home, he had written a simple rhyming poem of the sort that later would define his public persona. This one found its way to Afro-American newspapers and was published under the title "How Cassius Took Rome." It began:

> To make America the greatest is my goal
> So I beat the Russian, and I beat the Pole.

His goal after alighting on U.S. soil was to make himself the greatest. When Clay arrived at Idlewild Airport in New York, he posed for pictures with his fellow champs, Wilbert McClure and Eddie Crook. The waiting area bustled with fans, photographers, and reporters, including Jim McKay, the studio host for the CBS Olympic coverage, who sensed even then that the young boxer was good copy. Dick Schaap, *Newsweek*'s sports editor, who had met Clay in Manhattan before the squad left for Rome, joined the welcoming party and squired Clay around town again, taking him to Jack Dempsey's restaurant for lunch and to Birdland to hear jazz. Wearing his USA jacket, his light-heavyweight gold medal dangling, as always, from his neck, Clay was delightfully full of himself, joking that he had to sleep on his back the night before, "otherwise that gold medal would have cut my chest." Sashaying down Broadway, he stopped inside an arcade and composed a mock newspaper headline: "Clay Wins Heavyweight Title." Late that night he held court in his suite at the Waldorf-Astoria, where he jabbered away while leafing through a boxing scrapbook. The luxury suite had been provided gratis by William Reynolds, a Louisville businessman, one of many financiers who brightened at the idea of becoming Clay's professional sponsor.

The following day, on the morning of September 9, Clay arrived in Louisville in the company of Joe Martin, his first boxing mentor, who had started to mold the pugilist Clay when he was twelve and weighed eighty-nine pounds. Martin was a central character in the creation story, which revolved around one image: the old man teaching the young man to box after his bike was stolen. Their flight from New York was met at Standiford Field by family members, city officials, and hundreds of fans. "There's Gee!" his brother, Randolph Clay, yelped when Cassius appeared in the plane's doorway. Gee was his family nickname, soon to be overtaken by his other names and lost to history. With an all-white motorcycle police squadron clearing the way for a caravan of twenty-five cars, Clay rolled through his hometown in an open convertible. A fleeting glimpse of him drew gasps and cheers from the downtown crowds when the motorcade crossed Fourth and Broadway on the way to Central High, where a larger welcome awaited the teenage champ, whose success in Rome had transformed him from a failing student into a "conquering hero," as a local headline now described him.

On the high school steps, Mayor Bruce Hoblitzell, a sixty-three-year-old real estate and insurance man who was known around town as "Mr. Hobby," declared Clay a credit to the city. "He acts like you would like a young American to act after receiving so much acclaim and so many honors," the mayor said, slapping the young boxer on the back. Hoblitzell's border city was considered more advanced on matters of race than many southern towns, yet Clay, because of the color of his skin, could not eat in downtown restaurants or try on clothes in department stores. While he was training for his gold medal, civil rights activists in Louisville had spent 1960 organizing a voter registration campaign aimed at electing officials who would end the Jim Crow segregation. Now, inside the packed auditorium at Central High, after the roaring crowd quieted, principal Atwood

Wilson praised Clay as living refutation of any criticism of the American way. "When we consider all the efforts that are being made to undermine the prestige of America," Wilson declared, "we can be grateful we had such a fine ambassador as Cassius to send to Italy."

In the legend of Muhammad Ali, one of the defining stories holds that shortly after the young man returned to Louisville, he was refused service in a local restaurant because of the color of his skin, and the racist act infuriated him so much that he threw his gold medal into the Ohio River. How could a nation that gloried in his triumph treat him like a second-class citizen? The question is as valid as the story is phony. As several Ali biographers, including Thomas Hauser and David Remnick, later established, he did not throw his gold medal away, but lost it and devised a powerful fable to cover his own carelessness.

Wilma Rudolph and the Tennessee State relay team had joined the early exodus from Italy that Friday morning. Only two years earlier, the status of American track-and-field women was so low that Coach Temple wondered whether U.S. officials would agree to take them along for the groundbreaking dual track meet in Moscow. Now the whole world wanted to see them, especially Wilma. Picking and choosing from fifteen new invitations that came their way in Rome, they expanded a post-Olympics schedule of Athens and London by adding Amsterdam and a tour of Germany, with stops in Cologne, Wuppertal, Frankfurt, and Berlin. Ed Temple left Rome with conflicted feelings: drained of emotion; proud of his Tigerbelles, who had far exceeded expectations; haunted by a sense that they might never be that successful again; and awed by the newfound international charisma of Wilma Rudolph. Could this be the same gangly Skeeter who was so easygoing that they had to wake her to run the 100-meter dash? Not just her performance on the Stadio Olimpico track, but her charm and freshness had people clamoring for encores. German track fans would soon follow her every move, rocking the

Tigerbelles' bus at every stop, chanting a name—Rudolph! Rudolph! Rudolph!—that, they joked, sounded like one of their own.

Rafer Johnson, his gold medal mission complete, relieved to never have to compete in the decathlon again, headed the other way, toward home. He was joined by Dave Sime, whose time in Rome was less satisfying but who wanted no part of the extended European tour. Sime could only wonder which was more frustrating—the injury that left him off the Olympic team in 1956, when he was arguably the fastest runner in the world, or the achingly close disappointments four years later in Rome? He had entered 1960 as an afterthought in the Olympic considerations, still in the shadows of favorite Ray Norton, and then had overcome the flu and an adverse reaction to medicine to win a silver medal in the 100, nipped by Armin Hary in a photo finish at the tape, and a week later stormed from behind to cross the line first in the 4 X 100 relay, only to have that final shot at gold snatched from him because of Norton's disqualifying baton transfer. Off the track, along with his ailments, he had endured what he viewed as the bungling effort of the cocksure "Mr. Wolf," the American agent who had botched the effort to persuade Igor Ter-Ovanesyan to defect. Now Sime wanted no more to do with amateur track. While his teammates traveled to Athens, he headed the other direction, making his way back to medical school at Duke. More prized to him than his silver medal was an illicit totem he had seized on his last night in the city, when he, Don Bragg, and Al Cantello slipped out of the village on motor scooters determined to find souvenirs. Perhaps it was not fulfilling Avery Brundage's vision of the Olympic ideal, but the trackmen concluded their experience in Rome by shimmying up flagpoles to swipe Olympic banners. Actually, the less agile Sime needed a ladder, but in any case, one of the five-ringed flags came home with him in his suitcase.

• • •

THE OLYMPICS were not done. Events rolled in and ebbed in waves, and one of the final events was weight lifting, one of the oldest sports of Baron de Coubertin's modern Games, going back to the first competition in Greece in 1896. After training and waiting in Rome for weeks, the iron men would finally get their chance. Here was an East-West competition much like the high jump, only sevenfold; a direct contest between the superpowers, the Americans against the Soviets, for world supremacy in seven weight classes. The Americans held a slight edge during the two previous Olympics, taking home more gold medals from Helsinki and Melbourne, but the Soviets were getting stronger, they had won the first-ever dual meet in the U.S. two years earlier, and in terms of national attention, the rivalry was lopsided in their favor. There were only a few pockets of weight-lifting mania in the U.S. compared with the sport's broader popularity in the Soviet Union. Speed and hand-eye coordination were skills admired most by Americans, characteristics more applicable to the nation's indigenous team sports of baseball, basketball, and football, whereas raw strength was a prized physical attribute in Russia. This is what led Bob Hoffman, the U.S. weight-lifting coach, to assert that outside of sending the first man into space, winning the weight contests in Rome "would be our best propaganda weapon" in the cold war with the Soviets. And of all the individual weight-lifting contests, the biggest coup would be to take the heavyweight class, where the winner is crowned the world's strongest man.

The Soviet heavyweight was the confident Yuri Vlasov, whose star status was such that he carried his nation's flag at the Opening Ceremony, immediately assuring his place in Olympic accounts by toting the pole with a single outstretched hand. The U.S. hope was James Bradford, who, if not forgotten, remained virtually invisible despite his heavyweight hulk. Bradford was a thoroughly American product, his biography evoking the promise and contradictions of his country. He came out of Washington, DC, born and reared in a black neighborhood a few blocks north of the U.S. Capitol building. When he was fourteen, he weighed 247 pounds but was "pretty much of a butterball" until he leafed through a copy of *Strength and Health,* the weight-lifting magazine published by Hoffman's York Barbell Company in York, Pennsylvania. Inspired by the pictures and stories, he began working out at the 12th Street Y, where he emerged as a world-class young lifter with an unorthodox technique. He lifted the bar with virtually no split of the legs on the way up, only bending his back as he lifted over his head. This later became known as "the Bradford Press," and though it demonstrated his raw strength, he said it developed not from his prowess but from a fear of dropping the weights during his practices at the Y. There was no weight room there—the neighborhood was dominated by basketball—so he practiced on the basketball court, and he knew he would get kicked out if he dropped the barbells and scarred the floor.

Under the tutelage of Hoffman at York Barbells, Bradford won a silver medal at the 1952 Olympics in Helsinki, then rejoined the army. When he finished officer training school at Fort Benning, Georgia, and was leaving to serve with the 30th Infantry National Guard unit in the Korean War, the hardest part of his journey was getting out of the southern bus station. "Here I am a brand spanking new second lieutenant going overseas to defend America and willing to die—because we had been taught at Fort Benning that second lieutenants were cannon fodder, and our cry was 'Follow me!' The song we would sing was 'Follow Me and Die!'—yet when I left Fort Benning to get to the airport, I had the hardest time. I went into the bus station and happened to go into the wrong part, the whites-only part, and they wouldn't sell me a ticket. They called the sheriff on me and threw me out. And I'm thinking, What is this? A couple of other guys from the class were catching a cab, and they took me in the cab with them. And even then, when we got to the airport, some other cab drivers gave ours a hard time, and he was saying there was nothing he could do because these white fellows took me along."

Yet Bradford considered himself a patriot. "With all its problems,

America is still the greatest country on Earth," he would say. And it was his love of country that brought him out of retirement in 1960 to take on the resurgent Russians one last time in Rome. He was thirty-two by then, married (his wife, Grace Bradford, was an opera singer in the DC area), the father of three young children, and struggling to make payments on what would become his lifelong family home, a little row house at 641 Ingraham Street in Northeast Washington. The monthly mortgage was $105, while his federal paycheck as a documents clerk in the Library of Congress was $56 per week, meaningfully half his salary went into the house. If Big Jim accepted a few under-the-table loans and bonuses from York Barbells, it could not be said that they enriched him but barely helped him pay the bills. The enforcers of amateurism knew nothing about Hoffman's financial books, but they were made aware of an offer from Armour beef to provide Bradford and his family with all the meats he needed to train for the Olympics. "Avery Brundage said, 'If he takes one dollar, he's out!' " No deal for "the dog kids love to bite."

Working in the stacks of the world's largest library had made Bradford a perfect Olympian, at least in the sense that he acquired a keen awareness of the world, unlike many athletes who tended to focus narrowly on their sport. Day after day, from his perch in the government publications section of the Library of Congress, Bradford organized documents arriving from the United Nations. His assignment was to bind them in the proper books and folders. Some documents were in English, but many were in French, German, and Spanish, and while not fluent in foreign languages, Bradford, by sheer necessity, learned enough to get things in the right place. He started paying attention to world events and problems—hunger and disease in Africa, human rights in Asia, nuclear issues in Europe—and came to think of himself as a man of the world. When weight lifting took him overseas, he made a point of getting along with the local people. "For example, in 1959 we went to Warsaw, Poland, and it was still Communist, during the cold war, and other members of the team kept reminding me about that, but I seemed to get along so well with the people. In Poland you weren't supposed to go out at night without an escort, but I would go to the restaurants and drink beer. I would try to learn their language, and I would want to eat their food. I became native, whereas the other guys would want a hot dog or hamburger." Bradford also became a connoisseur of international airline food and became partial to KLM Royal Dutch Airlines. "Oh, gosh, with KLM, as soon as the plane would taxi down the runway, they were feeding you. Cheese, tea, or anything you wanted, and they fed you all the way from America to wherever you were going."

If Bradford was a welcome ambassador for America, he went largely unappreciated at home. A supervisor at the Library of Congress threatened to fire him for taking time off to attend the U.S. Trials and only grudgingly gave him permission to compete in Rome—and then only if he took an unpaid leave, which he could barely afford. Avery Brundage was a big proponent of unpaid leave, or uncompensated time, believing it was a key component of pure amateurism. But Brundage, the Chicago millionaire, and his IOC compatriots, like the Marquess of Exeter, with his lordly castles in the British countryside, did not have to punch a time clock or use half of their take-home pay to cover a monthly $105 mortgage. From Bradford's perspective, he was caught between a heartless employer and a haughty overseer, but he wanted to compete, and he loved to lift, so he accepted the leave without pay and went to Rome.

By the time Bradford took the stage, the Soviets had already snatched the team title. In the first contest, the U.S.'s Charles Vinci, a 4-foot-11 lifter nicknamed Mighty Mite, defended his gold medal in the bantamweight class, but the tone of the team match was set next when Isaac (Ike) Berger, who had also won in Melbourne, was upset in the featherweight division by Yevgenyi Minayev of Russia. Berger, the son of an Israeli cantor, grew up in the Brownsville section of Brooklyn and was a youth cantor himself before transforming his

body from that of a 5-foot-1 weakling into a sculpted little mus-
cleman at the gym on Pitkin Avenue. Since joining Hoffman's York-
based squad at age seventeen, he had beaten Minayev six times, and
he fully expected to win again in Rome. "I was the surest guy to win
on the squad, I was so far ahead of the competition," Berger said later.
But as the match dragged on—it took ten hours, the longest in Olympic history—Minayev got stronger, while Berger wore down. His
legs were weak, "like blubber," he would say later. Too late, he realized that he had made a mistake by overlifting in practice, going back
to the day of the Opening Ceremony when he had set a new world
record of 336½ pounds in the clean and jerk. "You can't do that. I
overtrained. I wanted to show off. Why did I lift so much in practice?
I felt good and wanted to see what I could do. It was really dumb." In
the end, Minayev beat him by ten pounds. It was such an upset,
Berger recalled, that Coach Hoffman approached him afterward and
snarled, "Someone must have paid you to lose!"

Berger was paid, but not as an enticement to lose. By his account,
the small sums of cash that he received each month came directly
from Hoffman himself or one of his men at York Barbell. The money
ostensibly was for Berger's work at Hoffman's high-protein-bar factory, though most of his time was spent working out at the gym. He
also received an apartment and could eat free at almost any restaurant in town by saying he was one of Hoffman's Olympians. Hoffman was the ultimate capitalist, always looking for a new product to
sell, a new way to fund his weight lifters through bodybuilding contests and exercise schemes, yet the subculture he developed in York
was in some ways much like that of a Soviet sports compound, where
the athletes enjoyed subsidies that allowed them to devote themselves
to sport.

There was another apparent connection between Hoffman and
the Soviets in 1960, involving the early use of anabolic steroids. Sports
historians John D. Fair at Auburn University at Montgomery and
John Hoberman at the University of Texas, both experts on sports

and the body, have traced the early use of anabolic steroids in the U.S. back to John Ziegler, a doctor from Olney, Maryland, who conducted steroid experiments on some of Hoffman's weight lifters in the run-up to the 1960 Olympics. Ziegler told Fair that he started his experiments after learning from a Soviet doctor at an international meet in Vienna that Russian lifters were getting stronger by ingesting a drug form of testosterone. Hoffman, according to Fair, had "been looking for a magic potion" to help his weight lifters. His fad of the moment was isometric exercises, but he became interested, if cautious, when Ziegler told him about the dramatic effects of the anabolic steroid Diabanol (whose generic name was methandrostenolone), a pill that was just then being manufactured by Ciba Pharmaceutical, which was not intended for athletes but for burn victims. Ziegler became known as "the father of Diabanol," a title that he regretted in his later years. Acknowledging to Fair that he tested steroids on some lifters, Ziegler lamented, "But I wish to God I'd never done it. I'd like to go back and take that whole chapter out of my life."

Small brown bottles of Diabanol made their way to Rome with the U.S. weight-lifting team. The effects were not established knowledge then, and steroid use was neither against the law nor specifically banned by the IOC. There is evidence that pills were administered to some U.S. weight lifters at the Olympic Village, but there were no indications that in this instance they improved performance. In his book *Muscletown USA,* Fair reprinted parts of a letter written by John Grimek, Hoffman's top assistant and a two-time Mr. America, to Ziegler from Rome on September 7, the first day of the weight-lifting competition, in which Grimek said that from the early results, it "didn't seem as if the 'pills' helped that much." Unlike the doping of the Danish cyclists, the use of steroids by Olympic strongmen went undetected and unreported at the time, but it was another seminal chapter in the long and troubled story of drugs and the Olympics. Harold Connolly, the defending champion hammer thrower who had lost unexpectedly in Rome, said later that he came back determined to strengthen his body by finding out what the weight lifters—he said it was the Russians, not the Americans—were taking. A doctor told him that "the only thing that could build lean muscle and tissue mass" like that was anabolic steroids, so Connolly decided that he wanted to try them. After Rome, the deluge. Doping and steroids became more tempting, more prevalent, and more of a problem year by year, altering the bodies, blood, strength, and endurance of athletes ranging from weight lifters to cyclists, from East German women swimmers to American sprinters.

The match between heavyweights Bradford and Vlasov had its own controversy apart from drugs. Olympic weight-lifting competitions in that era involved three types of lifts: the press, in which the barbell is lifted from floor to chest and then chest to overhead in what are supposed to be two smooth movements with a slight bend but no shifting of the feet; the snatch, in which the weight is lifted floor to overhead in one explosive movement, allowing the lifter to bend and shift his feet; and the clean and jerk, in which the weight is taken from floor to shoulder height, held there briefly, then lifted overhead with a squat and spring of the legs. Bradford was considered the world's best at the press, and he hoped to build a lead over Vlasov in the first of the three types of lifts. After spending hours meditating in his Olympic Village dorm room, visualizing his handling of the immense weights, he easily pressed 374½ pounds, but Vlasov matched him. Arkady Vorobyov, a Soviet weight-lifting expert, described the scene as "a competition between two schools—the old and the new. From the end of the last century, heavyweight weight lifters had been built like wardrobes, with boundless stomachs and backs the width of doorways. Nature had fashioned them with an axe rather than a chisel. Jim Bradford was clearly a representative of this ancient dynasty. When this lifter with the monstrously broad chest and great boulders of muscles appeared on the platform, the hall buzzed enthusiastically. His white costume crackled on his mighty black body. Bringing the weight up to his chest, he pressed with his arms alone. By comparison to his opponent, Vlasov seemed wiry and lean. It was just his massive legs which distinguished him."

More weight was added for the next round, raising it to 396½ pounds. Bradford made his press with apparent ease. Next up, Vlasov. "After smearing his palms with magnesia and adjusting his glasses," Vorobyov wrote, "Vlasov lifted the weight by a tremendous effort of willpower and pressed it. A magnificent performance!" To Soviet eyes, perhaps, but the Americans thought it was illegal, as did the panel of three judges, who disapproved the lift by a majority vote on the grounds that Vlasov paused too long on the way up. The match continued, with Vlasov lifting 11 pounds more than Bradford in the snatch—341½ to 330½. Bradford held a precarious lead, and it appeared that the gold medal would be decided by the clean and jerk, where Vlasov was superior. But just before they began their final lifts, Olympic officials announced that the initial ruling against Vlasov on the press had been overturned on appeal. Bradford, after thinking he was on his way to victory, was stunned. "I was ahead of everybody," he recalled later. "I was into the clean and jerk when I found out that the Russians had had the rules changed. In the middle of the contest! They went all the way back to the press and gave this guy the press. They tried to say he did the same amount I did. He was better at the clean and jerk, but I was better at the press. I said to an American official, 'Don't let them do that!' But he said, 'Well, we don't want to cause an international incident.' And I said, 'What does it take for me to win? I cannot beat somebody when they are going to do things like that.' To me that was very unsportsmanlike. It really killed a lot in me."

The ruling pushed Vlasov into a comfortable lead with his best lift still to come. Weight-lifting crowds traditionally sided with the athletes when judges rejected a lift, but this time the large and boisterous audience inside the Palazzetto dello Sport was on Bradford's side and "broke into loud boos when the Russian protest was upheld," according to a wire report.

For the rest of his life, Bradford would insist that had it not been for Soviet manipulation of the appeal, he would have won. Perhaps athletes deserve the prerogative of saying "if only," especially when something suspicious interferes with their hopes. In any case, Bradford knew that he could not match Vlasov in the clean and jerk, and as it turned out, Vlasov's margin there was so overwhelming that he would have had more points even without the appeal. When Bradford tried to lift 412 pounds, more than he ever had before, he tumbled over backward from the weight. The official Italian film of the Olympics shows him later leaning against a side wall, No. 5 in a white shirt, bowing his head and shaking it in dismay. Vlasov, now free from the pressure, strutted onto the platform thinking only of breaking the world record. A *Pravda* correspondent reported, "There was a lot of excitement in the audience" when Vlasov, after topping Bradford's best lift, asked for 446 pounds, a "weight that until recently was considered pretty much impossible for the human body. In a split second, this weight was up on his outstretched arms, and the audience burst into applause." When he jerked the record amount over his head, "people got up chanting bravo! And then endless applause, and the crowd surrounded Vlasov and picked him up on their shoulders." As Bob Hoffman's last man fell, his assessment of what weight lifting meant to the Soviets seemed correct. Vlasov's record-breaking performance, *Pravda* concluded, was "the biggest achievement of the Olympics" and the team's overall performance such "a convincing and full victory" that it "symbolized the strength and power of Soviet sports."

Over at the Palazzo dello Sport, the medals were being awarded after the basketball finals, which had taken place simultaneously. The U.S. team, never seriously challenged throughout the tournament, crushed Brazil for the gold medal, winning 90–63. After Jerry Lucas's early rebound basket, the first of a game-high twenty-five points for the Ohio State center, the Americans never trailed, playing what Coach Newell called their best game of the Olympics. Oscar

Robertson and Jerry West, though scoring only eighteen points between them, played brilliant floor games, and the Brazilians seemed to give up midway through the first half after big Walt Bellamy landed an elbow to the mouth of a Brazilian player and sent him sprawling to the court. Though it did not seem deliberate, Bellamy was ejected, but the Brazilians played timidly after that. "That was the end of the game for them," Robertson said later. "They were out of it at that point. They were not going to win anyway, but they didn't put up a big battle at all then."

The most compelling action at the Palazzo happened off the court. In a contest to determine the final positions below first place, the Soviets faced the Italians, and the crowd was fiercely partisan for the home team. There had been several near-fights in the game; the Italian fans thought the Russians were playing dirty. They jeered and whistled whenever a Soviet player stepped to the free-throw line, and several times tossed things onto the court, halting play. Loud chants of *"Italia! Italia!"* went up when the home team closed the gap, but the Soviets eventually prevailed, 78–70. Only a week earlier, in the same arena, Pete Newell had watched with apprehension as the Italian boxing crowd jeered and hissed through the playing of the national anthem, upset by a decision that favored the Americans. Newell viewed that response in a cold war context and wondered whether the audience was expressing a political as well as sporting rebuke of the United States. Now the sentiments had turned, and the Soviets were greeted with loud jeers when they took the second step on the medals podium, while Oscar Robertson and Jerry West, standing on the top rung for the U.S., received a rousing ovation. West was surprised by the emotions that overwhelmed him at that moment, as the flag rose, the anthem played, and he stood side by side with his teammate, representing his country at a difficult moment in history. Robertson was equally moved and felt a sense of brotherhood with his fellow captain. "It was a moment of jubilation for me, a very special moment," he said later. "Jerry and I being from different parts of the country . . . and neither of us had any money, and we are on the stands for the gold medal, one black and one white, with all the troubles that were going on in the country at that particular time, which people don't like you to talk that much about, the race relations then. For [the two of us] to stand there and take that medal for the country, it meant a lot."

NIKITA KHRUSHCHEV was on his way to New York by then. He had left the night before from the Soviet naval port of Baltiski on a ten-day sail from Estonia out the Baltic and across the Atlantic aboard the *Baltika,* accompanied by a cordon of leaders from Romania, Bulgaria, and Hungary. According to William Taubman, Khrushchev's biographer, he spent his time reading position papers, getting briefed by intelligence officers while lazing on a deck chair, consulting with the Eastern Europeans, and playing countless games of shuffleboard. He prided himself on not getting seasick. When he left, he was concerned about how he would be received at the United Nations, but as the trip toward New York progressed, he became exhilarated by the prospect of a bold confrontation with the West.

19

A THOUSAND
SENTINELS

AT THEIR assembly point atop the Campidoglio steps, sixty-nine distance runners warmed up before the start of the marathon. It was quarter after five on the Saturday afternoon of September 10, the last full day of the Rome Olympics. Sunlight glanced off the ruins of the Coliseum nearby, and church bells pealed in the distance as some athletes went through stretching routines and others jogged in tight orbits around shrubs and statuary. Lining the streets below, spectators jostled for position in the swelling crowd.

Gordon McKenzie, one of three Americans in the race, was nervous as he descended the steps and approached the starting line. McKenzie did not think of himself as a marathoner. He had been a miler at New York University and then a 10,000-meter specialist until earlier that year when he entered the Boston Marathon, where his wife, Chris, a fellow runner, had urged him on from the back of a motor scooter. For finishing second in Boston, he had won a bowl of stew, a laurel leaf, a trophy, and a spot on the U.S. Olympic team. His optimism in Rome now was tempered by uncertainty. He knew little about the marathon route and less about the field of competitors. Reports before the race had mentioned three Brits, two New Zealanders, two Soviets, a Moroccan, and an Argentine as the likeliest to head the pack. As he waited for the gun that would send the international horde off and running, McKenzie stood next to his teammate Allen Kelley, and not far from "a skinny little African guy in bare feet." How could someone think of running without shoes? McKenzie wondered.

"Well," he said to Kelley, nodding in the direction of the barefooted stranger. "There's one guy we don't have to worry about."

In bare feet, dark red trunks, bright green shirt, the two vertical lines of No. 11 defining his narrow, bony back—that was Abebe Bikila. He had running shoes with him when the Ethiopian team arrived from Addis Ababa nearly a month earlier, but the shoes were frayed and had to be replaced. In Rome he bought new ones, and wore them on several practice runs, but they did not fit the contours of his thin feet and caused blisters. On the day of the race, he decided it would be less painful to run with no shoes than with ill-fitting shoes, so there he was in his bare feet. If anyone's soles could be tough enough for the twenty-six-plus miles of pounding, Abebe Bikila's were, hardened by countless hours of barefoot running over Ethiopia's rugged terrain.

The crosswinds of change were blowing across black Africa that summer, with so many new nations being born: Benin, Cameroon, the Central African Republic, Chad, the Congo, Gabon, the Ivory Coast, Madagascar, Mali, Mauritania, Niger, Nigeria, Senegal, Somalia, and Togo. But to this point, the emergence of a new Africa had been felt only faintly in Rome. In the decision-making suites, Avery Brundage and his IOC executive board had averted their eyes from the blatant segregation in South Africa, putting it off to another time, while in the sporting arenas, the Africans, like fellow athletes from other emerging regions around the world, were mostly overwhelmed by the Soviets, Americans, and Europeans. Only two of the nearly one hundred competitors from sub-Saharan African nations had won medals (not counting the whites-only squad from South Africa, which claimed one silver and two bronze). Clement Quartey, a light welterweight from Ghana, had won a silver medal in boxing, and Abdoulaye Seye, a sprinter from Senegal, had taken a bronze in the 200-meter dash. Even then, Seye's feat had an Old World tint, since he ran wearing the colors of colonial France rather than his homeland.

The writer A. J. Liebling, who claimed a sentimental rooting interest in underdog nations ever since he "took Carthage's side against Rome," had spent his time at the Stadio Olimpico hoping that some newcomer would win an event "to encourage the others." He had been especially taken by the Flying Sikh, India's Milkha Singh, who had broken an Olympic record even as he finished fourth in the 400, barely missing a medal. But as the Rome Games neared an end, Liebling informed his *New Yorker* readers, "the notion that every jungle harbors instinctive high jumpers and every desert swift-footed runners was exposed as a romantic fallacy, and the new boys looked a couple of Olympiads away, by which time they would have had some coaching." The small Ethiopian squad, with the added incentive of competing in the capital city of a country that had invaded them twice, had been shut out so far, but here was one last chance.

Fallacy or not, some observers were immediately drawn to the romance of the shoeless Abebe Bikila. While the rest of the press corps was stuck in makeshift bleacher perches near the finish line, the Italian sportswriter Gian Paolo Ormezzano was lucky enough to hitch a ride in the back of an official Olympic film vehicle that would accompany the runners along the route. Ormezzano and his friend Sergio Valentini, a journalist working for the film company, decided to choose a runner to support "to make it more fun." One look at Abebe Bikila, and they had their man. Did he have a chance, or was he one guy no one had to worry about, as the American McKenzie

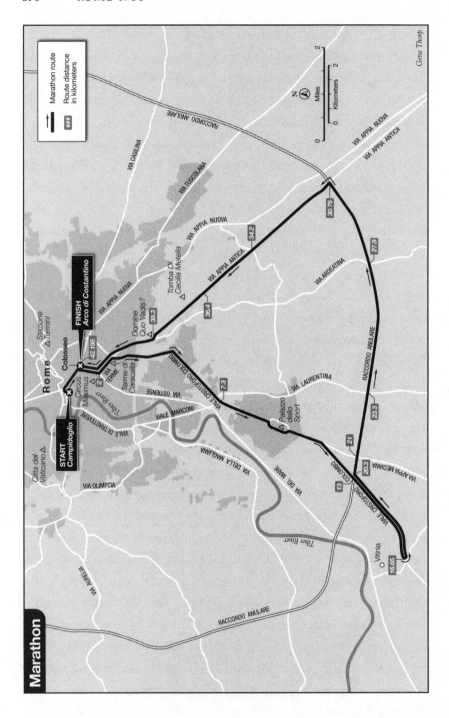

Marathon

Gene Thorp

assumed? There was at least one hint about his talent. Robert Pariente, a track expert for the French sports journal *L'Équipe,* happened to notice a recent running time of 2:21:35 next to the Ethiopian's name on an early marathon tip sheet. But Pariente quickly dismissed it, saying to himself, "Is not possible in the desert."

In the last seconds before the starting gun, Silvio de Florentis, wearing the colors of the home Italian team, was so nervous that he "pissed in [his] pants like a horse." Like McKenzie, he had never run a competitive marathon until that year, and he too had not heard of the Ethiopian. He thought the Russians were the ones to worry about. The New Zealand runners—Barry Magee, Jeff Julian, and Ray Puckett—were seen off by Arthur Lydiard, their renowned distance coach. Two from Lydiard's impressive stable of runners had won gold medals already, Peter Snell in the 800 and Murray Halberg in the 5000, and he now had high hopes for Magee, though the marathon course itself already had proved vexing for his team. Days earlier, they had tried to trace the route by car, five of them crammed into a compact Fiat, but their scouting mission encountered one calamity after another. First they were stopped by the cops for having too many passengers, then they were slowed by an accident in front of them involving a truck and a motor scooter, and finally, after only the first ten miles, the car gave out altogether, and they had to push it up a hill before giving up and hailing a cab to retreat, unenlightened, back to the Olympic Village.

There were only more frustrations for Lydiard now. After giving last-minute instructions to his runners, he thought he might follow the race on television at a bar, but he could not find one nearby, so as the race began he felt completely out of touch. His audacious Australian counterpart, Percy Cerutty, might have done something bold and out-of-bounds at that point, like seizing an official motor scooter to follow the race, but Lydiard and Cerutty were running gurus of opposite temperaments, and Lydiard went back to his hotel room.

At half past five the marathoners went off in an amoebalike mass, expanding and contracting, spilling out to the sides, elongating, flowing around the Coliseum down the Passeggiata Archeologica toward Viale Cristoforo Colombo and nine miles southward on the first leg of a triangle that led back to a finish line near the start. No modern marathon since the first one in Athens in 1896 had featured more tradition; much of the course was a spectacular tour of ancient Roman history. Yet at the same time, no modern marathon was more defiant of Olympic tradition. Marathons traditionally were held during daylight and ended with the runners entering the main stadium to the cheers of a vast throng. In the heat of Rome, the race began at twilight and proceeded into darkness; and the finish line was not inside the Stadio Olimpico but at the Arch of Constantine amid the Roman ruins.

Of all Olympic events, the marathon is most often connected to the Games of ancient Greece. Perhaps fittingly, it is also the most enveloped in myth. In the words of Olympic historian John A. Lucas of Pennsylvania State University, "the task of disentangling . . . fact from legend and myth . . . is a formidable one." One indisputable fact is that there was no comparable race at the ancient Games. The marathon was inspired by the legend of a messenger running approximately twenty-six miles from the small town of Marathon to Athens to announce a Greek victory over the Persians, but historians have concluded that the legendary run was only that, a legend, with no grounding in fact. While the story is often attributed to the *Histories* of the great Herodotus, he never wrote about it; instead he recounted the tale of a messenger named Pheidippides who was said to have run from Athens to Sparta, a much longer distance of 150 miles, to seek Sparta's help in the battle of Marathon. Nineteenth-century romantic poets, including Lord Byron, seized on Marathon as a symbol of freedom, and Robert Browning wrote a poem that placed Pheidippides in the heroic role of running from Marathon to Athens, confusing it with the run to Sparta. By then the story, real or myth, was so alluring that when Baron de Coubertin was planning his first Olympics at Athens in 1896, he was persuaded by a compatriot, Michel Breal—a scholar of Greek mythology at the Sorbonne—to include a race called the marathon.

In the early going, Gordon McKenzie stayed near the back of the second pack of runners. He had an empty stomach (this was before the days of pre-race carbo-loading), having not eaten in six hours. Abebe Bikila began not far from McKenzie, near the rear, on the left side of the street, but effortlessly moved up to the back of the first pack by the time they ran past the Axum Obelisk, the majestic fourth-century monument that Mussolini's army had looted from Ethiopia in 1937 and that now stood outside the United Nations Food and Agriculture Organization building. In the lead at that early stage was Arthur Keily of Great Britain, followed by Rhadi ben Abdessalem of Morocco, a distance runner of remarkable stamina who only two days earlier had finished fourteenth in the 10,000. The first leg of the triangle went south along Cristoforo Colombo, past the Palazzo dello Sport and the grandiose state buildings of Mussolini's EUR sector, then out into the Italian countryside on an up-and-back jag before turning east for the second shorter leg along the Grande Raccordo Anulare, the outer-ring highway around Rome.

McKenzie's plan had been to store energy for this stretch of the marathon. He was a slow starter and had it in mind to run his own race and not worry about what others were doing. But his legs started feeling sore after the first forty-five minutes, darkness fell over the Raccordo Anulare, and he soon became disoriented. He had no sense of where he was or where he was going. There was a severe pain in the left side of his stomach, a discomfort he later recorded in his daily diary, with another notation that his "left hamstring joining buttock was very tight." He was running in a pair of Hyde athletic shoes that had extra rubber soles in them, but his feet started to hurt. With every few paces, the night seemed darker, more alien. Now and then other runners passed him, but mostly he felt utterly alone, like he was "running in an isolation booth." Up ahead New Zealand's Barry Magee was also uncertain about where he was. He thought he was lagging in the middle of the field, but then a small pack led by Sergei Popov of the Soviet Union came up to join him. Popov was a favorite, holding the best time that year, so Magee figured he might be near the front, especially after they passed the early leader, Arthur Keily. By then he and Popov had moved ahead of their pack and were running alone. When Popov slowed at a water station, Magee took off by himself. It was then that he saw lights ahead of him, far in the distance.

Two competitors were up there, making the turn off the ring road and heading north, back toward the city, along the Appia Antica, the old Appian Way, queen of the Roman roads. What a strange and beautiful sight it was: a half moon glowing above, a thousand sentinels lining the ancient path, soldiers holding torches, stationed ten meters apart like human streetlights block after block; uneven cobblestones below, cypress trees and ancient ruins to the sides; a little convoy ahead, including a golf cart, two motorcycles, a station wagon carrying the film crew, and a lorry with photographers. All were focused on two small figures moving through the night: Rhadi ben Abdessalem and Abebe Bikila. They ran nearly side by side, No. 185 and No. 11. The soundman in the back of the station wagon picked up one noise in the silence, the steady *pat, pat, pat, pat, pat* of Abebe Bikila's bare feet.

Robert Creamer of *Sports Illustrated,* in charge of his magazine's coverage in Rome, had gone out to witness the marathon's start at the Campidoglio—"It was marvelous to watch the old thing begin as they went piling off toward the Coliseum"—then retreated to the *Time* bureau to monitor the remainder of the race on television. One of the office workers was an Italian woman who had lived in Ethiopia during the era of Mussolini's occupation. When she saw Abebe Bikila in the lead, Creamer recalled, "she got all excited and started shouting, 'We're winning! We're winning!' "

Over at the Olympic Village, the cyclist Jack Simes had plopped down on a comfortable chair in the canteen to watch the marathon with a group of American athletes. "We don't understand the Italian commentary, but that doesn't matter because the TV shots are great, with light trucks and cameras following the race," Simes wrote in his diary. "I'm surprised that the European TV is clear, too. Hartman [Jack Hartman, his cycling teammate] once said it's because they have more lines on the screen than we do, and that makes a better picture. I wonder how it can be that fifteen years ago the place was a pile of rubble, and now they have better TV than we do. I thought everything was supposed to be better in America and we invented TV. The marathon is at night to give the runners some relief from the Roman heat wave. [When there are only] a few guys off in front, someone says, 'Look, it's the guy from Africa.' And there are chuckles and comments as the camera closes in on his face. The camera pans down to his shoeless feet."

W. H. Strang, a British national who worked in Ethiopia, was on vacation back home in Northampton, watching the race on Eurovision. When he saw Abebe Bikila in the lead, he felt a rush of pride, he noted later in a letter to the *Ethiopian Herald*. It reminded him that running was such a routine part of everyday life in Addis Ababa. "It is a common sight to see dozens of men running to market every day along the Jimma road, past the old airport buildings, carrying heavily loaded baskets above their heads. It is men such as these as well as those who run for miles behind their donkeys, who have demonstrated what reserves of power there must be in their bodies to enable them to run such long distances in such difficult circumstances. There must be hundreds of Ethiopians with tremendous potentials of endurance."

Out of those hundreds came one now, padding down the uneven roadway of the Appian Way, breathing lightly, showing no outward signs of strain. During his adolescent years in the mountains near Debre Berhan, Abebe Bikila preferred riding to running. He could ride anything from a horse to an ox, and felt so natural bareback that when he was herding the oxen he would often ride one backward. At age seventeen, when he left the countryside and joined his divorced

mother in Addis Ababa, he started playing soccer and became infatu-
ated with the uniforms of Haile Selassie's Imperial Army, which he
joined two years later as a private in the Fifth Infantry Regiment of
the Imperial Body Guard. It was there that he began running and
eventually caught the attention of Onni Niskanen, the nation's director of athletics, who was putting together a team for the Rome Olympics. Abebe Bikila had been running the 5000- and 10,000-meter
races, and winning them regularly, but began training for the marathon. In early August, running in the desert near Debre Zeit, he finished a training marathon with a time bettering the winning mark at
the 1956 Melbourne Games. That was the time that leaked out to
Robert Pariente of *L'Équipe*, who could not believe it.

One Westerner who could believe it was LeRoy Walker, gold
medal hurdler Lee Calhoun's coach at North Carolina College. Earlier
that summer, the State Department had sent Walker to Ethiopia to
help train their Olympians, part of the larger cold war effort to win
friends in black Africa and counteract Soviet attacks on American racism. Walker was a sprint and hurdle coach who knew little about distance running, but for the rest of his life he jokingly claimed a role in
the development of the first great African distance men. As he would
later recount the story, with the hyperbole of a joyous legend, when he
first encountered six Ethiopian distance runners, he told them to warm
up by running around a little hill and back. "Thirty minutes go by,
then an hour or two. No sign of the runners. They musta got eaten by
lions or something. Two hours. They come back two and a half hours
later! Where the hell have you all been? 'Running,' they said. Well, it
turns out that little hill was a mountain some thirteen miles away."
Walker later told Dave Sime another story: all of the Ethiopians were
given a small amount of pocket money to take the bus from their homes
to the training facility. One runner was so poor that he kept the money
and ran the round-trip home and back, more than thirty miles. And
that was before and after their training runs.

Mile after mile, the marathon duel continued up the Appian Way, past the famed Chiesa del Domine Quo Vadis, the little seventeenth-century church near the spot where legend holds Saint Peter had a vision of Jesus (Q: "Lord, where are you going?" A: "I am going to Rome, to be crucified anew"), until finally they whisked through the St. Sebastian Gate and neared the Axum Obelisk. It was there that Rhadi tried to accelerate, but Bikila found another gear and pulled away, and word of a lone front-runner filtered back to a surprised press corps. The British writer Neil Allen, from his seat jammed amid his fellow journalists, feeling "the sudden chill of the night" and looking "dazedly at the floodlit Arch of Constantine," could not believe it when the loudspeaker crackled the name of the leader, Abebe Bikila. But when the name was repeated, he realized he had not misheard. "A completely unknown athlete from Ethiopia was going to win the Olympic marathon. Suddenly, faces lifted, the great crowd waited patiently. Journalists and officials edged forward in the wooden stands, peering along the darkness of the Appian Way hoping to be the first to spot this last and most unexpected hero of the Games." At last the lights of a convoy could be seen "twinkling in the distance," Allen recorded in his diary. "There was a brief tussle with one of the persistent Lambretta scooters before it was bundled out of the way, and then—here he came!"

At the Opening Ceremony seventeen days earlier, A. J. Liebling had looked down on the small Ethiopian team marching through the Stadio Olimpico and wondered what they were thinking. What could have been going through their minds on the approach into the Foro Italico as they passed marble blocks extolling the conquest of Addis Ababa and then as they stepped inside a stadium constructed by their oppressor, Mussolini? Liebling now thought he knew what one Ethiopian was thinking. "He had been thinking, correctly, that it would be a fine thing for the home folks if he could run barefoot all over Rome and win the marathon. So he did. It wasn't even a race; he just ran away from the field, accompanied most of the way by the Moroccan Rhadi, who had used the ten thousand meter as a tune-up.

The two Africans, symbolizing the escape of their continent from the people like the *Il Tempo* editorialist who suggested that all the troubles of the Western world had started with Italy's expulsion from Africa, fled through the night, leaving behind not only the representatives of the colonial powers but the Russians, whose intentions they apparently suspected. They moved so unobtrusively that half the people in the streets didn't know that the business end of the marathon had passed them by."

The official film crew focused solely on the barefoot Ethiopian striding toward the waiting crowd. The street widened, a bright white line down the middle, as the Arch of Constantine came into view, glowing in the darkness. Abebe Bikila ran on the right side, nearest the bleachers. A shadow cast by the strobe light ran with him, his only competition, and in the final steps, his shadow beat him to the finish. The time was 2:15:16. No one had run an Olympic marathon close to that time before. Abebe raised his hands above his waist and kept running until he was directly under the arch, prancing underneath, like a boxer in the ring awaiting the call of his name. Next came a little jig, then three toe touches, pushing his hands down to the ground as though he were unrolling a rug, finally throwing out his palms in an encompassing gesture—he was now everyone's runner, not just Ethiopia's—while sportswriters with pens in their mouths crafted deadline leads on portable typewriters for the world's newspapers. "A skinny barefooted palace guard in the Ethiopian Army of King Haile Selassie ran the fastest marathon in history tonight," wrote *Times* reporter Allison Danzig. Nearby, Jesse Abramson of the *Herald Tribune* tapped out a similar refrain: "In bare feet, an Ethiopian army corporal who had never run a race outside his isolated East African homeland . . ." Sportswriters tend to share thoughts with one another, so it was no surprise that Abramson, too, seemed interested in reading Abebe's mind, saying that "he might have asked at the end, if he could speak anything other than Amharic, 'Please, can we Ethiopians recover that statue which Mussolini pinched from us twenty-four years ago when I was a lad of four?'" What he did say, through a translator, was that he was not at all tired and could have run much farther. Neil Allen was reading into another source. Pliny was right, he thought: *ex Africa semper aliquid novi*—always something new from Africa.

In another twenty-five seconds, Rhadi came in, but then there was a two-minute wait for the bronze medalist, New Zealand's Magee. Coach Lydiard had left his hotel room to be at the finish line, where he waited "tensely" for his runner, he recorded in his diary. "Very pleased with Magee. Has vindicated my faith in him as a marathon runner." Magee had no idea he had won bronze until officials told him after the race. Gordon McKenzie was still out there, struggling, along with so many runners. What a terrible race, he thought. The course was full of cobblestones and potholes. It was like culture shock running on it. He was emotionally drained and demoralized. The entire effort had been nothing but hard, without incentive or adrenaline, only suffering. By the time he reached the finish, twenty-one minutes after the winner, the medals had been handed out and the crowds were leaving. There was still a massive traffic jam on the streets behind the arch; everyone had a place to go on this bustling Saturday night, but none on such a lonely mission as his. With 300 meters to go, he had given one last push to try to pass another runner, and his calves had seized. He walked five paces, then jogged in, losing three places at the very end, down to forty-eighth place. The only person waiting for him was his wife, Chris. He was told about the surprising winner, a skinny guy from Africa without shoes. "And I had laughed at the barefoot runner," he said later. "How do you like that? That will teach you not to make snap judgments."

A. J. Liebling, who did not have to run the race, but only watch it and write about it, agreed with McKenzie about the lesson of Abebe Bikila—"a man's a man for all that"—but had a brighter assessment of the grueling event. "It was," he wrote, "a glorious ending to the Olympic Games."

20

"THE WORLD
IS STIRRING"

Avery brundage once wrote in a memo to himself that as a student of history he was invariably disappointed when he compared the Closing Ceremony of the modern Olympics with the splendor of the ancient Greek Games. He loved the idea that in ancient Greece "the victors had to take part with their crown of oleaster on their head" and that the entire procession "sang old songs in honor of Herakles, the founder of the games." No modern ritual, however elaborate, matched those, he lamented. There were no songs in honor of the modern creator, Baron de Coubertin, and certainly none for the old Chicago businessman.

For the Closing Ceremony in Rome, many of the victors were gone, and the nations of the world were represented by lone flag bearers (including Ingrid Kraemer for the combined Germany, Abebe Bikila for Ethiopia, Yuri Vlasov for the Soviet Union, and gold medalist swimmer Mike Troy for the United States) who marched into the Stadio Olimpico single file early on the Sunday evening of September 11. They formed an arc in the infield as Brundage stepped to the rostrum to bring the Games to a formal end. "In the name of the International Olympic Committee . . . I declare the Games of the Seventeenth Olympiad closed," Brundage said. "And, in accordance with tradition, I call up the youth of all countries to assemble four years from now at Tokyo, there to celebrate with us the Games of the Eighteenth Olympiad. May they display cheerfulness and concord so that the Olympic torch will be carried on with ever-greater eagerness, courage, and honor for the good of humanity through the ages."

Capitoline trumpeters, outfitted in Roman red, sounded a triple fanfare, and the Choir of the National Academy of Santa Cecilia sang the Olympic anthem as the Olympic flame slowly went out and the five-ringed Olympic flag descended. All went dark until, on cue, tens of thousands of spectators brightened the night by lighting paper torches. In the distance, searchlights emblazoned the sky above Monte Mario. Brundage might have preferred old songs extolling the founders, but some observers were overwhelmed by the flickering scene and infused it with symbolic meaning. "There can never have been such a dramatic moment in Olympic history as that this evening . . ." Neil Allen recorded in his diary. "The whole stadium was a dancing shimmer of flame, living evidence that the ideals and spirit behind the Olympics can never go out." Wilfrid Smith, sports editor of the *Chicago Tribune,* noted the gentleness of the night, the faint illumination of national flags in the infield, and with a sense of wistfulness wrote of the "harmonious salute" at that time in history "with peace precarious."

Long after the stadium emptied, the black sky lit up again, this time with a midnight fireworks celebration. As glorious as the farewell rocketry was—with Brundage and his coterie watching from the terrace of Pincio Gardens overlooking the Piazza del Popolo, and thousands of Romans catching the show from rooftops, church steps, bridges, and the slopes of Monte Mario—the celebration also brought a reminder of how precarious life could be. Debris from the fireworks landed in the dry hills, sparking brushfires whipped by the winds. A momentary panic spread among thousands of spectators on the slopes, causing a stampede during which at least ten people were trampled and seriously injured. Several cars in the area burst into flames, and the gardens of private villas were scorched as firemen battled dozens of separate blazes all through the night. These fires, in a sense, were the true Closing Ceremony, deepening the inevitable feeling of something gone—these specific Olympics and the larger Olympic ideal—that could not be recaptured. Only a week later, rainstorms would bring floods to central Italy and turn the infield of the Stadio Olimpico into a lake.

THE MORNING after the Closing Ceremony, and before the floods washed out the roads from Rome north to Genoa, Gian Paolo Ormezzano, the young Italian journalist, left the city with his friend Livio Berruti, the gold medalist sprinter. As they drove north to Torino, where they both lived, they stopped for coffee at a bar in Civitavecchia across from a local prison. As soon as they emerged from the car, Berruti was recognized and mobbed by fans. Even the prison guards scurried over to congratulate the cool Italian in shades who had shocked the world by winning the 200. After the brief stop, Ormezzano drove on while Berruti napped. Weaving his car through Genoa, the writer ran a red light and was pulled over by traffic police. On the way down to the Olympics three weeks earlier, he had locked himself out of the car while stopping to relieve himself at the side of the road—and now this! He was worried that he might lose his license, and pointed over to his friend, who was slowly awakening. "I have your colleague in the car," Ormezzano said, remembering that Berruti had been given a job as a policeman even though he rarely reported for work. But when the officers asked to see Berruti's identification, he could not find it. Then, in a double take, they recognized him. "Look! It's Berruti!" They let Ormezzano go, but not without an unofficial fine.

Many of Ormezzano's colleagues from around the world were among the Olympic stragglers in Rome that Monday, enjoying one last meal on the Via Veneto and writing their final assessments of what they had witnessed. The statistical measurements were in hand. If the Games were a front in the propaganda battle of the cold war, the Soviets could claim victory. They had amassed the most medals, with forty-three gold, twenty-nine silver, and thirty-one bronze, compared to thirty-four gold, twenty-one silver, and sixteen bronze for the United States. In track and field, the U.S. men still prevailed over the Soviets, twenty-two medals to thirteen, but the Soviets accumulated their overall winning total by faring better in women's track and field (six gold medals to America's three won by Wilma Rudolph and the Tigerbelles), kayaking, fencing, gymnastics, shooting, weight lifting, and Greco-Roman wrestling. The two superpowers were followed in order of points by the combined German team, then Italy, Australia, Hungary, Poland, Japan, Great Britain, and Turkey. In all, forty-four nations received medals, including the first-ever medals for Ethiopia, Ghana, Taiwan, Iraq, Singapore, and the British West Indies.

As Arthur Daley of the *Times* examined the results and thought back on the competition, he reflected first on the stunning setting. "It must be admitted that it was a whale of a shindig while it lasted. Maybe it was the best. It's impossible to visualize or recollect any Olympic Games that could match the tone these noble Romans threw. The stadiums and arenas were more sumptuous and opulent than those of any predecessor's. Furthermore, the entire production was conducted with totally un-Italian efficiency but with typical Italian flair for drama and beauty." Yet for all that, Daley wrote, "in the cold light of the morning after, too many disquieting thoughts keep intruding." What haunted him were thoughts of Soviet prominence and of a world catching up to the United States. "The world is stirring not only politically," he noted. "It is stirring athletically, too. Nations that weren't in existence at the time of the Melbourne Games four years ago competed here with distinction. The U.S. scares not a soul any more. Once the Americans dominated the show. They don't any more, nor are they likely to do so again." Daley viewed the results through a cold war lens, which he said was all that mattered to the Soviets. "The totalitarian powers have the ability to marshal their youth for what they regard, among other things, as part of the propaganda war. They have said so, bluntly and unashamedly. And the Rome Olympics, on that basis, represented a resounding victory for Soviet Russia. The Red brothers beat us in total medals and in unofficial total points."

Also lingering in Rome were the Soviet correspondents Alexei Dyakov and Vitali Petrusenko of *Pravda,* who continued the Soviet courtship with the Italian public, lauding the "very friendly, almost Slavic-like hospitality of the local residents," who among other favors delivered a veritable greenhouse of bouquets to the Soviet embassy to send along to Russian athletes at the Olympic Village. "The village is deserted now," the Soviet sportswriters noted in their day-after column. "Everybody left. The last athletes are packing their suitcases. Very soon there will be children running around and new residents who were lucky to get these new apartments." Their fondness for the Italians was always considered apart from the Vatican, which remained a reliable villain. In a paragraph examining the financial benefits of the Games, *Pravda* asserted that hotels and restaurants did not fare as well as they hoped with the influx of foreign tourists because "the bulk of the revenue from tourists and guests of the Olympics somehow ended up in the safe deposit box of the Vatican."

Aside from political sniping, the central theme of the *Pravda* column was underscored in the question that Dyakov and Petrusenko said was constantly asked of the Soviet coaches in Rome: What is the secret of your success? "And our answer was our sports are for the masses, the people. We don't distinguish between important and nonimportant sports events. The country doesn't restrict financial means for sports establishments, stadiums, and the physical education of our young people. So that is our secret . . . It takes a lot of work from organizers and coaches to lead your team to victory. For example, Americans didn't win a single medal in gymnastics—the sport that is very good for the overall health and development of teenagers. The president of the IOC, Avery Brundage, pointed to this reason during his speech to the American Club of Rome. There are 800,000 gymnasts in Russia, he said, and it would be hard to find 800 in the USA."

Leaving aside the larger controversy over the state subsidization of athletics in the USSR and other Communist countries, the cold truth was that if gymnastics were not included, the Soviets would have had no reason to boast. More medals were awarded in gymnastics than any Olympic sport outside track and field, and the Soviets grabbed twenty-six, including ten gold medals, to a goose egg for the Americans. Without gymnastics, the U.S. could have claimed bragging rights to the overall medal count. Even though the men's and women's teams performed better in Rome than they had in previous Games, the shutout during the heat of the cold war represented a psychological bottoming out for U.S. gymnastic teams, who from that point began a long, slow rise toward the highest rungs, highlighted by Mary Lou Retton's all-around championship at Los Angeles in 1984 and a team gold medal in Atlanta in 1996.

But if Rome marked a motivational turning point for American gymnastics, there was also a deeper context. The concern that Brundage expressed during his speech at the American Club of Rome about the "soft life" in the United States, while easily mocked, had enough truth in it—and enough cold war ramifications—that the federal government soon became more invested in the Olympics and more involved in the physical fitness of the general population. Before the Olympics, the Eisenhower administration argued that it was not necessary to keep pace with the Soviets in ancillary interests such as sports. Science, space, mathematics, languages, military, yes, but not athletics. But immediately after the Olympics, the President's Committee on Information Activities Abroad was instructed to look further into the subject and reached the conclusion that "some Soviet sporting victories have had certain propaganda benefits" that needed to be counteracted. Although Eisenhower had created a national committee on physical fitness as early as 1956, it was Ike's successor, President Kennedy, who within six months after the Rome Olympics turned physical fitness into his personal crusade, naming Charles (Bud) Wilkinson, the former great football coach at the University of Oklahoma, a special consultant to the president and instructing his cabinet to "make it clearly understood that the promotion of sports participation and physical fitness is a basic and continuing policy of the United States."

Even before taking office, as president-elect, Kennedy wrote an article for the December 26, 1960, issue of *Sports Illustrated* that borrowed from Brundage in its message and title—"The Soft American." Kennedy began with an Olympian theme, reciting the history and mythology of the Games of ancient Greece 2,500 years ago. "The knowledge that the physical well-being of the citizen is an important foundation for the vigor and vitality of all the activities of the nation is as old as Western civilization itself," he wrote. "But it is a knowledge which today, in America, we are in danger of forgetting." Almost five years had passed since a landmark study showed that American children fared far worse in strength and flexibility tests than their European counterparts, Kennedy said, yet over the ensuing time there had been much talk but no change in the results. This "growing softness," he added, was a threat to national security and to "America's realization of its full potential as a nation." Soon enough, hundreds of thousands of elementary and junior high students across America were being tested for push-ups, sit-ups, chin-ups, cone-to-cone indoor sprints, and rope climbing as gym teachers attempted to answer the softness charge first sounded by Brundage and echoed by the new president.

From a divided nation that quickly would become a greater concern for President Kennedy, the officials and athletes of Germany left Rome with appropriately divided feelings. On their way out of the city, journalists for the *Frankfurter Allgemeine Zeitung* conducted an exit interview with Willi Daume, president of the German Sports Union and member of the IOC. The newspaper's sportswriters had already declared that the Germans were "the real surprise" of the Rome Games. They asked Daume whether he agreed, and whether he expected to see a combined German team again in Tokyo in 1964. "Our athletes were great winners, and when they had to be, great losers too," he said. "People spoke about a so-called third power. Well, Germany as a third power after Russia and the U.S. won't be a popular notion. But for us it is still a reason for joy to be the third power in terms of sports performance."

His answer then turned political. What pleased him most, Daume said, was that a majority of what he called the "classical Olympic medals" were won "by athletes whose home countries do not see the Olympic victory as a state act and whose victory is not the result of state breeding." Without defining what he meant by classical medals (presumably, it excluded gymnastics), he went on to claim that East German athletes would have been less successful had they not interacted in Rome with their freedom-loving western teammates. "So the relationship between team members was good on a sports companions' level, often even very warm. The joint successes contributed to this, naturally. The political bondage of the other side was quickly overcome by human contact. And I think that the East German athletes also felt that their good performances were not achieved due to the training according to Eastern principles but also because they were carried by the German mutuality and commonality in Rome." But unlike Brundage, who claimed a larger symbolism for a German team that transcended politics, Daume said it was nothing more than a fleeting merger for sports and should not be interpreted further. (That sentiment seemed to be shared by the political leaders of West Germany, including Chancellor Konrad Adenauer and Interior Minister Gerhard Schroder, who in their congratulatory telegrams made no mention of the unified nature of the German team.)

"As the overall German team was closely watched, and looked at in astonishment, especially in international circles, the term of the 'victory of sports over politics' came up again. This is nonsense," Daume said. "Sports cannot gain victories over politics just as arts cannot defeat sciences. We are happy that the mission, which wasn't easy, could be accomplished. And in both parts of our home country, people will be happy about that, too—but that's all. And I am not able to say how such a complex task will be solved in 1964." Four years was a long time, Daume said, full of political uncertainties.

THE SEPARATION of the combined team was a physical reality the day after the Olympics ended. While athletes from the West flew back to Bonn and Frankfurt or traveled on to other cities on the track circuit, Ingrid Kraemer and her teammates from East Germany spent an extra day in Italy, visiting Naples, before flying back to East Berlin on Tuesday. They arrived in four chartered Lufthansa jets at Schoenefeld airfield in the early afternoon of September 13 and were led through the Soviet zone in an elaborate parade, weaving past Adlergestell to the Karlshorter Landstrasse, past Stalinallee and Leninallee and Marx-Engelsplatz to the Haus der Ministerien. It was then, as Kraemer rode through the city in an open convertible, that she realized that her two gold medals in Rome had transformed her into a state hero. "There were people everywhere, cheering for me," she recalled later. "This proved the enthusiasm which people felt about my performance. And I was very proud then." Government posters with her picture on them were everywhere: *"Mit Ingrid Krae-*

mers Siegeswillen koennen wir den Plan erfullen." With Ingrid Kraemer's will for victory, we can fulfill the plan.

After her return, Kraemer was in constant demand for official
functions and factory visits throughout the GDR. She never felt relaxed at the banquets but enjoyed the visits with workers, where she
took pains to explain her "strong feelings of gratefulness" for the way
the socialist state organized her training and made it so that she and
her family did not have financial concerns. Over the months and
years to come, she would look back on Rome with wistfulness as the
world changed around her. The Berlin border closing during the
Olympics had gone largely unnoticed by German athletes in Rome,
but months later it took on an unavoidable physical reality when the
Berlin Wall went up. Kraemer called the construction of the wall "a
huge surprise . . . It was very cruel for many, especially the finality of
it. We were all shocked, as nothing had hinted to its erection before it
happened." The wall, and the cold war tensions that followed, made
a sham of Avery Brundage's insistence that the Germans bring another unified team to the Olympics in 1964. West German sports officials refused to have anything to do with their East German
counterparts after the wall went up, and fielded a combined team in
Tokyo in name only, barely able to "maintain the facade of being unified," in the words of historian Heather L. Dichter.

There were no scenes at the Tokyo Games comparable to the day
in Rome when East German official Manfred Ewald brought flowers to a West German woman swimmer who had won a silver medal.
In fact, Olympic photographers in Tokyo could not even lure athletes
from East and West to pose shaking hands.

If Brundage, busting with pride as the Germans marched into
Rome's Stadio Olimpico for the 1960 Opening Ceremony, thought
the combined team he saw below him was a triumph of sports over
politics, a bold manifestation of his Olympic Movement, events later
showed that he had been deceived by what was merely a transitional

opportunity in a world where sports and politics were becoming inseparable. By 1968 any pretense of one German team would end altogether; East Germany was on its own at Mexico City, beginning a two-decade period when it developed a national policy of winning by strengthening the human body with pharmaceuticals.

In the aftermath of Rome, Ingrid Kraemer had expressed shock at the role of drugs in the death of Danish cyclist Knud Enemark Jensen. "It seemed unbelievable to us that athletes would take that stuff which could apparently even be fatal," she said later. "The reaction to the death of the Dane was that we all assured ourselves that we would never take such things." But not for long. It was in the run-up to Tokyo that Kraemer noticed a marked change in her teammates. Her trainers said that muscle-building drugs would be counterproductive for divers, but not for other athletes. "We divers wondered about our fellow swimming athletes," she said. "The women suddenly got deeper voices and broader shoulders. Their bodies changed."

The mastermind of the East German athletic drug culture was none other than Manfred Ewald, who had led the Eastern delegation in Rome as deputy chief of mission of the combined German team. Upon his return from the 1960 Olympics, Ewald emerged as the most powerful figure at the nexus of sports and politics in East Germany as head of the GDR's sports ministry and member of the State Central Committee. In partnership with Manfred Hoeppner, his medical director, he began a program of strengthening East German athletes by putting them on a daily regimen of steroids and other performance-enhancing drugs. It was a massive effort, involving as many as ten thousand athletes over two decades, but there was a special concentration on young female swimmers. Many of them were started on hormone-altering drugs at the early ages of eleven and thirteen, being fed as many as thirty pills a day. In the great majority of cases, the girls were not told what they were taking and certainly were not informed of the adverse health effects. Most of them were told they were being given vitamins. According to East German records, the Stasi state police used another euphemism for the drugs: they were called "supporting means."

Ingrid Kraemer started noticing the deeper voices and broader shoulders of her teammates by 1964, but it took another decade before the full effect of the East German doping program became apparent to the world. At the 1972 Olympics in Munich, the East Germans for the first time accumulated more gold medals than the West Germans, despite a much smaller population. By the 1976 Olympics in Montreal, East German women swimmers were so dominant that they won eleven of thirteen possible gold medals. Despite the Olympic drug-testing procedures that began in 1968 and intensified in the 1970s, and despite the obvious physical changes in the East German women, it could not be proven that they had cheated. Ewald and Hoeppner had set up pharmaceutical labs that concentrated on finding ways to avoid detection.

It was not until the Berlin Wall fell in 1989, the two Germanys were reunified, and investigators could examine the meticulous records kept by East German officials that the full measure of the drug program was revealed. By then, many of the girls who had been drugged were adult females suffering various adverse consequences. Some had ovarian cysts, others liver dysfunction; some had babies born blind or with clubfeet. One woman, Heidi Krieger, a shotputter who had been fed testosterone pills since she was sixteen, felt her body and sensibility become so much like a man's that she underwent a sex-change operation. While the scientific effects of steroids were disputed then, as they would be thereafter, Ewald and Hoeppner were eventually taken to court on criminal charges for their abuse of hundreds of young women. During the testimony, one of the East German doctors, Ulrich Suender, stated the obvious, that the drugs were administered for a political purpose because "sport had a political function in the struggle between systems." To the dismay of many of his victims, Ewald, though found guilty in July 2000, received a light sentence, twenty-two months probation. He died two years later.

The reunification of Germany was not a fortuitous occasion for Ingrid Kraemer. Just as she was shocked by the erection of the Wall, she was also shocked by what happened to her after its fall. She felt that the West became obsessed with demonizing the sports system of the GDR, which she believed had strong benefits as well as obvious faults. She had liked the fact that in East Germany anyone who was talented was given opportunities regardless of their financial situation. It was, she said, based on her own experience, "a wonderful system in finding the most talented children, boosting and supporting them." When the Wall fell, she was working as a diving trainer, but she immediately lost her job, as did all but one of seventeen trainers in the East, she said. Without the same level of state support, the money was not there to sustain them. Some went to foreign countries and established successful teams abroad. Kraemer stayed in Dresden. She was forty-seven, depressed, and angry. Eventually she found a job as a teller in a bank.

A FLEET of Tupolev Tu-104s carried the Soviet Olympic team back to Moscow. Long jumper Igor Ter-Ovanesyan, weight lifter Yuri Vlasov, and their teammates reached Sheremetyevo Airport late on the evening of September 14. Nikita Khrushchev was still aboard the *Baltika* sailing across the Atlantic, not to arrive in New York Harbor for another five days, but the homecoming of the Olympic champions temporarily overshadowed the Soviet premier's historic voyage to the United Nations. Hundreds of people filled the arrival lounge as the athletes deplaned. Vera Krepkina, who was defeated by Wilma Rudolph in the 100-meter dash but won a gold medal in the women's long jump, spoke first for her teammates. "We are stepping on Moscow soil again—that is my first joy. My second joy is the victory over the American track-and-field team. And my third joy is that I got the gold medal."

The next day a public reception was held for the Soviet team at Lenin Stadium. Two years earlier, the huge stadium had hosted the first dual track meet between the USSR and the U.S., but it had taken a bit of manipulation of the scoring system for the Soviets to claim victory. This time, coming back from Rome, there was no doubt. "Here they are coming out," wrote a columnist for *Pravda,* describing the scene as though he were announcing it live. "Boris Shakhlin is at the head of the group, carrying the flag, the national red flag. [Shakhlin starred for the men's gymnastics team, winning a remarkable four gold medals for individual all-around, vault, parallel bars, and pommel horse.] The team of athletes is marching around the stadium, and in the center of the soccer field—the grass center—are delegations of gymnastic cheerleaders performing in honor of the athletes. [A smattering of Brundage's famous eight hundred thousand Soviet gymnasts, no doubt.] The athletes are lining up in front of the podium, where they are greeted by the secretary of the Central Committee of Komsomol [the youth brigade of the Communist Party]. Others who give speeches include the famous seamstress Serafima Kotova, secretary of the Moscow Communist Party, and the poet Lev Oshanin. Yuri Vlasov also gives a speech. He thanks the central committee for its constant care and emphasis on physical education. He reassures everyone that the Soviet athletes and the twenty-five million members of sports organizations and clubs will continue to work hard to represent their country in the future."

At the end, according to *Pravda,* the crowd chanted, "Long live the Communist Party of the Soviet Union and our beloved government!" And the athletes cheered back a chorus: "Glory! Glory! Glory!"

Later that week, several prominent Soviet Olympians, including Vlasov and Ter-Ovanesyan, were awarded Lenin state medals at another ceremony. As heroes of sport, they would be afforded even more special privileges, but the medals were also meant to inspire them to "perform even better," said N. N. Romanov, chair of the Central Sports Committee, who had led the Soviet delegation in Rome. This was the second major award ceremony for sports representatives in three years, *Pravda* pointed out, emphasizing the importance of sports in the cold war. "In the spring of 1957 a large group of leading athletes and organizers of the Melbourne Olympics were also given awards," the newspaper stated. "The Soviet athletes achieved decisive victory in Rome over the team of the leading capitalist country, USA. So now sports fans from all over the world recognize that the Soviet Union is the first and most powerful country in sports."

Not long after his return from Rome, Ter-Ovanesyan was at a training camp along the Black Sea. He had not won gold in 1960, but he had gained invaluable confidence in finishing third behind the two Americans, Ralph Boston and Bo Roberson. After his childhood reverence of Jesse Owens and his awe of the American long jumpers in Melbourne in 1956 and Moscow at the dual meet in 1958, he now realized his inferiority complex was gone, and so was any fear. Day after day at training camp, he was jumping freer and farther than ever before. By his own measurements, he was consistently eclipsing the world record set by Boston before the Olympics. He was so excited that he called the sports council in Moscow and said he was at the top of his game, ready to jump farther than anyone had ever jumped before, and was wondering whether there were any track meets where he could compete. They told him that a week later there would be a track meet in Yerevan in the Armenian republic. Ter-Ovanesyan grew up in Kiev, but Armenia was his homeland, the birthplace of his father. He quickly signed up for the Yerevan meet, and his expectations were met, as he surpassed Boston's record with a leap measured at 27 feet 3 inches. As he later recalled the scene, the Armenians embraced him as one of their own and celebrated his accomplishment with a countryside festival where they feasted him to fresh-killed meats roasted over an open fire.

In the decade after Rome, Ter-Ovanesyan made several trips to the United States to compete at track meets, and became so familiar with America that he could talk intimately of New York (its enormity and energy overwhelmed him) and Los Angeles (he loved Hollywood and once was invited to actor Gregory Peck's house). The lure of the Western world remained powerful, and the possibility that he still might defect was strong enough to make him someone that both American and Soviet agents watched closely. Ralph Boston, who remained his great rival, remembered a moment at the U.S.-Soviet dual meet at Stanford in 1962, a nationally televised two-day spectacle, when Ter-Ovanesyan backed him into a corner to talk. Ter-Ovanesyan asked him some questions about life in the U.S., and when Boston asked him why they were standing in such a peculiar place, crowded up against two corner walls, Igor explained that "there are lip readers on the Soviet team, and I have to be very careful about what I say." The next year, Ter-Ovanesyan led a Soviet team at an indoor meet at Madison Square Garden, and the CIA recruited David Sime, by then graduated from Duke Medical School and starting his residency, to fly up to New York for one last defection effort. "They got me a pass to go on the field to hook up with Igor to talk to him again," Sime recalled. "So I fly to New York, and I see him, and he sees me, and he looks away." Sime could tell that Ter-Ovanesyan looked uncomfortable, as though he were being monitored. "Shit, I gotta at least try," Sime said to himself. "So I catch him for a moment. 'Igor, how are you?' I ask. He says, 'Nice to see you, David. I can't talk to you anymore.'"

The next time Boston saw Ter-Ovanesyan, at the Olympics in Tokyo, there were security guards to his left and right. The hoped-for defection never happened. The West-loving long jumper won a bronze again in Tokyo, competed at two more Olympics, set the world record twice, and went on to become an esteemed coach, a professor of track and field at the Russian Sports Academy in Moscow, the vice president of the Russian Track and Field Federation, a lifetime honorable member of the International Association of Track and Field, and the founder of an organization called Sports Against Drugs.

The temptation of Igor Ter-Ovanesyan was played out in reverse in the story of James Bradford, the black American weight lifter. After having to take an unpaid leave of absence from his job at the Library of Congress to compete in Rome, Bradford returned to Washington as an Olympic silver medalist, but no one seemed to care. There was no celebration for him at work, barely any notice at all of his world-class achievement. "Nah, they just ignored it," Bradford said later. "I come back to my job, and that is it. That was par for the course then."

Bradford had been so discouraged by the finals in Rome, where he thought an appeal ruling cost him a gold medal, that he decided to give up competitive weight lifting, but he came out of retirement in 1961 at the urging of Yuri Vlasov, who called him and personally invited him to visit the Soviet Union for a series of weight-lifting events. Out of all his adventures overseas, this was a trip Bradford would never forget. Vlasov picked him up at the airport and drove him around in a specially built Russian car that was going to be given to President Eisenhower at the 1960 summit meeting that never happened because of the fallout from the U-2 spying incident. Instead of giving the car to Eisenhower, officials gave it to Vlasov when he returned from Rome. "So I was riding around in this car with a plaque on it that said 'Awarded to the President of the United States,' " Bradford remembered. It was the first sign to him that world-class athletes were treated differently in the Soviet Union.

Over the ensuing days, Vlasov offered him more evidence of the difference. "For example, all he did was weight lifting. He didn't have to work. He asked me how much did my government pay me for weight lifting. I said they didn't pay me anything. He said, 'Bullshit!' He couldn't speak that much English, but he got that much out. He didn't believe I had to work. He couldn't believe that in a rich country like the United States, that I worked. His apartment was free. All he had to pay was something like ten dollars a month for utilities. His wife went to the champions store to get food. She would just take her basket into this store and pick up any food she wanted and go home with it. He had the car. It was a Russian model sedan. And also they made him a captain in the army, so he got the captain's pay. And he was on some government council. And transportation was free, because he got a thing called Master of Sports and got a little pin that you put on, and he could go down to the airport and show this little pin and say, 'I'm Vlasov, I want to go to Leningrad.' If the plane was full, they would pull someone off."

The stories went on and on, and Bradford listened, thinking about how he was struggling to meet his mortgage on a little row house back on Ingraham Street in Northeast Washington and support a wife and three kids on $56 a week for his work at the Library of Congress, where no one seemed to know or care about his athletic prowess. Vlasov introduced Bradford to Valeriy Brumel, the great high jumper, who told him he had a job coaching high jumping at Moscow University. "I knew they were in a sense trying to pump me. I could feel this undercurrent of defection," Bradford said later. "They were saying, 'If you come over here, we could do this and we could do that.' " Bradford was impressed by the higher education system in the Soviet Union, and by the treatment of athletes, but he was not interested and came no closer to defecting than Ter-Ovanesyan had. He had fought against the Communists in the Korean War, and entered the Rome Olympics out of a patriotic urging to beat the Russians. At his hotel in Moscow, when he couldn't sleep in the middle of the night, he got up and went down to the lobby and tried to go outside for a walk, but he couldn't leave because the doors were locked. That was difference enough for Bradford. He felt more freedom in the United States, despite the reality that there were many places in America where he could not eat or sleep because of the color of his skin. "Say what you want," he would say. "I still think this is the greatest country on Earth, with all its problems."

There would come a time, decades later, when Yuri Vlasov would find himself in no frame of mind to sell the Soviet system to any outsider. With his dark-rimmed glasses and studious demeanor, Vlasov always had the look of an intellectual academic. He became a writer and poet after he retired from lifting, and one of his books, *The Special Region of China,* was about his father, who had been a Soviet spy executed in China by security forces. As a leader of the Soviet weight-lifting federation, Vlasov found himself increasingly disillusioned and started speaking out against a win-at-all-costs sporting philosophy and the massive use of steroids and other drugs in the pursuit of medals. "Gold medals have always been a yardstick of their work," Vlasov said of Soviet sports officials, "and at the same time a shield concealing their idleness and easy life. What was important was medals. How you got them—whether fattening athletes up on chemicals or swallowing white hot coals—was a secondary matter."

On the matter of steroids, Vlasov said they were widespread throughout the Soviet bloc sports system and in the international weight-lifting culture—and was ostracized for his outspokenness. Soviet officials restricted his travel, censored his books, and at one point, he claimed, even edited the film of the Rome Olympics to excise the shots of his famous entrance at the Opening Ceremony carrying the Soviet flag with one outstretched hand. He became known as a dissident, disenchanted with Communism, and was elected to the Soviet Duma—its parliament—in 1989, where at first he was affiliated politically with the liberal wing led by Boris Yeltsin. But his politics grew increasingly harsh after that, taking on a conspiratorial strain of anti-Zionism. Ter-Ovanesyan, who had considered Vlasov a friend, a fellow outsider within the restrictive Soviet system, was not surprised by the arc of his career. "He was considered an intellectual in sports, but he had an uneven temper," Ter-Ovanesyan said of the great weight lifter. "He was prone to depressions. He was very strong, but his character was kind of neurotic." In the Wild West atmosphere of post-Communist Russia, Vlasov became increasingly estranged, writing and theorizing as a lone wolf.

ABEBE BIKILA made his triumphant return to Addis Ababa on the afternoon of September 15. A felicitous saying by then had swept his homeland: "It had taken Italy a million-man army to defeat Ethiopia, but only one lone Ethiopian soldier to conquer Rome." The arrival of the marathon gold medalist at Haile Selassie the First Airport was witnessed by tens of thousands of countrymen shouting "Aaa-bbe! Aaa-bbe!" Makuria, the lion mascot of the Imperial Guard, was also there, wagging its tail. Abebe, draped in floral wreaths, rode through the crowded, noisy streets in the open bed of a white-painted Imperial Guard truck with the Olympic rings stenciled on its sides. Lampposts and windows were festooned with the green, yellow, and red Ethiopian flag. The caravan moved down Churchill Street and arrived at the Imperial Palace at Haile Selassie Square.

"With His own hands His Majesty the Emperor decorated Abebe Bikila with the Chevalier of the Order of the Star of Ethiopia," the *Ethiopian Herald* reported respectfully. Haile Selassie's remarks sounded rather stiff, if regal. "We are very much pleased, for you have ably shown to the world that sport is neither new nor foreign to Ethiopia," he said. "To win the laurel of world victory in a race which demands spiritual and physical strength is a significant event that brings global reputation to our country." Later that evening, a cocktail party was held for Abebe at the officers club, and Brigadier General Mengistu Neway promoted him from private to first corporal, the first of many military promotions that would accompany his running fame. This same General Neway would attempt a coup only three months later, in December, while the emperor was out of the country. The rebellion was swiftly crushed and many members of the palace guard were jailed, including Abebe, who got rounded up in the chaos. But he was above politics, and evidence showed that he was out running when the coup occurred, and he was quickly released.

Abebe was all of Africa's now, and the world's. In February 1961 he was invited back to Rome as a special guest of CONI, the Italian National Olympic Committee, for the premiere of the official film, *La Grande Olimpiade,* directed by Romolo Marcellini. In this gorgeous movie, as artistic and reverential of the human form as Leni Riefenstahl's *Olympia* but minus the Nazi sentiments of that tribute to the 1936 Berlin Games, there are many evocative scenes and characters. But Abebe Bikila unavoidably captures the imagination as he runs through the silent night, alone and barefoot down the torchlit path of the Appia Antica on his way to marathon history. During his return to Rome, he posed with Gina Lollobrigida and other film stars at the premier, and told reporters how his life had changed. He now had a house, he said, and a new car, and all the gasoline he needed, and a salary of $400 a month.

His reputation only grew in 1964, when he successfully defended his marathon gold medal at Tokyo, the first Olympian ever to win the grueling contest twice. He ran in socks and shoes this time, only two months after undergoing an appendectomy, and established a best-ever time of 2:12:11.2, four minutes better than his nearest opponent. The scene at the finish line in Rome, in the darkness near the Arch of Constantine, was haunting, but the ending in Tokyo gave Abebe more of a deserved moment in the sun. It was still daylight, and the final lap was run inside the Olympic Stadium, with eighty thousand spectators wildly cheering the thirty-two-year-old Ethiopian as he made his familiar long, level, incessant strides toward the tape. As in Rome, he jogged in place and did some calisthenics after finishing. He said later he could have run another six miles or more—

this despite difficult conditions that found several marathoners collapsing on the infield grass near the end and being hauled out on stretchers.

Upon Bikila's return to Ethiopia, he was promoted again, now to lieutenant. Only the emperor claimed higher status among his countrymen. His plan was to win a third gold medal at the Olympics in Mexico City, but after running ten miles, he dropped out of the race because of a fracture in his left leg. That moment in 1968 marked the beginning of his misfortune and decline. Five months later, driving to Addis Ababa from his hometown of Debre Behran on a rainy evening, he was run off the road by the bright headlights of a Land Rover. He was unconscious when he was discovered by startled passengers from a bus that had stopped to check on a wrecked car resting on its side. His spinal injuries were so severe that he spent nine months being treated at a hospital in Great Britain and returned in a wheelchair. Four years later, at age forty-one, he was dead. More than seventy-five thousand people attended his funeral at St. Joseph Church in Addis Ababa, including Haile Selassie.

On the day of his death, the *Ethiopian Herald* ran a poem that read in part:

> *He made our flag to fly*
> *Right above*
> *Dead and gone Mussolini*
> *Then and then*
> *Abebe led, Mamo followed*
> *Ethiopia led, Kenya followed*

The Mussolini allusion was obvious. The reference to Mamo was Mamo Wolde, a fellow Ethiopian who won the marathon at Mexico City after Abebe was forced to drop out. The last line carried his meaning into a larger realm. As the first black African to win a gold medal, Abebe Bikila paved the way for what would become a long and illustrious line of East African distance runners. Many were from Ethiopia but even more hailed from Kenya, led by the brilliant Kipchoge Keino, who won the metric mile at Mexico City, outpacing the American Jim Ryun, and took home the steeplechase gold four years later in Munich. Mamo Wolde, Miruts Yifter, Mohammed Kedir, Derartu Tulu, Haile Gebrselassie, Fatuma Roba, Milton Wolde, Gezahegne Abera, Kenenisa Bekele, Meseret Defar, of Ethiopia; Kipchoge Keino, Amos Biwott, Peter Rono, Naftali Temu, Charles Asati, Matthew Birir, Paul Ereng, Julius Korir, Reuben Kosgei, Noah Ngeny, John Ngugi, Hezahiah Nyamau, Robert Ouko, Julius Sang, William Tanui, of Kenya—Olympic gold medal runners all, and all in a sense the progeny of the barefooted palace guard who stunned the world in Rome. The rub of contradiction is evident in most legends, and there was a small cultural and semantic irony in the emergence of Abebe Bikila as the symbol of black Africa. Ethiopians had been dismissive of their brethren on the continent—so much so that the word for black African in Amharic translated as "slave." In the event, the rise of black Africa was paralleled by the Olympic decline and long-term disappearance of apartheid South Africa. Avery Brundage and his IOC inner circle had averted the issue in Rome, deciding to believe South African officials who claimed that no blacks were talented enough to make the Olympic team and that they did not discriminate against them—even though all sports in the nation were segregated, along with every other aspect of life. But with doubts persisting about that claim after Rome, with emerging nations around the world taking more active roles in IOC affairs, and with the threat of a boycott looming, the IOC voted to ban South Africa from the 1964 Games in Tokyo. Two years later, Brundage was still fighting a rear-guard action to bring South Africa back into the Olympic family. His reasoning was revealed in a May 3, 1966, letter to Reginald Stanley Alexander, a white IOC member from Kenya.

"The African question remains, and it is a most thorny problem," Brundage wrote.

*I am thinking of sending out a circular letter to all concerned along
the following lines: We cannot penalize a National Olympic Committee for something its government does, or we will not have any left,
since the perfect government has not yet been invented. We must view
the accomplishment of the South African NOC under IOC pressure in
obtaining permission to send a biracial committee composed of equal
numbers of white and nonwhite men to select their Olympic team as a
huge step forward in view of the prevailing conditions. Keeping South
Africa out of the Olympic Games is not going to change the government, but it is going to hurt the athletes both black and white who are
the most concerned.*

Brundage asked Alexander for his opinion, while advising the
former Nairobi mayor that he was "viewed as a colonial in some
quarters."

In a secret ballot the following year, the IOC executive committee
voted to readmit South Africa, but the fallout before Mexico City was
so intense, with as many as forty countries threatening to boycott,
that the decision was reversed. Questions of race and Africa continued to haunt the Games thereafter. In 1968 U.S. sprinters John Car-
los and Tommie Smith struck perhaps the most iconic pose of protest
in Olympic history, raising their fists and bowing their heads on the
medal stand to force the world to notice the lingering problems of
racism in America. In 1972 in Munich, several black African nations,
including Ethiopia, walked out in protest of the presence of white-
ruled Rhodesia. Four years later, at the 1976 Montreal Olympics, another boycott was staged by black African nations in protest against
New Zealand, whose most prominent rugby team had been touring
South Africa. The controversies would continue for more than three
decades after Michael Scott, representing the South African Sports
Association and the Campaign Against Race Discrimination in
Sport, arrived at the Luxor Hotel in Rome on that late August day in
1960 and sought his first meeting with Brundage and the IOC. It

would not end until South Africa was readmitted in July 1991, after the fall of its white supremacist government.

It would take fourteen more years for the correction of another historic misdeed. On April 19, 2005, the first section of the ancient Axum Obelisk was loaded onto a cargo plane in Rome and flown back to Ethiopia for its rightful restoration.

AFTER CLOSING the Rome Games, and before landing in Chicago in time for his seventy-third birthday late in September, Avery Brundage spent several days each in Lausanne, Paris, and London. If the IOC president shared the prevailing opinion that the Rome Olympics were a huge success, he was still haunted by problems that would not go away, many of which, one way or another, had to do with money. For all its upper-class pretensions, the IOC was always in need of funds. Brundage and his executive committee had been slow in realizing the financial possibilities of television, and now were paying for it. The Italian organizers had been able to cite the IOC's own rules in claiming that they had sole control over television contracts with CBS, Eurovision, and a Japanese network. In the end, despite Brundage's urgings and protests, the most he could get out of the pool of broadcast rights was a 5 percent take of $60,000.

With that modest amount, he had nothing to offer the various federations representing track and field, swimming, rowing, fencing, boxing, and all the other individual sports that had been pressuring him for what they considered their fair share of the proceeds. The IOC's desperation was evidenced in the weekly volley of letters that chancellor Otto Mayer sent to various Italian organizers seeking a final financial accounting of the Games, hoping more money might be headed his way at Mon Repos. But the Italians were not to be rushed. When Marcello Garroni of the organizing committee did compile a final report, it showed that they had expenses of $10.6 million (not including construction costs) and revenues of $7.3 million, resulting in a deficit of $3.3 million. For Brundage, that meant no juice to squeeze from the fruit beyond television revenue.

At the same time, Brundage and his IOC leadership remained obsessed about keeping the Olympic Movement clean, or from another perspective, keeping financial rewards away from the athletes who made the Olympics worth watching. Everywhere Brundage turned, he encountered stories of amateurism gone awry. One month after Rome, rumors about the questionable activities of Armin Hary busted into the open when a commission of the Deutscher Leichtathletik-Verban (DLV), the German Track and Field Association, began investigating the sprint champion for padding his expense accounts. In the brief time since his return to Frankfurt, Hary already had written an article critical of German functionaries, fallen into a spat with a movie company, ending his film career before it could begin, and bought a sports car. He believed that he was being targeted for his outspokenness and individualism, but the investigators had evidence. At least once, Hary had bogusly charged the federation for train tickets and then pocketed the transportation money while receiving a free ride to an event. Perhaps this did not sound like much, but it was enough to warrant a year's suspension.

German officials suspected the expense account padding was indicative of greater graft, though at the time they knew nothing of the much larger problem involving Hary and the shoe companies Puma and Adidas.

Brundage closely followed developments in Germany and exchanged correspondence on the Hary issue with the IOC's vice president, Lord Burghley, the Marquess of Exeter, who as president of the International Amateur Athletic Federation could review Hary's international status, including the validity of medals he won in Rome. If Hary's suspension survived an internal appeal in Germany, Exeter wrote in a January 18, 1961, letter to Brundage, "We naturally will give it 100 percent support, too. It will of course mean that he was a professional at the [Rome] Games, and will forfeit his gold medal, and presumably their relay team will also be disqualified, as he was on it, though it is very bad luck on the other three . . . I think there will be a temporary outcry but feel that this will be excellent for amateurism in the long run, and will make some prima donnas think twice before taking similar action, and it stops the criticism to which International Federations have laid themselves open, and that is that they do not enforce their rules strictly enough."

Hary was found guilty, as it turned out, but officials cut his suspension to a few months, by which time he had retired, his knee damaged from a car crash that occurred while he was speeding back from Berlin with a young female gymnast. The gold medals were never revoked, but his life grew only more troubled. In 1980, twenty years after his stirring late-afternoon sprint down the Stadio Olimpico track, Hary hit bottom, convicted of a 3.2 million deutsche mark swindle and served three years in jail.

Four months after the Rome Olympics, as the Hary story unfolded, *Sports Illustrated* published an article by Mike Agostini, a Trinidadian sprinter then living in London, who claimed that European promoters were paying amateur athletes to compete and that many countries provided a "happy hunting ground for trackmen," some of whom were getting as much as $10,000 a year for appearances. For his own part, Agostini said that he wrote his magazine exposé on a $100 typewriter he was awarded for finishing second in an event arranged by a promoter in Dortmund, Germany. Borrowing a term coined decades earlier by the New York newspaperman Paul Gallico, Agostini labeled this practice "shamateurism."

The IOC president had been alerted to the *SI* piece by an Associated Press reporter seeking his response. While saying little in public, Brundage fumed in letters to associates, belittling Agostini as a "tramp athlete" but nonetheless believing the basic charges, especially about Swedish promoters. Officials in Stockholm already had been asked to investigate charges that Dan Waern, their Olympic miler, had been paid to run at various meets. Swedish authorities eventually cleared Waern of professionalism charges on the grounds that whatever compensation he received was no higher than that of other runners around the world—hardly the sort of decision aimed to please Brundage. "This seems to indicate that they have no respect at all for rules and regulations," he complained in a letter to Lord Burghley. "Such a public repudiation of amateur principles should *not* be permitted to go unchallenged—it brings all amateur sport into disrepute." In another letter, he noted that *L'Équipe,* the French sports magazine, had broken a story of the Swedes sending a cable to the French track-and-field federation inviting two French athletes to a Swedish competition and asking, "What are their financial requirements, which we shall keep confidential?" It was, said Brundage, "such brazen defiance."

Brundage was not ready to give up on his vision of pure amateurism, but Rome was the beginning of the end. The shoe endorsement corruption that began with Armin Hary in 1960 became so widespread that by the 1968 Olympics in Mexico City, *Sports Illustrated's* John Underwood reported that runners from around the world received at least $100,000 in cash and $350,000 in equipment from Puma and Adidas alone—and that all but five American medal winners received something from them. Brundage, who insisted that his Olympic Movement was free of politics, or able to transcend politics, was caught in a tightening vise between two competing ideologies and economic systems. Capitalism was crushing him from one side, Communism from the other. Each side, in different but equally powerful ways, exposed the vulnerabilities of pure amateurism in a world where competition was either up for bid or totally controlled by the state.

JIM MCKAY'S daytime job with *The Verdict Is Yours* was gone when the Rome Olympics ended. The television courtroom drama had moved from New York to Los Angeles, and McKay had no desire to make the transfer. Besides, he had always preferred sports, and the notice he received as studio host for the first Olympics where an American network paid for broadcast rights afforded him more freedom to pursue that course. While TV critics gave him mostly positive reviews, it was one viewer in particular who proved most important to McKay's career. Roone Arledge, a young producer for ABC, was in the process of putting together a Saturday afternoon sports show, *Wide World of Sports,* the brainstorm of sports programmer Edgar J. Scherick. After watching McKay perform his Olympic duties with a universal touch, Arledge thought he would be the perfect host for the show, which would deal with a variety of sports, from track and field to gymnastics to car racing and surfing, and draw on athletes from around the world. McKay made the switch from CBS to ABC and was on camera when the first *Wide World of Sports* aired on the last Saturday of April 1961, televising the Penn Relays in Philadelphia. A colleague, Bill Flemming, the voice of Big Ten athletics, was sent to Des Moines to cover the Drake Relays for the same inaugural show.

Although their wide world encompassed more than Olympic sports, the production in many ways served as ideal preparation for Olympic coverage, and in the coming years, as the Games grew exponentially with the parallel rise of television, Roone Arledge and Jim McKay became the two most prominent figures of that relationship. ABC carried the Winter Olympics in 1964 from Innsbruck, Austria, and both the Summer and Winter Games many times thereafter. The Tokyo Olympics in 1964, carried by NBC, were the first to offer live coverage through the use of a satellite, Syncom III, positioned over the Pacific Ocean, but the 1968 Games in Mexico City, with McKay hosting for ABC, used the most extensive satellite coverage, forty-five hours' worth (compared to twenty hours in Rome), and also introduced slow-motion replays and color pictures—and went a long way toward establishing McKay as the voice and face of the Olympics, as familiar as the *Dah . . . Dah . . . duh-dah-dah dun-dun* fanfare theme song. (Working as a young researcher for McKay and Arledge in Mexico City was Dick Ebersol, who later was to become the lead executive for NBC's Olympic broadcasts.) Four years later, at the Summer Games in Munich, McKay established his anchorman credentials, reporting calmly hour after hour, accompanied by the expert reporting of newsman Peter Jennings, when Palestinian terrorists took eleven Israeli athletes and coaches hostage and eventually murdered them. His reporting of the tragedy earned McKay two Emmys.

It was all so minimal in Rome, with McKay in that little studio in New York, tapping out his own scripts on a portable typewriter, drawing information from the *Encyclopaedia Britannica*; and with Peter Molnar's crew of fewer than fifty in Rome filming and editing on the fly, literally trying to beat the clock every night with their canisters winging west toward New York City in the bellies of commercial jets. The televising of the Olympics grew from that infancy in Rome into an extravaganza, expanding every four years into an ever-larger enterprise that eventually entailed a broadcast army of more than three thousand people. The IOC, after a slow start getting in on the television money, eventually adapted to the lucrative new world, changing its rules so that the international body held more control along with the organizing committees for host cities.

Television revenues rose dramatically every four years from Rome, going up to about $10 million at Mexico City, and then doubling and tripling every quadrennial from there until they exceeded $1.2 billion at Athens in 2004. At Rome, television revenues made up about $1 of every $400 it cost to host the Games, while by Munich in 1972, the ratio was $1 of every $50, and by 1984 in Los Angeles it was $1 of every $3, according to an analysis that John Slater of Western Carolina University presented at the Fourth International Symposium for Olympic Research. When Roone Arledge tapped Jim McKay for *Wide World of Sports*, influenced by the work he had seen in those archaic early shows detailing the Games in Rome, it was a crucial early step along that road to riches, down an Olympian path that Arledge later would say was "worth every penny—every single million bucks—you have to spend for it."

IN WASHINGTON a few days after the Rome Games ended, the ambassador from the Republic of China was invited to the State Department for a meeting with J. Graham Parsons, assistant secretary for Far Eastern Affairs, and Larue R. Lutkins, acting director for Chinese Affairs. The purpose of the meeting was to hold a postmortem on the politics of the Olympics. According to a memorandum of conversation, Parsons began by berating his visitor, telling him how unhappy the U.S. was with the way his government handled the Olympic dispute over what the island nation should be called. The State Department, he said, had been "vigorously supporting the Chinese efforts to secure affiliation with the IOC under name Olympic Committee of the Republic of China" for several years. "And in recent months, particularly intensive efforts made by U.S. throughout the world toward this end," the memo noted, paraphrasing Parsons's criticisms. But during the Olympics, he complained, the "Chinese cut the ground out from under their own position by (1) agreeing to participate in basketball tourney in Bologna as Taiwan, and (2) subsequent leak from Taipei that they were prepared to accept designation as Taiwan in Rome Games, albeit under protest."

These actions, Parsons argued, "were effectively exploited by Brundage and doubtless had an effect on the decisive nature of the vote [forcing the Republic of China to participate only as Taiwan]." Parsons said he understood that news leaks do occur but predicted that this particular leak would "sour private American citizens whose cooperation had been actively solicited and to make it more difficult for us in the future to enlist their cooperation for the cause."

The next morning, C. K. Yang arrived triumphantly in Taipei. As he descended the ramp of a chartered jet that had brought his team home from Rome, he carried a Republic of China flag—the very banner Olympic officials would not let his squad display at the Opening Ceremony inside the Stadio Olimpico. But he also carried a silver medal, the first Olympic medal ever won by his country, which served as a proud physical representation of the reason C.K.'s delegation leaders had refused to follow the State Department's recommendation that they boycott the Rome Games. In a drenching rain, Yang now was mobbed by well-wishers, including his parents and sisters. His mother burst into tears when she saw him for the first time in a year. The family accompanied him in an open jeep that took them on a parade route through the streets to a luncheon at the Hero's Hostel on Yenping South Road. After that, he flew across the island to his home town of Malan, where an ancestor, Khras Mahanhan, had been a chieftain of Taitung's Ami tribe and known for his athletic prowess. Yang met with the island's sportswriters and talked of marriage and the future. He expected to be ready to win gold in Tokyo.

When word reached Taipei of the chewing-out their ambassador had received at the State Department, American diplomats there were called in for lunch with Foreign Minister Hsu Shao-chang. In polite tones, he expressed regret that the Americans did not appreciate Taiwan's dilemma. The only alternative, he said, according to a cable later sent to the State Department, was to "withdraw from the Rome Games, alienate the IOC, and open the door to Chinese Communist participation in future Olympics." He conceded that the press leak was unfortunate and the decision to participate in the pre-Olympic basketball Trials in Bologna might have been a tactical error, but argued that neither of these mistakes was decisive because Brundage in fact had "long ago made up his mind that [we] must accept the Taiwan label or get out."

Republic of China or Taiwan—the issue of nomenclature would not go away, with the IOC swinging one way and then another and then back again. In 1968 the team was allowed to compete as the Republic of China, but eight years later in Montreal it was ordered to revert to Taiwan and left the Olympics rather than accede again to that demand. There was no Chinese representation, island or mainland, in Montreal or four years later at Moscow, but for the 1984 Olympics in Los Angeles, the Taiwanese returned as Chinese Taipei at the same time that the People's Republic of China, after ending its long exile by appearing in the 1980 Winter Games, finally rejoined the Summer Games. With the largest population in the world to draw upon, the mainland Chinese quickly rose into the top ranks of competition, finishing fourth in the gold medal standings at Los Angeles and up to second twenty years later at Athens in 2004. For 2008, nearly a half century after the furious debate in Rome, something perhaps unimaginable then would come to pass, with the Beijing Olympics.

In the days after Rome, Frenchy Grombach, the erstwhile American spook and retired brigadier general, would not let go in his Ahab-like pursuit of an unlikely white whale, Lord David Burghley, the Marquess of Exeter. Grombach was convinced that Lord Burghley was the insidious force behind the IOC's decision to make Taiwan compete as Taiwan, and on October 6, less than a month after the Games ended, he sent a letter to the Anglo-American Detective Agency on Lower John Street in London, retaining gumshoes there in the hopes of uncovering the marquess's business connections to mainland China. Word of the investigation reached Avery Brundage before it went public. On February 9, 1961, Brundage dictated a heads-up letter to Lord Burghley:

> *Dear David:*
>
> *A few minutes ago I had a long-distance telephone call from a British journalist in New York, named Coulter, who said that he had a telephone call from his London office, asking him to investigate a report that a General Grombach had asked some London detective agency to investigate you because you were supporting Red China and Russia in the Olympic Movement. Imagine! Coulter asked me if I*

knew anything about this and who I thought Grombach was repre-
senting. Naturally, I told him it was outrageous.

Grombach (I know him very slightly) is a very officious individ-
ual, who made himself extremely obnoxious at the time of the rumpus
about Formosa, following our meeting in Munich. He may be em-
ployed by the "China Lobby." He did his best to try to induce me,
without success, to help him get the United States agency for the Olym-
pic film. He was in Rome during the Games, writing a column in the
English newspaper there . . .

I don't know what he is up to, but certainly no good.

Sincerely,
Avery Brundage

Three days later, the story exploded in the British press, first with
a banner headline in *The People* newspaper: "General Orders: Probe
Lord Burghley. Americans Spread Vile Witch-Hunt to Britain."

"For the past three months," the article by Patrick Kent began,
"an American intelligence agency has been conducting a secret, high-
powered check-up on one of Britain's bluest-blooded aristocrats—
because they think he may be a Communist." The story characterized
the investigation as "this ridiculous witch-hunt" and said it was insti-
gated by "a mysterious group of suspicious Americans" led by Grombach. "Speaking to General Grombach on the transatlantic phone, I
pointed out that Lord Burghley was educated at Eton and Cambridge,
was an officer in the Guards, and for twelve years a Conservative MP.
Did that sound like a Communist background?" Kent wrote.

" 'Well,' said General Grombach, 'there are still many people who
wonder why the Marquess is so keen to help Russia and Red China
in the Olympics.' "

Kent then called Exeter "at his stately home in Stamford, Lincs
[Lincolnshire], where he keeps his own pack of foxhounds" and told
him of the spying.

"At first he was flabbergasted—then he roared with laughter.

'My godfathers! Me a Red! You'd better tell that investigator fellow that I've got a radio transmitter under my bed!'"

After handling the press, the marquess dashed off a return note to Brundage. "I have treated it all with ridicule, which seems to have produced the desired result," he wrote. Then he rid himself of the nuisance altogether by buying out the London detective agency that had been hired to snoop on him.

Grombach, frustrated at every turn, made one last plea with his congressional contacts on the Senate Internal Security Subcommittee. He had been pushing them to investigate Brundage, Exeter, and the IOC for two years, with no luck. This time he urged them to subpoena him to testify, and went so far as to write out in advance what questions he should be asked and how he would answer them. He used a journalist friend, John A. Clements, as an intermediary to slip his material to the staff of subcommittee chairman James O. Eastland of Mississippi. But now Grombach appeared so toxic that even the staunch anticommunists on the subcommittee were wary. "Mr. Grombach's proffered testimony, which was transmitted to you by John A. Clements of Hearst Newspapers, would have been more timely a year ago" when the subcommittee might have been willing to hear him, staff counsel Jay Sourwine wrote in a memo to Senator Eastland. "Now, having gotten himself into the glare of notoriety through hiring a detective agency to investigate a British peer, he wants an early hearing." Grombach never got it.

SCHOOL AWAITED many Americans when they got home. John Thomas, back at Boston University, returned to a stuffed mailbag. Most of it was hate mail lambasting him for losing to the Russians. "People still remember that you lost to a Russian," he said later. "You can win a thousand times, but if you lose once to a Russian, that's a no-no." When Anne Warner came back to Menlo-Atherton High for her junior year, the principal took her to lunch, and that was it.

Her career was essentially over—the same for most of the young female swimmers who had no college scholarships in their futures. Four years later, Warner fumed when that same principal hailed Dick Roth, a swimmer on the 1964 Tokyo squad, as the school's first Olympian. "He meant first *male* athlete," Warner said later, in those few words evoking years of frustration.

Dave Sime came back from Rome to report for his medical residency at the VA hospital in Durham, North Carolina. The chief resident, Stuart Boganoff, told him, "Oh, you're the famous runner; well, we have a famous case for you." There was a patient with a bad case of prostatitis who needed his prostate massaged, Sime was told. He prepared to do as instructed, until he noticed that the other residents "were all laughing so hard they had tears coming from their eyes." Welcome home, hotshot. Sime remained in great shape, and in the years after Rome occasionally thought about trying a comeback to finally gain the gold medal that had so cruelly eluded him. In 1971, when he was thirty-five, he competed at a meet in Miami and ran a 9.6 100-yard dash—yards, not meters, but still impressive. But he kept his focus on medicine, eventually becoming one of the most respected eye doctors in South Florida. His patients over the years included baseball legend Ted Williams, jockey Eddie Arcaro, Nixon pal Bebe Rebozo, and Eleanor Holm, the champion swimmer. Holm became best known for her most humiliating moment out of the pool, when Avery Brundage kicked her off the 1936 Olympic squad for misbehavior, alleging public drunkenness during the team's voyage across the Atlantic aboard the SS *Manhattan* on the way to Berlin. Holm always acknowledged that she had had a few glasses of champagne but claimed that Brundage held a grudge against her. In conversations decades later with Sime, a fellow Olympian, she finally revealed what she believed to be the underlying reason for the grudge. It was not her drinking that upset the publicly upright Brundage, she told her eye doctor, but rather the fact that this unlikely Don Juan had propositioned her, and she had turned him down. Here was just one more reason for Dave Sime to view the Olympic ideal with a healthy dose of skepticism.

What Rafer Johnson most wanted to do after winning his gold medal in Rome, he said, was nothing more than take a walk in the dark and stare up at the moon. Beyond that, he had few plans. He knew he would never compete in the decathlon again. His days as a track-and-field star were done. "That chapter was definitely over," he said later. "But at that moment, I didn't have a clue what I was going to do next." Some of the Olympic boxers and basketball players—Cassius Clay, Oscar Robertson, Walt Bellamy, Bob Boozer, Adrian Smith, Jerry Lucas, Jerry West, among others—could keep doing what they were doing and get paid for it in the pros. Some of the track stars, including Ray Norton, Stone Johnson, and Rink Babka, were planning to switch sports and try to make it in the National Football League. Rafer considered that option after being drafted by the Los Angeles Rams, but he had not played football since high school, and being a twenty-eighth-round draft choice did not establish him as much of a prospect.

The favorite son returned to Kingsburg, his hometown up on Freeway 99 in the middle of the San Joaquin Valley, halfway between Los Angeles and San Francisco, to see his mother and siblings and unwind in the hot, dry balm of that embracing place. Kingsburg had followed Johnson's every move in Rome; the audio of the television coverage even blared on the small town's public address system. They held a parade in his honor and gave him the keys to the city. With his gold medal finally secured, he felt that he had come full circle since the day his high school coach first took him twenty miles down the valley to Tulare to see Bob Mathias compete in a decathlon. Mathias had inspired him, and now he had surpassed his inspiration, breaking Mathias's records. Many awards would come Johnson's way as the best amateur athlete of the year, but a testimony in his hometown newspaper, the *Kingsburg Recorder*, seemed to move him most.

The community should be proud of Rafer Johnson, not only as an athlete but as an individual. Tobacco-chewing, beer-drinking, loud-talking athletes received the plaudits of the crowd so long as they can hit a baseball or run with a football. There are communities proud of being their hometowns. But how proud can they be of the individual as an individual, not just as an athlete?

Quantities of character are at least as important as physical ability, even in this day when standards seem to be no higher than the gutter. When character and ability are combined, you have an unusual individual. They are combined in Rafer Johnson. Writers have come to Kingsburg to try and discover what makes him as he is. They seem baffled. Why it should be unusual to have a young American with high moral standards and outstanding athletic ability is a question. Perhaps fame does something to the head, and to the heart; makes one bigger and the other smaller.

Johnson was a first in many ways. He had made history by setting a world record in the decathlon and by being the first black to captain a U.S. Olympic team and carry the American flag at the Opening Ceremony. Yet in some sense, even as he won deserved praise from his hometown newspaper, he found himself limited by the same positive characteristics the paper enumerated: his athletic prowess, his universal sensibility, and his integrity. He was a good youngster who turned into a better man, a story that does not have the dramatic arc of a tough kid who reformed or a young hero who slipped. His life was certainly not without obstacles. He had to deal with an angry, alcoholic father. Growing up as one of the few black kids in an overwhelmingly white community presented constant challenges, even as Kingsburg encouraged and comforted him. At UCLA, when he was elected student body president, he received a steady stream of hate mail from bigots who were particularly upset by a photograph showing him posing with two white female assistants. But Johnson absorbed these conditions and transcended them. He rejected his father's anger without turning away from him, understanding that the son had opportunities that the old man never had. He did not grow embittered or disillusioned from his experiences in the white world but instead developed what might now be called a post-racial sensibility in his dealings with people of all races at the same time that he remained proud of who he was.

Was he being manipulated by white officials, who used him as a paragon of athletic virtue and as a powerful answer to charges of American racism? The letter that air force general Lauris Norstad wrote from Rome after the Opening Ceremony, in which he referred to the magnificence of "this colored boy being in the lead," captured the mixture of awe and cultural condescension with which Johnson was regarded. Yet Rafer himself seemed largely untroubled by the ambiguity. If society was uncertain and contradictory, he was not. His philosophy was simple and consistent, summed up by the title of the autobiography he eventually wrote, *The Best That I Can Be.* He figured that his best answer to the problems of the world was his own excellence. His personality came without rough edges, without obvious imbalances or obsessions. Perhaps he saw too much, beyond himself.

In later years, Johnson would try acting (among other roles, as a Buffalo Soldier in *The Red, White, and Blue*), television (reporting from the Tokyo Olympics and doing sports on a local station in Los Angeles, where his colleagues included Tom Brokaw), and various corporate jobs. He became friendly with the Kennedy family and was drawn into their orbit, both as an official for the Special Olympics and as a strong supporter of Robert F. Kennedy's presidential campaign in 1968. Not only was he at the Ambassador Hotel in Los Angeles on the night that RFK was assassinated, but he and former NFL lineman Roosevelt Grier wrestled the gun from Sirhan Sirhan's hand on the hotel's kitchen floor. Johnson, dazed and depressed, went home that night with the gun still in his coat pocket and only realized days later that he was in possession of the murder weapon, which he then returned to the police. Throughout the years, he maintained a close association with the Olympics. Nearly a quarter century after his brilliant performance in Rome, he was chosen to light the flame at the 1984 Games in Los Angeles. He ascended the steps of the Coliseum looking as though he could still go out and win the decathlon one last time.

In Rome, among the athletes, Rafer Johnson was an undisputed leader. No one could match him. He was smart, regal, empathetic, handsome, and superbly skilled. He did not disappear or shrink when the Games ended, nor did he transform himself into something mythic. He remained forever Rafer Johnson, while one of his younger teammates, Cassius Clay, evolved into Muhammad Ali, the best-known athlete on the planet. Who was the superior figure, really, between the two? One could imagine some envy, or even dismay, seeping into Johnson's soul as he watched the clown prince of Rome become the self-styled king of the world.

But Johnson would not let that happen. He felt close to the young boxer from the first time they met at the Olympic Village in Rome. Months after they had won their gold medals, they toured the South together on a speaking tour of predominantly black colleges. They were roommates on the road and stayed up late at night as Clay told Johnson precisely how he planned to become an unforgettable character as well as the heavyweight champion of the world. Many of the cocky phrases and poems that Clay—and later Ali—brought to the world, he first tried out on Rafer Johnson in their hotel rooms. Johnson saved those discussions for posterity on a small tape recorder. The friendship, for Johnson, was an attraction to an opposite, or a repressed part of self, and he was self-aware enough to appreciate it, saying of Cassius Clay: "I loved the way he talked. He was just brash and challenged people, and he said it the way he felt it, and he talked about it. I am not that type of person. I carry it inside. I talk about it a little bit, but I don't need to say everything. He seemed to need to say everything. He wanted to talk about the beginning, and how he was going to do it, and the end, how he was going to finish. I just couldn't do that. That just wasn't my makeup. But I loved him for being that kind of person. I loved him for that."

Johnson shook his head in amazement as he reminisced about Clay, as did Tennessee State coach Ed Temple when recalling another incident that occurred shortly after he returned from Rome. He was at home preparing to leave for school one morning when his wife looked out the window and gasped. "Who do you know who drives a pink Cadillac convertible?" she asked. Temple was not sure, nor was he surprised when it turned out to be the brash kid from the boxing team who had such a huge crush on one of his Tigerbelles. "Coach," Cassius Clay said when he reached the door. "Can you tell me what room Wilma's in? I came here from Louisville, and I just want to holler at her."

Coach Temple and the Tigerbelles had arrived home on the Thursday afternoon of September 29, more than two weeks after the closing of the Rome Games. They had toured Europe and stopped in Detroit and Chicago on the way back to the Tennessee State campus, where more than five thousand students and local supporters packed the campus gym to greet them. The next Monday they were guests at the Tennessee state capitol, where they were honored with scrolls and praised by Governor Buford Ellington, the same politician who had campaigned as a segregationist two years earlier while Temple's women competed for their nation at the first dual track meet in Moscow.

The triumph of Wilma Rudolph temporarily transformed the racial landscape of her home turf, but the change did not come merely because of her grand accomplishments in Rome. It came because she insisted on it. When the Clarksville town fathers announced they wanted to hold a parade and banquet in her honor and proclaim Tuesday, October 4, Wilma Rudolph Day, she said she would attend only if all events were integrated. "So I sort of broke that barrier in my hometown," she said later. "I probably did everything that I wasn't supposed to do, but it was to pave the way for other blacks in the town."

The banquet at the armory marked the first time blacks and whites in Clarksville sat together at racially integrated tables for an official event. Rudolph was joined on the dais by Martha Hudson and Barbara Jones, two of her teammates on the relay team, along with Ralph Boston, the gold medalist long jumper, and Eddie Crook, the army sergeant from nearby Fort Campbell who had won the middleweight title in Rome. Nearby were Mayor W. W. Barksdale, chamber of commerce president Walton N. Smith, Burt High School principal G. W. Brooks, and Dr. W. S. Davis, president of Tennessee State. Among the more than eleven hundred people in the audience were her parents, Eddie and Blanche Rudolph. On the wall behind the dais was an oversized American flag, and above that a banner that read "Welcome Wilma." The chamber president gave her a silver tray. The college president called her "the queen of the Olympics." The high school principal said it was not the prevailing wind but her own determination that carried her to the finish line. The mayor handed her a copy of the Wilma Rudolph Day proclamation extolling her "magnificent victories" and introduced her to a standing ovation. Amid her happiness, Rudolph said, she remained aware of her responsibilities as a champion. "In every effort I have been motivated by one thing: to do justice to those who believe in me and to use my physical talents to the glory of God and the honor of womanhood."

She did more than justice to both. The same magnetism that prompted her hometown to desegregate for a day drew people of all kinds toward her for the rest of her life. A few months after the banquet, President Kennedy, hearing that she was in Washington to receive an award, called her over to the White House and was so taken by her that he missed his rocking chair as he sat down next to her in the Oval Office, and then talked to her so long that he left his next appointment waiting for an extra half hour. He told her how much he enjoyed watching her run on television and asked her the story of her life.

But it was the last phrase of her banquet speech—the honor of womanhood—that resonated deepest and longest. She was by no means the first great woman Olympian, but a unique combination of personal and cultural forces—her style and attractiveness, her candor and pride in who she was and where she was from, the leg braces of her childhood, the fact that she flashed onto the scene so brilliantly at the first commercially televised Olympics, her international esteem—made her a powerful symbol of the rise of women in sports. If there were a Mount Rushmore of women athletes, her profile would be one of the four chiseled faces. "For every woman athlete who came after, she was the person who opened the door," Ed Temple said later. "Wilma opened that door, and for all women, not just in track and field. She had that smile. She had that charisma."

One December afternoon more than four and a half decades after the sprints at the Stadio Olimpico, Temple, now eighty-four, sat at Swett's restaurant in North Nashville, not far from Tennessee State, and thought back on the unlikely rise of the Tigerbelles. It was at this same restaurant that Wilma Rudolph made her last appearance in public, one week before she died from brain cancer at the early age of fifty-four on November 12, 1994. "We came in, and David Swett [the proprietor] was here, and he carried her tray, and we sat right over there," the old coach said, pointing to a table in the corner. "And this was the last place . . ." His voice trailed off. In the hours before they shared a last meal that day, he and his star runner met one final time at their old college. They walked slowly around the track and talked about her days as a high school basketball player at Burt High in Clarksville, and how she buzzed around like a skeeter and had that loping stride and unstoppable hook shot. They remembered Temple's unforgiving summer track camps, and how much she hated them at first; and how they had no money, no scholarships, no office, no bus, not even a regulation track; and those exhausting overnight car rides to Tuskegee and Alabama State, when the Tigerbelles, with no safe place to stop, would eat peanut butter and jelly sandwiches from brown paper bags. They talked about her family and the fullness of life, her four children and seven grandchildren; and all the generations of girls and women who found encouragement from her story—and about how she twisted her ankle in that hole on a grassy practice field but recovered in time for those few days of magic and history at the Olympic Games in Rome.

APPENDIX

I. HOST CITIES OF OLYMPIC GAMES

1896	Athens, Greece		1956	Melbourne, Australia
1900	Paris, France		**1960**	**Rome, Italy**
1904	St. Louis, USA		1964	Tokyo, Japan
1908	London, England		1968	Mexico City, Mexico
1912	Stockholm, Sweden		1972	Munich, Germany
1916	Cancelled, WWI		1976	Montreal, Canada
1920	Antwerp, Belgium		1980	Moscow, Soviet Union
1924	Paris, France		1984	Los Angeles, USA
1928	Amsterdam, Holland		1988	Seoul, South Korea
1932	Los Angeles, USA		1992	Barcelona, Spain
1936	Berlin, Germany		1996	Atlanta, USA
1940	Cancelled, WWII		2000	Sydney, Australia
1944	Cancelled, WWII		2004	Athens, Greece
1948	London, England		2008	Beijing, China
1952	Helsinki, Finland			

II. AWARD OF MEDALS AT 1960 OLYMPIC GAMES AT ROME

	Gold	Silver	Bronze
Soviet Union	43	29	31
United States	34	21	16
Italy	13	10	13
Germany	12	20	10
Australia	8	8	6
Hungary	6	8	7
Poland	4	6	11
Great Britain	2	6	12
Japan	4	7	7
Romania	3	1	6
Turkey	7	2	0
Czechoslovakia	3	2	3
Bulgaria	1	3	3
Denmark	2	3	1
Sweden	1	2	3
Switzerland	0	3	3
France	0	2	3
Finland	1	1	3
Belgium	0	2	2
Iran	0	1	3
Holland	0	1	2
South Africa	0	1	2
New Zealand	2	0	1
Yugoslavia	1	1	0
Pakistan	1	0	1
Austria	1	1	0
Argentina	0	1	1
West Indies	0	0	2
Brazil	0	0	2
United Arab Republic	0	1	1
Canada	0	1	0
Norway	1	0	0
Venezuela	0	0	1
India	0	1	0
Spain	0	0	1
Ethiopia	1	0	0
Formosa (Taiwan)	0	1	0
Ghana	0	1	0
Greece	1	0	0
Iraq	0	0	1
Morocco	0	1	0
Mexico	0	0	1
Portugal	0	1	0
Singapore	0	1	0

Selected 1960 Olympic Results

III. MEN'S TRACK AND FIELD MEDALISTS

Decathlon		Points
1 Rafer Johnson	USA	8392
2 Chuan-Kwang Yang	Formosa	8334
3 Vasily Kuznetsov	USSR	7809

100-meter Dash		Time
1 Armin Hary	Germany	10.2
2 David Sime	United States	10.2
3 Peter Radford	Great Britain	10.3

200-meter Dash		Time
1 Livio Berruti	Italy	20.5
2 Lester Carney	USA	20.6
3 Abdoulaye Seye	France	20.7

400-meter Dash		Time
1 Otis Davis	USA	44.9
2 Carl Kaufmann	Germany	44.9
3 Malcolm Spence	South Africa	45.5

800-meter Dash		Time
1 Peter Snell	New Zealand	1:46.3
2 Roger Moens	Belgium	1:46.5
3 George Kerr	West Indies	1:47.1

1500-meter Run		Time
1 Herb Elliott	Australia	3:35.6
2 Michel Jazy	France	3:38.4
3 Istvan Rózsavölgyi	Hungary	3:39.2

5000-meter Run		Time
1 Murray Halberg	New Zealand	13:43.4
2 Hans Grodotzki	Germany	13:44.6
3 Kazimierz Zimny	Poland	13:44.8

10,000-meter Run		Time
1 Petr Bolotnikov	USSR	28:32.2
2 Hans Grodotzki	Germany	28:37.0
3 David Power	Australia	28:38.2

Marathon		Time
1 Abebe Bikila	Ethiopia	2:15:16.2
2 Rhadi ben Abdessalem	Morocco	2:15:41.6
3 Barry Magee	New Zealand	2:17:18.2

20,000-meter Walk		Time
1 Vladimir Golubnichiy	USSR	1:34:07.2
2 Noel Freeman	Australia	1:34:16.4
3 Stanley Vickers	Great Britain	1:34:56.4

50,000-meter Walk		Time
1 Donald Thompson	Great Britain	4:25:30.0
2 John Ljiunggren	Sweden	4:25:47.0
3 Abdom Pomich	Italy	4:27:55.4

110-meter High Hurdles		Time
1 Lee Calhoun	USA	13.8
2 Willie May	USA	13.8
3 Hayes Jones	USA	14.0

400-meter Hurdles		Time
1 Glenn Davis	USA	49.3
2 Clifton Cushman	USA	49.6
3 Richard Howard	USA	49.7

3000-meter Steeplechase		Time
1 Zdzislaw Krzyszkowiak	Poland	8:34.22
2 Nikolay Sokolov	USSR	8:36.4
3 Semen Rzhistchin	USSR	8:42.2

400-meter Relay	Time
1 Germany (Cullmann, Hary, Mahlendorf, Lauer)	39.5
2 USSR	40.1
3 Great Britain	40.2
(U.S. best time, 39.4, but disqualified for passing baton beyond legal zone)	

1600-meter Relay	Time
1 USA (Yerman, Young, Glenn Davis, Otis Davis)	3:02.2
2 Germany	3:02.7
3 West Indies	3:04.0

High Jump		Distance
1 Robert Shavlakadze	USSR	7-1 (gold due to fewer misses)

2 Valeri Brumel	USSR	7-1
3 John Thomas	USA	$7\frac{1}{4}$

Broad Jump — Distance

1 Ralph Boston	USA	$26\text{-}7\frac{3}{4}$
2 Bo Roberson	USA	$26\text{-}7\frac{1}{4}$
3 Igor Ter-Ovanesyan	USSR	$26\text{-}4\frac{1}{2}$

Pole Vault — Distance

1 Donald Bragg	USA	$15\text{-}5\frac{1}{8}$
2 Ronald Morris	USA	$15\text{-}1\frac{1}{8}$
3 Eeles Landstrom	Finland	$14\text{-}11\frac{1}{8}$

Hop, Step, and Jump — Distance

1 Jozef Schmidt	Poland	$55\text{-}1\frac{1}{4}$
2 Vladimir Goriaev	USSR	$54\text{-}6\frac{5}{8}$
3 Vitold Kreer	USSR	$53\text{-}10\frac{3}{4}$

Shot Put — Distance

1 William Nieder	USA	$64\text{-}6\frac{3}{4}$
2 Parry O'Brien	USA	$62\text{-}8\frac{1}{2}$
3 Dallas Long	USA	$62\text{-}4\frac{1}{2}$

Hammer Throw — Distance

1 Vasiliy Rudenkov	USSR	$220\text{-}1\frac{5}{8}$
2 Gyula Zsivotzky	Hungary	$215\text{-}10\frac{1}{8}$
3 Tadeusz Rut	Poland	$215\text{-}4\frac{1}{4}$

Javelin — Distance

1 Viktor Cybulenko	USSR	$277\text{-}8\frac{3}{8}$
2 Walter Kreuger	Germany	$260\text{-}4\frac{5}{8}$
3 Gergely Kulscar	Hungary	$257\text{-}9\frac{3}{8}$

Discus — Distance

1 Al Oerter	USA	194-2
2 Rink Babka	USA	$190\text{-}4\frac{1}{4}$
3 Richard Cochran	USA	$187\text{-}6\frac{3}{8}$

IV. WOMEN'S TRACK AND FIELD MEDALISTS

100-meter Dash — Time

1 Wilma Rudolph	USA	11.0
2 Dorothy Hyman	Great Britain	11.3
3 Giuseppina Leone	Italy	11.3

200-meter Dash		Time
1 Wilma Rudolph	USA	24.0
2 Jutta Heine	Germany	24.4
3 Dorothy Hyman	Great Britain	24.7

800-meter Run		Time
1 Shevtsova-Lysenko	USSR	2:04.3
2 Brenda Jones	Australia	2:04.4
3 Ursula Donath	Germany	2:05.6

400-meter Relay	Time
1 USA (Hudson, Jones, Williams, Rudolph)	44.5
2 Germany	44.8
3 Poland	45.0

80-meter Hurdles		Time
1 Irina Press	USSR	10.8
2 Carole Quinton	Great Britain	10.9
3 Gisela Birkemeyer	Germany	11.0

Broad Jump		Distance
1 Vera Krepkina	USSR	20-10¾
2 Elzbieta Krzesinska	Poland	20-6¾
3 Hildrun Claus	Germany	20-4½

Javelin		Distance
1 Elvira Ozolina	USSR	182-8
2 Dana Zatopkova	Czechoslovakia	176-5¼
3 Birute Kaledene	USSR	175-4½

Shot Put		Distance
1 Tamara Press	USSR	56-9⅞
2 Johanna Luettge	Germany	54-5⅞
3 Earlene Brown	USA	53-10⅜

High Jump		Distance
1 Iolanda Balas	Romania	6¾
2 Jaroslawa Jozwiakowska	Poland	5-7⅜
2 (tie) Dorothy Shirley	Great Britain	5-7⅜

Discus		Distance
1 Nina Ponomareva	USSR	180-8¼
2 Tamara Press	USSR	173-6½
3 Lia Manoliu	Romania	179-1¾

V. BASKETBALL

Score

1 USA	8–0
2 USSR	6–2
3 Brazil	6–2

USA versus Soviet Union, September 3, 1960
USA 81, USSR 57

USA	FG	FT	Pts
West, Jerry	9	1	19
Robertson, Oscar	6	4	16
Lucas, Jerry	6	0	12
Smith, Adrian	4	1	9
Bellamy, Walt	3	1	7
Boozer, Bob	1	2	4
Dischinger, Terry	1	0	2
Imhoff, Darrall	2	0	4
Lane, Lester	4	0	8
Arnette, Jay	0	0	0
Haldorson, Burdette	0	0	0
Kelley, Allen	0	0	0

USSR	FG	FT	Pts
Muiznieks, Valdis	2	4	8
Valdman, Maigonis	2	2	6
Valjtin, Albert	2	0	4
Minashvili, Guram	0	0	0
Zubkov, Viktor	6	1	13
Ugrekhilidze, Vladimir	0	0	0
Krumins, Janis	0	0	0
Semenov, Michael	0	2	2
Korneyev, Yuri	1	4	6
Petrov, Alexandr	4	3	11
Volinov, Gennadiy	2	2	6
Ozers, Ceaser	0	0	0

ACKNOWLEDGMENTS

In a family of siblings fluent in foreign languages, I emerged grievously lacking that useful gene, so I feel obliged to start by thanking the interpreters and translators without whom this book would not have been possible. Knesia Boitsova and Anastazie Harris helped me with Russian interviews and documents. Nancy Hart and Kathryn Wallace, expats in Rome from the U.S. and Great Britain, were delightful and invaluable as my guides, interpreters, and translators in the Eternal City. Kim Vergeront accompanied my wife and me to Lausanne and translated Olympic documents written in French with the perfection of the great teacher that she is. Petra Krischok in Berlin did amazing work tracking down German documents, newspapers, and interview subjects, and rendering them all understandable to me. David Edminster helped with German translations and Jean Alexander, my sister, with Russian.

For the third time, I felt great joy enlisting my son, Andrew Maraniss, to participate in the project when he could from Nashville, the home track of Coach Temple and the Tigerbelles. David Baumgarten, one of my ace students during a teaching stint at Princeton University, spent a few months helping me track down people and documents in Washington and at the Eisenhower Library in Kansas before heading off to Harvard Law. Francis Harris came to my aid in London. Madonna Lebling, a crack researcher at the *Washington Post,* once again worked her magic ferreting out addresses and telephone numbers. Brian Brown of NBC Olympics knows how grateful I am for his help, as does Joe Gesue.

Librarians and archivists, unsung heroes to every nonfiction writer, made my work easier around the world. They included Wayne Wilson at the LA84 Foundation in Los Angeles; Ruth Beck-Perrenoud and Patricia Eckert at the Olympic Studies Centre in Lausanne; Donatella Minelli, Paolo Pedinelli, and Barbara Monteduro at the Italian National Olympic Committee (CONI) in Rome; Dwight Strandberg at the Eisenhower Presidential Library; Rodney A. Ross at the National Archives in Washington; Tim Nenninger at the National Archives in College Park, Maryland; Sara Velez at the New York Public Library for the Performing Arts; and Chris Prom and Linda Stahnke at the Avery Brundage collection at the University of Illinois Urbana-Champaign.

Donald E. Graham, chairman of the Washington Post Company, shared with me his memories of spending part of his fifteenth summer in Rome as an assistant to the legendary sportswriter Shirley Povich, and for that and a thousand other favors, I thank this most generous man. The *Post* has been my working family for more than thirty years and sustains me even when I'm not there, with its high standards and embracing atmosphere. Thanks to Bo Jones, Leonard Downie, Phil Bennett, Bill Hamilton, R. B. Brenner, Michel du Cille, Bob Kaiser, Ellen Nakashima, Zachary Goldfarb, Dana Priest, and my great friend and CD-burning music supplier Anne Hull for making my forays into the newspaper so comforting and productive. John Feinstein, though late for pancakes, was helpful as usual with contacts in the sporting world. Thanks also to Jim Warren (always one of my first and best readers) and Cornelia Grumman, Neil Henry, Mike (Stormin') and Beth Norman, Jane and Rick (Scribbler) Atkinson, Andy Cohn and Kim Vergeront, Michael Weiden and Peggy Vergeront, Peter and Carrie Ritz, Ben and Judy Sidran, Joanne and Bob Skloot, Rick and Sue Corley, Eric Simonson, the terrific *The Only Thing* cast and crew, Sam Schwartz, Dave Foster, Dave Marshall, Rebekah and Michael (Mordecai) Weisskopf, Chip (Struc) Brown and Kate Betts, Blaine Harden and Jessica Kowal, Suey Kong Wong, Karl Harter, John Roach (fellow new hipster), Dr. Rogerson and his great staff, Dr. Olson and the nurses at Meriter and Associated Physicians, Dan Siebens and Linda Krumholz, Frank and Kathy Roloff, Dick and Mary Anne Porter, Trip and Heddy Reid, Bob Woodward and Elsa Walsh, Jim Wooten and Patience O'Connor, Robert Caro, Doug and Cathy Williams, Pat and Ritchey Porter, Carol and Ty Garner, Jean and Michael Alexander, Jim Maraniss and Gigi Kaeser, George Raine, Elizabeth Johnson, and the entire wonderful block of Knickerbocker neighbors.

I feel blessed that Simon & Schuster has published all of my books. Thanks to the people who have been supportive all the way, Carolyn Reidy and David Rosenthal, Victoria Meyer and Rebecca Davis, the amazing Roger Labrie and Karen Thompson and the inimitable Alice Mayhew, whose friendship, energy, wisdom, and passion keep me going as an author. Thanks also to first-class copy editors Phil Bashe and Kathleen Rizzo and the legal eye of Elisa Rivlin. Rafe Sagalyn, my agent, who claims some mystical bond with Rafer Johnson, was greatly supportive, as were his assistants Bridget Wagner and Shannon O'Neill.

Everything I do is in honor of my late parents, Elliott and Mary Maraniss, and my sister Wendy, and now my big Uncle Joe, all gone and irreplaceable but never forgotten. Along with loss there is also renewal, and in our family it came this year with the joyous addition of another Maraniss, Alison, who married our son Andrew. There are long periods of loneliness in the writing of any book, but my mood always brightened at the thought of the two redheads out in New Jersey, our daughter Sarah and bubbly granddaughter Heidi, along with Sarah's husband Tom Vander Schaaff. It was exactly eleven years ago that I turned to my wife Linda and uttered the immortal loving words, "How would you like to move to Green Bay for the winter?" Her first response was "Brrrrr," but she quickly agreed, and that is when research on my biography of Vince Lombardi began. It goes without saying that it was easier to ask her whether she would like to spend time in Rome and Lausanne to research *Rome 1960*. Linda, the quirky saint, is my first editor, my photographer, my eyes and nose, my constant companion, my rock, and my salvation.

Washington, DC
March 22, 2008

BIBLIOGRAPHY

Abebe, Tsige. *Triumph and Tragedy: A History of Abebe Bikila and His Marathon Career.* Printed in Ethiopia by Tsige Abebe, 1996.

Abrahams, Harold, editor. *XVII Olympiad, Rome 1960.* Cassell & Co. Ltd., London, 1960.

Allen, Neil. *Olympic Diary: Rome 1960.* Nicholas Kaye Limited, London, 1960.

Arnold, Peter. *The Olympic Games.* Optimum Books, London, 1983.

Biracree, Tom. *Wilma Rudolph: Champion Athlete.* Chelsea House, New York, 1988.

Brasher, Chris, editor. *The Road to Rome.* William Kimber and Co., London, 1960.

Carlson, Lewis H., and John J. Fogarty. *Tales of Gold: An Oral History of the Summer Olympic Games.* Contemporary Books, New York, 1987.

Cuthbert, Betty, and Jim Webster. *Golden Girl: The Autobiography of Betty Cuthbert.* Pelham Books, London, 1966.

Durant, John. *Highlights of the Olympics.* Hastings House Publishers, New York, 1965.

Eatwell, Roger. *Fascism: A History.* Pimlico, London, 1995.

Fair, John D. *Muscletown USA.* Pennsylvania State University Press, University Park, PA, 1999.

Findling, John E., and Kimberly D. Pelle. *Historical Dictionary of the Modern Olympic Movement.* Greenwood Press, Westport, CT, 1996.

Fleischer, Nat. *50 Years at Ringside.* Corgi Books, London, 1960.

Fursenko, Aleksandr, and Timothy Naftali. *Khrushchev's Cold War.* W. W. Norton & Company, Inc., New York, 2006.

Giamoni, Romolo; Marcello Garroni; Enrico Vignolini; Elena Baggio (translation, Edwin Byatt). *The Games of the XVII Olympiad, Rome 1960, The Official Report of the Organizing Committee, volumes 1 and 2.* Organizing Committee of the Games of the XVII Olympiad, Rome, 1960.

Gilmour, Garth. *Arthur Lydiard, Master Coach.* Exisle Publishing, Auckland, 2004.

Guttman, Allen. *The Games Must Go On.* Columbia University Press, New York, 1983.

Hoberman, John M. *Testosterone Dreams.* University of California Press, Berkeley, CA, 2005.

————. *Sport and Political Ideology.* University of Texas Press, Austin, 1984.

Italian State Tourist Department. *Olympiad 1960: Games of the XVII Olympiad.* Rome, 1960.

Johnson, Rafer. *The Best That I Can Be.* Doubleday, New York, 1998.

Kieran, John, and Arthur Daley. *The Story of the Olympic Games.* J. B. Lippincott Company, Philadelphia and New York, revised edition, 1961.

Kindred, David. *Sound and Fury: Two Powerful Lives, One Fateful Friendship.* Free Press, New York, 2006.

Lebedev, Lev. *USSR-USA Sports Encounters.* Progress Publishers, Moscow, 1977.

Lechenperg, Harald, editor. *Olympic Games 1960: Squaw Valley, Rome.* A. S. Barnes and Co., New York, 1960.

Le Masurier, John. *Track Speed.* Stanley Paul, London, 1972.

Lentz, Arthur G., editor. *United States 1960 Olympic Book: Quadrennial Report of the United States Olympic Committee.* Walker-Rackliff Co., New Haven, CT, 1961.

Mangan, J. A., editor. *Shaping the Superman: Fascist Body as Political Icon.* Frank Cass Publishers, London, 1999.

Masson, Georgina. *The Companion Guide to Rome.* Prentice-Hall, Inc., Englewood Cliffs, NJ, 1965.

McKay, Jim. *The Real McKay: My Wide World of Sports.* Plume, New York, 1999.

Monoco, Franco. *XVII Olympiad: Olympic Guide Book, Rome 1960.* Banco Nazionale del Lavoro, Rome, 1960.

Moore, Kenny. *Bowerman and the Men of Oregon.* Rodale, New York, 2006.

Paul, C. Robert, and Jack Orr. *The Olympic Games: From Ancient Greece to Mexico City.* The Lion Press, New York, 1968.

Phillips, Dennis H. *Australian Women at the Olympic Games.* Kangaroo Press, Sydney, 1992.

Piley, Phil, editor. *Official Report of the Olympic Games 1960, The British Olympic Association.* World Sports, London, 1960.

Powell, John T. *Origins and Aspects of Olympism.* Stipes Publishing Company, Champaign, IL, 1994.

Remnick, David. *King of the World.* Vintage Books, New York, 1999.

Roghi, Bruno, supervisor. *Games of the XVII Olympiad.* Italian Olympic Committee (CONI) production, Rome, 1960.

Schoebel, Heinz. *The Four Dimensions of Avery Brundage.* Edition Leipzig, Leipzig, German Democratic Republic, 1968.

Sims, Graem. *Why Die? The Extraordinary Percy Cerutty.* Lothiam Books, South Melbourne, 2003.

Smit, Barbara. *Pitch Invasion: Adidas, Puma and the Making of Modern Sport.* Allen Lane, London, 2006.

Smith, Red. *Red Smith's Sports Annual, 1961.* Crown Publishers, New York, 1961.

Tanner, J. M. *The Physique of the Olympic Athlete: A Study of 137 Track and Field Athletes at the XVII Olympic Games, Rome 1960.* George Allen and Unwin Ltd., London, 1964.

Taubman, William. *Khrushchev: The Man and His Era.* W. W. Norton & Company, Inc., New York, 2003.

Teske, Knut. *Sprinter of the Century: The Breathtaking Career of Armin Hary.* Goettingen, Berlin, 2007.

Tipping, E. W. *The Tipping Olympics. Melbourne 1956-Rome 1960.* Peter Isaacson Pty. Limited, Australia, 1972.

Wallechinsky, David. *The Complete Book of the Summer Olympics: Athens 2004 Edition.* SportClassic Books, New York, 2004.

SOURCES

The narrative branches of this book are rooted in primary sources: thousands of archival documents, along with personal diaries, oral transcripts, and scores of interviews with athletes, coaches, officials, journalists, and observers from around the world who were at the 1960 Rome Olympics. Many subjects were interviewed several times. Among the documents, the vast majority were found in the fourteen archives listed below. In addition to books listed in the bibliography, the forty-four newspaper and magazines named here, the first drafts of history, were also invaluable, and are cited in the text and chapter notes.

PRIMARY ARCHIVAL SOURCES

Amateur Athletic Foundation of Los Angeles (LA84 Foundation)
Avery Brundage collection, University of Illinois at Urbana-Champaign
Clarksville-Montgomery County Public Library, Tennessee
Columbia Broadcasting Company (CBS)
Comitato Olimpico Nazionale Italiano (CONI), Rome
Dwight D. Eisenhower Presidential Library and Museum, Abilene, Kansas
Georgetown University Lauinger Library, Special Collections
German National Archives (Bundesarchiv), Berlin
Library of Congress, Newspaper and Current Periodical Reading Room
Nashville Public Library Special Collections Division, Tennessee
National Archives and Records Administration, College Park, Maryland
National Archives and Records Administration, Washington, DC
National Broadcasting Company (NBC), *The Wonders of Rome* archive
Olympic Studies Centre, International Olympic Committee Museum, Lausanne, Switzerland

NEWSPAPER AND MAGAZINE SOURCES

Amateur Athlete, American Mercury, Baltimore *Sun, Boston Globe, Chicago Tribune, China Daily News,* Clarksville *Leaf-Chronicle, Columbus Post-Dispatch, Die Welt, L'Echo Illustré, L'Équipe, Ethiopian Herald, Frankfurter Allgemeine Zeitung, IOC Official Bulletin, Izvestia, Journal of Sport History, Kingsburg Recorder, Life, Los Angeles Times,* Louisville *Courier-Journal, Il Messaggero, Nashville Banner,* Nashville *Tennessean, Neues Deutschland, Newsweek, New Yorker,* New York *Herald Tribune, New York Times, Olympic Review, Pakistan Times, Pravda, la Repubblica, Ring* magazine, *Rome Daily American,* San Francisco *Chronicle, Sport, Sports Illustrated, Time, Times of India, Times* of London, *Track & Field News, Tuttosport, Wall Street Journal, Washington Post.*

NOTES

<hr/>

CHAPTER 1: ALL THE WAY TO MOSCOW

1 *Darkness fell slowly:* Ints., Dallas Long, Gordon McKenzie, Ed Temple, Rafer Johnson, Rink Babka, David Edstrom, Lucinda Williams; also *Amateur Athlete*, Sept. 1958. *Amateur Athlete* was the monthly magazine of the Amateur Athletic Union, at a time when the AAU was the dominant amateur body in the United States, more powerful than the U.S. Olympic Committee and the National Collegiate Athletic Association.

2 *As he was preparing to leave:* Ints., Ed Temple, Lucinda Williams.

5 *Aside from those two black Southern colleges:* Frances Kaszubski correspondence; Ints., Ed Temple, Lucinda Williams; *Amateur Athlete*, Aug. 1958.

7 *The home and away exchange:* Record group 59, box 2127, NARA-College Park. Also on the U.S. negotiating team were Loftus E. Becker and Malcolm Toon; Joseph Turrini, " 'It Was Communism versus the Free World': The USA-USSR Dual Track Meet Series and the Development of Track and Field in the United States, 1958–1985," *Journal of Sport History,* vol. 28, no. 3.

8 *By the time the roster:* Int., David Edstrom; also *Time*, July 7, 1958.

9 *Kaszubski approached him:* Int., Ed Temple; also Kaszubski correspondence.

9 *A National Security Council task force:* White House Office, National Security Council staff papers, OCB central file, box 112, Eisenhower Presidential Library.

10 *"Clipper AAU" was painted on the side: Amateur Athlete*, Sept. 1958.

10 *This was Rafer Lewis Johnson:* Int., Rafer Johnson. In early 2007, when Johnson was interviewed at length at his office at the Special Olympics of Southern California in Culver City, California, he looked like he could win the decathlon still at age seventy-two;

also ints., David Edstrom, Dallas Long, Rink Babka, Lucinda Williams; "An Olympian's Oral History: Craig Dixon," Amateur Athletic Foundation of Los Angeles.

12 *When the Americans landed:* Int., Ed Temple; *Amateur Athlete,* Sept. 1958; *Amateur Athlete*, June 1958 ("Hailed as Mr. AAU of the District of Columbia, Eddie Rosenblum . . . was honored Tuesday evening, May 27, at a testimonial civic dinner in the main ballroom of the Willard Hotel in Washington, DC," began an article under the headline "Eddie Rosenblum Paid Tribute for 40 Years of Service."

13 *With his heavy-framed glasses:* Int., Igor Ter-Ovanesyan; also "Testing Service to the 'Queen,' " Gavriel Korobkov, *Candidate of Pedagogical Sciences,* Former Coach of the Soviet Athletic Team, LA84 Foundation library; *Stanford Magazine*, May/June 2005; Letter to *Stanford Magazine* from Robert Coe, July/Aug. 2005.

14 *After the eerie bus ride:* Ints., Rink Babka, David Edstrom, Rafer Johnson, Dallas Long, Lucinda Williams.

16 *Ed Temple experienced a starkly different variation:* Int., Ed Temple.

17 *On the eve of the track meet:* Int., Rafer Johnson; also *The Best That I Can Be,* Rafer Johnson.

17 *A huge, clamorous crowd filled:* Ints., David Edstrom, Igor Ter-Ovanesyan; also *Track & Field News,* Aug. 1958; *New York Times,* July 28, 1958.

18 *After reading day after day:* Ints., Ed Temple, Rink Babka; also Nashville *Tennessean,* July 28, 1958; *New York Times,* July 28, 1958.

19 *The most disconcerting event:* Int., Gordon McKenzie; also *Track & Field News*, Aug. 1958; *Amateur Athlete,* Sept. 1958; *New York Times,* July 28, 1958.

20 *The crowd the next afternoon:* Ints., Lucinda Williams, Ed Temple, Rink Babka, Rafer Johnson, David Edstrom; also *Track & Field News,* Aug. 1958; *New York Times,* July 29, 1958.

22 *The atmosphere at the end:* Ints., Rafer Johnson, Igor Ter-Ovanesyan; also *Track & Field News,* Aug. 1958; *New York Times,* July 29, 1958; *Amateur Athlete,* Sept. 1958. In a "Memo from the Publisher" in that issue, Harold O. Zimman, writing from his office in Lynn, Massachusetts, noted: "International Olympic Committee president Avery Brundage, who has served as AAU president and U.S. Olympic chairman, was enthusiastic about the international meets as a means of spreading the Olympic doctrine of understanding among the nations of the world. He recently told me in Chicago that he had no fear that such meets detract from the Olympic Games, which, he pointed out, cover a much greater range of events."

CHAPTER 2: ALL ROADS TO ROME

24 *Two weeks before the opening:* Department of State, memorandum of conversation, Aug. 12, 1960, Participants: Mr. Gabriele Paresce, press counselor, Italian embassy; John G. Kormann, Department of State. State Department central files, NARA-College Park.

25 *"About what?" Sime wondered:* Int., David Sime. This was not the first time that Sime had worked with the U.S. government. He presumed that one reason he had been approached for this assignment was because of an earlier trip he had taken to Burma with a delegation of athletes and performers sponsored by the State Department. One of the performers on that trip was the singer Eartha Kitt. His Burmese hosts gave him a gorgeous hand-carved ivory boat, which he said he swapped for a car when he got home.

29 *To Igor Ter-Ovanesyan, not quite twenty-two:* Int., Igor Ter-Ovanesyan. While he knew some English, Ter-Ovanesyan spoke mainly in Russian. The interview was interpreted by Knesia Boitsova.

33 *More than half of the U.S. contingent: New York Times,* Aug. 16, 1960; Associated Press report, Aug. 15, 1960.

34 *No one looked sharper: 1960 United States Olympic Book,* pp. 38–41. Casual and formal outfits for the 420 members of the U.S. delegation (including administrative staff) were donated by American manufacturers. The clothing value was estimated at $106,300.

34 *Beneath his composed exterior:* Int., Rafer Johnson; also "An Olympian's Oral History: Craig Dixon, LA84 Foundation: Conversation with C. K. Yang and Rafer Johnson, LA84 Foundation."

37 *That night, after an informal reception:* Ints., Rink Babka, Ed Temple, Lucinda Williams, Jerry Armstrong, Nikos Spanakos; diary of Jack Sikes; Wilbert McClure oral history, NBC, *"The Wonders of Rome,"* an excellent documentary that aired during the 1996 Atlanta Olympics; also *Amateur Athlete,* Sept. 1960; Associated Press report, Aug. 16, 1960.

40 *The Ethiopians came early to Rome: Ethiopian Herald,* Aug. 12–20, 1960; *Rome Daily American,* Aug. 13–16, 1960; *The Games of the XVII Olympiad, Rome 1960, The Official Report of the Organizing Committee.*

43 *West and East, two political systems:* Note for the files, regarding negotiations between the NOCs of the GDR and FRG, 10-8-59, Herbert Vollstadt, secretary. German National Archives; Report on the Annual Meeting of the NOC-West in Hannover, Mar. 3, 1960. Heather L. Dichter, "Building Walls, Dividing Teams," Sixth International Symposium for Olympic Research 2002; G. A. Carr, "The Involvement of Politics in the Sporting Relationships of East and West Germany, 1945–1972," *Journal of Sport History,* spring 1980.

44 *Ewald, at age thirty-six, had moved: New York Times,* obituary, Oct. 26, 2002; the *Independent* (London), obituary, Oct. 25, 2002.

45 *While Cerutty, known for his special diets:* Int., Cord Nelson; *Why Die?,* Graem Sims.

46 *Pete Newell, the U.S. Olympic basketball coach: Amateur Athletics,* June 1960; Newell oral history, NBC archive; *1960 United States Olympic Book;* Associated Press account, Aug. 21, 1960.

47 *The track-and-field team faced:* Account of U.S. track-and-field team in Switzerland and on its way to Rome from: Ints., Rink Babka, Dallas Long, Rafer Johnson, John Thomas, David Sime, Jim Beatty, Joe Faust; *Sports Illustrated,* Aug. 29, 1960; *Nashville Banner,* Aug. 21–23, 1960; *New York Times,* Aug. 21–23, 1960; Associated Press accounts, Aug. 21, 1960; *Track & Field News,* Sept. 1960; oral histories, Ray Norton, Oscar Robertson, Pete Newell, NBC archive.

CHAPTER 3: NO MONARCH EVER HELD SWAY

52 *When Avery Brundage . . . arrived in Rome:* Brundage handwritten diary, Aug. 1960; Brundage "To whom it may concern" letter of recommendation for Edward Cernaez, Sept. 10, 1960, Brundage collection, University of Illinois; cablegram, U.S. embassy to State Department, Aug. 18, 1960, NARA-College Park; Associated Press account of arrival, Aug. 17, 1960; The Nineteen-Ten Illio, box 299, Brundage collection.

55 *The first order of business:* Minutes, Rome session 1960, Executive Board Meeting, IOC, Rome file, IOC Olympic Studies Centre, Lausanne; also letter from Otto Mayer to the Marquess of Exeter, Mar. 9, 1959, Otto Mayer file, OSC, Lausanne; also box 50, Brundage collection.

56 *Then, at a decisive session in Munich:* 55th Session, IOC, Munich, May 25–28, 1959, box 79, Brundage collection; Chinese question, protest letters, box 129, Brundage collection.

59 *In the run-up to the Olympics:* Outgoing telegram, Department of State, Embtel 558, 5:20 p.m., Aug. 11, 1960. State Department central file, NARA-College Park. Douglas Roby was in regular contact with State during the China dispute, keeping his government apprised of what he was thinking and where he could be reached at all times. It was a delicate situation because IOC custom forbade blatant political operations by members, and the U.S. often complained about the political connection between Eastern bloc delegates and Communist leaders in their countries. It was for this reason, according to a June 17 memorandum of conversation involving a State Department official, "Mr. Roby, as he had done previously, requested that we keep in confidence the fact that he has had discussions with the Department of State on these matters."

61 *opening dinner of the 57th Session: Olympic Bulletin,* Sept. 1960, no. 21, Solemn Inauguration of the 57th Session of the IOC, Olympic Studies Centre, Lausanne; remarks of Avery Brundage, Rome, Italy, Aug. 20, 1960, Brundage collection.

62 *The next morning, in his room at the Hotel Luxor:* Letter to Brundage from Michael Scott, delivered Aug. 21, 1960, South Africa file, box 144, Brundage collection; Letter from Otto Mayer to Antony Steel, Aug. 10, 1960, Mayer file, OSC, Lausanne. In concluding his letter to Steel, Mayer wrote: "Furthermore, I must say that our agenda is already so heavy that some other most important problems have to be discussed, that we shall have hardly any time to bring other items on the table. I am sure that you will understand our point of view and that this problem can be postponed for our next session."

64 *Appended to Emery's letter were news clippings:* Apr. 14, 1960, letter to Brundage from Ira G. Emery of South African Olympic and Commonwealth Games Association, Johannesburg, South Africa file, Brundage collection. Certain passages had been underlined in the clippings, including a section that said detectives discovered files on Otto Mayer and Brundage when they raided Brutus's home.

65 *Yet Brundage was a chronic doodler:* From examination of voluminous handwritten notes in Brundage collection; handwritten notes from Rome IOC meeting, box 249, Brundage collection.

67 *But beneath that argument ran:* Letter to Carl Diem, Sept. 27, 1935, box 129, Brundage collection. In the letter, Brundage asked Diem for information that might help him fight the attempted boycott. "The more definite data which you can furnish to me which establishes the fact that Jews are going on about their business in Germany so far as sport is concerned, and that the pledges made to the International Olympic Committee and to me are kept, the better equipped I will be to offset the vicious propaganda which is being released in this country."

An earlier letter from Diem had praised Brundage for remarks he made on radio in support of the Berlin Olympics. "The transmission to Germany had unfortunately been troubled so that we were not able to hear by ourselves your words, but the telegraphical news say that you sent a warm appeal for a strong and intensive preparation for the Olympic Games and that you declined the newly fomented baiting against the American participation," Diem wrote.

68 *In the manuscript of an autobiography:* For *The Olympic Story,* by Avery Brundage, chapter 8, box 330, Brundage collection.

68 *A week after he returned to America: New York Times,* Oct. 5, 1936, "Brundage Extols Hitler's Regime—At German Day Observance Here He Says 'We, Too, Must Stamp Out Communism'—20,000 Cheer Him Wildly—He Praises Olympic Spirit of Reich as Greatest Since Greek Era." Brundage chose this setting to make his first speech upon his return from Berlin. During his time at the Olympics, he said, he "found Germans friendly, courteous, and obliging."

CHAPTER 4: MAY THE BEST MAN WIN

70 *Paolo was five years old then:* Int., Paolo Pedinelli at CONI headquarters, Rome. Decades later, Pedinelli came to work at the Rome Olympics site as historian and archivist. He regarded every chunk of loose cement near the Stadio Olimpico as an irreplaceable jewel.

71 *The U.S. men's team was housed:* Ints., Lance Larson, Jim Beatty, David Sime, Ed Temple, Nikos Spanakos, Jerry Armstrong, James Bradford, Ike Berger, Rafer Johnson, John Thomas, Joe Faust, David Edstrom, Otis Davis; also Jack Simes diary, Ray Norton oral history, NBC archive.

73 *After a few days at the village:* Int., Anne Warner (Cribbs).

73 *There was a decidedly sexist tone:* Ints., Abe Grossfeld, Anne Warner, Ed Temple, Lucinda Williams; UPI report, Aug. 23, 1960, "Muriel Nearly Outpoints Gina"; Frances Kaszubski correspondence; Dennis H. Phillips correspondence; *Rome Daily American,* Aug. 23, 1960; *New York Times,* Aug. 23, 1960; San Francisco *Chronicle,* Aug. 27, 1960, "Bikinis Confound Swim Expert."

76 *Within a few days, Clay had established himself:* Ints., Nikos Spanakos, Jerry Armstrong, Ed Temple, John Thomas, Rink Babka; Wilbert McClure oral history, NBC archive; "An Olympian's Oral History: Paula Jean Myers Pope," AAFLA.

78 *Igor Ter-Ovanesyan and his Soviet teammates:* Int., Igor Ter-Ovanesyan (Knesia Boitsova, interpreter), also *Pravda* and *Izvestia,* Aug. 17–24, 1960.

80 *The Soviet public relations campaign: Rome Daily American,* Aug. 24, 1960; UPI dispatch, Aug. 24, 1960; Int., Anne Warner (Cribbs); Bill Mulliken oral history, *Tales of Gold.*

82 *Concealed under the green carpet:* Description of Foro Mussolini based on author observations under expert guidance of historian Paolo Pedinelli.

83 *. . . an address and benediction from Pope John XXIII:* Description of papal address to athletes based on *New Yorker,* Aug. 31, 1960; Ints., Lucinda Williams, Joe Faust; Williams oral history, NBC archive; Baltimore *Sun,* Aug. 25, 1960; *Rome Daily American,* Aug. 25, 1960; *Boston Globe,* Aug. 25, 1960.

85 *Il Paese . . . offered further detail:* Department of State Foreign Service dispatch from Stanislaus B. Milus, Refugee and Migration Section: "There are enclosed for your information translations of three articles from Italian newspapers which may be of interest, as they deal with anticipations of propaganda efforts of both the East and West concerning the oncoming Olympic Games to be held in Rome," State Department central file, NARA-College Park.

86 *The West German press corps: Frankfurter Allgemeine Zeitung,* Aug. 25, 1960.

87 *August 24 . . . had been a full day for Avery Brundage:* Brundage handwritten schedule, box 249, Brundage collection.

87 *The myth of white supremacy, Scott argued:* Address for presentation to the International Olympic Games Committee, Rome, Aug. 1960, by Rev. Michael Scott, representing South African Sports Association and Campaign Against Race Discrimination in Sport, box 144, Brundage collection. Scott concluded: "In order to bring to an end as far as is possible by official action this anachronism of racial discrimination in international sport in this world of 1960, we feel we must ask you, for the sake of Africa and for the sake of posterity, not to allow the South African team to compete until it is truly representative of all the South African people and until the assurances that were given . . . have been carried out."

88 *Here is but a small, random sample: The Games of the XVII Olympiad, Rome 1960, Volume One,* sports equipment, table 1.

89 *Everything set to go, except . . . Virgilio Tommasi:* Int., Rino Tommasi.

89 *Reaching the Olympics along the road to Rome:* Int., Gian Paolo Ormezzano (Kathryn Wallace, interpreter).

CHAPTER 5: OUT OF THE SHADOWS

93 *Carrying the flag for the Greeks:* Depiction of the Opening Ceremony of the XVII Olympiad based on Ints., Rafer Johnson, John Thomas, Anne Warner (Cribbs), Igor Ter-Ovanesyan, Livio Berruti, Gian Paolo Ormezzano, Rino Tommasi, Dallas Long, Ingrid Kraemer, David Sime, Isaac Berger, Nikos Spanakos, Lance Larson, Otis Davis, Ed Temple, Lucinda Williams; also *Los Angeles Times,* Aug. 26, 1960; *Washington Post,* Aug. 26, 1960; UPI account, Aug. 25, 1960; Associated Press account by Eddy Gilmore, Aug. 25, 1960; *New York Times,* Aug. 26, 1960; New York *Herald Tribune,* Aug. 26, 1960; Baltimore *Sun,* Aug. 26, 1960; *Chicago Tribune,* Aug. 26, 1960; *Die Welt,* Aug. 26, 1960, *Frankfurter Allgemeine Zeitung,* Aug. 26, 1960; *Neues Deutschland,* Aug. 26, 1960; *Pravda,* Aug. 26, 1960; *Izvestia,* Aug. 26, 1960; *Rome Daily American,* Aug. 26, 1960; *China Daily News,* Aug. 26, 1960; *New Yorker,* Aug. 31, 1960; also incoming airgram from American embassy in Rome to Department of State, Aug. 27, 1960, State Department central file, NARA-College Park: "The Chinese ambassador telephoned to the reporting officer on August 25 stating that in spite of his best efforts with all authorities, the IOC had had its way, and it was going to be necessary for the Chinese teams to march in the opening ceremony under the inscription 'Formosa' without any mention of the name 'Republic of China'"; also manuscript for *The Olympic Story* by Avery Brundage, chapter 12, box 330, Brundage collection; Neil Allen, *Olympic Diary* (pp. 34–36); Kieran and Daley, *The Story of the Olympic Games* (pp. 330–332); *1960 United States Olympic Book* (p. 28); *Golden Girl,* Betty Cuthbert: "I rested up the next day as well. I had no choice. The opening ceremony was on, and those of us with events early in the programme weren't allowed to march"; *Red Smith's Sports Annual 1961* (pp. 112–114); *The Games of the XVII Olympiad, Rome 1960,* vol. 2 (pp. 13–18); *Newsweek,* Aug. 29, 1960; *Life,* Sept. 19, 1960; *Olympic Review,* Sept. 1960 (pp. 79–81).

CHAPTER 6: HEAT

110   *Friday morning was infernally hot:* "The Games of the XVII Olympiad, Cycling Regulations," Olympic Studies Centre, Rome; *Rome Daily American,* Aug. 27, 1960.

110   *One of the U.S. cyclists:* Ints., Bob Tetzlaff, Jack Simes, Allen Bell.

111   *The Danes were among the better teams:* Depiction of collapse of Knud Enemark Jensen drawn from: *Ekstra Bladet,* Aug. 27, 1960; *Politiken,* Aug. 27–30, 1960; *Politiken,* Sept. 20, 1998, "The Doping Case That Changed the World," Lars Bogeskov; *Politiken,* Apr. 9, 2001, "The Doping Mystery Without a Solution," Lars Bogeskov; Int., Bob Tetzlaff; *Life,* Sept. 1960.

114   *Though weak from strep throat:* Ints., David Sime, Igor Ter-Ovanesyan.

114   *Across the warm-up field:* Int., Rafer Johnson; UPI account, Aug. 26, 1960; "An Olympian's Oral History: Craig Dixon," AAFLA; *China Daily News,* Aug. 20–26, 1960.

116   *Doubts about the Tigerbelles persisted:* Ints., Ed Temple, Lucinda Williams; Frances Kaszubski correspondence.

117   *Most American sportswriters were looking elsewhere:* Int., John Thomas; *Track & Field News,* Aug. 1960; *Nashville Banner,* Aug. 27, 1960; *Washington Post,* Aug. 27, 1960; UPI account, Aug. 26, 1960; Tim Horgan, "Six O'Clock Jumper," *Amateur Athlete,* Aug. 1960.

121   *This was a mysterious character:* Obituary, Assembly, June 1983, Register of Graduates, West Point, 7204A, John Valentin Grombach; Studies in Intelligence 48, no. 3, Mark Stout, "The Pond: Running Agents for State, War, and the CIA"; Cecil B. Lyon Papers, box 10, folder 25, Georgetown University Special Collections; Grombach file, box 26, Brundage collection; Senate Internal Security Subcommittee record group 46, Grombach file, NARA-Washington.

123   *Left alone in the dressing room:* Int., Nikos Spanakos; also New York *Herald Tribune,* Aug. 27, 1960; *Los Angeles Times,* Aug. 27, 1960; *Ring,* Sept. 1960.

CHAPTER 7: QUICKER THAN THE EYE

125   *Not much had gone as planned:* Ints., Lance Larson, Anne Warner (Cribbs); *Time,* Aug. 15, 1960, "Game Try"; *Sports Illustrated,* July 26, 1996, "Olympic Flashback: The Beginning of an American Dynasty."

127   *Watching from the press section:* Account of 100-meter freestyle drawn from Ints., Gian Paolo Ormezzano, Lance Larson; also *Tuttosport,* Aug. 28, 1960; New York *Herald Tribune,* Aug. 28, 1960; *New York Times,* Aug. 28, 1960; R. Max Ritter, "The Case of Larson vs. Devitt," *Amateur Athlete,* Dec. 1960. Ritter began his article: "I now respectfully submit to you the evidence which caused me as the United States representative to protest this hastily announced result of the 100-meter freestyle race, and I ask you to judge for yourselves if I was the 'willful' official who dared to question this result or if I was justified in trying to protect the interest of a competitor, who, in my opinion, had been placed unfairly and in an irregular manner."

132   *When U.S. officials began preparing their appeal:* Ints., Jim McKay, Bud Palmer, Frank Chirkinian; "CBS News Reveals Coverage Plan for 1960 Olympic Games in Rome," CBS News archive; *New York Times,* Aug. 21, 1960, "CBS Plans Same-Day Telecasts of Rome Olympic Games."

133   *By coincidence, an experimental U.S. communications satellite:* Associated Press report,

NOTES **447**

Aug. 12, 1960, "U.S. Launches Echo 1 Message Satellite"; Baltimore *Sun,* Aug. 29, 1960, "Survival Tests Passed by Echo"; San Francisco *Chronicle* editorial, Aug. 23, 1960, "A Look at 'Echo' Raises Questions." The *Chronicle* editorial took note of the civil war raging in the Congo, likening it to a proxy war between the superpowers, the U.S. and Soviet Union, and concluded: "Russians and Americans should look at their satellites and be ashamed. So long as satellites are designed primarily to spy on or kill other human beings, we are not in a position to proclaim the glories of Western culture to underdeveloped peoples."

133 *The contract with CBS News . . . was negotiated:* CBS News Agreement, Brundage collection. Agreement made as of the 8th day of June, 1959, by and between CBS News, a division of Columbia Broadcasting System, Inc., 485 Madison Avenue, New York, New York, and the Gardner Advertising Corporation, a Missouri corporation having a business office at 9 Rockefeller Plaza, New York, New York, as agent for the Comitato Organizzatore dei Giochi della XVII Olympiade, Via Crescenzio 14, Rome, Italy.

134 *For its Olympic coverage, CBS News assembled:* Ints., Jim McKay, Bud Palmer, Frank Chirkinian; also *New York Times,* Aug. 21, 1960; "Television in the Olympic Games, the New Era," IOC International Symposium, Lausanne, Oct. 20, 1998.

136 *Critics offered mixed reviews:* Boston *Globe,* Sept. 2, 1960, "Too Much Swimming Made Olympics Dull," John Crosby; *New York Times,* Aug. 29, 1960, "CBS Coverage of Olympics Shows an Awareness of the Broader Aspects": Baltimore *Sun,* Sept. 4, 1960, Donald Kirkley. "Sound reporting has been the rule," Kirkley wrote, "and there has been no attempt to sensationalize even the peaks of action. The story is being handled with skill and good judgment, as was the case in coverage of the national convention."

138 *News broke that morning that Oluf Jorgensen: Akfuelt,* Aug. 27, 1960; UPI account, Aug. 28, 1960; *Sports Illustrated,* Sept. 12, 1960; *New York Times,* Aug. 29, 1960. Robert Daley wrote that doping of bike racers was common in Europe. A Swiss rider had died in that country's amateur championships the year before, and an autopsy had shown drugs in his system. And in the spring of 1960, Daley reported, a French cyclist, Jean Graczyk, said that he took drugs but planned to stop. He said French cyclists used amphetamines. In the UPI account, Dr. Rene Mathieu, the chief doctor for the French Olympic team, said he had no evidence that the Danes took stimulants, "but I have had long experience in the stimulant problem with cyclists, and they certainly had all the symptoms of people who had taken something before the race."

140 *Suspicions of doping haunted Olympic history: The First Thirty Years of the International Olympic Committee Medical Commission,* Dr. Albert Dirix, IOC Medical Commission Archivist; *Origins and Aspects of Olympism,* chapter 8, John T. Powell.

141 *After Knud Enemark Jensen died:* Letter from Brundage and Otto Mayer to Danish authorities, Sept. 7, 1960, Mayer file, Olympics Studies Centre. "We would be very grateful if you would have a detailed report about the matter of your unfortunate deceased athlete sent to us as soon as your investigation is finished. Please let us know additionally what precautions you will take to avoid a repeat of such actions and what sanctions you will impose on those who were responsible"; also *Politiken,* Apr. 9, 2001, Lars Bogeskov.

142 *President Eisenhower had written:* State Department central files, NARA-College Park. The letter was written Aug. 26, 1960, but by Aug. 28 the State Department was still unable to get the message to Norman Armitage. In an outgoing telegram that day, State advised the Rome embassy: "If embassy unable deliver President's message to

Armitage by 11 a.m. Rome time, deliver message to Avery Brundage, making arrangements for earliest possible release in Rome."

143 *In the meantime, the Soviets staged: Pravda,* Aug. 29, 1960.

144 *At dinner, the conversation slowly turned toward the future:* Ints., David Sime, Igor Ter-Ovanesyan.

145 *That weekend . . . a Soviet athletic planning official:* UPI account, Tony Austin, Aug. 28, 1960; *Cleveland Call & Post,* Aug. 28, 1960; Ed Temple oral history, Nashville Public Library special collections.

CHAPTER 8: UPSIDE DOWN

148 *Manfred Ewald . . . was seen walking: Die Welt,* Aug. 30, 1960.

148 *To a brilliant old crank like A. J. Liebling: New Yorker,* Aug. 31, 1960.

150 *Kraemer knew less about the Americans:* Int., Ingrid Kraemer (German interpreter, Petra Krischok).

151 *Any medal showing was heralded: Neues Deutschland,* Aug. 28, 1960, "Ingrid Kraemer's Perfect Triumph."

153 *Germany in the late summer of 1960:* Ian Fleming, "Spying Is Big Business in Berlin," (London) *Sunday Times,* Aug. 7, 1960. Along with his fascination with the rubble from WWII and the veritable army of spies, Fleming took an interest in the transvestite nightclubs of Berlin. Of a bar named Eden he wrote: "The 'waitresses' were most ingenious at serving one while somehow keeping their huge hands and feet out of sight and modulating the deep tones of their voices when they took your order, but otherwise they were buttressed, bewigged, and made-up as extremely handsome and decorous 'ladies.' "

154 *At the White House that summer:* National Security Council, Operations Coordinating Board Report on U.S. Policy Toward Germany, series OCB, box 5, Eisenhower Presidential Library.

155 *East German officials said they felt compelled: Die Welt,* Aug. 29, 1960; *Frankfurter Allgemeine Zeitung,* Aug. 31–Sept. 4, 1960; Reuters report, Aug. 31, 1960.

156 *"They get along well with each other": Die Welt,* Aug. 30, 1960.

156 *Ingrid Kraemer had also emerged:* Int., Ingrid Kraemer; in Kurt Vonnegut's *Slaughterhouse-Five,* the main character, Billy Pilgrim, an American prisoner of war, survives the massive firebombing by taking shelter in an airtight meat locker in the basement of a former Dresden slaughterhouse.

158 *Whether that happened: Neues Deutschland,* Aug. 31, 1960; *Frankfurter Allgemeine Zeitung,* Aug. 31, 1960; *Los Angeles Times,* Aug. 31, 1960; "An Olympian's Oral History: Paula Jean Myers Pope," LA84.

159 *Was it really another proxy battle in the cold war?:* Int., Ingrid Kraemer; also *Frankfurter Allgemeine Zeitung,* Aug. 31–Sept. 1, 1960; *Die Welt,* Aug. 31–Sept. 1, 1960; *Neues Deutschland,* Sept. 1, 1960.

CHAPTER 9: TRACK & FIELD NEWS

161 *Riding a streetcar from the YMCA hotel:* Ints., Cordner Nelson, Nancy Nelson.

162 *From depth charts listing:* Ints., Cordner Nelson, Nancy Nelson. In keeping with *Track*

& Field News's dismissive attitude toward female athletes, the Nelson Competition involved only men's events.

163 *Print still ruled: Nashville Banner,* Aug. 10–23, 1960; San Francisco *Chronicle,* Aug. 18–25, 1960; Red Smith, "Road to Rome," New York *Herald Tribune,* Aug. 21, 1960: "Little Becky Trueheart took the hills like a bird. Little Becky is a Peugeot sedan that was picked up in Paris, and not even the hairpin turns and dizzying heights of the Grossglocknerhochalpenstrasse could faze her. She made it a comfortable journey."

163 *Shirley Povich . . . brought along . . . his own aide-de-camp:* Int., Don Graham; also *The Games of the XVII Olympiad, Rome 1960.*

164 *It was a movable feast:* Int., Robert Creamer; *The Games of the XVII Olympiad, Rome 1960.*

165 *Aside from the private parties: New Yorker,* Aug. 31, 1960.

165 *Most foreign correspondents were not:* Int., Gian Paolo Ormezzano; *The Games of the XVII Olympiad, Rome, 1960.*

166 *Dave Sime arrived at the stadium:* Ints., Dave Sime, Joe Faust; also *1960 United States Olympic Book.*

168 *For the quarterfinal round:* Ints., Dave Sime, Don Graham; Ray Norton oral history, NBC archive; *The Tipping Olympics; Il Messaggero,* Sept. 2, 1960; *Die Welt,* Sept. 3, 1960.

169 *Hary did his own part:* Int., Lute Mason; Scripps Howard syndicate, Jesse Owens as told to Paul G. Neimark, Aug. 31, 1960; UPI account, Aug. 31, 1960; also *Sprinter of the Century,* Rome chapter.

170 *About the time the cheering died down:* Int., Dallas Long; also Parry O'Brien oral history, *Tales of Gold; Sport,* Aug. 1960; *1960 United States Olympic Book; Track & Field News,* Sept. 1960.

173 *In the cafeterias at the Olympic Village:* Ints., Dave Sime, Robert Creamer; also Ray Norton oral history, NBC archive; *Los Angeles Times,* Sept. 1, 1960; *New York Times,* Sept. 1, 1960; *Sprinter of the Century,* Rome chapter; Scripps Howard syndicate, Jesse Owens as told to Neimark, Sept. 1, 1960.

CHAPTER 10: BLACK THURSDAY

176 *Late in the afternoon, at a quarter after five:* Ints., Dave Sime, Don Graham, Robert Creamer, Cordner Nelson, Ed Temple, Lucinda Williams, Joe Faust, Livio Berruti; also Ray Norton oral history, NBC archive; *Sprinter of the Century,* Rome chapter; *Track & Field News,* Sept. 1960; *Sports Illustrated,* Sept. 5, 1960; *Time,* Sept. 12, 1960; *Life,* Sept. 1960; *Los Angeles Times,* Sept. 2, 1960; *Washington Post,* Sept. 2, 1960; *1960 United States Olympic Book; The Road to Rome,* "The Biggest Sprint of All, Peter Radford."

182 *Even in sprinting, the most elemental sport:* Official film of the 1960 Rome Olympics; *Sprinter of the Century,* Rome chapter.

183 *The finger tightened on the trigger:* Description of the 100-meter final drawn from Ints., Dave Sime, Ed Temple, Don Graham; *Olympic Diary,* Neil Allen; *1960 United States Olympic Book; Die Welt,* Sept. 2, 1960; *Frankfurter Allgemeine Zeitung,* Sept. 2, 1960; *Track & Field News,* Sept. 1960; Scripps Howard syndicate, Jesse Owens as told to Neimark, Sept. 2, 1960; *Sports Illustrated,* Sept. 5, 1960; *New York Times,* Sept. 2, 1960; New

York *Herald Tribune,* Sept. 2, 1960; *Rome Daily American,* Sept. 2, 1960; *Pravda,* Sept. 3, 1960; *Los Angeles Times,* Sept. 2, 1960; *Nashville Banner,* Sept. 2, 1960; *Times* of London, Sept. 2, 1960; *Sprinter of the Century,* Rome chapter; *Pitch Invasion* (pp. 67–68); Notes, box 246, Brundage collection (first cited *The Games Must Go On,* Guttmann, p. 168).

189 *In the Boston area that morning: Boston Globe,* Sept. 1, 1960.

190 *"This is a sensation!": Izvestia,* Sept. 2, 1960.

191 *But Nason was worried:* Description of high-jump final drawn from Ints., John Thomas, Cord Nelson, Joe Faust; also *Boston Globe,* Sept. 2, 1960; *Track & Field News,* Sept. 1960; *Sports Illustrated,* Sept. 5, 1960; *Pravda,* Sept. 2, 1960; *Izvestia,* Sept. 2, 1960; "Testing Service to the Queen," Gavriel Korobkov; *Chicago Tribune,* Sept. 2, 1960; New York *Herald Tribune,* Sept. 2, 1960; *Nashville Banner,* Sept. 2, 1960.

193 *His parents were fine:* New York *Herald Tribune,* Sept. 2, 1960; *Los Angeles Times,* Sept. 2, 1960; *Newsweek,* Sept. 5, 1960.

195 *At the Palazzetto dello Sport:* UPI account, Sept. 1, 1960; Pete Newell oral history, NBC archive.

196 *Shatkov was anything but crude:* Ints., Bud Palmer, Lute Mason, Nikos Spanakos; *Ring,* Oct. 1960; Mikhail Lukashev, "The Discovery of Boxing America."

197 *Traditionalists thought his style . . . : Chicago Tribune,* Apr. 29, 1959; Jim Doherty, "At 17, Ali Charmed Madison," *Wisconsin State Journal,* Oct. 26, 2005.

198 *The Olympic Trials were held:* San Francisco *Chronicle,* May 18–20, 1960.

199 *Gennady Shatkov, like Clay:* Mikhail Lukashev, "The Discovery of Boxing America."

INTERLUDE: DESCENDING WITH GRATITUDE

200 *It could be said that Joe Faust:* Story of Joe Faust based on interviews and correspondence with Joe Faust and meeting at his house in Los Angeles; also *1960 United States Olympic Book; Track & Field News,* July, Aug., Sept. 1960.

CHAPTER 11: THE WIND AT HER BACK

205 *Ed Temple was so worried:* Int., Ed Temple.

206 *During a training jog with the Tigerbelles:* Ints., Lucinda Williams, Ed Temple; also Nashville *Tennessean,* Sept. 3, 1960.

207 *As a child, Wilma was underweight:* Ints., Ed Temple, Lucinda Williams; Yvonne Rudolph oral history, NBC archive; Alex Haley, May 1961 *Rotarian* magazine; Vivian Bernice Lee Adkins, "The Development of the Negro Female Olympic Talent," Indiana University thesis, 1967; *Wilma Rudolph, Champion Athlete,* Biracree; Barbara Heilman, "Like Nothing Else in Tennessee," *Sports Illustrated,* Nov. 14, 1960.

210 *When the Tigerbelles returned:* Int., David Halberstam.

212 *Now, on this Friday afternoon . . . in Rome:* Int., Ed Temple.

212 *Until Wilma Rudolph awoke:* New York *Times,* Sept. 3, 1960; *Detroit Times,* Sept. 3, 1960; Eddy Gilmore, Associated Press account, Sept. 2, 1960; *Washington Post,* Sept. 3, 1960; Ints., Lucinda Williams, Rafer Johnson, John Thomas.

215 *Winning . . . was by no means only an American obsession: Rome Daily American,* Sept. 3, 1960; Associated Press account, Sept. 3, 1960. "Sports experts said it was the first time such a fix charge had ever been made in the Olympics. The allegation had the whole Olympic Village talking the next day."

216 *The Olympic spirit was also under assault:* UPI account, Sept. 3, 1960; *New Yorker,* Aug. 31, 1960; Letter from Brundage to Count Henri Latour regarding boxing at 1936 Berlin Olympics, boxes 129, 248, Brundage collection.

217 *Once again, the Germans:* Int., Lute Mason; UPI account, Sept. 3, 1960; also *Sprinter of the Century.*

219 *It was that versatility . . . that made Davis like a brother:* Int., Rafer Johnson; Glenn Davis oral history, *Tales of Gold; New York Times,* Sept. 3, 1960; New York *Herald Tribune,* Sept. 3, 1960; *Die Welt,* Sept. 3, 1960; *Columbus Dispatch,* Sept. 3, 1961.

221 *When not extolling the virtues: Rome Daily American,* Aug. 25–Sept. 10, 1960; Grombach file, box 26, Brundage collection; Otto Mayer file, OSC, Lausanne; Senate Internal Security Subcommittee record group 46, Brundage file, Grombach file, NARA-Washington.

222 *In the . . . stadium sat Jesse Owens:* UPI account, Sept. 3, 1960; Scripps Howard syndicate, Jesse Owens to Neimark, Sept. 3, 1960; *Nashville Banner,* Sept. 3, 1960; Nashville *Tennessean,* Sept. 3, 1960; Ints., Ed Temple, Lucinda Williams; *Track & Field News,* Sept. 1960, *Amateur Athlete,* Oct. 1960.

223 *Next came Ter-Ovanesyan:* Int., Igor Ter-Ovanesyan (Knesia Boitsova, interpreter); also *Track & Field News,* Sept. 1960.

224 *All that remained was the final jump:* Nashville *Tennessean,* Sept. 3, 1960; *Los Angeles Times,* Sept. 3, 1960; Brett Hoover, "The Bo You Didn't Know," *Ivy League Sports Newsletter.* In this intriguing article, Hoover quotes Jeremy Schaap, the son of sportswriter Dick Schaap, who was a classmate of Bo Roberson's at Cornell, saying, "He was convinced Bo Roberson was the best natural athlete ever in the Ivy League."

225 *Only twenty minutes earlier:* Int., Ed Temple; also *Nashville Banner,* Sept. 3, 1960; official film of the Rome Olympics.

CHAPTER 12: LIBERATION

228 *What a bella festa:* Int., Gian Paolo Ormezzano (Kathryn Wallace, interpreter).

229 *There was one other thing:* Ints., Livio Berruti, Gian Paolo Ormezzano, Rino Tommasi.

230 *The 200 had always been:* Int., Dave Sime.

230 *With Sime gone to the coast:* Ints., Dave Sime, Livio Berruti; Ray Norton oral history, NBC archive.

231 *Perhaps because it was a Saturday:* Ints., Cordner Nelson, Nancy Nelson.

231 *He was ahead at 70 meters:* Ints., Livio Berruti, Gian Paolo Ormezzano, Don Graham, Cordner Nelson; also *Rome Daily American,* Sept. 4, 1960; Associated Press account, Sept. 3, 1960.

232 *Off to the side stood Ray Norton:* Ray Norton oral history, NBC archive; Int., Rafer Johnson; Nashville *Tennessean,* Sept. 3, 1960, Raymond Johnson column.

234 *Tickets were so tight:* Letter of thanks from Zellerbach to Avery Brundage, Brundage collection.

234 *Some of the best views in the house:* Int., Dallas Long.

234 *The United States . . . had dominated Olympic competition:* National Basketball Hall of Fame archive, Springfield, Massachusetts.

235 *Spandarian was further encouraged: Pravda,* Sept. 2, 1960; UPI account, Aug. 24, 1960.

235 *In preparing his team:* Newell oral history, NBC archive.

236 *The consequences of East-West tensions:* Jerry West oral history, NBC archive; Geoff

Calkins, "West Knows the Horror of War All Too Well," Memphis *Commercial Appeal,* March 31, 2003. Calkins began his compelling story: "Thirteen-year-old Jerry West went to go fetch the mail for his mother Cecile. This was 1951 in Cheylan, West Virginia. Going to fetch the mail back then didn't mean walking to the end of the driveway. It meant walking to the post office in Cabin Creek. Jerry, a good son, volunteered for the job. When he arrived at the post office, he ran into a neighbor. All these years later, West still flinches at the memory. 'He told me my brother had been killed in Korea.' "

236   *Meaning comes from life experience:* Oscar Robertson oral history, NBC archive.

236   *After West scored the first basket: 1960 United States Olympic Book; Los Angeles Times,* Sept. 3, 1960; San Francisco *Chronicle,* Sept. 3, 1960; Newell oral history, NBC archive.

240   *It had been a trying year:* Int., Peter Bos; also USNA athletic department archive, 1960 Navy crew; *Sports Illustrated,* July 18, 1960, "The Old Navy Way"; *The Years of MacArthur,* vol. 1, Dorris Clayton James (pp. 138–139).

243   *Inspiration in heavyweight rowing: Frankfurter Allgemeine Zeitung,* Sept. 4, 1960; *Die Welt,* Aug. 26, 1960.

245   *Bynum Shaw of the Baltimore* Sun: Bynum Shaw, Sept. 9, 1960, "New Republic on the Rhine," Baltimore *Sun.* Aside from the Olympic coverage, Bynum wrote of East German television, "The rest of the TV day, about four hours at best, is given over to documentary films, dull interviews, boring political lectures, or a piece of heavy drama. Ballet or opera makes the grade occasionally, and on Sunday the children have a dubbed version of *Lassie.*"

246   *That night, Dave Sime and Jim Beatty:* Ints., Dave Sime, Jim Beatty, Eraldo Pizzo.

CHAPTER 13: THE RUSSIANS ARE COMING

248   *The second Sunday of the Olympics:* A. Dyakov, B. Petrusenko, and C. Narinyani, "Big Day of Friendship," *Pravda,* Sept. 5, 1960. Their account of the journey began: "It is a hot, sunny day, and on the way to new Appia there are four large buses driving fast, bypassing little villages and great plantations around them. Soviet songs can be heard from the buses."

249   *Another day of propaganda:* Associated Press report, Sept. 5, 1960.

250   *The American press and public began:* "What I Saw in Three Weeks Behind the Iron Curtain," Avery Brundage speech to Economic Club of Detroit, box 245, Brundage collection; also *Saturday Evening Post,* Apr. 30, 1955, "I Must Admit—Russian Athletes Are Great!" by Avery Brundage. The article was ghostwritten by sportswriter Will Grimsley and edited by Harry T. Paxton at the *Saturday Evening Post.* In one editing exchange with Brundage, Paxton wrote: "I can appreciate your fears about being mistaken for a Communist sympathizer, but it seems to me that you have already taken care of this with such statements as, 'I do not mean we should adopt Russia's methods. That would not be the American way.' And 'The Russians were well aware of my view on Communism.' I had been denounced frequently as 'an imperialistic agent and a shameless capitalist.' If you want to spell this out even more explicitly, wouldn't the purpose be served by inserting a sentence to the effect that you went to Russia solely to pass judgment on their sports program, and not on their political system?" That sentence was indeed inserted into the article.

253   *The Domus Mariae, headquarters for foreign correspondents: Olympic diary,* Neil Allen;
      Observer, Sept. 4, 1960; *Times* of London, Sept. 5, 1960; *New York Times,* Sept. 5, 1960;
      Die Welt, Sept. 4, 1960; Nashville *Tennessean,* Sept. 4, 1960; *Pravda,* Sept. 4–5, 1960.

255   *Rome teemed with spies:* Correspondence with Ieva Lesinska-Geibere, daughter of the
      late Imants Lesinskis; Benjamin Smith, "How a Double Agent's Daughter Dealt with
      Life after Defection," *Wall Street Journal,* July 6, 2001. In Smith's fascinating account,
      Lesinskis finally gave up his life as a double agent and openly defected to the U.S. with
      his daughter in 1974. "Some Latvian émigrés suspected that he was not a defector but a
      Soviet plant," Smith wrote. "Asked by the American Latvian Society 'to set the record
      straight,' [a CIA spokesman] would only state that . . . 'Mr. Lesinskis' courage, dedica-
      tion, and true patriotism were well known to most of us here."

257   *There were KGB agents circling around the team:* Int., Igor Ter-Ovanesyan; also tran-
      scripts, Igor Ter-Ovanesyan, Lev Markov, Konstantin Gyanov, *The Red Files,* PBS.

257   *Sime did not know what to expect this time:* Ints., David Sime, Igor Ter-Ovanesyan.

259   *In the capital of the Free World: Washington Post,* Sept. 5, 1960.

259   *Johnson had spent much of that Sunday evening:* Int., Rafer Johnson.

CHAPTER 14: THE GREATEST

261   *The dense sky was familiar:* Int., Rafer Johnson; also *China Daily News,* Sept. 6, 1960;
      New York Times, Sept. 6, 1960; New York *Herald Tribune,* Sept. 6, 1960.

263   *Although a test of endurance:* Int., David Edstrom; *1960 United States Olympic Book;*
      Track & Field News, Sept. 1960.

265   *He knew how important:* Int., Rafer Johnson; conversation with Rafer Johnson and
      C. K. Yang transcript, LA84; *Track & Field News,* Sept. 1960.

266   *Across the Tiber . . . that lunch hour:* Jack Simes diary.

267   *"You have to be in Rome on a rainy day": L'Équipe,* Sept. 6, 1960.

267   *It was almost three o'clock:* Ints., Rafer Johnson, David Edstrom.

268   *Calhoun, the defending gold medalist:* Ints., Gwen Calhoun, Roger Gimbel, Harrison
      Dillard; also Lee Calhoun oral history, *Tales of Gold; New York Times,* Aug. 9, 1957;
      Track & Field News, Jan. 1958, Sept. 1960; *Chicago Defender,* Aug. 5, 1957; *Los Angeles
      Times,* Sept. 6, 1960; *Olympic Diary,* Neil Allen; *L'Équipe,* Sept. 7, 1960. When Calhoun
      was suspended, Ferris pointed to General Rule VII, Section 1d, of the AAU code that
      said no athlete could capitalize on his athletic fame.

272   *Earlier in the competition:* Ints., Ed Temple, Lucinda Williams, Anne Warner (Cribbs);
      1960 United States Olympic Book; Nashville *Tennessean,* Sept. 6, 1960.

276   *By then the conditions:* Int., Rafer Johnson; conversation with Rafer Johnson and C. K.
      Yang transcript, LA84; C. K. Yang oral history, NBC archive; New York *Herald Tri-
      bune,* Sept. 6, 1960; *Los Angeles Times,* Sept. 6, 1960; *1960 United States Olympic Book;*
      Washington Post, Sept. 6, 1960.

277   *The rains continued:* Ints., Bud Palmer, Lute Mason, Jerry Armstrong, Nikos Spanakos,
      Rino Tomassi; Wilbert McClure oral history, NBC archive; Pete Newell oral history,
      NBC archive; *Olympic Diary,* Neil Allen; *Red Smith's Sports Annual 1961; Washington
      Post,* Sept. 6, 1960; *Ring,* Sept.–Oct. 1960; official film of the Rome 1960 Olympics; *1960
      United States Olympic Book.*

283   *Their competition had resumed:* Int., Rafer Johnson.

CHAPTER 15: THE LAST LAPS

285 *Everyone seemed up and about:* Ints., Lucinda Williams, Dallas Long, Nikos Spanakos, David Sime, Ed Temple; Louisville *Courier-Journal,* Sept. 7, 1960.

287 *Rafer Johnson was also up early:* Int., Rafer Johnson.

288 *The seventh event:* Int., Rafer Johnson; transcript of conversation with Rafer Johnson and C. K. Yang transcript, LA84; C. K. Yang oral history, NBC archive; *Track & Field News,* Sept. 1960, *Sports Illustrated,* Sept. 12, 1960; *1960 United States Olympic Book;* official film of 1960 Rome Olympics; *Los Angeles Times,* Sept. 8, 1960; *New York Times,* Sept. 8, 1960; *Pravda,* Sept. 9, 1960.

290 *Of that group, the most exotic: Times of India,* "A Commentary by AFST"; *Sikh Heritage,* "The Flying Sikh," 2006.

291 *Davis came from Bill Bowerman's renowned track program:* Ints., Otis Davis, David Edstrom, Cordner Nelson; New York *Herald Tribune,* Sept. 8, 1960; Associated Press account, Sept. 7, 1960; *Bowerman and the Men of Oregon* (pp. 110–112); *Track & Field News,* Aug.–Sept. 1960.

295 *Here was an impressive assortment:* (London) *Sunday Times,* Sept. 5, 1960; *Why Die? The Extraordinary Percy Cerutty.*

296 *Elliott and Cerutty made a lasting impression:* Ints., Cordner Nelson, Nancy Nelson.

297 *At the race's start:* Ints., Jim Beatty, Don Graham, Cordner Nelson; official film of the 1960 Rome Olympics; *New York Times,* Sept. 8, 1960; *The Tipping Olympics,* E. W. Tipping; *Olympic Diary,* Neil Allen; Associated Press account, Sept. 7, 1960; *Times* of London, Sept. 8, 1960; *Le Miroir des Sports,* Sept. 8, 1960.

300 *Darkness had fallen:* Ints., Rafer Johnson, Lucinda Williams, Ed Temple, David Edstrom, Don Graham, John A. Lucas, Cordner Nelson; C. K. Yang oral history, NBC archive; Pete Newell oral history, NBC archive; conversation with Rafer Johnson and C. K. Yang transcript, LA84; *Track & Field News,* Sept.–Oct. 1960; *Sports Illustrated,* Sept. 12, 1960; *Pravda,* Sept. 9, 1960; *1960 United States Olympic Book; New York Times,* Sept. 8, 1960; *Los Angeles Times,* Sept. 8, 1960; American diplomatic legation, Budapest, dispatch to State Department, Nicholas Feld, Oct. 3, 1960, State Department central file, NARA-College Park. While the Hungarians refused to acknowledge Yang, Feld reported that in other respects the Olympics promoted some measure of goodwill between his legation and Hungarian officials. "When the reporting officer paid a call on a Foreign Ministry official on the day the American swimmers had won several events, the official was quick to offer congratulations, which were duly reciprocated by congratulations on the pentathlon victories of the Hungarians. This is the kind of reciprocity which the legation, unfortunately, does not enjoy in its other dealings with the Hungarian regime."

306 *Yang's silver medal was the top story: China Daily News,* Sept. 8, 1960.

CHAPTER 16: NEW WORLDS

308 *Before President Eisenhower held a press conference:* Briefing Papers for the President's Press Conference, September 7, 1960, and Official White House Transcript of President Eisenhower's Press and Radio Conference No. 191 (filmed, taped, and shorthand reported). Held in room 474, Executive Office Building, Wednesday, September 7,

1960, 10:30 o'clock a.m., Press Conference Series, box 8, Eisenhower Presidential Library.

309 *There was growing concern:* Incoming telegram from Rome to Secretary of State, No. 1026, September 8, 4 p.m., State Department Rome file, NARA-College Park.

311 *Hours before . . . Rafer Johnson appeared:* Int., Rafer Johnson; Associated Press account, Sept. 8, 1960.

311 *Also breaking ground was Ljudmila Shevstova-Lysenko:* Minutes of IOC session, Munich, May 25, 1959; *1960 United States Olympic Book*; Mary Leigh and Therese Bonin, 1977. Sheila Mitchell, *Journal of Sport History,* vol. 4, no. 2. Bridget Mary Handley, Rhodes University thesis, 1976; UPI account, Sept. 8, 1960; Int., Don Graham; *Los Angeles Times,* Sept. 9, 1960.

315 *Eight long days and nights had passed:* Int., Rink Babka; Otis Chandler obituary, *Los Angeles Times,* Feb. 27, 2006.

321 *That was too much of a bump-up for Morris:* Don Bragg oral history, *Tales of Gold; Track & Field News,* Sept. 1960; *Sports Illustrated,* Sept. 12, 1960.

321 *One more day of track and field: New York Times,* Sept. 8, 1960; *1960 United States Olympic Book.*

322 *At his press conference in Washington:* Official White House Transcript of President Eisenhower's Press and Radio Conference, Press Conference Series, box 8, Eisenhower Presidential Library.

322 *That night in Moscow:* Incoming telegram from Moscow to Secretary of State, No. 686, September 7, 11 p.m., Herter papers, box 13, Eisenhower Presidential Library.

CHAPTER 17: THE SOFT LIFE

324 *Only three days of competition remained: New Yorker,* Sept. 11, 1960. "Once the seats [inside the Stadio Olimpico] seemed hard and narrow; at the end we had become hardened and narrowed to them," Liebling wrote.

324 *On the go from dawn to midnight:* Handwritten daily diary, August–September 1960, Brundage collection; *Rome Daily American,* Sept. 8, 1960.

325 *This meant the Olympic Movement:* Rome, Sept. 8, 1960, handwritten notes for speech to the American Club of Rome, box 246, Brundage collection. The outlines of Brundage's speech were on eleven note cards. The day after the speech, Brundage received a letter from Gordon E. Dawson, a retired colonel who was president of the club, thanking him for a "frank and stimulating talk, and adding: Personally I agree with you 100% on all your points. As far back as when I was an undergraduate, I was out of sympathy with the 'big business' aspect of college athletics at the expense of a wide program for everyone . . . Your words of yesterday and the final U.S. showing in this Olympiad should do something to awaken our political leaders to the need for a nationwide athletic and physical fitness program."

327 *Red Smith of the* Herald Tribune: Red Smith, "Avery of Sparta," New York *Herald Tribune,* Sept. 12, 1960.

327 *There was . . . far more to the contradiction: Sports Illustrated,* Aug. 4, 1980, "The Man behind the Mask," William Oscar Johnson. This other side of Brundage, revealed five years after his death, still seemed shocking, Johnson wrote. "After all, Brundage was considered so straitlaced that a barber at Chicago's LaSalle Hotel, which Brundage owned, would censor the stories that were being told as soon as the boss walked into

the shop. In retrospect, these stories were probably nothing compared to the ones Avery himself could have provided."

328 *In a letter to Brundage:* July 4, 1960, letter to Brundage, Burghley file, OSC, Lausanne.

328 *Many athletes had individual stories:* Int., Abe Grossfeld; May 16, 1960, open letter to Avery Brundage and Dan Ferris (AAU president) from Washington lawyer Melchior Savarese, Brundage collection, amateurism file. Savarese argued that Rafer Johnson's injuries might prevent him from defeating Vasily Kuznetsov, and that Mathias's request to qualify as an amateur was thus motivated by his patriotic duty to beat the Soviets. He asked how Ferris and Brundage could reject Mathias as a professional because of his acting career and yet allow the Soviets to compete even though they were sponsored by the state. "There is no question in anyone's mind that the Communists use all things to advance the cause of Communism," Savarese wrote. "There is no field of endeavor too big or small in which they do not dabble"; also letter from K. S. Duncan of British Olympic Assn. to Col. Ansell of British Horse Society, Nov. 20, 1959, amateurism file, OCS, Lausanne.

329 *Most were of a pettier nature:* Ints., Nikos Spanakos, Isaac Berger, James Bradford, Don Graham, Rino Tommasi.

330 *Brundage's view of amateurism:* Brundage memo to self, undated, early 1950s, Brundage collection.

331 *But could he ever win his "perpetual battle"?:* 34th IOC Session, Warsaw, 1937 session, box 75, Brundage collection.

331 *Led by delegate Albert Mayer: L' Echo Illustré,* Geneva, Aug. 20, 1960.

332 *For the athletes from Germany's Eastern zone: Neues Deutschland,* Sept. 9, 1960; also *Neues Deutschland,* Aug. 26–Sept. 10, 1960.

334 *But journalists from West Germany: Die Welt,* Sept. 9, 1960; *Frankfurter Allgemeine Zeitung,* Sept. 8–9, 1960.

335 *First up was the men's 4 x 400:* Ints., Otis Davis, Cord Nelson; *Track & Field News,* Sept. 1960; *Columbus Dispatch,* Sept. 9, 1960; Nashville *Tennessean,* Sept. 9, 1960; New York *Herald Tribune,* Sept. 9, 1960; *Die Welt,* Sept. 9, 1960; UPI account, Sept. 8, 1960; *Times of India,* Sept. 10, 1960; *1960 United States Olympic Book; Olympic Diary,* Neil Allen.

336 *At six that morning, back in Nashville:* Ints., Ed Temple, Lucinda Williams; *Sports Illustrated,* Nov. 14, 1960; *Sports Illustrated,* Sept. 12, 1960; "The Development of the Negro Female Olympic Talent," Adkins; *Nashville Banner,* Sept. 9, 1960; Nashville *Tennessean,* Sept. 9, 1960; *Frankfurter Allgemeine Zeitung,* Sept. 9, 1960; *Pravda,* Sept. 9, 1960; *Rome Daily American,* Sept. 9, 1960; *1960 United States Olympic Book.*

341 *Now here came Sime and his teammates:* Ints., Dave Sime, Cordner Nelson, Don Graham, Ed Temple, Lucinda Williams, Jim Beatty; Ray Norton oral history, NBC archive; *Track & Field News,* Sept. 1960; *Die Welt,* Sept. 9, 1960; *Frankfurter Allgemeine Zeitung,* Sept. 9, 1960; *Sprinter of the Century,* Rome chapter; New York *Herald Tribune,* Sept. 9, 1960; *New York Times,* Sept. 9, 1960; *Sports Illustrated,* Sept. 12, 1960; *1960 United States Olympic Book.*

344 *Almost every night since August 31:* Ints., Cordner Nelson, John Lucas; "Testing Service to the Queen," Gavriel Korobkov.

CHAPTER 18: "SUCCESSFUL COMPLETION OF THE JOB"

348 *They competed for the world championship:* The accounts of field hockey in Pakistan and India and of the gold medal game are drawn from: *The Games of the XVII Olympiad Rome 1960,* vols. 1 and 2; *Times of India,* Sept. 10, 1960; *Pakistan Times,* Sept. 10, 1960; Official White House transcript of President Eisenhower's Press and Radio Conference, Sept. 7, 1960, box 8, Eisenhower Presidential Library; *Times* of London, Sept. 10, 1960; official website of the Pakistan Hockey Federation; *World Hockey News,* Apr. 20, 2005; Melbourne *Age,* Mar. 19, 2006; *Indian Hockey,* Sept. 9, 2004.

351 *In the U.S. delegation, among the first to depart:* Int., Anne Warner (Cribbs); San Francisco *Chronicle,* Sept. 1, 1960.

352 *The boxers returned at the same time:* Ints., Jerry Armstrong, Nikos Spanakos; Louisville *Courier-Journal,* Sept. 7–10, 1960; *King of the World,* Remnick; *Muhammad Ali,* Hauser.

354 *Wilma Rudolph and the Tennessee State relay team:* Ints., Ed Temple, Lucinda Williams.

355 *He was joined by Dave Sime:* Int., Dave Sime.

356 *The U.S. hope was James Bradford:* Int., James Bradford; also *Washington Post,* June 17, 1960; *Rome Daily American,* Sept. 11–12, 1960; *Pravda,* Sept. 10–12, 1960; Artie Drechsler, "The Jim Bradford Story," *Iron Game History,* vol. 6, no. 3.

360 *There was another apparent connection:* John D. Fair, *Muscletown USA;* Terry Todd, *Journal of Sport History,* vol. 14, 1987 (pp. 188–189).

364 *Over at the Palazzo dello Sport, the medals were being awarded:* Ints., Bud Palmer, Lute Mason; also Newell, Robertson, West oral histories, NBC archive; *Rome Daily American,* Sept. 12, 1960; *Los Angeles Times,* Sept. 10, 1960.

366 *Nikita Khrushchev was on his way:* Taubman, *Khrushchev: The Man and His Era* (pp. 473–474). "Khrushchev decided to travel to New York by ship," Taubman wrote. "He dreamed of arriving there like the first American settlers he had read about in his youth . . ."

CHAPTER 19: A THOUSAND SENTINELS

367 *At their assembly point atop the Campidoglio:* Official film of the 1960 Rome Olympics.

367 *Gordon McKenzie, one of three Americans in the race:* Int., Gordon McKenzie.

369 *Only two of the nearly one hundred competitors:* Statistics gleaned from *The Games of the XVII Olympiad, Rome 1960; 1960 United States Olympic Book.*

369 *He had been especially taken:* A. J. Liebling, *New Yorker,* Sept. 11, 1960.

369 *Fallacy or not:* Int., Gian Paolo Ormezzano. The Italian journalist recalled that he finally met Abebe Bikila years later, after the accident that had placed the great Olympian in a wheelchair, and tried to remind him about how they had been cheering him on along the marathon route, "but Bikila spoke very little English [or Italian] and didn't understand."

371 *In the last seconds before the starting gun:* Int., Silvio deFlorentis (Kathryn Wallace, interpreter); also *Arthur Lydiard, Master Coach* (pp. 72–73).

371 *At half past five the marathoners went off:* Official film of the 1960 Rome Olympics.

372 *By then the story, real or myth:* John A. Lucas, "A History of the Marathon Race," *Journal of Sport History,* vol. 3, no. 2, 1976; also manuscript of *The Olympic Story* by Avery Brundage, chapter 3, Brundage collection. Brundage wrote of the first marathon in

1896: "When an unknown Greek shepherd boy, Spiridon Loues, followed by two of his countrymen, led the line of runners into the stadium, all disappointments were forgotten. Hailed by the princes who escorted him to the finish and then to his majesty, the king, for congratulations, Loues became the hero of the Games. There was a tremendous surge of national pride and enthusiasm, and all Greece was on fire. Greece thus became the first country converted to the Olympic idea."

373 *In the early going:* Description of the race drawn from Ints., Gordon McKenzie, Silvio deFlorentis, Robert Creamer, Don Graham, Dave Sime, Ed Temple, Jim Beatty, Cordner Nelson, Gian Paolo Ormezzano; Gordon McKenzie diary, 1960 (McKenzie kept a daily diary throughout his running career; little black books that recorded statistics on his eating habits, physical condition, sleeping hours, and how he felt running that day); Jack Simes diary; *Olympic Diary,* Neil Allen; official film of the 1960 Rome Olympics; *Ethiopian Herald,* Sept. 11–14, 1960; *1960 United States Olympic Book; Track & Field News,* Sept.–Oct. 1960; *Sports Illustrated,* Sept. 12, 1960; *Times* of London, Sept. 12, 1960; UPI account, Sept. 10, 1960; *New Yorker,* Sept. 11, 1960; *Pravda,* Sept. 11, 1960; *Arthur Lydiard, Master Coach* (p. 73); *Bowerman and the Men of Oregon; Los Angeles Times,* Sept. 11, 1960; *Washington Post,* Sept. 11, 1960; *Boston Globe,* Sept. 11, 1960; Reuters, Sept. 10, 1960; New York *Herald Tribune,* Sept. 11, 1960; *New York Times,* Sept. 11, 1960.

CHAPTER 20: "THE WORLD IS STIRRING"

380 *Avery Brundage once wrote:* Undated Brundage memo, Brundage collection.
380 *For the Closing Ceremony in Rome:* Official film of the 1960 Rome Olympics; Ints., Rino Tommasi, Livio Berruti, Ingrid Kraemer; *The Games of the XVII Olympiad, Rome 1960; 1960 United States Olympic Book;* "Olympic Bulletin Newsletter," Oct. 1960; *Rome Daily American,* Sept. 12, 1960; *Pravda,* Sept. 12, 1960; *Frankfurter Allgemeine Zeitung,* Sept. 12, 1960; *Neues Deutschland,* Sept. 12, 1960; *Washington Post,* Sept. 12, 1960; *New York Times,* Sept. 12, 1960; *Boston Globe,* Sept. 12, 1960; New York *Herald Tribune,* Sept. 12, 1960; *Ethiopian Herald,* Sept. 12, 1960; *Los Angeles Times,* Sept. 12, 1960; Reuters report, Sept. 11–12, 1960; A. J. Liebling, *New Yorker,* Sept. 11, 1960.
382 *The morning after the Closing Ceremony:* Ints., Gian Paolo Ormezzano, Livio Berruti.
383 *Many of Ormezzano's colleagues:* Statistics drawn from *1960 United States Olympic Book.*
383 *As Arthur Daley of the* Times *examined:* New York Times, Sept. 12, 1960. Daley added: "Once every four years the U.S. stirs slightly and discovers that it has to assemble teams in sports it has been ignoring. The Russians are prepared, and so is up-and-coming Germany, the most intensely nationalistic nation of any here, even though a divided Germany competed under a compromise flag."
384 *Also lingering in Rome were:* Pravda, Sept. 12, 1960. The *Pravda* account also cherry-picked positive comments about the Soviet team from newspapers around the world. Perhaps something was lost, or changed, in translation, but from *Pravda's* account, there was global unanimity on the Soviet domination.
385 *Leaving aside the larger controversy:* U.S. officials had been aware of the Soviet advantage in gymnastics for many years and from the start were concerned about how that advantage could be used in propaganda. A September 30, 1954, White House memorandum on a meeting with United States Information Agency officials stated: "The Soviets lay great emphasis on gymnastics in their athletic program and as a conse-

quence generally far surpass other competitors in these events to such a degree it permits them to claim unofficial top score in the games though they may be overshadowed in the other events which are regarded as much more important by all other nations."

385 *But if Rome marked:* White House central files, box 734, Eisenhower Presidential Library; *Sports Illustrated,* Dec. 26, 1960, "The Soft American." In the article, Kennedy presented a four-point plan to restore America to physical health. His plan included establishing a White House Committee on Health and Fitness, ordering the Department of Health, Education, and Welfare to conduct research on the best physical fitness programs for public schools, inviting the governors to an annual Youth Fitness Congress, and making it clear that the promotion of physical fitness was a continuing policy of the U.S. government.

387 *From a divided nation: Frankfurter Allgemeine Zeitung,* Sept. 12, 1960.

388 *The separation of the combined team:* Int., Ingrid Kraemer; also *Neues Deutschland,* Sept. 12–14, 1960; "Building Walls, Dividing Teams," Dichter.

390 *The mastermind of the East German athletic drug culture:* Int., Ingrid Kraemer; *Times* of London obituary, Oct. 26, 2002; *Independent* (London) obituary, Oct. 25, 2002; *New York Times,* Nov. 5, 2007; CBC Sports, Jan. 19, 2003; *Indian Express,* Aug. 19, 1998.

392 *A fleet of Tupolev Tu-104s:* Ints., Igor Ter-Ovanesyan, Dave Sime; Ralph Boston oral history, NBC archive; *The Red Files,* PBS archive; also *Pravda,* Sept. 13–16, 1960.

396 *Bradford had been so discouraged:* Int., James Bradford.

399 *Abebe Bikila made his triumphant return:* National Olympic Committee of Ethiopia profile, Ethiopia OC file, OSC, Lausanne; *Ethiopian Herald,* Sept. 13–17, 1960; *Triumph and Tragedy,* Rome chapter; *New York Times,* Feb. 3, 1961, Oct. 21, 1964, March 14, 1965, March 5, 1967, Aug. 16, 1972; Associated Press obituary, Oct. 25, 1973; David DuPree, "Hurdles Are Many for African Runners," *Washington Post,* July 23, 1975.

402 *"The African question remains":* South Africa file, Brundage collection: IOC sessions, 1965–68, OSC, Lausanne; *The International Olympic Committee and South Africa,* Keba Mbaye, IOC publication.

404 *After closing the Rome Games:* Brundage handwritten daily diary, Brundage collection; Letter from Bruno Zauli, secretary general of CONI, to Otto Mayer, IOC chancellor, Oct. 14, 1961, Mayer file, OSC, Lausanne.

405 *Everywhere Brundage turned:* Letters between Brundage and Marquess of Exeter, Jan. 26, 1961, July 22, 1961, Aug. 14, 1961, amateurism file, OSC, Lausanne; *Sports Illustrated,* Jan. 30, 1961; Associated Press report, Jan. 7, 1961; *Sprinter of the Century.*

407 *Jim McKay's daytime job:* Int., Jim McKay.

409 *Television revenues rose:* Slater, Fourth International Symposium for Olympic Research, Changing Partners, table 3, page 56, "The Relationship Between the Mass Media and the Olympic Games."

410 *In Washington a few days after:* Memorandum of conversation, Handling of Olympic Affiliation Problem; participants Dr. George K. C. Yeh, J. Graham Parsons, Larue R. Lutkins, Sept. 13, 1960, State Department central files, China, NARA-College Park.

410 *The next morning C. K. Yang: China Daily News,* Sept. 14–16, 1960.

411 *When word reached Taipei:* Incoming airgram from American embassy Taipei to Secretary of State, Sept. 20, 1960, State Department central files, China, NARA-College Park.

412 *In the days after Rome:* Account of Grombach obsession with Lord Burghley drawn from letter from Industrial Reports Inc., 113 West 57th St., New York, to Mr. C. Chrys-

tall, Anglo-American Detective Agency, 3, Lower John St., London, W.1., signed by John Grombach, Grombach file, OSC, Lausanne; confidential letter from Brundage to Exeter, Feb. 9, 1961, Lord Burghley file, Brundage collection; *The People* (London), Feb. 12, 1961; *Times* of London, Feb. 13, 1961; *News of the World,* Feb. 13, 1961; May 1961 memorandum to Senator Eastland from Jay Sourwine, Senate Internal Security Subcommittee, record group 46, Brundage file, NARA-Washington.

414 *School awaited many Americans:* Ints., John Thomas, Dave Sime, Anne Warner (Cribbs).

416 *What Rafer Johnson most wanted to do:* Int., Rafer Johnson; also *Kingsburg Record,* Aug. 30–Sept. 15, 1960.

420 *Coach Temple and the Tigerbelles:* Ints., Ed Temple, Lucinda Williams; Nashville *Tennessean,* Sept. 29–Oct. 3, 1960; Clarksville *Leaf-Chonicle,* Oct. 2–5, 1960.

INDEX

461

ABOUT THE AUTHOR

David MARANISS is an associate editor at *The Washington Post*. He is the winner of the 1993 Pulitzer Prize for National Reporting and was a part of a team of *Post* reporters who won the 2008 Pulitzer for coverage of the Virginia Tech tragedy. He was a Pulitzer finalist two other times for his journalism and again for *They Marched Into Sunlight,* a book about Vietnam and the sixties. Also the author of bestselling works on Bill Clinton, Vince Lombardi, and Roberto Clemente, Maraniss is a fellow of the Society of American Historians. He and his wife, Linda, live in Washington, DC, and Madison, Wisconsin.